WORKERS' COMPENSATION AND EMPLOYEE PROTECTION LAWS

IN A NUTSHELL

Fourth Edition

JACK B. HOOD
Former Adjunct Professor of Law
University of Georgia School of Law

BENJAMIN A. HARDY, Jr.
Associate Professor
Jacksonville State University

HAROLD S. LEWIS, Jr.
Walter F. George Professor of Law
Mercer University School of Law

THOMSON
WEST

Mat #40250277

COPYRIGHT © 1984, 1990 WEST PUBLISHING CO.
COPYRIGHT © 1999 WEST GROUP
© 2005 West, a Thomson business
   610 Opperman Drive
   P.O. Box 64526
   St. Paul, MN 55164–0526
   1–800–328–9352
Printed in the United States of America

ISBN 0–314–15311–X

TEXT IS PRINTED ON 10% POST CONSUMER RECYCLED PAPER

TO
Pat, Sara, and Laura
Linda and Andy
Leslie, Ethan, and Isabel

*

PREFACE

Our purpose in writing this Nutshell is to provide an overview of the laws affecting employees in the workplace. It is our hope that the sections on workers' compensation and employment discrimination will provide both students and lawyers with insight into the most common questions in the field. Only summaries have been attempted in the sections dealing with other employee protection legislation, because the subject areas were too large for detailed explanations.

An excellent and comprehensive treatment of workers' compensation is to be found in Larson's multi-volume treatise on the subject, and we have given citations to that work at relevant points. We have also given numerous cites to the very useful three volumes of Modern Workers Compensation (Westlaw database "mwc"). In the areas of employment discrimination, one may find helpful Lewis and Norman's treatise, Litigating Civil Rights and Employment Discrimination Cases (Thomson/West 2004), and Lewis and Norman's hornbook, Employment Discrimination Law and Practice (2d ed. Thomson/West 2004). The Nutshell by Professor Leslie on Labor Law (Thomson/West 2000) is also of assistance, along with Rothstein, Craver, Schroeder, and Shoben's hornbook, Employment Law (Thomson/West 2004).

We would like to acknowledge and thank the University of Alabama and Mercer Law Schools, and our research assistants and Alabama Law School students, Jason H. Cromey and Amy L. Alexander, of Birmingham, Alabama. We also express our appreciation to the law libraries at the Cumberland School of Law of Samford University, the University of Mississippi, and the University of Alabama.

JACK B. HOOD
BENJAMIN A. HARDY, JR.
HAROLD S. LEWIS, JR.

December, 2004
Birmingham, Alabama

OUTLINE

PART 2. THE LAW OF WORKERS' COMPENSATION

OUTLINE

OUTLINE

TABLE OF CASES

References are to Pages

A

B

C

D

E

TABLE OF CASES

G

H

I

J

K

L

M

N

O

P

Q

R

S

T

U

V

W

Y

Z

WORKERS' COMPENSATION AND EMPLOYEE PROTECTION LAWS

IN A NUTSHELL

Fourth Edition

*

PART 1

HISTORICAL BACKGROUND OF COMPENSATION LEGISLATION

CHAPTER 1

EMPLOYMENT RELATED ACTIONS AND LEGISLATION

A. EMPLOYEE'S COMMON–LAW REMEDIES

The common-law imposed a number of duties on employers for the protection of their employees, and an action existed for the breach of these duties; however, as a practical matter the common-law failed to provide adequate remedies for such injuries and deaths. The common-law duties imposed upon the master were as follows:

(1) to provide a safe place to work;

(2) to provide safe appliances, tools and equipment;

(3) to give warnings of dangers of which the employee might reasonably be expected to remain in ignorance;

(4) to provide a sufficient number of fit, trained, or suitable fellow servants to perform assigned tasks; and

(5) to promulgate and enforce rules relating to employee conduct which would make the work safe.

1

Employee remedies based upon a breach of the foregoing duties were restricted by the "unholy trinity" of common-law defenses: (1) fellow-servant doctrine; (2) contributory negligence; and (3) assumption of risk. See Prosser and Keeton on Torts § 80 (5th ed. 1984).

1. FELLOW–SERVANT DOCTRINE

Unless there was an express contract the rule at common law was that a master was not liable to a servant for injuries due to the negligence of a fellow servant. Priestley v. Fowler (1837); see Murray v. South Carolina Railroad Co. (1841). The doctrine provided that the negligence of a co-employee was not to be imputed to the master; of course, the injured employee, for what it was worth, could still sue a co-employee. The fellow-servant rule was not founded in abstract or natural justice, and the rule was an exception to the rule of agency and the general rule that a master was responsible for injuries caused to third persons by the negligence of servants who were acting within the scope of their employment. In support of the fellow-servant doctrine it was said that the negligence of a fellow-servant was one of the risks incident to employment, and the risk was assumed by the servant as an implied term of the employment contract. Public policy in support of the doctrine was to the effect that the rule would make servants careful and watchful with regard to each other, thus promoting greater care in the performance of their duties.

The harshness of the fellow-servant doctrine was lessened by the recognition of certain exceptions. For example, servants who did not have a common master and who were not engaged in the same enterprise were not barred from recovery by the fellow-servant rules. Furthermore, if they were employed in different departments of the same enterprise, the employees were not generally to be treated as fellow-servants. The most important exception involved the negligence of a "vice-principal" because the fellow-servant bar did not apply to the vice-principal. One approach required that the vice-principal be a supervisory employee, representing the employer in his duty toward the employee. The vice-principal exception has been held to apply to any servant, as opposed to just superior servants. The key inquiry aimed at an employer's liability was whether a servant (alleged vice-principal) owed an obligation to the injured employee to meet the common-law duties of the employer. In order for the master to be liable, these duties were viewed as being non-delegable. The vice-principal exception was subject to an important qualification. It was not applicable to those incidental dangers which arose out of the operational details of a fellow-servant's work. No duty was owed by the master with regard to these risks. See generally, J. Lee and B. Lindahl, 4 Modern Tort Law: Liability and Litigation § 43:9—Fellow Servant Doctrine (2d ed. 2003).

2.   CONTRIBUTORY NEGLIGENCE

An employee or servant was required to exercise reasonable care for his own safety, and his failure to use the precautions that ordinary prudence required, barred any recovery under the contributory negligence defense. Exceptions existed on the basis of the last clear chance doctrine and in situations in which the master's conduct was willful or wanton. As a result of the doctrine's harshness, statutes sometimes abrogated the defense and statutorily imposed requirements for worker safety, placing certain servants in a special, protected category. In some jurisdictions comparative negligence statutes aided employees. In others, the courts have adopted comparative fault principles. See Carroll v. Whitney (Tenn. 2000) (history of change to comparative negligence); but see Williams v. Delta Int'l Machinery Corp. (Ala. 1993) (retaining contributory negligence and rejecting comparative fault principles).

3. ASSUMPTION OF RISK

The assumption of risk defense was grounded in the notion that the servant or employee had voluntarily agreed to assume the dangers normally and ordinarily incident to the work. Risks were covered which a mature worker was presumed to know, regardless of whether one had actual knowledge. The employee further assumed such extraordinary and abnormal risks of which he had knowledge and appreciation. Assumption of risk was customarily based upon contract theory, as opposed to contributory negligence which was based upon tort theory. Contributory negligence involved the notion of fault and a breach of duty to one's self, whereas assumption of risk could exist in the absence of fault because of its contractual nature. Employees or servants did not assume those risks growing out of the negligence of the master, or a vice principal. Generally risks arising out of the non-delegable duties doctrine were not viewed as the ordinary sort of risks which one could assume; these were treated as extraordinary risks which one did not assume. It should be kept in mind that recovery could still be barred by one's contributory negligence. See Jenkins v. Union Pacific R. Co. (9th Cir. 1994) (discussion of history of assumption of risk, the statutory abolition in FELA cases, and the interplay of the FELA's modified contributory negligence principles with comparative fault).

In summary, the foregoing "unholy trinity" may be explained in large part on the basis of the highly individualistic attitude of the common-law courts and society's desire to encourage industrial expansion and development by lessening the financial costs upon industry for industrial injuries and deaths. See R. Epstein, The Historical Origins and Economic Structure of Workers' Compensation Law, 16 Ga. L. Rev. 775 (1982); see generally, Dodd, Administration of Workmen's Compensation, § 7 (1936); Horovitz, Injury and Death Under

Workmen's Compensation Laws (1944); Prosser and Keeton on Torts § 80 (5th ed. 1984).

B. EMPLOYERS' LIABILITY ACTS

Employers' liability acts came into being in response to rising industrial injury and death rates in the 19th Century, and in response to dissatisfaction with the common-law remedies available to employees. For example, in 1855, the State of Georgia enacted a statute making railroads liable to employees and others for negligence in situations previously barred by the fellow-servant defense. By 1908, almost every American jurisdiction had passed similar legislation. Congress, in 1908, placed interstate railroad employees under an employers' liability act system and later extended this same coverage to seamen. The state and federal acts generally barred the use of the fellow-servant rule, substituted comparative negligence for pure contributory negligence, and later barred the use of the assumption of risk defense. These employers' liability laws were, however, soon found to be unsatisfactory for several reasons: workers or their survivors had to bring law suits for damages; the employers' defenses, while considerably weakened, still made it difficult for workers to prosecute their cases; the outcome of the cases were always uncertain; actions were costly to bring and were lengthy; cases produced ill-will between the employers and employees and posed a constant threat to job security. For a view on the role of insurance in the historical development of this area, see J. Witt, Toward a New History of American Accident Law: Classical Tort Law and the Cooperative Firstparty Insurance Movement, 114 Harv. L. Rev. 690 (2001).

C. EUROPEAN COMPENSATION LEGISLATION

The historical origins of modern workers' compensation legislation may be found first in Germany and then in England. Philosophers and politicians, especially socialists, were of great influence in the development of European compensation legislation which later influenced the development of similar compensation legislation in the United States.

1. GERMANY

The German influence began in 1838 with the enactment of an employers' liability act that was applicable to railroads. In 1873 Germany extended coverage to workers in factories, mines and quarries. In 1884, Germany enacted a compulsory system of accident insurance which is regarded as the first true workers' compensation act, and it covered all employees engaged in manufacturing, mining and transportation. Similar workers' compensation laws were enacted in Austria in 1887, Norway in 1894, Finland in 1895, and Great Britain in 1897.

2. GREAT BRITAIN

The Workmen's Compensation Act of 1897 provided the prototype, and was the forerunner of the majority of compensation acts passed in the early 1900's in the United States. The Act contained important limitations: only hazardous employments were covered; there were no insurance provisions; and the employer bore the complete burden of compensation benefit costs. The statute also gave rise to the key phrase, "arising out of and in the course of employment," which is generally found today in compensation statutes in the United States. The British legislation differed from the German. Germany attempted to provide broader coverage in the area of social insurance and to provide a more complete compensation system. The British Act gave a workman only moderate recovery, with the cost being borne by the employer as an expense of doing business.

D. STATE COMPENSATION ACTS

There was a gradual recognition after the turn of the century that the common-law remedies of employees injured or killed on the job, were filled with inequities. The states were slow, however, to adopt workers' compensation laws, and initial attempts to do so faced legal and political opposition. Early compensation legislation was very limited and legislators exercised great caution in replacing the common-law recovery system. While it is beyond the scope of this work to address the various attempts of the states to enact compensation legislation, a sampling is necessary for historical appreciation of workers' compensation legislation in the United States.

1. MARYLAND

In 1902, Maryland passed the first workers' compensation act in the United States. It applied to death cases only, and provided coverage to a limited number of workers. This act was declared unconstitutional in Franklin v. United Railways and Electric Co. (1904), because it was held to deprive the parties of the right to jury trial and said to be violative of the separation of powers doctrine (an insurance commissioner, under the executive branch, was performing judicial functions). In 1910, Maryland enacted a voluntary workers' compensation statute, but apathy on behalf of employers and employees rendered the legislation ineffective.

2. MONTANA

In 1909, Montana enacted a compulsory workers' compensation statute, which was designed for employees in the coal industry. The employer and employee were both required to contribute to a state fund, and a covered employee or his beneficiaries could elect to sue at law or receive compensation from the fund; however, workers could not receive the benefits of both. This legislation was declared unconstitutional in Cunningham v. Northwestern Improvement Co. (1911), because it was held that employers were denied equal protection of the laws, in that there was the potential for double liability (employers had to contribute to the state compensation fund and additionally were open to suit if an employee or beneficiary so elected).

3. MASSACHUSETTS

Massachusetts, in 1908, passed a voluntary workers' compensation statute. The voluntary nature of the act was designed to avoid some of the theoretical constitutional problems concerning compensation acts. As a result of the voluntary nature of the act, both employers and employees had no incentive to commit themselves to the scheme. Thus, the Massachusetts act proved to be ineffective.

4. NEW YORK

In 1909, in New York, a commission on Employers' Liability was created (popularly known as the "Wainwright Commission"). It was to inquire into the liabilities of employers to employees for industrial accidents, and to compare and study: efficiencies, costs, justice, merits and defects in the laws of the other industrial states and countries. The Commission reported that the current common-law system with its employers' liability act exceptions provided insufficient compensation; was wasteful in terms of resources; caused unsatisfactory delays and was essentially antagonistic in nature. The Commission proposed two statutes in light of constitutional problems. One proposal was aimed at employers and employees when especially dangerous employments were involved. The other statute was designed as an elective statute to cover employments outside of the especially dangerous work categories. In 1910, both compulsory and voluntary acts were passed. Predictably, the voluntary statute suffered from employer indifference, and the compulsory statute was declared unconstitutional in Ives v. South Buffalo Railway (1911). Employers were viewed as having been denied due process under both the state and federal constitutions in that employers' property, i.e., money, was taken without consent and without fault.

In 1913, New York amended its constitution to permit the enactment of a compulsory workers' compensation statute and in 1914 the New York legislature passed a compulsory workers' compensation law that applied only to hazardous employments. In Jensen v. Southern Pacific Co. (1915), the New York Court of Appeals upheld the statute as a valid exercise of police power. As might be expected, thereafter mandatory coverage was extended and broadened in New York.

5. CALIFORNIA

In 1911, California passed the Roseberry Act which created its first workers' compensation laws, and in 1917, the Workman's Compensation, Insurance and Safety Act was enacted. Subsequent amendments were frequent in the 1900's, and included the 1937 provisions that consolidated workers' compensation into the state's Labor Code. Important amendments to the Labor Code were made with the passage of the Workers' Compensation Reform Act of 1989, and several important subsequent amendments in the 1990's were also enacted. See generally, Grossmont Hosp. v. Workers' Comp. Appeals Bd. (1997); Mathews v. Workmen's Comp. App. Bd. (1972); West's Ann. Cal. Lab. Code § 3200, et. seq.

In 2004, new reform legislation was passed at the urging of business groups and the California Chamber of Commerce because of perceived high insurance costs and low benefits. Among other items, the reform legislation attempted to: increase benefits for workers with severe permanent disabilities; decrease benefits for minor permanent injuries; cap temporary disability benefits for most injuries at 2 years; remove subjective factors in physician determined impairment ratings; require physicians to employ national standards in impairment determinations; encourage reinstatement of injured employees; and give employers a better ability to apportion liability by requiring physicians to address causation issues in their disability evaluations and by requiring employees to disclose all prior physical impairments and permanent disabilities.

Whether or not these reforms will allow California to control program costs remains to be seen. Many other states are watching these developments closely.

6. FLORIDA

By 1920, most states had adopted some form of workers' compensation legislation. The last state to adopt a compensation act was Mississippi in 1949. In 1935 the State of Florida enacted its first workers' compensation act which was elective in theory. The development of the law in this area in Florida is typical of its development in the United States. For example, from 1935 forward, practically every session of the Florida legislature amended the compensation act. It must be pointed out, however, that the Florida legislature in 1978, because of its concern over excessive awards and a backlog of claims, initiated a study of the problems. In 1979 the legislature enacted a Workers' Compensation Reform Act which "re-established the centrality of the wage-loss principle," and represented a departure from the development in many other jurisdictions. The current theory in Florida is that awards should not be based on the medical nature of the injury alone but should focus on the economic impact of the injury. Florida's wage-loss approach is designed to avoid compensating a worker for an injury per se, or basing an award on conjecture as to the future course of a specific injury; instead, its goal is to provide compensation for an employee's economic losses as they arise. See Abinger & Granoff, Legislative Overview: The Florida Workers' Compensation Act, 1979, 4 Nova L.J. 91 (1980). This approach was used by Florida in an advertising effort to attract new industry. In 1990, as a result of a Governor's Task Force on Worker's Compensation, the legislature enacted legislation returning an impairment (medical loss) schedule to Florida's compensation program. See generally, A. Watson and M. Valen, A Historic View of Workers' Compensation Reform in Florida, 21 Fla. St. L. Rev. 501 (1993). The Florida experience exemplifies the continuing political battles fought in legislatures between employees in the work force and employers and insurance carriers.

E. FEDERAL LEGISLATION

There are a variety of federal acts designed to provide compensation or recovery for certain employees injured or killed on the job. Additionally, there has been federal legislation aimed at regulation of safety practices, labor standards, discrimination, social security benefits, etc. and which may affect employees' rights in the workplace. Provided below is a brief history and introduction of the more important federal acts providing compensation or recovery; other employee protection laws will be addressed in Part III.

1. FEDERAL EMPLOYEES' COMPENSATION ACT

In 1908, Congress enacted a workers' compensation act for a limited group of federal employees, and, in 1916, it expanded the coverage to all civil employees of the United States government without regard to the hazards of their employment. An extensive revision of the FECA was undertaken in 1949, and today, the FECA, 5 U.S.C.A. § 8101 et seq., is considered to be one of the most liberal workers' compensation acts in existence, and provides coverage for federal employees and their dependents for death or disability resulting from personal injury "sustained while in the performance of duty." Congressional appropriations finance all administrative and benefit costs, thus making the government a self-insurer. The Secretary of Labor supervises administrative claims procedures through the Office of Workers' Compensation Programs. The Employees' Compensation Appeals Board reviews appeals from final decisions. When an employee is covered by the FECA, all other rights against the government are barred. See Noble v. United States (11th Cir. 2000) (exclusive remedy case). Third party actions may be commenced when appropriate, and there may be an election of civil service retirement benefits (assuming eligibility), as opposed to compensation benefits. The Supreme Court, in Westfall v. Erwin (1988), indicated that co-employee liability was possible in FECA situations; however, Congress legislatively overruled Westfall by enacting the Federal Employees Liability Reform and Tort Compensation Act of 1988 (28 U.S.C.A. § 2679). The FECA's exclusive liability provision does not directly preclude third-party indemnity actions against the United States. Lockheed Aircraft Corp. v. United States (1983).

Members of the armed forces of the United States are not covered by the FECA; however, analogous legislation does provide them with disability compensation and death benefits. 10 U.S.C.A. Ch. 61 & 75; 38 U.S.C.A. § 301 et seq. Coverage is allowed in cases of service-connected disability or death. The military scheme requires a "line of duty" determination to be made in each case, and either the particular branch of service and/or the Veterans Administration provides the machinery for the claims process and supervision. See Federal Benefits for Veterans and Dependents, VA Pamphlet 80–92–1.

It should be noted that the *Feres* doctrine precludes servicemen's recoveries under the Federal Tort Claims Act against the United States for injury, death, or loss "incident to service." Feres v. United States (1950). Furthermore, service personnel cannot generally maintain damage actions against superior officers for violation of constitutional rights. Chappell v. Wallace (1983).

It should also be noted that the Prison Industries Fund, 18 U.S.C. § 4126, provides an exclusive remedy for federal prisoners. See Vander v. U.S. Department of Justice (9th Cir. 2001) (fund held exclusive remedy for prisoner who made claim under the Federal Tort Claims Act for delay in medical treatment). In some circumstances, federal prisoners can have valid constitutional tort claims for ill treatment. See, e.g., Magluta v. Samples (11th Cir. 2004) (prisoner could sue bureau of prisons employees for unlawful solitary confinement).

2. FEDERAL EMPLOYERS' LIABILITY ACT

In 1906, Congress passed the first Federal Employers' Liability Act, but the United States Supreme Court held the Act unconstitutional because it infringed upon state rights in that the Act applied to intrastate as well as interstate commerce. Howard v. Illinois Central Railroad (1908). This first FELA was held constitutional, however, as far as the District of Columbia and the territories of the United States were concerned. El Paso & Northeastern Railway v. Gutierrez (1909). In 1908, Congress enacted a second FELA which applied to common carriers engaged in interstate commerce only. It is this second FELA statute which remains effective to this day and is codified at 45 U.S.C.A. §§ 51–60. The FELA is not a true workers' compensation act for it requires an employee to prove negligence even though the burden of proving that negligence has been greatly liberalized by the courts. The FELA at the time of its passage was considered the most progressive of the various employers' liability acts that existed at the time. Comparative fault replaced contributory negligence and the fellow-servant rule was abolished completely. In 1939, Congress amended the act with an eye toward the elimination of the assumption of risk defense. Subsequent court decisions make it clear that there is no assumption of inherent risks based upon the risk of ordinary railroading; nor can there be assumption of risk for obvious dangers knowingly encountered by the railroad employee, but of course, comparative fault may come into play.

In recent times, some have advocated that the FELA should be repealed and replaced with traditional workers' compensation systems. See generally, T. Baker, Why Congress Should Replace the Federal Employers' Liability Act of 1908, 29 Harv. L. Rev. 79 (1992); V. Schwartz and L. Mahshigian, The Federal Employers' Liability Act, A Bane for Workers, A Bust for Railroads, A Boon for Lawyers, 23 San Diego L. Rev. 1 (1986).

One should note that the Safety Appliance Act and the Boiler Inspection Act impose absolute and mandatory duties upon the defendant carriers, which can provide the basis for liability under the FELA. The traditional common-law tort compensatory approach is taken toward personal injury damages under the FELA, but the Supreme Court has remained receptive to new claims, especially in the emotional distress area. Norfolk & Western Ry. Co. v. Ayers (2003) (mental anguish damages resulting from fear of cancer can be recovered under FELA by railroad worker suffering from actionable injury asbestosis caused by work-related exposure to asbestos); Atchison, Topeka & Santa Fe Ry. Co. v. Buell (1987); see also, Consolidated Rail Corp. v. Gottshall (1994) (fear of cancer). In death cases, a pecuniary loss approach is employed for beneficiaries. Most courts have held that punitive damages are not recoverable. Actions may be filed in state or federal courts; if filed in state court the action cannot be removed to federal court.

3. THE JONES ACT

Historically, under the general maritime law, seamen were allowed maintenance and cure which consisted of subsistence, medical care and unearned wages, but they had no effective negligence remedy. At the turn of the Twentieth Century, the Supreme Court began fashioning the doctrine of unseaworthiness, which provided a proper cause of action, but a limited remedy for seamen. See The Osceola (1903). Because of concern for the welfare of seamen, Congress enacted the Seamen's Act of 1915, which abolished the fellow-servant defense, but this legislation was effectively nullified in Chelentis v. Luckenbach Steamship Co. (1918). In 1920, Congress passed the Merchant Marine Act of 1920, commonly known as the Jones Act. It provided seamen with the same negligence remedy that is available to railroad employees under the Federal Employers Liability Act. 46 App. U.S.C.A. § 688 et seq. Both state and federal courts may entertain these actions and comparative negligence applies. In the 1940's, the Supreme Court transformed the unseaworthiness doctrine into an effective liability basis for recoveries by seamen. The unseaworthiness doctrine essentially imposes liability without fault on the part of a shipowner who fails to provide a safe and seaworthy vessel. The determination of a worker's status as a seaman is of critical importance. Chandris, Inc. v. Latsis (1995); see Harbor Tug & Barge Co. v. Papai (1997); Stewart v. Dutra Constr. Co. (1st Cir. 2003) (issue of whether a floating work platform being used as a dredge to excavate a tunnel in Boston Harbor was a vessel in navigation for Jones Act purposes). Thus, today once a person is classified as a seaman he may join actions for maintenance and cure, Jones Act negligence and unseaworthiness in order to obtain compensation for his personal injuries. Fitzgerald v. United States Lines Co. (1963). Punitive damages appear to be unavailable to seamen in actions against their employers or vessels. See generally, Guevara v. Maritime Overseas Corp. (5th Cir.1995).

Sometimes there can be an overlap between seamen's rights to recovery under the aforementioned theories and the various state workers' compensation laws. This area is sometimes called a "twilight zone" of coverage. See Ch. 9, C., infra.

In Miles v. Apex Marine Corp. (1990), the Supreme Court recognized that seamen have a general maritime law cause of action for wrongful death. This action is generally limited to pecuniary damages. Beyond one marine league from shore the Death on the High Seas Act of 1920, 46 U.S.C.A. §§ 761–767, is generally applicable, but seamen's damages are pecuniary in nature regardless of whether they are sought under the Jones Act, general maritime law, or the Death on the High Seas Act. See also, Dooley v. Korean Air Lines Co. (1998). As a result of the Miles decision, the lower courts have generally held that seamen can only recover for general and special damages in claims for personal injuries. See generally, T. Schoenbaum, Admiralty and Maritime Law, Chapter 8. Wrongful Death (4th ed. 2004).

It should be noted that the penalty wage statute, 46 U.S.C.A. §§ 10313(f)–(i), 10501(b)–(d), permits an action for delayed payment of wages. In appropriate circumstances, this action may be joined with other seamen's remedies. Griffin v. Oceanic Contractors, Inc. (1982).

4. LONGSHORE AND HARBOR WORKERS' COMPENSATION ACT

In 1927, Congress enacted a national workers' compensation statute for the benefit of longshoremen and other persons engaged in maritime employment on navigable waters. The Longshoremen's and Harbor Workers' Compensation Act (hereinafter "LHWCA") was prompted by the case of Southern Pacific Co. v. Jensen (1917), which had nullified a New York workers' compensation statute as applied to longshoremen. See generally, R. Force, Deconstructing Jensen: Admiralty and Federalism in the Twenty–First Century, 32 J. Mar. L. & Com. 517 (2001). Coverage under the 1927 legislation was said to exist only if the accident occurred on navigable waters; Nacirema Operating Co. v. Johnson (1969); and the fact that a worker's employment was maritime in nature was not a coverage issue. Calbeck v. Travelers Insurance Co. (1962). By decisions of the Supreme Court, covered workers were also given an unseaworthiness remedy against a vessel, Seas Shipping Co. v. Sieracki (1946), and the vessel owner was given an indemnity action against the stevedore employer, Ryan Stevedoring Co. v. Pan-Atlantic Steamship Corp. (1956).

In 1972, Congress significantly amended the LHWCA. In summary, the amendments increased benefits, eliminated the unseaworthiness remedy against vessels, abolished the vessel owner's right of indemnity against stevedore employers, and instituted needed administrative changes. Most importantly the 1972 amendments broadened coverage, by using both "situs" and "status" for coverage. The situs test is no longer confined to navigable waters, but it includes dockside workers on adjoining shore areas. See Northeast Marine Terminal Co. v. Caputo (1977). The status test is met if a worker is engaged in "maritime employment." 33 U.S.C.A. § 902(3). See Chesapeake & Ohio Railway Co. v. Schwalb (1989).

In 1984, Congress amended the LHWCA, restricting coverage and changing the name of the act to the Longshore and Harbor Workers' Compensation Act; 33 U.S.C.A. § 901 et seq. All private maritime employments upon navigable waters or adjoining land areas are generally covered by the LHWCA. See Cunningham, Jr. v. Director, OWCP (1st Cir. 2004) (pipe-fabrication facility 4 miles from shipbuilder's main shipyard was not an "adjoining area" for coverage by LHWCA). Specifically excluded are seamen and government employees. Also excluded are clerical employees, recreation employees, temporary employees not engaged in longshore or harbor work, agricultural employees, employees on certain small commercial vessels, and employees who repair or break recreational vessels under 65 feet in length, so long as there is state workers' compensation coverage for these employees.

As might be expected, jurisdictional battles arise because claimants wish to assert seaman status, while employers prefer to claim immunity from suit under the LHWCA. Seaman status is usually a jury question. Southwest Marine, Inc. v. Gizoni (1991). See generally, J. Hillsman, Still Lost in the Labyrinth: the Continuing Puzzle of Seaman Status, 15 U.S.F. Mar. L. J. 49 (2003).

When there is an overlap of coverage due to state workers' compensation law, the LHWCA does not necessarily pre-empt. The Supreme Court's concurrent jurisdiction doctrines (sometimes applied in twilight zone cases) indicate that generally, an employee covered by both has an option. See Sun Ship, Inc. v. Pennsylvania (1980). See Ch. 9, C., infra.

It should be pointed out that the receipt of LHWCA benefits does not preclude the initiation of a third-party action based upon traditional negligence concepts. 33 U.S.C.A. § 905(b); see Scindia Steam Navigation Co., Limited v. De Los Santos (1981). Furthermore, a longshoreman can pursue a negligence remedy under the LHWCA against a vessel owner who acts as his own stevedore, despite the fact that the longshoreman has received compensation under the LHWCA from the stevedore-vessel owner. Jones & Laughlin Steel Corp. v. Pfeifer (1983). But ship repairers' actions are barred by § 905(b).

The LHWCA has been applied by Congress to employees other than longshoremen and maritime workers. The Defense Base Act applies the LHWCA to injuries on deaths of certain persons engaged in public works contracts outside the continental United States and to certain persons employed at military bases outside the United States. 42 U.S.C.A. § 1651 et seq. The War Hazards Compensation Act (42 U.S.C.A. § 1701 et seq.) provides a compensation remedy for death, injury, or detention of certain persons employed overseas by U.S. government contractors or by the United States government; benefits, disability, etc., are determined by reference to the LHWCA. Administration of these claims is accomplished under the Federal Employees' Compensation Act. Subject to certain criteria, employees of nonappropriated fund instrumentalities of the United States are also entitled to the benefits of the LHWCA. 5 U.S.C.A. §§ 8171, 8172.

In 1928, Congress extended the substantive and procedural provisions of the LHWCA to employees in the District of Columbia (D.C. Code §§ 36–501, 36–502 (1973)). These provisions were replaced by the District of Columbia Workers' Compensation Act. D.C. Code 1981, § 1–233; See District of

Columbia v. Greater Washington Central Labor Council, AFL-CIO (1982). For the current workers' compensation provisions, see D.C. Official Code, 2001 Ed. § 32–1501 et seq. See also e.g., Washington Post v. District of Columbia Dept. of Employment Services (D.C. 2004) (disability is an economic concept rather than a medical condition for purposes of workers' compensation).

Finally, the Outer Continental Shelf Lands Act (43 U.S.C.A. §§ 1331–1343) incorporates the provisions of the LHWCA for the benefit of certain employees engaged in natural resources exploration, development, transportation, etc., outside the states' seaward boundaries on the continental shelves. See Herb's Welding, Inc. v. Gray (1985); Mills v. Director (1989). See generally, W. Hastings, To Avoid Drowning in the Gaps of Workers' Compensation Coverage on the Outer Continental Shelf, 35 J. Mar. Law & Com. 35 (2004).

The U.S. Department of Labor maintains a useful website at: http://www.dol.gov/asp/programs/guide/longshor.htm.

5. FEDERAL BLACK LUNG BENEFITS LEGISLATION

As an incident to the Federal Coal Mine Health and Safety Act of 1969, a basic income maintenance program was established for certain coal miners and their dependents. 30 U.S.C.A. § 801 et seq. The program was designed to provide compensation benefits in certain cases in which coal miners had suffered or died from pneumoconiosis ("black lung"). In 1972, Congress passed the Black Lung Benefits Act, and thereby authorized a national workers' compensation program to be administered under the U.S. Department of Labor. Since that time several important amendments have occurred. In 1978, Congress passed the Black Lung Benefits Reform Act of

1977 and the Black Lung Benefits Review Act of 1977. Later, Congress enacted the Black Lung Benefits Revenue Act of 1981, the Black Lung Benefits Amendments of 1981 and the Consolidated Omnibus Budget Reconciliation Act of 1985. Because of the controversial and political nature of this federal workers' compensation legislation, there is no doubt that future amendments and revisions will occur. For a more detailed description of the black lung compensation legislation, see Chapter 15, infra.

6. ENERGY EMPLOYEES

The United States government created a workers' compensation system pursuant to the Energy Employees Occupational Illness Compensation Act of 2000 (Pub. L. 106–398, 114 Stat. 1654) and the Energy Employees Occupational Illness Compensation Amendments of 2001. The legislation provides a compensation program for employees, or their survivors, of the Department of Energy, its contractors, subcontractors, and related private companies, who have suffered occupational illnesses from exposures to the unique hazards associated with nuclear weapons development and testing processes. Specifically targeted are beryllium-related diseases, radiation-related cancers, silica-related diseases, special exposure cohorts, uranium miners, and other occupational diseases. The U. S. Department of Labor has primary responsibility for administering the compensation and medical benefit programs. The Department of Energy's Office of Worker Advocacy provides the Department of Labor with medical and employment records necessary for claims. Claimants pursuing state workers' compensation benefits are also provided assistance. Ten resource centers are open near Department of Energy sites to provide further assistance to workers and their families: Hanford, Washington; Idaho Falls, Idaho; Las Vegas, Nevada;

Espanola, New Mexico; Denver, Colorado; Aiken, South Carolina; Portsmouth, Ohio; Paducah, Kentucky; Oak Ridge, Tennessee; and Anchorage, Alaska.

The Department of Energy made public an initial list of facilities to be covered, including beryllium vendors, and Department of Energy sites where radioactive materials were used and facilities where atomic weapons workers may have been employed. The list includes 317 sites in 37 states, Puerto Rico, the District of Columbia, and the Marshall Islands. Claimants may be entitled to medical benefits and compensation in the amount of $150,000. Information can be obtained from the Department of Energy's website at http://www.eh.doe.gov/advocacy. Similarly, information can be obtained from the U.S. Department of Labor's website at http://www.dol.gov.

7. RADIATION EXPOSURE CLAIMS

In 1990, Congress enacted the Radiation Exposure Compensation Act (42 U.S.C.A. § 2210) that provided for compensation to the victims of certain diseases and cancers which resulted from radiation exposure during nuclear tests or because of employment exposure to radiation in mines. On July 10, 2000, Congress enacted the Radiation Exposure Compensation Act Amendments of 2000 (Pub. L. 106–245), 114 Stat. 501). These amendments expanded coverage to include broader classes of claimants and additional diseases, lowered exposure requirements, and modified medical documentation requirements. There are five groups of claimants: onsite participants; downwinders; ore transporters; uranium millers; and uranium miners. Eligible miners, millers and transporters may be entitled to compensation payments of $100,000 each. Onsite participants may be entitled to compensation payments of $75,000 each, and downwinders may be entitled to compensation payments of $50,000 each. This program is administered by the Department of Justice, and information can be obtained its website at http:// www.usdoj.gov/civil/torts/const/reca/.

8. SEPTEMBER 11TH VICTIM COMPENSATION FUND

The United States government created a special compensation fund to provide a no-fault alternative to tort litigation for individuals who were physically injured or killed as a result of the aircraft hijackings and crashes on September 11, 2001. See the Air Transportation Safety and System Stabilization Act of September 22, 2001, Pub. Law 107–42, 115 Stat. 230, and the Victims of Terrorism Relief Act of 2001 of January 23, 2002, Pub. Law 107–134.

Eligibility is generally limited to (1) individuals on the planes at the time of the crashes (of course excluding the terrorists); and (2) individuals present at the World Trade Center, the Pentagon, or the site of the crash in Pennsylvania at the time of the crashes or in the immediate aftermath of the crashes. A claimant filing for compensation under this legislation waives any right to file a civil action or be a party to a civil action in any state or federal court for damages sustained as a result of the terrorist crashes, except actions to recover collateral source obligations. Determinations of eligibility are to be made by a Special Master. See 28 C. F. R. Part 104. There are two basic claims: personal injury and death. The program contains presumed economic and noneconomic losses.

Administration is conducted by the U. S. Department of Justice, and information can be obtained from its website at http://www.usdoj.gov/victimcompensation/.

*

PART 2

THE LAW OF WORKERS' COMPENSATION

CHAPTER 2

THEORIES AND POLICIES OF WORKERS' COMPENSATION

A. CONSTITUTIONAL THEORIES

Traditionally there have been several key constitutional objections to workers' compensation legislation. Most of these objections have centered on the following constitutional issues: due process of law, equal protection, impairment of contract obligations, trial by jury, and the privileges and immunities of the citizens of the different states. Initially, many of these constitutional objections were sustained; however, most constitutional problems have fallen by the wayside, particularly with the adoption by most states of specific constitutional amendments that authorize workers' compensation legislation. These constitutional problems are not always of just historical interest. They can be of importance to a modern day analysis of a particular compensation scheme; for example, see State ex rel. Doersam v. Industrial Commission (1988); Reed v. Brunson (1988). See also, Kline v. Berg Drywall, Inc. (Minn. 2004) (exclusion of claimant's legal counsel in early stages of ADR process violated collective bargaining statute; constitutional issues not addressed); Repass v. Workers' Compensation Division (2002) (adoption of AMA Guides as the exclusive measure for disability determination conflicted with several other statutory provisions and was therefore invalid).

1. FREEDOM OF CONTRACT

The U.S. Constitution prohibits the states from enacting laws that impair contract obligations. U.S. Const. Art. 1, § 10. As a result of this general prohibition and the parallel provisions sometimes found within state constitutions, some workers' compensation acts were held at one time to be violative of these provisions. However, the general view is to the effect that even if a workers' compensation act impairs an existing contract obligation between an employer and employee, the impairment may nevertheless be valid because a proper exercise of the police power has occurred. The health, safety and welfare of the people are of overriding importance.

2. ELECTION

Many of the original workers' compensation acts were said to be "elective" in order to avoid the constitutional difficulties imposed by the impairment of contract clause. An elective compensation act could thus be said to be a part of or to be "read into" every contract of employment, and the act contained provisions for employers or employees to opt in or out. There were usually penalty provisions that encouraged coverage. Later, most elective acts were said to be presumptive, that is, the employer and employee were presumed to be covered unless they had taken specific steps in accordance with the act to avoid coverage. Many acts appear to retain their elective and contractual character because of the manner in which they were written, despite the fact that today most state workers' compensation acts are compulsory. See generally, 1 Modern Workers Compensation, Part 2 Compulsory/Elective Coverage (2004).

The majority of states have enacted constitutional amendments that eliminate the constitutional difficulties originally posed in this area. See e.g., California Constitution, Article XIV § 4. Virtually all states today have compulsory coverage. Any system other than a compulsory one appears to be at odds with the purposes and policies of workers' compensation. It should be recalled that when coverage fails for one reason or another, the employee must then rely upon the common law remedies, or those remedies provided by the employers' liability acts.

3. PRESUMPTIVE COVERAGE

As previously mentioned, many compensation acts were elective, thus affording the employer and employee the right to accept or reject coverage. While most acts today are compulsory in character, the few remaining elective acts can pose coverage problems. For example, an employer could refuse on the basis of costs to carry workers' compensation insurance, and some employees may not be sufficiently knowledgeable of their rights to make intelligent elections. Consequently, some of the elective acts contain presumptive coverage provisions. In other words, the acts may provide for an election, but, coverage is presumed unless specific steps are taken by the employee or employer to preclude coverage.

4. COMPULSORY COVERAGE

A majority of states employ a compulsory coverage system of workers' compensation. This has generally been accomplished by state constitutional amendments authorizing workers' compensation statutes; see Schmidt v. Wolf Contracting Co.

(1945). These state amendments grant the necessary legislative power for the enactment of workers' compensation laws. These grants include the power to enact all reasonable and proper provisions necessary to effectuate the law and to fulfill the objectives of the constitutional provisions. Needless to say, the legislation cannot exceed whatever limitations exist in the constitutional provision.

5. EXCLUSIVENESS OF REMEDY

Regardless of whether a workers' compensation act is compulsory or elective, it generally affords the exclusive remedy for employees or dependents against employers for personal injuries, diseases, or deaths arising out of and in the course of employment. The exclusivity provision of workers' compensation acts is the keystone of all such legislation. The employee or dependents recover without regard to fault, and the employer is spared the possibility of large tort verdicts. Initial assaults on the exclusive remedy provided by workers' compensation were based on allegations of denial of due process of law. Common law and statutory actions were being abrogated along with common law defenses. There was strong early resistance (just as there is today) to the adoption of no-fault statutory systems of compensation. Needless to say, constitutional controversies surrounded meanings of employment, requirements to secure payment of compensation, and the hazardous employment classifications. Additionally, equal protection arguments were made. For a discussion of constitutional issues see generally Cudahy Packing Co. v. Parramore (1923); Arizona Employers' Liability Cases (1919); Jensen v. Southern Pacific Co. (1915). Most constitutional issues have been laid to rest by state constitutional amendments and by more liberal and realistic judicial decisions.

B. SOCIAL AND ECONOMIC POLICIES

1. EMPLOYEE–EMPLOYER "BARGAIN"

It is sometimes said that the employee and employer have entered into an "industrial bargain." The employee has given up his right to sue his employer for negligence and possibly receive a potentially greater damage award, and the employer has surrendered the common law defenses available in negligence actions. In exchange the employee is entitled to prompt but modest compensation for injuries, (or one's dependents for death) arising out of the employment relationship regardless of fault. The employer avoids costly litigation, and faces fixed and limited liability that can be covered by insurance.

2. INDUSTRIAL BURDEN FOR INJURIES AND DEATH

An important economic and social theory underlying the workers' compensation idea is that the cost of employment related injuries, diseases and deaths ultimately should be borne by the purchasers' and consumers' products and services. In other words, built into the cost of any product is the employer's insurance premium for the cost of workers' compensation or the cost of self-insurance. Thus, the costs of employment related injuries, diseases and deaths are properly distributed throughout society.

3. MEDICAL LOSS AND WAGE LOSS

The benefits payable vary from jurisdiction to jurisdiction. An essential inquiry to be made in each jurisdiction is whether the particular statute is based upon a medical loss theory, a wage loss theory, or both. A medical loss theory dictates, for example, that in the case of one who has lost an arm, compensation is required for the loss of that limb regardless of whether there has been an adverse impact upon earning capacity or lost wages. On the other hand, the wage loss theory is based upon the idea that a person should be compensated for loss of wages or diminished earning capacity and not for any pure medical losses that have occurred. Many jurisdictions mix the two theories and provide compensation based upon wage and medical losses. One may find in a purportedly wage loss jurisdiction the utilization of an injury schedule which provides compensation for pure medical losses enumerated in the schedule. For example, one would be entitled a specific amount of compensation for the loss of an arm regardless of any diminution in earning capacity.

It is worthy of note that the State of Florida in recent years attempted to employ an almost pure wage loss theory. As a result, Florida reduced the costs to employers of its workers' compensation system. Florida later added a schedule (medical loss) back into its system. Recent legislative reforms based upon medical loss and wage loss theories have not always produced better or more efficient systems. Regardless of the theory chosen, it should be kept in mind that generally workers' compensation benefits remain modest and have failed to keep abreast of inflation. See generally, M. McCluskey, The Illusion of Efficiency In Workers' Compensation "Reform," 50 Rutgers L. Rev. 657 (1998).

4. SOCIAL INSURANCE

It must be emphasized that workers' compensation in the United States is privately funded with an insurance base, whereas, in some countries, as for example, in Great Britain, a comprehensive social insurance system encompassing workers' compensation exists. There have been reform proposals in the United States aimed at establishing a more comprehensive national system, however, the American system remains a private one grounded in insurance. Certainly, a legitimate criticism of the current system can be made because compensation allocations are made regardless of need. It would at first appear that the general public bears the costs of workers' compensation, however, the actual costs are probably borne by limited groups of consumers of particular products and services. As a result of the fact that workers' compensation is a statutory no-fault scheme, many lose sight of the relevance of tort law and its notions of culpability and fault. For example, intoxication on the job and intentional self-injuries can prevent the recovery of compensation despite the no-fault theory of the system. For a further discussion of compensation as social insurance, see 1 A. Larson and L. Larson, Larson's Workers' Compensation Law, §§ 1.01–1.04 (2004) [hereinafter cited as "__ Larson § __"].

5. ECONOMIC APPRAISAL

In comparison with the tort compensation system, workers' compensation provides a more efficient economic model. For example, in the case of automobile accidents the tort system provides recovery to victims and families of only 44% of the sums provided by the system, with the remainder of the costs consumed by the inefficiency of the system itself, i.e., court costs, lawyers fees, insurance administration, etc. Workers' compensation ordinarily does not require lengthy and costly hearings; attorney's fees are regulated by statute; and while issues of fault do creep into compensation decisions, ordinarily compensation is assured when a work related injury or death is demonstrated, as opposed to the perils of the tort system.

In evaluating the workers' compensation system one must consider, however, the economic status of today's industrial worker. Wages generally have not kept up with inflation and

workers' compensation payments do not reflect current costs
of living; further the system fails to provide the amounts
necessary for effective educational retraining and vocational
rehabilitation. Compensation benefits simply do not reflect the
degree of economic harm suffered by a worker and his family;
all persons are treated in a uniform manner by the particular
workers' compensation act. Additionally, there is generally no
provision allowing for increases and escalations due to inflation. As a final criticism, workers' compensation benefits vary
a great deal from state to state. Because of this disparity a
National Workers' Compensation Standards Act has been proposed.

The U.S. Chamber of Commerce compiles annual surveys of
state and federal compensation law changes which are useful
in evaluating policy changes from jurisdiction to jurisdiction.
Its website address is: http://www.uschamber.com. An abbrevi-
ated annual survey of workers' compensation and unemployment insurance laws is available from the AFL–CIO, Department of Occupational Safety and Health. Its website is http://
www.aflcio.org.

A complete legal survey workers' compensation laws is
compiled each year by the American Insurance Association,
whose website is: http://www.aiadc.org. It should be noted that
the terrorists' acts of September 11, 2001 combined to create
the most costly catastrophic events in insurance industry
history. These events have had a serious economic impact on
workers' compensation and other insurance. Congress stepped
in and enacted The Terrorism Insurance Act (P.L. 107–297,
Title I, §§ 101–108, Nov. 26, 2002, 116 Stat. 2322) which
stabilized the insurance markets by providing federal back-
stops to reimburse insurers for terrorism losses above established thresholds. However, this legislation sunsets December
31, 2005, unless extended. The forgoing website maintained by
the American Insurance Association provides an analysis of

the issues and provides projected event scenarios for the future. See Towers Perrin, Workers' Compensation Terrorism Reinsurance Pool Feasibility Study (March 2004). See generally, 3 Modern Workers Compensation, Chapter 321 Statutory Comparison Table (2004); L. Dhooge, A Previously Unimaginable Risk Potential: September 11 and the Insurance Industry, 40 Am. Bus. L. J. 687 (2003).

C.　LIBERAL CONSTRUCTION OF COMPENSATION ACTS

Traditionally, it was generally said that there is to be a liberal construction of all workers' compensation acts because such legislation is remedial in nature. In fact, many workers' compensation acts have an express provision requiring liberal construction. The humane and beneficient purposes of workers' compensation legislation are certainly taken to heart by judges and compensation commissions. For example, see Ex parte Byrom (Ala.2004); Flores v. United Air Lines, Inc. (1988); Pacific Employers Insurance Co. v. Industrial Accident Commission (1945). While as a general rule workers' compensation acts are to be liberally construed, liberality of construction should not rise to the level of judicial legislation.

In recent times, in an effort at cost savings, some states have backed away from the tradition of liberal construction that favors the workers. These states have enacted statutes that attempt to provide neutrality of construction that neither favors the worker nor the employer. See e.g., N.M.S.A. § 52–5–1 (1998); Fla. Stat. § 440.015 (1997).

CHAPTER 3

WORKERS' COMPENSATION AND THE LAW OF TORTS

A. COMMON LAW AND STATUTORY ACTIONS

The common law remedies, and the statutory actions provided by the various employers' liability acts, form the underlying layer of law upon which a remedy can be based when the applicable workers' compensation act fails to provide coverage. Thus, common law and statutory actions still remain important. Common law and statutory actions are also extremely important when there is third party involvement and recovery is sought against them. Third parties are not covered by the act and are not allowed to limit their liability in the same manner as an employer. See generally, 1 Modern Workers Compensation, Chapter 102 Remedies Against Employer (2004).

B. THE STRUGGLE FOR COVERAGE AND NON–COVERAGE

Workers are constantly searching for greater compensation than that provided by the applicable workers' compensation system. Whenever possible, and certainly in situations in which there has been no fault on the part of the worker, attempts will be made to obtain increased recoveries through the utilization of traditional tort theories. Attorneys have certainly been creative in this area and there have been many attempts to circumvent the limitations on tort recovery imposed by workers' compensation legislation. Needless to say, because of the potential economic harm posed by large tort damages awards, employers want to insure that workers' compensation remains as a viable shield to tort recoveries. The more important areas in which the struggle for coverage and non-coverage exists are: co-employee suits, dual capacity situations, property damages, negligent inspectors; bad faith liability, products liability, negligent physicians, intentional torts, nonphysical torts and retaliatory discharge.

1. CO–EMPLOYEES

The majority of states provide co-employees with immunity from ordinary tort liability in connection with the employer immunity provisions found in the workers' compensation acts. In a few states, however, common law or statutory actions may be brought against all persons other than one's employer, and this would include a right against a co-employee who may have negligently injured or killed a fellow employee. The co-employee immunity which exists in the majority of states can be found both in statutes and in judicial decisions. For an example of a statutory provision creating co-employee immunity, see New York-McKinney's Workers' Compensation Law § 64.29; for an example of a judicial decision in favor of co-employee immunity which was grounded on public policy, see Miller v. Scott (1960). Even when immunity exists, it will not be available to a co-employee in most intentional tort situations. See e.g., Olszewski v. BMC West Corp. (Mont. 2004) (worker failed to meet burden of proof to show intentional tort exception to exclusive remedy provision); Torres v. Parkhouse Tire Service, Inc. (2001) (worker required to prove that co-employee acted with intent to cause injury in order to show exception to exclusive remedy rule). Immunity does not extend to all acts of persons who happen to be co-employees. See Sauve v. Winfree (Alaska, 1999).

2.　DUAL CAPACITY EMPLOYERS

Despite the fact that the employer is generally immune from tort liability, the dual capacity doctrine may place an employer in a position to be sued in an alternative capacity, thus avoiding the immunity provided by a workers' compensation act. The majority of courts are reluctant to find a dual capacity on the part of an employer. See Wilder v. United States (1989) (noting the doctrine to be disfavored). There have been rare instances of success on the basis of dual capacity theories. See generally, 1 Modern Workers Compensation § 102:9 Dual capacity doctrine (2004). One should contrast the similar dual persona doctrine in which an employer is sometimes sued in tort by a worker because the employer has a different legal identity, usually by way of merger or successor in interest. See, e.g., Van Bebber & Associates, Inc. v. Cook (Fla. App. 2004) (rejecting application of dual persona exception to particular facts); Herbolsheimer v. SMS Holding Co. (2000) (discussion of dual capacity and dual persons concepts). See generally, 1 Modern Workers Compensation § 102:10 Dual persona doctrine (2004).

3.　PROPERTY ACTIONS

It should always be remembered that the exclusive remedy provisions granting immunity to employers do not deny a worker's tort claim for any property damage. See Superb Carpet Mills, Inc. v. Thomason (1987) (property action allowed but no punitive damages permitted); Haddad v. Justice (1975). Liberal and modern views of what constitute property interests raise questions with regard to what types of actions might be maintainable against employers. See Brewer v. Monsanto Corp. (M.D. Tenn. 1986) (property damage claims for nuisance by employees not barred by Tennessee's exclusive remedy provision); Silkwood v. Kerr–McGee Corp. (10th Cir. 1981)

(Oklahoma's workers' compensation law does not bar employee property damage claims).

4. NEGLIGENT INSPECTORS

Some jurisdictions extend the employer's immunity to insurance carriers and others that may conduct safety inspections. In other jurisdictions, however, an insurance carrier or, for example, a union or union inspector, may be held liable under traditional tort concepts for the negligent performance of such an inspection. Compare Bryant v. Old Republic Insurance Co. (1970) with Nelson v. Union Wire Rope Corp. (1964). See also, Coker v. Deep South Surplus of Georgia, Inc. (2002) (action against third party hired by compensation carrier to perform safety inspection allowed).

5. BAD FAITH

The possibility exists of a successful bad faith action against either the employer or the insurance compensation carrier based upon the manner in which an employee's claim for workers' compensation benefits is administered. See Simkins v. Great West Cas. Co. (1987). A strong argument for bad faith on the part of an insurance company can be made when it fails to process an employee's legitimate claim for workers' compensation in a manner which demonstrates good faith. Thus, the potential exists for a large tort recovery even if a simple or fairly minor injury has occurred. See generally, J. Lee and B. Lindahl, 4 Modern Tort Law: Liability and Litigation, § 43.38 Claims against employer's Workers' Compensation insurer (2d ed. 2003).

6.   PRODUCTS LIABILITY

Perhaps the area of greatest interest for third party consideration is that of products liability. In practically every workers' compensation case when an employee has been injured by a particular product or instrumentality, attorneys should consider that deeper pocket provided by the product manufacturer. This is especially true today in light of the impact of Section 402A of the Restatement (Second) of Torts, and its strict liability approach. See generally, American Law of Products Liability 3d (2004).

Furthermore, the possibility exists for a products liability action by a worker against his employer through a dual capacity theory. For example, an employee of a company manufacturing a product may be injured in the normal course of his employment through the use of that particular product. See generally, Schump v. Firestone Tire and Rubber Co. (1989). See generally, D. Owen, M. Madden and M. Davis, 2 Madden & Owen on Product Liability, § 19:7 Employers As Manufacturers (3d ed. 2004).

7.   PHYSICIANS

Ordinarily a physician who commits malpractice on an injured employee who is covered by workers' compensation is liable in tort to the employee just as the physician would be to any other patient in the particular jurisdiction. However, workers' compensation acts providing co-employees with immunity may provide protection to a physician employed by the employer. See, e.g., Hayes v. Marshall Field & Co. (1953). It should be noted that the dual capacity theory could be used to impose tort liability on an employer for the negligence of a physician employee which causes additional harm to a worker. See Davis v. Stover (1987) (action allowed against physician who also happened to be a co-employee). Furthermore, a physician employee could be viewed as an independent contractor and thus subject to tort liability as a third person.

8. INTENTIONAL TORTS OF EMPLOYERS

Generally there is tort liability on the part of an employer for intentional torts committed against a worker. See generally, Smolarek v. Chrysler Corp. (1989) (retaliation and discrimination); Paroline v. Unisys Corp. (1989) (sexual assault); Childers v. Chesapeake & Potomac Tel. Co. (1989) (intentional infliction of emotional distress). Problems are posed by those difficult cases in which an employer has knowledge of a continuing dangerous condition to a worker and then knowingly fails to take appropriate action to eliminate the hazard. It is possible for the employer's conduct to be characterized as an "intentional tort" which is outside the coverage of the act. For example, see Johns–Manville Products Corp. v. Contra Costa Superior Court (1980); Blankenship v. Cincinnati Milacron Chemicals, Inc. (1982); but see, Kofron v. Amoco Chemicals Corp. (1982). See generally, J. Lee and B. Lindahl, 4 Modern Tort Law: Liability and Litigation, § 43.29 Intentional Injuries—By Employer (2d ed. 2003).

It should be noted that there is a growing trend in some states to provide enhanced workers' compensation awards for intentional torts in the workplace. These provisions punish the employer while providing a more efficient remedy to the employee who would otherwise have to resort to a traditional tort action with its cost, delay and uncertainty.

Further, there is a recent trend to impose criminal responsibility for certain employer conduct that injures or kills employees. See Illinois v. Chicago Magnet Wire Corp. (1989) (aggravated battery charged for exposing employees to hazardous substances in the workplace; no federal preemption by

OSHA). These criminal proceedings can be of assistance to claimants pursuing compensation and other civil remedies.

9. NONPHYSICAL TORTS

The exclusive remedy provisions of workers' compensation acts generally do not bar what are sometimes referred to as nonphysical torts. These would include actions for false arrest or imprisonment, libel and slander. Additionally, actions for sex, race and handicap discrimination, etc., would not be excluded. See generally, Cole v. Fair Oaks Fire Protection District (1987); Boscaglia v. Michigan Bell Tel. Co. (1984); Dorr v. C.B. Johnson, Inc. (1983) (slander). See generally, 6 Larson, §§ 104.01–104.07 (2004).

10. RETALIATORY DISCHARGE

Retaliatory discharge actions are permitted in most states when an employer discharges an employee for filing a workers' compensation claim. See e.g., Tyson Foods, Inc. v. McCollum (Ala. 2003) (retaliatory discharge claim under the workers' compensation act can be based upon a constructive discharge); City of Moorpark v. Superior Court (1998) (disability discrimination arising out of a workers' compensation claim could form the basis for a common-law wrongful discharge claim). Griess v. Consolidated Freightways Corp. (1989) (public policy supports retaliatory discharge claim). See also Lingle v. Norge Div. of Magic Chef, Inc. (1988) (retaliatory discharge action arising out of the filing of a workers' compensation claim is not preempted by 301 of the Labor Management Relations Act).

CHAPTER 4

THE EMPLOYEE–EMPLOYER RELATIONSHIP

A. EMPLOYEES AND EMPLOYERS GENERALLY

The common law defined a master as one who employed another to perform services and who controls or has a right of control over the other's conduct in performing such services. The master had to have not only the power to control, choose, and direct the servant with regard to the object to be accomplished but also had to possess the power to control the details of the work. The common law definitions are still of importance in establishing who is an employer and employee; however, definitions provided in workers' compensation legislation are controlling. Typically, an employee for workers' compensation coverage purposes is defined as one who works for, and under the control of, another for hire. A liberal construction should be given to the definitions of employer and employee because of the objectives of workers' compensation and the need to make coverage as expansive as possible. The Restatement (Second) of Agency § 220 relating to master and servant provides the basic definitions of employee and employer. The Restatement places primary emphasis on the employer's right to control the details of the work in order for a sufficient employment relationship to exist. Professor Larson has criticized this test and advocates in its place that an inquiry be directed at the nature of the claimant's work in relation to the employer's regular business. He argues that if the particular work has become a part of the cost of the product or services, then the particular work and thus the employee should be covered by compensation. Professor Larson indicates that the right of control test is a false one and that the independent contractor-employee classification issue can lead to unsatisfactory results. See 3 Larson, §§ 60.01–60.05 (2004). Despite this criticism, the traditional test of the employer/employee relationship continues, and the following factors, inter alia, are to be considered: who has assumed the direction and control of the employee; who possesses the power to hire and fire or recall; who bears responsibility for wages and compensation; in whose work was the employee engaged and for whose benefit was the work primarily being done; who furnished any equipment to be used by the employee; and who bore responsibility for the employee's working conditions.

B. EMPLOYEES

On the basis of statutes and judicial decisions, particular classes of employees are sometimes specifically included in or excluded from workers' compensation coverage. Typical employee classifications are provided hereinafter.

1. CASUAL EMPLOYEES

Casual employees are sometimes excluded from workers' compensation coverage. Real difficulties exist in determining who is a casual employee because of a failure to distinguish properly between casual and non-casual employments. Determinations may be based upon the following issues: the contract of hire; the nature of the service or work to be rendered; the scope and purpose of the employment; and the duration and regularity of the service. Ordinarily employment may be casual if it is temporary in nature and limited in purpose, or if it is incidental, accidental or irregular. The casual classification is not determined solely by a lack of frequency or length. As might be expected, the law in this area varies greatly from jurisdiction to jurisdiction, but the majority view may well be to exclude an employment from compensation coverage only if the employment is both casual and outside of the course of the employer's business. See e.g., Stoica v. Pocol (2001) (carpet layer employer's argument that claimant was a casual employee was rejected where claimant worked 30 per cent of the time); Riden v. Kemet Elecs. Corp. (S.C. App. 1993) (duct cleaner worker was not exempt from workers' compensation as a casual employee).

2. AGRICULTURAL EMPLOYEES

The majority of workers' compensation acts specifically exclude agricultural and farm laborers from coverage. See Eastway v. Eisenga (Mich. 1984) (exclusion of agricultural worker from compensation coverage held constitutional). Difficulties in this area exist with regard to the appropriate label; for example, one who trained a race horse was not an agricultural employee. See Tuma v. Kosterman (1984). The focus ordinarily is upon the substance of the employee's work as opposed to the employer's class of business. Because of the great number of workers employed in activities incidental to farm enterprises, the line between compensation coverage for ordinary employment and non-coverage for agricultural workers can be a perplexing one. For example, one employed as an agricultural worker, whose duties also include the repair of farm buildings, might not be covered; while one specially employed to repair a farm building would receive the benefits of workers' compensation coverage. See Cannon v. Industrial Accident Commission (1959).

3. DOMESTIC EMPLOYEES

Most compensation acts exempt domestic and household employment from coverage. The test for domestic or household employment is generally whether or not the duties performed are directed at the maintenance of the home. Some jurisdictions treat domestic employees as "casual" employees; others exclude them from coverage because of the "non-business" nature of their employment; and they are excluded in other jurisdictions because of the coverage exception applicable to employers who have less than the statutory requisite number of employees. It should be noted that the 1972 Report of the National Commission on State Workmen's Compensation Laws recommended that household workers be covered at least to the extent they are covered by federal social security insurance.

4. LOANED EMPLOYEES

The case law addressing the issue of loaned employees is confusing and conflicting. The common law rules are relevant to a determination of who is a lent employee and who occupies the status of the employee's general or special employer. The traditional test of special employment focuses on whether the employee has moved out of the control of the general employer and into the direction and control of the special employer. The inquiry is frequently made in tort cases in an effort to establish the proper employer for purposes of vicarious liability. It must be stressed that the issue in workers' compensation cases is simply the need to find an employer who can provide coverage. While in some states lent employee issues are resolved by statute, other states address the questions through case law which may impose compensation liability on the general or special employer, or both. See generally, 1 Modern

Workers Compensation § 105:9 Borrowing and loaning employers (2004).

5. STATE AND MUNICIPAL EMPLOYEES

State, municipal and public agency employees may be covered by the provisions of state workers' compensation acts, or by some alternative state compensation system. Workers' compensation statutes vary considerably and each state's act must be consulted individually in an effort to learn if a particular public employee is covered. Some of the more common issues are: whether municipal corporations are "employers" under the act; whether one is a state officer or official and thus outside coverage or is an employee. Generally, individuals exercising some portion of a state's sovereign power are considered officials. Police officers and firemen, in particular, have posed problems with regard to workers' compensation coverage. Generally, they are not viewed as "workmen" or "employees," and thus, are not covered; however, many workers' compensation acts have special provisions covering for these occupations.

6. FEDERAL EMPLOYEES

Employees and civil officers of the various branches of the United States Government or any of its wholly owned instrumentalities who are injured or killed in the performance of their duties are provided compensation under the Federal Employee's Compensation Act, 5 U.S.C.A. § 8101 et seq. The FECA is liberally construed, administered by the Secretary of Labor, and provides federal employees with their exclusive remedy against the United States for injuries or deaths sustained in the performance of their duties. Traditional third-party liability is not disturbed. The term "employee" under the Act is defined by statute and various classes of employees are specifically covered and others are specifically excluded. See 5 U.S.C.A. § 8101. The amounts and duration of compensation payable under the Act are among the most liberal in the United States. The amount of compensation payable under the FECA is generally based on the employee's monthly pay. Disputed claims for compensation are handled administratively under the Department of Labor. Hearings may be had and final decisions of the Secretary of Labor are subject to review by the Employees' Compensation Appeals Board within the U.S. Department of Labor.

Active duty members of the military services are not covered by state compensation acts or the FECA. They are subject to special federal statutory provisions that cover injury and death sustained in the line of duty. See Chapter 1, E, supra.

7. PARTICIPATION OF EMPLOYEES IN ENTERPRISE

Originally, workers' compensation acts excluded executives, partners, corporate officers and the like, from coverage because they did not fall under the definition of a workman. Additionally, it was felt that workers' compensation legislation was not intended to apply to these groups. Today, the fact that a claimant is a corporate officer does not generally preclude coverage. Even if an injury occurs while one is acting in a managerial capacity, one may still be considered an employee under an act. It is possible, however, because of stock ownership and a controlling interest for one, in effect, to be the business. In these instances there would be no coverage, unless perhaps one could be classified as an employee on the basis of the activities one was engaged in at the time of injury (i.e., non-executive activities). This result is reached on the basis of the dual capacity doctrine (not to be confused here with the dual capacity doctrine concerning an employer's potential tort liability; see Chapter 3, B., 2.), which makes it possible for an executive, who at the time of injury was acting as an employee rather than as an executive, to recover compensation. See Hirsch v. Hirsch Brothers, Inc. (1952). See generally, 82 Am. Jur. 2d, Workers' Compensation § 111 Partnerships; Joint Ventures.

Partners are treated differently because there is no separate employer entity; partners share equal liability and possess comparable rights in management. In the absence of special legislation, partners are not considered to be employees within compensation coverage even if they have been injured in situations in which they would have been entitled to compensation had they been employees.

8. VOLUNTEERS

One who works for another as a volunteer is not generally entitled to the benefits of workers' compensation because one is not deemed to be an employee. Under most acts only those persons who perform a service for hire are employees and, therefore, volunteers are excluded. See generally, 1 Modern Workers Compensation § 106:63 Volunteers, generally (2004).

9. ALIENS

The term "employee" in the various workers' compensation acts includes all persons who perform services for hire and includes aliens. It should be pointed out, however, that some acts require that one be a state resident in order to receive workers' compensation benefits. States are not uniform in this regard and in the absence of a provision to the contrary, it is generally said that residency is not a requirement for compensation. It should be noted that certain classes of nonresident alien dependents are often excluded from the receipt of death benefits. See Jurado v. Popejoy Constr. Co. (1993) (constitutional challenge); Alvarez Martinez v. Industrial Commission (1986). See generally, 1 Modern Workers Compensation § 106:9 Aliens (2004).

10. MINORS

Generally, any person may be an "employee" for the purposes of workers' compensation coverage, and one is not excluded from such coverage simply because of minority. Most states have specific provisions in their compensation acts regarding minors. In some states minors are entitled to double compensation, and in others minors may either opt for compensation or sue for damages. A minor's unlawful employment may itself provide a separate tort basis for liability. See Restatement (Second) of Torts § 286 Comment e (1966). See generally, 1 Modern Workers Compensation § 106:46 Minors (2004).

11. ILLEGAL EMPLOYMENTS

Illegally employed workers can present unique coverage problems. The difficulty usually relates to the question of whether the employment itself is prohibited by statute; for example, prostitution would be a prohibited employment in most jurisdictions, and thus if one is employed to perform acts in violation of a penal statute, coverage would be denied. On the other hand, one who has been illegally employed still enjoys coverage when the employment contract is unlawful because of a provision relating to the legality of such an agreement; for example, laws prohibiting the employment of a minor should not interfere with coverage if a minor is injured in an otherwise lawful employment.

12. INDEPENDENT CONTRACTORS

If one is classified as an independent contractor, rather than the servant or employee of another, one may lose the right to workers' compensation coverage. The independent contractor issue is one of the most frequently litigated questions in the law of workers' compensation. The Restatement (Second) of Agency, § 220 provides the usual definition and tests utilized in this area. The most common factors considered are: the right of control; the method of payment; the providing of materials, tools, or supplies; control over the work site; and the right to discharge the employee. See generally, 1 Modern Workers Compensation § 106:31 Independent contractors (2004).

Independent contractor decisions are often conflicting and irreconcilable. The difficulty in this area stems from attempts by the courts to resolve independent contractor issues in tort cases in which the question is one of vicarious liability. It is questionable whether an inquiry aimed at the avoidance of vicarious liability should be of any relevance to a determination of workers' compensation coverage, given the social and economic policies underlying workers' compensation legislation. See Laurel Daily Leader, Inc. v. James (1955). See also 3 Larson, §§ 61.01–61.08 (2004). Professor Larson argues that a relative nature of work test should be used because it is supported by workers' compensation theory. This test provides that any worker whose efforts are regularly and continually included in the costs of products or services should receive compensation from the manufacturer of such products, or the provider of such services.

13. PROFESSIONAL EMPLOYEES

While often professionals may be viewed as independent contractors, it is certainly possible for them in certain employment circumstances to be employees for purposes of workers' compensation coverage. For example nurses and interns regularly employed by hospitals are generally employees and included within coverage. Additionally, it is possible for an attorney to have an employer and be an "employee" for workers' compensation coverage. See Egan v. New York State Joint Legislative Committee (1956). See generally, 1 Modern Workers Compensation, Part 5 Covered Employers/Employees/Dependents (2004).

C. EMPLOYERS GENERALLY

Workers' compensation acts must be consulted for the definition of "employer." As in the case of "employees" the statutory definition of "employer" is the controlling one to the extent that common law concepts of master and servant are modified. Typically, "employer" means a master or principal who employs another to perform services for hire; who controls or has the right of control of the other; and who usually pays another's wages directly. Situations may arise in which an employee appears to have two employers. For example, an employer's employee may hire another without informing the hiree of the true employer's identity. Since an employer for workers' compensation coverage is usually provided on agency theories, the employee is permitted to elect a covered "employer" for compensation purposes. See Hesse v. J. J. Oys & Co. (1958).

1. MINIMUM NUMBER OF EMPLOYEES

A minority of workers' compensation acts contain provisions that mandate coverage only in situations in which an employer has a specified number of regular employees. Typical provisions of this nature would, for example, require coverage in the case of three or more employees. Minimum employee requirements are liberally construed in favor of coverage. See Jackson v. Fly (1952). See generally, 1 Modern Workers Compensation § 105:6 Number of employees (2004).

Furthermore, the usual requirement of workers "regularly" employed does not necessarily mean constant or continuous employment in order to meet the minimum threshold for coverage.

2. GENERAL AND SPECIAL EMPLOYERS

General and special employer issues usually arise in loaned employee cases. The term "general employer" refers to a worker's original employer, while the term "special employer" refers to the one to whom a worker is loaned. It is possible for one to be the employee of both at the same time, and thus seek compensation against one or both. Special employment relationships require the consent and knowledge of the employee. The basic test for determining one's employer in the loaned employee situation is: who had the right of control and direction over the worker at the relevant time. The pertinent factors, inter alia, include: the power to fire; who paid the wages; and whose business was being furthered. See also Chapter 4, A.4., Loaned Employees, supra. See generally, 1 Modern Workers Compensation § 105:9 Borrowing and loaning employers (2004).

3. SUBCONTRACTORS AND STATUTORY EMPLOYERS

A majority of states have provisions in their workers' compensation acts which are designed to prevent a general contractor from shielding himself from compensation liability through the use of subcontractors. These "statutory employer" or "contracting under" provisions are intended to provide protection for employees injured or killed while working for uninsured or judgment proof subcontractors. In order to successfully maintain a compensation claim against a statutory employer, the subcontractor's employee must establish that the work that gave rise to the injury was a part of the regular business of the statutory employer. The statutory employer may also be benefited in that tort liability can be precluded. See Black v. Cabot Petroleum Corp. (1989) (exclusive remedy protection involving upstream and downstream contractors); Kelpfer v. Joyce (1961). It must be pointed out, however, that issues of primary versus secondary liability, the status of the statutory employer as guarantor or insurer under some acts, and the subcontractor's failure to carry insurance, may affect third party tort liability on the part of the statutory employer, even if he has paid workers' compensation benefits. See 4 Larson, §§ 70.01–70.06 (2004). The possibility exists for a statutory employer to obtain reimbursement from a solvent subcontractor. See, e.g., New York-McKinney's Workers' Compensation Law § 56. See generally, 1 Modern Workers Compensation § 103:14 Statutory employers (2004).

4. CHARITABLE ORGANIZATIONS

Employees of charitable or nonprofit organizations may not be covered by workers' compensation in some states. Some acts expressly exclude charitable employers. Charities and nonprofit organizations may be excluded as employers because they involve employments not carried on "for pecuniary gain." In those jurisdictions that require that one be engaged "in the trade or business of the employer" in order to be covered there are conflicting decisions with regard to the coverage of an employee of a charitable organization. The better view allows coverage. See Smith v. Lincoln Memorial University (1957). See generally, 1 Modern Workers Compensation § 106:16 Charity or nonprofit organization personnel (2004).

5. CONCURRENT EMPLOYERS

An employee may have more than one employer for workers' compensation purposes. These employers may be characterized as either concurrent employers or as joint employers. When one is injured or killed in the service of such employers, several approaches have been taken toward compensation. Liability may be joint, or apportioned, or placed upon only one employer. In apportionment situations employers may be required to provide compensation in proportion to the wages they paid the employee. See Newman v. Bennett (1973). See generally, J. Lee and B. Lindahl, 4 Modern Tort Law: Liability and Litigation, § 43.23 Covered "employees" (2d ed. 2003).

6. SUCCESSIVE EMPLOYERS

It is not uncommon for an employee to have successive employers, and difficulties can arise in determining which employer is the "employer" for workers' compensation purposes. One method of determining one's responsible employer is to focus simply on the date of injury, and to view the employer at that time as the appropriate one. In those cases in which a disability or injury has resulted from successive employments, the various employers may be required to provide compensation on the basis of their contribution to such disability or injury. Some injuries and certainly death, as in tort cases, can be viewed as single and indivisible, or as incapable of apportionment, with entire liability imposed upon the employers.

In cases of occupational disease and successive employers the following possibilities exist: liability is placed upon the employer in whose service the disease was contracted; liability is borne by the last employer in whose employ the worker was last exposed to the disease's hazards; or liability may be apportioned among several employers. Statutory variations exist with respect to the foregoing possibilities, but given the objectives and policies of workers' compensation, there should be complete compensation for employment related diseases whenever a solvent contributing employer exists. See generally, 1 Modern Workers Compensation, Chapter 116 Subsequent Injuries (2004).

CHAPTER 5

THE COVERAGE FORMULA NECESSITY FOR A "PERSONAL INJURY BY ACCIDENT ARISING OUT OF AND IN THE COURSE OF EMPLOYMENT"

A. THE COVERAGE INQUIRY

Since the inception of workers' compensation legislation, there have been difficulties in fixing and defining the boundaries of coverage. Problems in this area have largely been the result of a failure to properly identify and inquire into the issue of the scope of the risk. The early cases took a tort law, proximate cause approach toward the risk inquiry. Needless to say, a fault based risk analysis is totally incompatible with the objective and policies of workers' compensation. Subsequent decisions developed various doctrines aimed at defining the scope of the risk, e.g., the "peculiar risk" doctrine, see infra.

One can best understand scope of the risk questions by reference to three broad categories of risks. First, there are definite employment related risks, as the loss of limb by a machinery operator; all would agree that this type of injury is within the scope of the risk of employment and covered by workers' compensation. Second, there are personal risks, such as an injury produced by an epileptic seizure while at work, but unrelated to the employment; this injury might be covered by hospital insurance, but not by workers' compensation because the injury arose from a purely personal condition and was unrelated to a risk of employment. Third, there are neutral risks, such as acts of God, or random acts of violence unrelated to one's employment. These risks are neutral because they bear no relation to one's employment, and they cannot be classified as personal risks. Neutral risks are the cause of a great deal of conflict and confusion.

In a further effort to define the boundaries of coverage, an inquiry is made with regard to whether a sufficient relation exists between one's employment and one's injury. Factors such as time, place and circumstances are considered; however, scope of the risk issues with concomitant confusion also arise in this context. For example, an employee traveling to and from work could be excluded from coverage because at the time of injury the employee was not at work and was off the employer's business premises. While time, place, and circumstances may be relevant, the true question in to and from work situations may be whether the perils of such a journey should be within the scope of the risk created by one's employment, given the policies and purposes of workers' compensation.

An additional inquiry which must be made in an effort to define coverage boundaries is that of factual cause. This refers to the necessity for a factual connection between one's activities at the time of injury and the injury of which one complains; i.e., did the employment in which one was allegedly engaged produce the medical complaint for which one now seeks compensation. For example, did one's employment activity contribute to or cause a heart attack that occurred while one was at work.

In summary, the principal elements directed at coverage in workers' compensation cases are:

1. scope of the risk;

2. sufficient relation to employment, and;

3. factual cause.

The preceding issues arise in the context of the statutory language or coverage formula found in workers' compensation legislation. The coverage formula used in the vast majority of workers' compensation acts requires a "personal injury or death by accident arising out of and in the course of employment." The "arising out of" requirement refers to the scope of the risk issue previously discussed in this section and which will be more fully discussed hereinafter. The "in the course of" requirement refers to the sufficient relation to employment issue (time, place, and circumstances factors) which was discussed above and which will be more fully developed later. Factual causation issues will also be discussed.

The coverage formula requirements of "personal injury by accident" have posed problems in cases involving diseases, mental illnesses, and injuries to artificial limbs. Originally, injuries to artificial limbs were not considered "personal injuries," and disabilities from disease that developed over long time periods were excluded from coverage because no personal inquiry "by accident" had occurred.

It should be noted that while the coverage formula speaks in terms of "personal injury," workers' compensation legislation also provides coverage for death cases. Thus, much of what ordinarily is stated with regard to injuries is also applicable to death situations. Therefore, the analysis of various circumstances producing injuries in the following sections is also applicable when those circumstances have resulted in death. See generally, 1 Modern Workers Compensation § 110:1 Work nexus is essential (2004).

B. THE "ARISING OUT OF" CONCEPT

One can best understand the "arising out of" concept by comparing it to the scope of the risk question asked and resolved by courts on the basis of policy considerations in tort cases. Sometimes this issue is dealt with in tort cases through the use of proximate cause terminology. It is important to remember that this is a question of law and policy exclusively for the court, and certainly scope of the risk issues should be approached in a similar fashion in workers' compensation cases. In light of the objectives and policies of workers' compensation it is submitted that a much broader approach should be taken toward the scope of the risk than is taken in tort cases. See generally, 1 Modern Workers Compensation § 110:4 Arising out of requirement (2004).

There appears to be five basic risk doctrines employed by the courts to determine the scope of the risk.

1. THE FIVE BASIC RISK DOCTRINES

a. *Proximate Cause*

Originally judges had difficulty divorcing themselves from tort law with its proximate cause and fault concepts, and some early cases, therefore adopted the fault-related proximate cause test for the "arising out of" concept, which required that one's employment be the proximate cause of one's injury. This approach is much too narrow, and it is incompatible and in conflict with the objectives of any statutory no-fault compensation system.

b. *Peculiar Risk*

An early device which resulted in hardship to employees was the peculiar risk doctrine. This risk concept excluded coverage for injuries caused by risks which, admittedly were within the course of one's employment, but which were commonly shared by others, even though the employee was exposed for a longer period of time by virtue of the nature of the employee's employment. For example, an employee who suffered a sunstroke while delivering coal for his employer was viewed as not having been "peculiarly exposed" to the danger of sunstroke because he was not subjected to a materially greater risk of sunstroke than other outdoor workers. Dougherty's Case (1921). The peculiar risk theory is generally rejected in modern compensation cases because it is unrealistic and allows only limited coverage.

c. Increased Risk

A modern approach which provides broader coverage than the peculiar risk test is the increased risk doctrine. This approach includes within the scope of the risk those risks to which an employee has been exposed for a longer period of time than the public, even though the risk is commonly shared by all. If one's employment results in a greater exposure to a risk there would be coverage even though the risk is not one that is qualitatively different from that shared by others. For example, one constantly exposed to extreme heat on the job and who suffers from heatstroke should be entitled to compensation under the increased risk theory.

d. Actual Risk

A liberal approach toward the scope of the risk issue can be found in the actual risk doctrine. The sole question to be answered is whether the risk realized was in fact a risk of one's employment, regardless of whether the risk is commonly shared by the public. For example, heat prostration would be compensable if the nature of the employment exposed the employee to the risk; the fact that the risk is common to all who are exposed to the sun's rays on a hot day would be immaterial. Hughes v. Trustees of St. Patrick's Cathedral (1927).

e. Positional Risk

The positional risk doctrine is the most liberal of the scope of the risk theories, and it has been adopted in a minority of jurisdictions. The only inquiry under a positional risk theory is whether one's employment was responsible for one's being at the time and place where an injury occurred.

Even the most neutral of risks can be included; for example, an employee at work who was accidentally struck by an arrow fired by a small boy next door, would be covered. Gargiulo v. Gargiulo (1952).

2. A MISCELLANY OF RISKS

a. Acts of God

While acts of God such as windstorms, tornadoes, exposure, lightning, floods, earthquakes, etc., would at first appear to be outside the employment risk, it is generally agreed that if one's employment has enhanced or "increased" the risk of injury from these sources, the injury would be compensable. In addition to an increased risk approach to recovery, it may be possible to recover on the basis of "actual risk" or "positional risk" theories. The "proximate cause" or "peculiar risk" approaches would disallow compensation. See generally, 1 Modern Workers Compensation § 113:3 Act of God defense (2004).

b. Street Risk Doctrine

Frequently employees find themselves on the streets and highways in the course of their employment. Early decisions denied recovery to employees who were injured as a result of the realization of risks associated with the use of streets and highways because these were viewed as common risks or hazards to the general public and not risks peculiar to one's employment. The situation is somewhat different today, and an employee who is subjected to a greater exposure to the risks of the street, despite the fact that such risks are common to the public, may be covered. Coverage in these cases can be provided on the basis of the increased risk approach; also, coverage can be had on the basis of the actual risk or positional risk doctrines. See generally, 1 Modern Workers Compensation, Chapter 111 Travel & Commuting (2004).

c. Imported Dangers Doctrine

It is not uncommon for employees to be exposed to a risk of harm which they or their fellow employees have imported to the worksite; e.g., matches, explosives, firearms, etc. Traditionally, risks imported by the injured employee were viewed as "personal" and outside of the scope of the risk of employment. A danger imported by one's co-employee, while it may appear to be a neutral risk, could nevertheless give rise to recovery on the basis of increased, actual or positional risk theories. In Ward v. Halliburton Co. (1966), compensation was denied to an employee who was killed when his hunting gun accidentally discharged while he was getting a work uniform from his car; the court indicated that recovery would have been allowed if the gun had belonged to another employee. Additionally, an employee might be able to recover for the realization of a personal risk that the employee has imported, if it could be established that the employment had increased such a risk. See generally, 1 Modern Workers Compensation § 110:8 On-premises injuries—Personal risks (2004).

d. Assault

Assaults are held to be within the scope of the risk and to arise out of one's employment when the nature of the employment (e.g., policeman or security guard) increases the likelihood of such an occurrence, or if the assault has grown out of a controversy that is work related. Ordinarily assaults are not within the scope of the risk if they have been prompted by malice or personal motives; however, even these assaults may be included if in some manner one's work has contributed to the occurrence. Assaults in some cases, such as those by strangers, lunatics, children, etc., may be viewed as neutral risks outside coverage; however, it may be possible for these to be covered through the use of the positional risk doctrine. See generally, 1 Modern Workers Compensation, Chapter 114 Assaults or Firearms (2004).

Early cases recognized the aggressor defense which denied compensation to an aggressor in work-related assaults. The aggressor defense has been discredited today because it creates a fault based defense in a no-fault system. Despite the rejection of the aggressor defense, a substantial minority of jurisdictions by statute exclude from coverage those who have been harmed as a result of their "willful intent to injure" others. Generally these statutes require a greater degree of fault and wrongdoing than is required for the aggressor defense.

e. Horseplay

Frequently injuries occur in the workplace as a result of horseplay. There is little difficulty in providing coverage for a non-participant who is a victim of a horseplay injury; such an injury is viewed as being within the scope of the risk of one's employment. Difficult problems are posed, however, when one instigates or actively participates in horseplay and receives an injury. These cases may be disposed of on the basis of whether they occurred "in the course of" employment; however, the better analysis is one that focuses on the scope of the risk inquiry with the increased, actual, or positional risk doctrines determining coverage. In any event, an instigator or willing participant may be able to recover on the basis of the longevity and customary nature of the practice. See generally, 1 Modern Workers Compensation § 115:3 Horseplay (2004).

f. Heart Cases

One of the most problematic areas in the law of workers' compensation is that of heart cases. Commonly these cases are approached on the basis of whether or not a personal injury "by accident" has occurred. This approach requires that "unusual" strain or exertion precipitate the heart attack. This is an impractical and unsatisfactory test for coverage in heart cases; distinctions between "usual" and "unusual" strains are practically impossible to make, and serve to confuse the issue. See generally, J. Lee and B. Lindahl, 4 Modern Tort Law: Liability and Litigation, § 43:40 Heart attacks (2d ed. 2003).

The better approach is one that focuses on the scope of the risk; thus if one's employment has contributed to the heart attack because of exertion or other work-related circumstances, the attack may be found to have arisen out of one's employment; otherwise heart attacks occurring on the job would involve personal risks. Professor Larson advocates the utilization of both a legal test and a medical test in heart cases. The legal test would be met on the basis of work-related exertion, and the medical test would simply require proof of a causal connection between such work-related exertion and the heart attack. This inquiry would be the same as that previously characterized as factual cause and would necessitate expert medical testimony.

As a result of the difficulties in this area, some jurisdictions have special provisions directed at heart and exertion cases.

g. Pre-existing Injury or Disease

It is certainly not uncommon for employees to bring pre-existing medical problems to the workplace. The difficulty posed in this area stems from the fact that pre-existing medical problems constitute personal risks which would fall outside of coverage; however, if one is able to demonstrate that one's employment exacerbated or aggravated a pre-existing medical problem, then recovery may be permitted. The obvious problem facing employees is that of factual cause and medical proof. One must establish through expert medical testimony the fact of aggravation and a causal connection between one's employment and the claimed injury. Some jurisdictions address this problem area through special provisions in their workers' compensation act. See generally, 1 Modern Workers Compensation § 116:2 Employment aggravation of pre-existing condition (2004).

h. Unexplained Accidents

Coverage questions arise in cases of unexplained deaths, unexplained falls, and idiopathic falls. A strict application of the neutral risk or personal risk theories could result in a denial of coverage, even if a fall or death occurred in the course of employment. An application of the positional risk doctrine can result in recovery even if the cause of a fall or death is unknown, because of the employment relation that existed at the time. The positional risk doctrine could also permit recovery in idiopathic fall situations in which the fall was the result of a purely personal condition, if, for example, the fall occurred at work. See generally, 1 Modern Workers Compensation § 116.10 Idiopathic conditions (2004).

In an effort to resolve the problems posed by an unexplained employee death, courts will generally employ a presumption that the death was one that arose out of employment if the death occurred at the appropriate time and in the appropriate work situation. Given the objectives and policies of workers' compensation legislation every effort should be made to resolve unexplained injury and death cases in favor of the employee or his survivors.

C.   THE "IN THE COURSE OF" CONCEPT

1.   AN INTRODUCTION AND PERSPECTIVE

The statutory formula for workers' compensation coverage generally requires a personal injury by accident arising out of and "in the course of" one's employment. The "in the course of" requirement refers to the necessity for a sufficiently close relationship between one's employment and injury. This inquiry focuses on considerations of time, place, and circumstances, as they relate to one's employment.

Problems in this area usually occur for two reasons. First, the "in the course of" concept may be confused with the vicarious liability requirement of the same terms used in tort cases to establish liability; for example, a master is liable for the torts of a servant committed in the course of employment. The vicarious liability "in the course of" requirement certainly may be of assistance in many workers' compensation cases in establishing the requisite employment connection or relation; however, it should not be determinative in those cases in which it conflicts with the policies and coverage objectives of workers' compensation legislation. For example, if one's employment has produced an injury which occurs or manifests itself while one is not at work and off the employer's premises, there should still be coverage. In other words, one need not be acting within the course and scope of one's employment when an employment related harm produces injury. The only issue is one of causal connection between one's employment and injury. Rogers v. Allis Chalmers Manufacturing Co. (1949); see 1 Larson, §§ 12.01–12.02 (2004). In Technical Tape Corp. v. Industrial Commission (1974), the inhalation of chemical fumes at work produced residual intoxication causing an employee to have an automobile accident after leaving the work-place; compensation was allowed.

The second cause of difficulties in this area stems from confusing the "in the course of" requirement with the scope of the risk inquiry which is made in conjunction with the "arising out of" requirement. In other words, the time, place, and circumstances considerations involved in the "in the course of" question may be permitted to dictate the answer to the scope of the risk issue. The scope of the risk issue should always be viewed as a question directed at the scope of workers' compensation coverage, with the necessity for a liberal and broad approach toward employment risks. The "in the course of" requirement really should do no more than establish the necessary relation to one's employment required for workers' compensation coverage. The more liberal a jurisdiction's approach toward the selection of a risk theory, then the less that will probably be required to meet the "in the course of" test. If a positional risk theory is employed, little would probably be required to establish the necessary employment relation. For example, a salesman who suffers harm some distance from the employer's place of business, and on the premises of another, could be covered. See Wiseman v. Industrial Accident Commission (1956).

2. COMMON "IN THE COURSE OF" PROBLEMS

a. *Going to and From Work*

Injuries occurring while employees are traveling to and from work have constituted a large portion of workers' compensation litigation, and there is a lack of uniformity in this area. It should be noted at the outset that the problems posed with regard to coverage stem from a failure to recognize that many of these cases should be addressed on the basis of the "arising out of'' requirement with its concomitant scope of the risk inquiry.

Generally, those accidents that take place while one is on the way to or from work are viewed as outside the course of one's employment; however, if one is on the employer's premises (having not yet arrived at work or in the process of leaving work) ordinarily there would be coverage. The key issue thus becomes the boundaries of the employer's premises. Various devices have been employed to resolve coverage issues for those injured off of but near the employer's premises; included are: the parking lot exception; the "so-close" rule; the "proximity" rule; and the "threshold" doctrine. Some jurisdictions have special provisions in their compensation laws to deal with "going to and from work" problems.

An employee may well be found "in the course of" in the following special circumstances, even if the injury has occurred while going to or coming from work. These special circumstances exist if: the employer provides the transportation or travel expenses; the employer compensates the employee for time spent in travel; or the employee is on call and travel constitutes a significant portion of employment duties. In many situations employees are required, as a regular part of their employment, to spend time away from home or office and difficult questions arise here because of the myriad of circumstances in which one might receive an injury; e.g., sleeping, eating, recreation, etc., in conjunction with work-related travel. Again it must be emphasized that the crux of the "in the course of" problem is to be found in a failure to address many of these cases on the basis of the scope of the risk. See generally, J. Lee and B. Lindahl, 4 Modern Tort Law: Liability and Litigation, § 43.17 Going to and coming from place of employment (2d ed. 2003).

b. Mixed-Purpose Trips

An area in which the rules of vicarious liability have created confusion with regard to workers' compensation coverage is that of mixed-purpose trips. On occasion an employee may be injured while on a trip that is both for the employee's benefit and for that of the employer; these are sometimes called "dual purpose" cases. Certainly, if the trip is primarily for the benefit of the employer there should be coverage despite the fact that the trip also involves some personal benefit or personal purpose; this is generally called the dominant purpose rule. Marks' Dependents v. Gray (1929). See generally, 1 Modern Workers Compensation § 111:18 Dual purpose travel (2004).

Just as in cases of vicarious liability, issues of frolic and detour arise. It should be kept in mind that in vicarious liability situations the issue is one of possible employer liability to a third person, whereas in compensation cases the issue is one of coverage for the injured employee. Given the question in workers' compensation cases a more liberal approach is required and less emphasis should be placed upon the vicarious liability meaning of "in the course of." Little should be required in the way of employment connection, and the major inquiry should focus on the scope of the risk. In some jurisdictions a liberalizing trend is evident in this area. For example, coverage was extended to an employee who, prior to going to work, was injured in an accident while driving his child to school in a company truck; this would certainly appear to have been a personal trip, but the presence of the company's name and address on the truck seemingly determined the outcome. Thomas v. Certified Refrigeration, Inc. (1974).

c. Recreation

Various approaches have been taken toward compensation coverage when accidents have occurred during recreational or social activities. There may be liability when injuries from these sources have occurred on the employer's premises. Some decisions take a scope of employment approach toward the activity that produced the injury, while others insist upon some kind of benefit to the employer, direct or indirect. Recreational cases may frequently involve "going to and from" work and personal comfort issues (see infra). The more liberal a jurisdiction's risk theory, the greater the likelihood of coverage in recreation cases, and the less that is required for an activity to be "in the course of" employment. See generally, J. Lee and B. Lindahl, 4 Modern Tort Law: Liability and Litigation, § 43.14 Recreational activities (2d ed. 2003).

d. *Personal Comfort Doctrine*

Employees who are injured while engaged in activities aimed at their personal comfort, e.g., drinking, eating, resting, smoking, using toilet facilities, etc., generally enjoy compensation coverage if their activities bear the necessary relationship to their employment. An employee may, however, remove oneself from the course of employment if, in efforts to satisfy personal needs, one abandons one's work or employs means which move the employee outside of the employment relation, thus indicating that a purely personal or neutral risk has been realized. For example, a deliveryman injured while attempting to dislodge a rabbit from a culvert was denied compensation. Ranger Insurance Co. v. Valerio (1977). See generally, J. Lee and B. Lindahl, 4 Modern Tort Law: Liability and Litigation, § 43.13 Personal comfort (2d ed. 2003).

e. *Emergencies*

Employees injured while attempting rescues, or otherwise in emergency situations, are viewed as having acted within the course of their employment if an interest of the employer was furthered by the effort or activity. The good will of the employer alone may constitute a sufficient interest for coverage. As a matter of policy, very little should be required for a finding of "in the course of" when employees receive injuries during rescue attempts. The positional risk theory should be employed to provide coverage when an employee, motivated by common humanity and decency, is injured while attempting to rescue a stranger who bears no relation to the employer's business. See Food Products Corp. v. Industrial Commission of Arizona (1981). See generally, 1 Modern Workers Compensation § 110:11 Emergencies (2004).

f. *Wilful Misconduct and Violation of Laws, Regulations and Safety Rules*

The question of wilful misconduct on the part of an employee may arise in two important contexts: (1) it may provide the basis for a statutorily created defense in a minority of jurisdictions or, (2) in the absence of such a statute, it may be relevant to the issue of whether an employee was outside of the course of employment at the time of injury. The wilful misconduct defense is usually a difficult one to establish, because employee fault should not bar recovery under workers' compensation theory. The term "wilful" is strictly construed, and gross negligence will not suffice. The issue of wilful misconduct may also arise in the "in the course of" context in conjunction with questions concerning personal comfort, going to and from work, recreation, etc.

Some jurisdictions provide the employer with a statutory defense when an employee has wilfully violated safety rules, regulations, or statutes. The wilful violation defense is in some ways comparable to the assumption of the risk defense in tort cases. The employer must establish actual knowledge of the rule or statute and an appreciation of the risk connected with non-compliance. Additionally, excuses may exist for non-compliance. The justification and wisdom of the wilful violation defense is open to question in light of the no-fault nature of workers' compensation and the inevitability of employee injuries which are in large part the result of human frailty. See generally, 1 Modern Workers Compensation, Chapter 115 Employee Misconduct (2004).

g. *Intoxication*

Employee intoxication is addressed statutorily in a majority of jurisdictions, and it may constitute a separate defense to coverage. The key question in employee intoxication cases is one of causation. The "sole cause" approach taken by some statutes appears to be the one most compatible with the policies of workers' compensation legislation; if there has been some work-related contribution to the injury, there should be coverage.

The coverage question in intoxication cases may also be addressed on the basis of a scope of the risk inquiry, an "in the course of" requirement, or as an issue of whether an injury "by accident" has occurred. See generally, 1 Modern Workers Compensation § 115:18 Alcohol or drug abuse (2004).

h. *Suicides*

Suicides have traditionally posed problems because they may be viewed as the result of a wilful act on the part of an employee, which severs the causal connection between a job related injury and one's death. The minority view, which parallels the traditional tort view, would only allow recovery in those cases in which one committed suicide in a state of delirium or as a result of an uncontrollable impulse evidencing an inability to make a conscious decision with regard to the taking of one's life. Under the minority approach there would need to be medical testimony of a mental disorder sufficiently serious to deprive one of volition.

A more liberal approach is generally taken in many jurisdictions, and if an unbroken chain of causation can be established between a work related injury and a mental condition that leads to a suicide, then compensation may be permitted. See City of Tampa v. Scott (1981).

Given the difficulties involved in establishing the requisite causal relation between employment related injuries and suicides, a better approach would be one requiring simply a demonstration of some contribution to the suicide by an employment related physical or psychic injury. See Lopucki v. Ford Motor Co. (1981). A broad approach should be taken toward the scope of the risk in suicide cases, and such deaths should be viewed as in the course of one's employment when a work relation can be shown. See generally, J. Lee and B. Lindahl, 4 Modern Tort Law: Liability and Litigation, § 43.42 Suicide (2d ed. 2003).

D. THE NECESSITY OF "PERSONAL INJURY BY ACCIDENT"

1. THE PROBLEMS

Traditionally most workers' compensation acts have required as a part of their coverage formula a "personal injury by accident" or "accidental injury." Difficulties have arisen in interpreting the meanings of "accident" and "personal injury." Historically, problems have existed in this area because of the failure to take a pragmatic and liberal approach toward these requirements as they relate to the scope of the employment risk.

Furthermore, difficulties in this area were compounded by factual causation issues which were disposed of under the guise of "personal injury by accident," and which more appropriately should have been addressed as a part of the employment risk question, with very little required in the way of the cause in fact.

The personal injury by accident requirement has caused confusion and worked hardships in the following three major areas: occupational diseases; mental illness; and diseases, illnesses or injuries that have developed over a gradual period of time. Additionally controversies sometimes exist as to whether injuries to artificial limbs are excluded from coverage by the "personal injury" or "accidental injury" requirement. See Self v. Riverside Companies, Inc. (1980). A growing number of jurisdictions treat artificial limb injuries by special statutory provisions.

Initially, occupational diseases were excluded from workers' compensation coverage because it was generally thought that this was an area for private health insurance. There was thus no provision for disease coverage in early compensation legislation, and the courts refused to find coverage because no "personal injury by accident" had occurred; after all, all diseases were considered to be personal or neutral risks commonly shared by everyone. In more modern times the necessity for occupational disease coverage has been candidly recognized either by broad judicial interpretations of the formula wording, or by special occupational disease provisions in the compensation acts.

Another difficulty with the "personal injury by accident" requirement is that presented by mental illnesses. Certainly today, on the basis of medical science, mental illness is recognized as a legitimate form of injury that may be causally connected to a risk of one's employment. The basic employment-related, mental illness fact patterns that commonly arise are: (1) physical trauma producing a nervous disorder; (2) nervous shock producing a physical disorder; (3) nervous shock producing a nervous condition or neurosis; (4) mental distress produced by prolonged work-related stress and anxiety; and (5) compensation neurosis; i.e., an unconscious desire to prolong compensation or a fear that compensation will not be paid. Little difficulty is presented for coverage by the foregoing first two fact patterns; however, coverage issues exist in the latter three. There is authority for compensation recovery in all five areas, and given the current state of medical science, there should be coverage for all the patterns when a mental illness is proven and the requisite employment connection is established. Given the pace and complexity of the modern industrial state with its rapid technological changes, mental disorders may well be within the scope of the risk of one's employment. See generally, Wade v. Anchorage School Dist. (1987).

Originally the formula coverage requirement of an "accident" was generally said to necessitate an "unusual," or "unforeseen," or "unexpected," or "external" event as the cause of an injury. In addition to an "unexpected event," it was also generally said that an injury had to have been sustained on a definite occasion or at a certain time. This approach created insoluble coverage problems because of the apparent necessity of distinguishing between "unexpected" or "unusual" and "expected" or "usual" risks; e.g., was the strain, exertion or hernia caused by an unusual or usual work related event. Furthermore, the definite occasion requirement in "accident" cases resulted in the exclusion of occupational diseases which had gradually developed over a long period of time. See generally, 1 Modern Workers Compensation, Chapter 108 Accidents & Injuries (2004).

2. THE SOLUTION

The enormous coverage problems caused by the "accident" interpretations in many jurisdictions prompted the National

Commission on State Workmen's Compensation Laws to recommend the elimination of this coverage requirement. It should be pointed out that the confusion created by the language "personal injury by accident" can be avoided simply by focusing upon scope of the risk, work connection, and factual cause.

E. OCCUPATIONAL DISEASE

1. COVERAGE SCHEMES

General compensation coverage for occupational diseases is currently provided in all jurisdictions, but the coverage methods vary considerably. The exclusive remedy provisions in the various acts, in recent years, have provided an increasingly important area of employer immunity. See Buford v. American Tel. & Tel. Co. (7th Cir.1989). At least five schemes of occupational disease coverage are identifiable: (1) use of a general definition of occupational disease in the workers' compensation act; (2) use of an expanded definition of "injury" or "personal injury" to include occupational disease; (3) use of a scheduled list of occupational diseases coupled with a general disease catch-all definition; (4) use of an unrestricted disease coverage provision; and (5) use of a separate occupational disease act. In addition to the foregoing general occupational disease coverage schemes, it is not uncommon to find specific legislative provisions dealing with loss of hearing, hernias, radiation, and various diseases of the lungs. Finally, the area of coal miner pneumoconiosis or "black lung" has virtually been preempted by federal legislation and programs; see supra Chapter 1, E., 5. and infra Chapter 15. See generally, 1 Modern Workers Compensation, Chapter 109 Diseases (2004).

2. COVERAGE PROBLEMS

a. *Occupational Disease Versus Accident*

As mentioned previously, early workers' compensation acts contained no provision for occupational disease coverage, and most courts interpreted the formula "personal injury by accident" to exclude all diseases from workers' compensation coverage. As might be expected, the grey area between the definition of personal injury and disease became a conceptually difficult one. With the passage of special occupational disease legislation, however, the distinctions between disease and injury by accident definitions became less important. It should be kept in mind that an occupational disease can in fact occur through accidental means; for example, one can contract many diseases as a result of an accidental cut or skin breakage that is work related. See Wilson Foods Corp. v. Porter (1980).

b. *Occupational Disease Versus Common Diseases*

The major problem area today in occupational disease cases is to be found in the identification of those ordinary diseases of life that are said to be common to the public and not distinctively associated with a particular employment. Most jurisdictions attempt to give a detailed definition of the term "occupational disease," and despite the wording chosen, the ultimate issue of coverage is usually decided by the particular jurisdiction's approach to the scope of the employment risk of the disease in question. This is probably the case even though many jurisdictions fail to realize that their decisions are being made on this basis. For example, coverage problems of this nature could easily arise for a delivery man who is regularly exposed to rain, sleet and snow in the winter months, and who claims that his pneumonia is sufficiently work-related to be compensable. Pneumonia may be an ordinary disease of life, common to the public, and certainly not peculiar to his employment; however, deliveries made in winter weather may increase the risk of pneumonia, or make it an actual risk of employment, or place the delivery man in a position to contract the disease.

c. *Occupational Disease and Medical Causation*

In the foregoing example of the delivery man who contracted pneumonia in the winter months, difficulties also arise with regard to medical causation. A medical expert might testify that the employee's exposure because of his working conditions was a minor causative factor in the contraction of the pneumonia, or the expert might testify that the employee was subjected to both employment and non-employment related exposure, either of which could have caused the disease. The key inquiry should be whether the employment exposure caused or substantially contributed to the pneumonia. If the employment relation, as the cause in fact of the disease, is unclear, vague, or uncertain in the medical sense, then there is a likelihood that no coverage will be found. See Florida State Hospital v. Potter (1980).

The medical cause in fact inquiry poses real difficulties because of the frequent merger of the scope of the risk issue with the medical-factual causation question, and the surrounding confusion that this produces. The entire area of occupational disease is confusing and troublesome, and as recognized by the 1972 Report of The National Commission on State Workmen's Compensation Laws, "the determination of the etiology or 'cause' of a disease in a medical sense is often difficult or even impossible."

3. SPECIAL COVERAGE RESTRICTIONS

It has been fairly common for various states to place unique restrictions on recovery for certain occupational diseases.

Those diseases which receive restrictive treatment are generally diseases of the lungs, such as silicosis, asbestosis, black lung, etc. Typical restrictions are those that preclude recovery unless death or disability has occurred within a certain number of years from the date of last injurious exposure or from the date of the last employment in a particular area. Another example of restriction is to be found in the denial of benefits to one who has suffered less than total disability as a result of a particular occupational disease. Sometimes one finds that employees are precluded from compensation unless they can demonstrate their exposure to the hazards of a particular disease for a specified period of time. The policies and practices of each jurisdiction should be examined. In some instances there are even special provisions granting greater compensation than normal for certain lung diseases. See generally, 1 Modern Workers Compensation, Chapter 109 Diseases (2004).

CHAPTER 6

DEATH

A. DEATH BENEFITS GENERALLY

Death benefits are provided by workers' compensation legislation to certain classes of beneficiaries. These benefits include burial expenses, with a statutory limit placed on the expenses, and compensation for the beneficiaries that is calculated on the basis of the appropriate statutory formula of the particular jurisdiction. The right to death benefits is a right created by statute, and it is not dependent upon any rights of the deceased worker. Therefore, a worker's release, compromise, or settlement, or unfavorable compensation decision, would be no bar to the claims of beneficiaries. A beneficiary's claim is legally separate and distinct from the worker's claim for compensation during his lifetime, and the worker generally has no right to control or dispose of the claims of the beneficiaries. See generally, 1 Modern Workers Compensation § 200:44 Death (2004).

B. DEPENDENCY AND PARTIAL DEPENDENCY

As a general proposition only those beneficiaries who are viewed by the compensation act as "dependents" are entitled to death benefits. The acts vary, but generally compensation statutes require a showing of either actual dependency (complete or partial), and/or membership in a designated class or group before there can be recovery. In many instances those bearing certain relationships to the deceased, e.g., wife or child, enjoy a presumption of dependency and need not demonstrate actual dependency.

It is always important at the outset to determine who can be classified as complete or total dependents as opposed to partial dependents, because the former group is given preference and may recover compensation to the exclusion of the latter group. Anyone claiming death benefits other than one who enjoys a statutory presumption of dependency, must prove actual dependency, and membership in the statutory class entitled to compensation. The statutory classes are defined differently from jurisdiction to jurisdiction. Some acts provide fixed lists of persons, e.g., widow or widower, child, parent, brother, etc. Other acts use classes defined by the terms "next of kin," or "member of the employee's family," or "member of the employee's household." While the term "next of kin" may sometimes mean blood relatives only, a liberal approach should be taken toward the classifications, and for example, an unadopted dependent child living in the deceased's household should be included as a beneficiary. See generally Ryan–Walsh Stevedoring Co., Inc. v. Trainer (5th Cir.1979).

In those cases in which one does not receive the benefit of a presumption of total dependency, either total or partial dependency actually must be proven. Generally, total dependency may be proven despite the fact that a dependent had some other minor sources of support; however, one would not be totally dependent if a substantial source of support was received from other than the deceased. Partial dependency is a question of fact, and can be found to exist even if one's own sources provide substantial support. A majority of jurisdictions take a liberal approach toward the definition of "dependent"; see Tabor v. Industrial Accident Fund (1952). See generally, 1 Modern Workers Compensation, Chapter 107 Dependents (2004).

C. WIDOW

In a majority of jurisdictions a widow is conclusively presumed to be totally dependent upon the deceased for workers' compensation purposes. Widowers should receive equal treatment. See Wengler v. Druggists Mutual Insurance Co. (1980). When no legal presumption exists, proof of dependency would be required. A claimant's marital status at the time of the death of the employee is often a key factor because some jurisdictions fix compensation rights as of the time of death. Other jurisdictions, sometimes with inequitable results, fix relationships and dependency as of the time of the accident or injury producing death. See generally, Dunn v. Industrial Commission (1994). For example, widows have been denied death benefits when they married an employee after the date of an injury that ultimately produced death. See generally, 1 Modern Workers Compensation § 107:7 Spouse or cohabitant (2004).

1. LIVING WITH OR APART

In most jurisdictions a surviving spouse enjoys a presumption of dependency only if living with the deceased employee at the time of injury or death. "Living with" does not necessarily mean residing together; for example, economic necessity or considerations of health might dictate a separation. Additionally, a separation may be the result of desertion or other wrongful conduct on the part of the deceased employee's spouse which does not affect the legal obligation to provide support. If a separation has occurred that relieves the deceased employee's spouse of the legal obligation to provide support, the "living with" requirement would not be met, and there would be no presumption of dependency.

2. COMMON–LAW MARRIAGE

The domestic relations laws of a particular jurisdiction control whether a surviving common-law spouse may recover death benefits. For example, a common-law wife may be viewed as a "widow" or "wife" for workers' compensation purposes. See National Union Fire Insurance Co. v. Britton (1960). Even in jurisdictions in which the relationship is considered illicit, one may be entitled to compensation benefits as an actual dependent member of the deceased's "household." Furthermore, in some jurisdictions an illicit relationship is no bar to recovery if it was entered into in a "good faith" belief in legality by the surviving spouse. See Dawson v. Hatfield Wire & Cable Co. (1971). Bigamous marriage situations are often resolved on the basis of the "last marriage rule," which presumes that the last marriage was the legal one for compensation purposes. See Gibson v. Hughes (1961).

D. CHILDREN

Death benefits are generally provided for the "child" or "children" of a deceased employee on the basis of specific statutory language that includes them within the group conclusively presumed to be dependent. Illegitimate children, stepchildren, posthumous children, and other children who were not the subject of a legal obligation for support on the part of the deceased employee, have posed coverage problems. Coverage has sometimes been afforded under the dependent classifications of "member of the family" or "member of the household," and under specific statutory provisions addressing acknowledged illegitimate children. Today the difficulties previously posed by illegitimate children have been largely eliminated by the Supreme Court decision of Weber v. Aetna Casualty & Surety Co. (1972), in which the Louisiana Workers' Compensation Act was declared unconstitutional in so far as unacknowledged illegitimate children were denied coverage. This was held to be violative of the Equal Protection Clause of the Fourteenth Amendment. Proof problems with regard to paternity still remain. See generally, 1 Modern Workers Compensation § 107:8 Children (2004).

E. FAMILY AND HOUSEHOLD MEMBERS

While the exact statutory language may vary, many workers' compensation acts permit the recovery of death benefits to one who can qualify as a "member of the family" or "member of the household." On the basis of the creation of these classifications it may be possible for stepchildren, stepgrandchildren, stepmothers, illegitimate children, nephews, mothers-in-law, and even unrelated children, etc., who can establish some dependency upon the deceased to receive death benefits. The liberal approach taken toward these groupings is supported by the humane objectives of workers' compensation. See generally, 1 Modern Workers Compensation, Chapter 107 Dependents (2004).

F. PRIORITIES

Death benefit priorities are statutorily established in workers' compensation acts. Family relationships and/or dependency dictate priorities and benefits. For example, it is sometimes provided that a surviving spouse and minor children are to receive an entire award to the exclusion of others claiming dependency. Ordinarily that class which consists of total dependents are entitled to receive death benefits even if this means no recovery for partial dependents. When more than one wholly dependent claimant exists, there may be an equal division of benefits or statutorily fixed proportions may be allocated. It is possible, however, on the basis of some acts, for both total and partial dependents to receive compensation, but this should only occur after full compensation has been had by total dependents. As a caveat, it should be noted that compensation accrued and due a deceased employee must be paid either to the deceased's estate for distribution, or to the dependents under a compensation act, depending upon the jurisdiction. See generally, 1 Modern Workers Compensation, Chapter 107 Dependents (2004).

CHAPTER 7

MEDICAL EXPENSES, DISABILITIES AND BENEFITS

A. INTRODUCTION TO RECOVERIES

The three broad categories of recovery under workers' compensation are: (1) medical and related expenses; (2) disability benefits; and (3) death benefits. Under the first group, medical expenses, rehabilitation costs, nursing costs, drugs, etc., are recoverable. Disability benefits are designed to provide compensation for the loss of earnings or earning power, and they are usually determined on the basis of either medical loss or wage loss theories, or some combination thereof; these benefits are determined by statutory formulas that may result in weekly, monthly, or sometimes lump sum payments. Death benefits are paid to the dependents of a deceased worker and such benefits are based on a statutory formula; additional amounts are specified for funeral or burial expenses. For reference and comparison purposes, the U. S. Chamber of Commerce compiles, on an annual basis, comprehensive charts of the state, federal and Canadian compensation requirements and benefits. U. S. Chamber of Commerce, Analysis of Workers' Compensation Laws. See generally, 2 Modern Workers Compensation, Part 9 Compensation & Benefits (2004).

B. MEDICAL EXPENSES AND REHABILITATION

At one time workers' compensation acts placed limitations on the amounts recoverable for medical expenses. Today most jurisdictions permit the recovery of unlimited medical expenses so long as a worker's condition necessitates continued treatment and care. A liberal approach is taken toward medical expenses, and commonly the costs of doctors, nurses, specialists, hospitalization, medical equipment, prosthetic devices, psychiatric treatment, drugs, medicines, etc. are included. It should be noted that in those cases in which an injured worker's spouse provides home nursing services, there can be recovery for the value of such services under the heading of medical expenses. See Kushay v. Sexton Dairy Co. (1975). See generally, 2 Modern Workers Compensation, Chapter 202 Medical Benefits (2004).

There is a lack of uniformity among workers' compensation statutes with regard to the recovery of physical and vocational rehabilitation costs. Ordinarily, those costs reasonably necessary for medical rehabilitation are recoverable, however, very few statutes provide complete coverage for the costs of vocational rehabilitation and related expenses necessary for a worker's return to full employment. See generally, 2 Modern Workers Compensation, Chapter 203 Vocational Rehabilitation (2004).

It should be remembered that in those cases in which medical complications, bad results, and even greater disabilities from medical malpractice occur, these events can be viewed as a part of the employee's original "injury", and all increased medical costs and benefits should be recoverable. See, e.g., Mallette v. Mercury Outboard Supply Co., Inc. (1959).

It should also be noted that the avoidable consequences rule has been applied to workers' compensation cases by statutes or case law. Employees who unreasonably refuse to submit to medical aid and treatment may jeopardize their rights to benefits. See Commonwealth, Department of Highways v. Lindon (1964).

C. SELECTION OF PHYSICIAN

The right to choose freely one's physician has been the subject of a great deal of controversy under workers' compensation laws. Some acts permit an employee to select a physician and others require that a selection be made from a panel of physicians chosen by the employer. Other acts require that treating physicians be approved by the medical profession for workers' compensation practice.

The physician selection controversy revolves around the need for physician-patient confidentiality and confidence on the one hand, versus the need to control medical costs and to provide effective medical treatment on the other hand. No matter what the physician selection rule of the particular jurisdiction may be, an injured employee cannot generally seek medical assistance without the employer's prior knowledge and consent, except for emergency situations. Of course, if after notice, an employer fails to provide the necessary medical care, an employee is free to procure medical assistance and submit claim for reimbursement. It should be noted that osteopaths and chiropractors may be selected. See Wetzel v. Goodwin Brothers, GMC Truck (1981). See generally, 2 Modern Workers Compensation § 202:35 Selection of physician (2004).

D. MEDICAL LOSS AND WAGE LOSS

The key to understanding compensable disabilities is to be found in medical loss and wage loss theories; both theoretically compensate an injured worker for loss of earnings or earning power, but they achieve this result by different methods. The medical loss theory focuses upon the physical injury or impairment suffered by a worker. Compensation may be based on "pure" medical losses; for example, workers' compensation acts usually contain "schedules" which provide a predetermined amount of compensation for specific enumerated medical losses; i.e., a schedule might provide a specified amount of compensation for the loss of a hand, regardless of the economic impact of such a loss. In other words, certain enumerated medical losses, are clearly recognized as disabilities and a loss of earnings or earning power is conclusively presumed on the basis of the inclusion of the loss in a medical loss schedule.

The wage loss theory attempts to provide compensation for an injured employee on the basis of the employee's actual earnings that have been lost due to an injury. For example, a "pure" wage loss approach might award compensation to an injured employee on the basis of actual lost wages incurred during the period of incapacity. In many jurisdictions wage loss determinations are made by comparing actual earnings prior to the date of injury with one's "earning capacity" after the injury. This "diminished earning capacity" concept permits an injured worker to recover compensation even if there has been no actual loss of earnings. See, e.g., Karr v. Armstrong Tire & Rubber Co. (1953).

No compensation system today employs pure medical loss or pure wage loss theory, rather, one finds that compensation acts utilize both in varying degrees. For example, a compensation act that contains an injury schedule may also provide compensation for an unscheduled injury that has resulted in a medical impairment. The severity of the impairment and the degree of one's disability (i.e., temporary total, permanent total, temporary partial, and permanent partial) commonly are used to determine the duration and amount of the employee's economic losses.

A tremendous amount of controversy exists with regard to the proper use of medical and wage loss theories in the determination of the appropriate amount of compensation for injured workers. See A. Larson, "The Wage–Loss Principle in Workers' Compensation," 6 Wm. Mitchell L.Rev. 501 (1980). While it is desirable for compensation awards to bear a reasonable relation to one's past wages, and to be based upon a reduction in one's earning capacity, rather than on the basis of arbitrary amounts dictated by the type of medical injury sustained, it must be stressed that no wage loss or medical loss approach actually attempts to provide compensation on the basis of the injury's true economic impact on the particular worker or on the worker's earning power or earning capacity. All legislation in this area represents compromises which have resulted in a no-fault system of reduced but fairly certain compensation for work-related injuries. See generally, 2 Modern Workers Compensation, Chapter 200 Basis For Compensation (2004).

E. THE AVERAGE WAGE AND FORMULAS

The cornerstone of compensation calculations is an employee's average wage, commonly specified as an "average weekly wage" or as some other average wage based upon a unit of time such as months or days. The average weekly wage, average monthly wage or the like represents an average earnings figure, which, when multiplied times a jurisdiction's fixed statutory percentage (ranging from 50 to 66⅔%), produces the employee's basic weekly or monthly benefit. Statutory formulas vary from jurisdiction to jurisdiction, but commonly, compensation benefits are determined on the basis of weeks or months of eligibility. In addition, it is commonly provided that maximums and minimums are to be placed on the amount of the weekly or monthly benefits; further, limitations may be placed upon the number of weeks or months of eligibility.

Frequently, issues arise with regard to the composition of the average weekly wage, and whether, for example, tips, fringe benefits, bonuses, meals, transportation, etc., should be considered. Every effort should be made to make the employee's average weekly wage computation as complete as possible. See Jess Parrish Memorial Hospital v. Ansell (1980); but see Morrison–Knudsen Construction Co. v. Director, OWCP (1983).

Difficulties may also arise because of an employee's temporary, irregular, or erratic work history. The average wage may sometimes be calculated with reference to the wages of a comparably situated employee. Most statutes permit calculations of average wages in a discretionary manner, if a just and fair result for the employee cannot be obtained by the use of the normal statutory formulas. See generally, 2 Modern Workers Compensation, Chapter 200 Basis for Compensation (2004).

F. DISABILITIES

1. DISABILITIES GENERALLY

Workers' compensation statutes ordinarily provide four classifications of disability. These classifications are determined by the severity or extent of the disability with the disability characterized as either partial or total. Additionally, disabilities are affected by their duration and are characterized as either permanent or temporary. The four common disability classifications are: temporary partial, temporary total, permanent partial, and permanent total. These disability classifications in conjunction with the employee's average wages, and appropriate statutory formulas provide the basis for disability benefit computation. See generally, 2 Modern Workers Compensation § 200:1 Generally (2004).

2. TEMPORARY PARTIAL

A temporary partial disability is present when an employee, who has been injured on the job, is no longer able to perform that job, but for the period of disability is able to engage in some kind of gainful employment. Temporary partial disability compensation is designed to pay an injured worker for lost wages, and thus wage loss theory is generally employed in making awards. Additionally, this classification promotes the prompt return of an injured employee to the workforce. Examples of injuries that commonly produce temporary partial disabilities are sprains, minor fractures, contusions and lacerations. See generally, 2 Modern Workers Compensation § 200:7 Temporary partial disability (2004).

The critical factor in determining the temporary partial classification may be the impairment of the employee's earning capacity. For example, an employee who has received a minor injury that has resulted in no loss of time at work and who has suffered no actual wage losses, may still be entitled to temporary partial compensation if some impairment to earning capacity can be proven.

3. TEMPORARY TOTAL

The condition of temporary total disability exists when an employee is unable to work at all for a temporary but undetermined amount of time. One may be totally disabled even though not completely helpless or wholly disabled. Examples of injuries that can result in temporary total disability are serious illnesses, heat exhaustion and disabling back injuries. Temporary total disability is designed to provide compensation to an injured worker for the economic losses incurred during a recuperative period. See generally, 2 Modern Workers Compensation § 200:8 Temporary total disability (2004).

4. PERMANENT PARTIAL

A permanent partial disability may be found when a permanent and irreparable injury has occurred to an employee, i.e., one that probably will continue for an indefinite period with no present indication of recovery. For example, one who loses a foot on the job will experience a period of temporary total disability during hospitalization and recuperation. At the point in time when maximum medical improvement has been attained, the disability should be classified as permanent partial; a foot has been lost, but the employee is able to perform some gainful work. The purpose of permanent partial disability is to provide compensation for the employee's reduced earning capacity, even though this is often accomplished through the use of a medical loss schedule. It should be noted that the majority view is to the effect that if a scheduled injury produces additional disability to other parts of the body, the employee will be able to recover an amount in excess of that provided in the schedule, for example, loss of a foot could produce traumatic neurosis. See Gonzales v. Gackle Drilling Co. (1962). See generally, 2 Modern Workers Compensation § 200:9 Permanent partial disability (2004).

5. PERMANENT TOTAL

The condition of permanent total disability exists when an employment related injury renders an employee permanently and indefinitely unable to perform any gainful work. An employee need not be entirely helpless or completely incapacitated in a medical sense. The so-called "odd-lot" doctrine permits the finding of a permanent total disability for workers who are not completely incapacitated, but are handicapped to such an extent that they cannot become regularly employed in any well-known branch of the labor market; the worker is said to have been left in the position of an "odd lot" in the labor market. Cardiff Corp. v. Hall (1911). One may receive a permanent total disability on the basis of a scheduled loss; for example, loss of sight in both eyes can be a scheduled loss that requires compensation as a permanent total disability. It is difficult to generalize about permanent total disabilities, but the following factors are generally relevant to such determinations: age; experience; skills and training; education; nature and extent of injury; employment history and nature of employment at the time of injury. See generally, 2 Modern Workers Compensation § 200:9 Permanent total disability (2004).

6.   DISFIGUREMENT

The great majority of jurisdictions address disfigurement by special provision. Compensation for disfigurement is generally provided in much the same way that compensation is provided for scheduled injuries. In the absence of special disfigurement provisions it may be difficult for a worker to establish an impairment to earning capacity because of disfigurement, scars or the like. These special provisions candidly recognize the need for compensation in disfigurement cases, and thus like medical loss schedules, conclusively presume a wage loss that dictates compensation. Occasionally, the issue may arise with regard to whether an employee may receive compensation both on the basis of a disability classification and disfigurement. It may be possible to obtain compensation on the basis of both. For example, compensation has been awarded for permanent partial disability resulting from burns with additional compensation awarded for disfigurement. Kerr–McGee Corp. v. Washington (1970). See generally, 2 Modern Workers Compensation § 200:19 Disfigurement (2004).

G. MULTIPLE AND SUCCESSIVE INJURIES

Difficulties sometimes arise when multiple injuries are received by a worker from the same accident. Often this problem is addressed statutorily in the particular workers' compensation act. In the absence of a specific provision an approach should be taken that provides the injured employee with the greatest possible coverage and compensation for the most serious degree of disability that can be demonstrated. For example, a worker might receive concurrent injuries to two different fingers on the same hand. These injuries could result in the complete loss of use of both fingers, and the compensation paid could simply amount to twice the scheduled amount for the loss of a finger. This amount might be less than the compensation to which the worker would be entitled on the basis of a percentage disability to the hand as a whole. In other words, an employee should not be confined to an injury schedule when multiple injuries have been sustained and the disability is greater than the sum of the scheduled losses. The reverse should also be the case, and when the sum of the scheduled losses provides greater compensation than the percentage of disability, then the greater amount should be awarded. See Emerson Electric Co. v. Powers (1980); Holcombe v. Fireman's Fund Insurance Co. (1960). See generally, 2 Modern Workers Compensation § 200:22 Overlapping disability (2004).

Successive injuries may present problems because the cumulative effect of the injuries may produce a greater degree of disability and dictate greater compensation than the amount that would have been paid on the basis of separate scheduled injuries. For example, an employee who has lost one hand may lose the other hand in another work-related accident. The worker has thus suffered a much greater loss than the sum of single hand losses on a schedule. Three possible approaches are taken to the problem. First, the employer can be required to provide compensation for the entire resulting disability. Second, there may be apportionment statutes requiring the employer to provide compensation on the basis of the disability the employee would have experienced without taking into effect the previous disability. It should be noted that if a greater disability is suffered because of some pre-existing illness, disorder, weakness, or disease on the part of the employee, apportionment may not be permitted; as a general rule, an employer takes an employee as he finds him with regard to latent and pre-existing conditions that result in greater disabilities than otherwise would have been suffered. Third, "second injury funds" may exist (discussed infra) and therefore assure that an employee is fully compensated for an entire disability. See generally, 2 Modern Workers Compensation § 200:25 Successive injuries (2004).

H. SECOND INJURY FUNDS

Second injury funds (sometimes called "subsequent injury funds") offer the best solution to the problem of the worker who suffers a greater degree of disability, as the result of a work-related injury, because of some pre-existing disability or condition. The second injury fund is designed to encourage the employment and retention of handicapped workers. There is little incentive for their employment if the last employer faces entire liability for a disability in part due to pre-existing causes. The second injury fund provides an equitable solution to the problem of the handicapped employee by allowing the employer to pay only that amount he would have been required to pay in the absence of the pre-existing difficulty. An issue exists in second injury situations with regard to what will qualify as an "injury" or "disability" for purposes of the utilization of the second injury fund. Traditionally employers take their employees as they find them; however, it is questionable whether the last employer of an injured employee should bear the complete burden of an employee's disability that is in part the result of a previous work related injury or disability. It is also questionable whether the last employer should bear the complete burden of an employee's disability that is in part the result of a previous nonwork-related injury. See Lawson v. Suwannee Fruit & Steamship Co. (1949). It should be noted that second injury fund liability cannot be established when the sequence of injuries is reversed; subsequent nonwork-related accidents make no difference in compensation awards.

A liberal approach should be taken toward the utilization of second injury funds because handicapped workers are often the subject of job discrimination. Furthermore, workers' compensation legislation should strive to provide compensation for the entire extent of a disability suffered as a result of a work-related injury regardless of whether that disability has been contributed to by some purely personal condition or previous work-related injury. It should be noted that the Americans With Disabilities Act, 42 U.S.C.A § 12101 et seq., promotes employment of physically disabled workers by providing remedies for employment disability discrimination. Because of this special protection, some have argued that second injury funds are no longer needed. See C. Dowd, Comment, Oklahoma's Special Indemnity Fund: A Fund Without a Function?, 30 Tulsa L. Rev. 745 (1995). This is one of the reasons that Colorado, Kansas, and Georgia, have repealed their second injury fund laws. See generally, 2 Modern Workers Compensation § 204:4 Second injury fund claims (2004).

I. DEATH AFTER DISABILITY

When death follows disability several issues may arise. In analyzing the problems in this area it should always be remembered that an employee's right to compensation benefits is separate and distinct from the right of an employee's dependents to death benefits. (See supra Chapter 6, A.) For that reason, death benefits should not be reduced by compensation paid to an injured worker prior to the worker's death unless there is a statutory provision to the contrary; for example, some jurisdictions statutorily reduce the dependency period by the period of disability compensation payments. An additional problem area is that of accrued compensation benefits that have not been paid prior to a worker's death. Generally these accrued amounts are paid to the employee's estate or to the employee's dependents, depending on the jurisdiction. Reference should be had to particular statutes that address this issue. See generally, 2 Modern Workers Compensation § 200:44 Death (2004).

J. DEATH COMPENSATION BENEFITS

In the case of complete or total dependents, death compensation benefits are generally computed on the basis of statutorily fixed percentages of a workers' average wage, just as in the case of computing a worker's disability compensation benefits. The majority of compensation acts place maximum limits on death benefits. Statutes vary considerably with regard to the computation of death benefits for those classified as partial dependents. A popular method of computing benefits for partial dependents is to provide compensation on the basis of the amounts of the deceased worker's contributions. It must be stressed that the formulas and methods employed in computing death benefits for all dependents vary considerably, and generalizations are inappropriate regarding exact computations. Usually, the most important legal issues involved in this area are those mentioned in Chapter 6, supra. See generally, 2 Modern Workers Compensation § 200:44 Death (2004).

CHAPTER 8

ADMINISTRATION

A. INTRODUCTION

A statutory scheme of no-fault compensation can be no better than its administration. Efficient and effective administration is especially necessary in the workers' compensation context, because a majority of claims are uncontested, and the prompt delivery of compensation benefits is of critical importance to a worker and the worker's family.

According to the 1972 Report of the National Commission on State Workmen's Compensation Laws there are six primary obligations of administration:

(1) to take initiatives in administering the act;

(2) to provide for continuing review and seek periodic revision of both the workmen's compensation statute and supporting regulations and procedures, based on research findings, changing needs, and the evidence of experience;

(3) to advise employees of their rights and obligations and to assure workers of their benefits under the law;

(4) to apprise employers, carriers, and others involved of their rights, obligations, and privileges;

(5) to assist voluntary resolutions of disputes, consistent with the law; and

(6) to adjudicate disputes which do not yield to voluntary negotiation.

The National Commission clearly pointed out that the adjudication of disputes should be the least burdensome of the six obligations when the other five obligations are properly executed. See generally, 3 Modern Workers Compensation, Part 12 Administrative Proceedings (2004).

B.　COMMISSIONS VERSUS COURTS

Only a few jurisdictions permit the initial judicial adjudication of disputed compensation claims. The great majority of the states have administrative agencies that supervise, administer, and adjudicate workers' compensation matters, subject to subsequent judicial appellate review.

It is generally accepted that the judiciary is ill equipped to administer adequately and effectively compensation matters and accomplish the six primary obligations of administration identified by the National Commission on Workmen's Compensation, supra, Chapter 8, A. Furthermore, the adversary nature of judicial proceedings insures unhealthy conflict between employers and employees and is incompatible with the goals and objectives of workers' compensation. State systems of administration vary, however, the best approach appears to be the one recommended by the National Commission on State Workmen's Compensation Laws. Under its recommendation there would be an executive officer and staff who devote their time solely to administration, with a separate and independent board of compensation appeals. The appellate board would review the decisions of hearing officers in contested compensation cases. An informal procedures unit would handle all claims initially, and those claims that are incapable of voluntary resolution would be forwarded to a hearing officer for a formal determination. Only questions of law from the appellate board would receive judicial review. See generally, 3

Modern Workers Compensation, Part 13 Judicial Proceedings (2004).

C. NOTICES

Almost all workers' compensation acts contain provisions requiring that an employee promptly inform the employer of an injury. Some statutes may require that notice of injury be given within a specified period of time. The purpose of the notice requirement is to facilitate prompt medical treatment and care, and to minimize the extent of an employee's injury. Additionally, notice provides the employer with a timely opportunity to investigate the causes and conditions of injury.

A rigid approach should not be taken, and generally it is not taken toward notice requirements. The employee's failure to comply with the notice requirement should be excused if there is actual knowledge on the part of the employer or one whose knowledge can be imputed to the employer. Certainly, knowledge can be found on the basis of compensation or medical payments to an employee. Additionally, an employee's lack of compliance should be excused if it has not resulted in prejudice to the employer. Many reasonable excuses can exist for non-compliance with formal notice requirements. See generally, 3 Modern Workers Compensation, Chapter 303 Notice & Claim; Pleadings (2004).

D. STATUTES OF LIMITATION

There are generally two types of limitation statutes that govern the timely filing of workers' compensation claims for disability. In one type of statute, the limitation period runs from the date of injury, and in the other type of statute the period commences on the date of the employee's accident. In jurisdictions using date of injury, a liberal approach is usually taken, and the appropriate date may be the time when the injury became apparent or reasonably should have become apparent to the employee. In date of accident jurisdictions, an inflexible and literal approach is sometimes taken toward the time of the accident; this may result in the loss of a worker's claim, because of a personal failure to discover the injury or its work connection prior to the running of the statute. This type of statute of limitations has been the subject of a great deal of criticism. See 7 Larson § 126.06[2] (2004).

Generally in death cases, statutes of limitation begin to run at the date of an employee's death; however, some statutes of limitation commence at the time of the accident or injury producing death. A literal approach should not be taken to date of accident or injury statutes in recognition of the fact that dependents' rights do not arise until the date of an employee's death.

The possibility always exists for a finding of a waiver of the limitations period on the part of the employer. A recognition of liability, the payment of compensation or medical benefits, or the failure to raise the defense of the statute of limitations in a timely manner, can result in waiver. See generally, 3 Modern Workers Compensation, Chapter 301 Time Limitations (2004).

E. WAITING PERIODS

Waiting periods may be found in workers' compensation statutes. These provisions authorize compensation only after the passage of a specific amount of time from the date of an employee's injury. Waiting periods are generally inapplicable to medical benefits and to death benefits. In an effort to discourage malingering and to promote a prompt return to the workforce, many waiting period provisions are directed specifically at temporary total disability claims.

By way of illustration, the Council of State Government's Model Act, Part III, Section 15, proposes a waiting period of three days, with retroactive payment if the total period of disability exceeds fourteen days. This follows the recommendation of the 1972 Report of the National Commission on State Workmen's Compensation Laws. As a general proposition, it should be noted that the longer the waiting or qualifying periods, then the less the costs of workers' compensation programs; however, this results in reduced benefits for workers. See generally, 2 Modern Workers Compensation § 200:45 Waiting period (2004).

F. HEARINGS, EVIDENCE AND REVIEW

In practically all jurisdictions, disputed workers' compensation cases are handled by an administrative process rather than by the courts. A less formal, more expeditious and more flexible approach is taken than in a normal judicial civil trial. It is always desirable for some part of the administrative machinery to be available for the resolution of contested claims through the use of an informal procedure; however, a formal administrative adjudicative process must be available for those contested claims which cannot otherwise be resolved informally. See generally, 3 Modern Workers Compensation, Part 12 Administrative Proceedings (2004).

The workers' compensation administrative process may vary somewhat from jurisdiction to jurisdiction, and despite occasional commentary to the contrary, the proceedings in contested cases are all marked by a degree of practical formality consistent with the adjudication of substantive rights. One should exercise some caution when one encounters the often repeated phrase that compensation proceedings are to be informal with the ordinary rules of evidence relaxed.

In every jurisdiction, administrative compensation decisions can ultimately be the subject of judicial review. In most jurisdictions, judicial review is limited to questions of law, and administrative findings of fact will not generally be disturbed.

The common law rules of evidence generally do not apply to compensation proceedings; however, they can serve as a guide. Appellate review sometimes occurs because of the admission of hearsay evidence. Wide discretion is permitted in compensation hearings, and the admission of evidence that would be inadmissible in a court of law is allowed. While the admission of hearsay evidence may not constitute error, if an undue amount of weight has been given to such evidence in the administrative decision, then error may have been committed. A jurisdiction's approach to the treatment of hearsay is particularly important to claimants who are prone to present a great deal of hearsay evidence; indeed, in many cases, only hearsay evidence may be available on key issues. In reviewing compensation decisions, four different approaches have been taken toward the use of hearsay evidence. First, hearsay is admissible and may provide the basis for the decision. Second is the residuum and majority rule which permits administrative decisions to be based upon hearsay evidence, but some of the evidence supporting the decision must have been admissible. Third, the admission of the hearsay is not reversible error; however, if the decision would not have been rendered but for the hearsay evidence, the decision must be reversed. Finally, there is some authority declaring hearsay evidence inadmissible and its admission to be reversible error. See generally, 3 Modern Workers Compensation, Chapter 306 Admissibility of Evidence (2004).

Generally the standard of review in appeals of administratively decided compensation cases is whether there is substantial evidence to support the decision. For variations on the above standard of review, see 8 Larson § 130.03 (2004). See generally, 3 Modern Workers Compensation, Chapter 315 Scope of Review (2004).

G. COMPROMISE, SETTLEMENT, AND LUMP SUM COMMUTATION

The policy considerations in workers' compensation cases differ from those found in the adversary and uncertain environment of the tort system with regard to compromises, agreements, and settlements. As a result of these differences most jurisdictions by statute or by judicial decision deny the claimants the right to settle, adjust, or compromise a claim for less than the statutory amount regardless of whether the claim is disputed or undisputed. See Southern v. Department of Labor and Industries (1951). The minority view would permit compromises and settlements for less than the statutory amounts when disputed questions of liability exist; even so, approval of the compromise, agreement, or settlement would ordinarily be required by the appropriate workers' compensation authority.

It may be possible for a claimant to receive compensation benefits in a "lump sum" rather than by way of periodic payments, depending upon the jurisdiction. This method of payment is subject to criticism given the objectives of compensation benefits to replace lost wages and to provide economic benefits over a period of time. Lump summing generally takes the form of a reduction of periodic benefits to present value with the use of a percentage discount. There may be some situations in which the best interests of a claimant can dictate a lump sum approval, as for example, in the cases of a worker who needs the entire amount for legitimate educational, retraining, or rehabilitation costs. Tremendous potential for harm exists, however, when lump summing is indiscriminately permitted because of the likelihood that the entire award will be quickly and unwisely spent. See Malmedal v. Industrial Accident Board (1959). The use of lump sums and the difficulties that surround their use have been exacerbated by the desire of some claimants' attorneys to obtain their entire fees at once rather than over a period of time. See generally, 2 Modern Workers Compensation Chapter 204 Compensation Agreements (2004).

H. REOPENING, MODIFICATION, TERMINATION, AND REDISTRIBUTION

Statutes vary from jurisdiction to jurisdiction with regard to the details of reopening and modification of compensation awards; however, reopening and modification is usually permitted on the basis of a disabled worker's changed condition. Modification may take the form of increased or decreased benefits, or a cessation of benefits. Time limits for reopening can be found in a majority of jurisdictions. Fraud, mutual mistake of fact, and sometimes "any good cause" can provide grounds for reopening. A minority of jurisdictions permit reopening at any time for changed conditions.

In death benefit cases, the possibility exists for termination or redistribution of benefits based upon certain dependents' changes in status. For example, the remarriage of a widow may result in the termination of benefits; a redistribution could also occur as a result of the death of a minor dependent. See generally, 3 Modern Workers Compensation, Chapter 309 Award (2004).

I. INSURANCE

There are three methods of insuring workers' compensation benefits. First of all there is the private insurance system, which provides a majority of the benefits paid in the United States, and which may be utilized in the vast majority of states. Secondly, there is self-insurance, which is also available in a vast majority of states, but which provides a small overall percentage of the benefits paid in the United States. Third, there are state insurance fund systems, which provide almost a fourth of the benefits paid in the United States; six states mandate participation in the state fund, while twelve states permit private insurance competition with their state insurance funds. It is difficult to determine whether any one insurance method is superior to another, and as long as proper controls exist for the adequate protection of compensation claimants, any of the methods accomplish their purposes. Perhaps, lower insurance costs can be achieved through the use of state insurance funds.

It must be stressed that the object of insurance in workers' compensation systems is to provide security for the payment of benefits. If for some reason the insurance carrier or employer is unable to provide insurance or to guarantee benefits, then machinery and resources should be in existence to provide workers and their dependents the benefits to which they are entitled. For example, Michigan has a self-insurer's security fund. See McQueen v. Great Markwestern Packing Co. (1974). Most states do not have direct security systems, but rely upon indirect or administrative supervision of insurance carriers and self-insurers. The Council of State Government's Model Workmen's Compensation and Rehabilitation Law contains special fund provisions which would provide payments in the case of insolvent employers or insurers. See Part IV, Insurance; Section 55, Special Fund.

Workers' Compensation insurance is designed for the benefit and protection of both the employee and the employer. In an effort to maximize the security of the employee and dependent claimants, the defenses which could be used by an insurer against an employer should not be available against claimants. For example, the employer's failure to pay a premium should not provide an effective bar to an otherwise eligible compensation claimant. See Home Life & Accident Co. v. Orchard (1920).

Each state has a workers' compensation insurance regulatory authority which establishes rates based upon experience ratings and loss experiences. Rate making service organizations have a direct impact on this process. While a few states have independent data gathering organizations, the majority of states use the National Council on Compensation Insurance (NCCI) to collect data for rate making purposes. Its website address is: http://www.ncci.com.

J. REMOVAL

Under 28 U.S.C.A. § 1445, actions brought under the FELA and Jones Act in state court generally cannot be removed to federal court. The same code section also prohibits removal of actions under workers' compensation laws of the state in which the federal district court is sitting. This would include suits for retaliatory discharge for filing a worker's compensation claim. See Wallace v. Ryan–Walsh Stevedoring Co. (1989). The federal statute reflects a Congressional policy of allowing states local control over their workers' compensation systems without federal court interference in the local administrative process. It should be noted that 28 U.S.C.A. § 1332(c), the direct action provision, does not apply to actions initiated in federal court by a workers' compensation insurer; actions against such an insurer initiated in federal court are not allowed. Northbrook National Insurance Co. v. Brewer (1989).

CHAPTER 9

EXTRATERRITORIAL PROBLEMS AND OVERLAPPING COVERAGES

A. CONFLICT OF LAWS

Conflict of laws and full faith and credit problems often arise in workers' compensation cases because of the inevitable multi-state contacts which are encountered by today's employees. For example, an employee may reside in Texas, sign a contract of employment in Oklahoma, work for a company whose home office is in Arkansas, on a job based in Wyoming, and receive a compensable injury while on company business in Louisiana. Conflicts questions ordinarily are concerned with which state's workers' compensation statute is applicable. As a general rule, the rights provided by the workers' compensation act of one state cannot be enforced in other states. See 9 Larson §§ 140.01–140.03 (2004).

The following fact patterns usually give rise to most conflicts problems: (1) the accident is local and the employment contract is foreign; (2) the employment contract is local and the accident is foreign; (3) both the accident and the employment contract are foreign; and (4) the accident is foreign to the state of the employer's principal place of business or legal residence. Most states have specific statutory provisions which address conflict of laws issues. Normally, if a compensable injury has taken place within a state, that fact alone may provide a basis for the utilization of local law.

State statutes addressing out of state injuries commonly provide for the application of the law of the forum on the basis of the contract of employment being entered into within the forum state, or on the basis of employment connections, relations, or contacts with the forum state. Where both the employment contract and state of injury are foreign, a proceeding under the law of an unrelated forum is generally inappropriate. Finally, the domicile or residence of the claimant, and/or the location of the employer's home office or legal residence, can affect the application of a particular state's workers' compensation act. In order to avoid the conflicts difficulties in workers' compensation cases, the Report of the National Commission on State Workmen's Compensation Laws recommended that a worker or dependents have the choice of claiming compensation in the state where the injury or death occurred, or where the employment was principally localized, or where the employee was hired. This recommendation would probably eliminate the problem of the employee who could be without compensation coverage in any state, because of multi-state contacts. The Restatement (Second) of Conflicts § 181 takes a liberal and expansive approach toward the circumstances that may bring the workers' compensation law of the forum into play. It is suggested that resort should be had to this restatement section when statutes of a forum state fail to address a workers' compensation conflict problem. This restatement section is compatible with the objectives and policies of workers' compensation legislation. See generally, 1 Modern Workers Compensation, Part 4 Governing Law (2004).

B. FULL FAITH AND CREDIT

The full faith and credit clause has posed two major problems for workers' compensation: (1) the extent to which the workers' compensation laws of one state should be recognized and given weight in the decisions of another state; and (2) to what extent should successive compensation awards be permitted from state to state for the same injury or death.

The primary difficulties created in the first situation were the result of Bradford Electric Light Co. v. Clapper (1932), in which the Supreme Court held that New Hampshire was forced to recognize the Vermont workers' compensation statute under the full faith and credit clause. A subsequent series of Supreme Court decisions have virtually abolished the Clapper doctrine, and the full faith and credit clause's requirement of the recognition of foreign law, now presents few problems when the forum state wishes to apply its own workers' compensation act. See Carroll v. Lanza (1955); Kelly v. Guyon General Piping, Inc. (4th Cir.1989) (Virginia would apply North Carolina exclusive remedy provision to bar tort claim arising out of accident in South Carolina).

The full faith and credit clause has been the source of a great deal of controversy because of the difficulties posed when more than one state awards compensation to a claimant for the same injury or death. The Supreme Court resolved a major area of controversy in Thomas v. Washington Gas Light Co. (1980). This case held that one jurisdiction has no legitimate interest in preventing another jurisdiction from awarding supplemental compensation, when that second jurisdiction had the power in the first instance to apply its compensation law and to make an award. The full faith and credit clause is not to be construed in such a way as to bar another state's successive award of workers' compensation, so long as credit is given for the prior state's award. In other words, a worker is entitled to receive the largest single amount of compensation to which one would be entitled under the applicable compensation acts. See generally, 1 Modern Workers Compensation § 104.6 Full faith and credit requirements (2004).

C.　THE PROBLEM OF OVERLAPPING COVERAGE

The coverage boundaries between state workers' compensation acts and certain federal remedies and programs are unclear. These vague boundaries create difficulties for claimants because of the possibility of federal preemption, and an improper election of remedies which could result in a denial of compensation or in a lesser award than that to which a claimant could be entitled. The federal remedies that pose potential problems in this area are: the Longshore and Harbor Workers' Compensation Act (LHWCA); personal injury and death actions by seamen or their survivors based upon Jones Act negligence, general maritime law unseaworthiness, and maintenance and cure; and personal injury and death actions based upon the Federal Employers' Liability Act.

In LHWCA situations the "twilight zone" doctrine has been recognized by the Supreme Court. Davis v. Department of Labor & Industries (1942). This doctrine eliminates the risk of an initial mistake on the part of a claimant, by allowing a presumption of coverage under the first act providing a basis for the claim. Additionally, the Supreme Court has indicated that concurrent jurisdiction may exist in borderline cases, particularly in regard to injuries or deaths occurring on land. Sun Ship, Inc. v. Pennsylvania (1980). The possibility of successive and supplementary awards exists in the LHWCA area by analogy to the policies contained in Thomas v. Washington Gas Light Co., supra, even though the constitutional bases would be different. Certainly, no double recovery should be permitted. It should be noted that the LHWCA generally provides more generous benefits than the various state compensation acts.

The coverage problems of seamen involving either the LHWCA or state workers' compensation acts usually depend upon a factual determination of one's status as a seaman. The LHWCA specifically excludes from coverage a master or member of the crew of a vessel. Borderline cases involving state compensation acts may also receive "twilight zone" doctrine treatment. See Maryland Casualty Co. v. Toups (5th Cir.1949). But see Anderson v. Alaska Packers Association (1981). Successive awards are sometimes allowed on the basis of concurrent jurisdiction theories when federal seamen's remedies are pursued after an acceptance of state workers' compensation benefits. See Manuel Caceres v. San Juan Barge Co. (1st Cir.1975).

The Federal Employers' Liability Act (FELA) provides a negligence remedy for all interstate railway workers whose jobs affect interstate commerce, including employees engaged in auxiliary activities related to interstate railroads. Motor carrier, airline, and other interstate transportation workers are not covered by the FELA. If an employee is covered by the FELA, then it is said to be the exclusive remedy because of federal preemption in the field of interstate commerce, and thus state compensation acts have no application. The LHWCA provides the exclusive remedy for covered workers and bars actions under the FELA. See Chesapeake & Ohio Railway Co. v. Schwalb (1989).

As an additional note on overlapping coverages, it should be remembered that the payment of workers' compensation benefits may have a direct impact upon one's social security benefits, because the Social Security Act provides for the reduction of benefits to the extent that they are duplicated by state or federal workers' compensation payments. See 42 U.S.C.A. § 424a; 20 C.F.R. § 404.408; Sciarotta v. Bowen (3d Cir.1988). In 14 states, however, there are statutory provisions that reduce worker's compensation benefits when a worker is entitled to social security. The FELA is not considered a workers' compensation law or plan for the purposes of 42 U.S.C.A. § 424a.

In settlement situations involving Medicare beneficiaries, the Centers for Medicare and Medicaid Services (formerly the Health Care Financing Administration), pursuant to the Medicare secondary payor statute (42 U.S.C.A. § 1395y), may undertake actions to collect moneys in situations in which workers' compensation settlements have been reached without the agency's knowledge or consent. Both insurance carriers and workers' attorneys may be at risk for failure to obtain Medicare approval of settlements and for failure to set aside the proper funding amounts to cover workers' future medical expenses. Medicare generally resists all attempts by insurance carriers to shift liability for lifetime medicals to Medicare in workers' compensation cases (42 U.S.C.A § 411.46(d)(2)). A Medicare Set Aside Trust or Custodial Agreement is frequently used to avoid problems with Medicare, with savings to the workers. Only the medicals that Medicare would normally cover are placed in a trust or under a custodial agreement, leaving out allocations for nursing homes, prescriptions, custodial care and any other medicals not covered by Medicare.

In addition, approximately one-half of the states treat workers' compensation payments as disqualifying income for unemployment compensation purposes. There is a lack of uniformity on this issue. See Page v. General Electric Co. (1978).

It should also be noted that tensions can arise in the context of the Americans with Disabilities Act (ADA) and workers' compensation. For example, settlement of permanent partial disability claims usually involve carefully crafted releases. Other issues include the effects of ADA violations on state claims for compensation. See Caldwell v. Aarlin/Holcombe Armature (1997). In 1996, the EEOC published a guide entitled, Workers' Compensation and the Americans with Disabilities Act (Pub. No. 915.002).

Finally, an issue of claim preclusion can arise when a workers' compensation or social security disability claimant alleges total disability but seeks to maintain an ADA action. See Dush v. Appleton Electric Co. (8th Cir.1997); Swanks v. Washington Metro. Area Transit Authority (D.C.Cir.1997). See generally, 1 Modern Workers Compensation, Part 4 Governing Law (2004).

CHAPTER 10

THIRD PARTY ACTIONS

A. EXCLUSIVE NATURE OF COMPENSATION ACT

Workers' compensation legislation provides employees and their dependents with their exclusive remedy against the employer and insurance carrier for all injuries and deaths which arise out of and in the course of employment. The exclusivity provisions of workers' compensation acts have generally withstood constitutional attacks for the most part in recent times, and their continued vitality remains the keystone of compensation legislation. Constitutional questions concerning exclusivity may, however, be of importance in certain areas. See Chapter 3, B., supra. See also Fleischman v. Flowers (1971). Generally, the immunities provided to the employer and others are difficult to avoid. Kimball v. Millet (1988).

The exclusive nature of the workers' compensation remedy can sometimes result in a denial of compensation in cases in which damage has clearly occurred. For example, injuries to sexual organs, the senses, the psyche and sometimes disfigurement, and non-disabling pain and suffering may go uncompensated, if the injuries producing these results fall within the workers' compensation formula, because most workers' compensation acts fail to provide compensation for these results.

It should always be remembered that an employer may be sued in tort despite the exclusivity provision, on the basis of intentional tort theories and in situations giving rise to nonphysical torts. Lopez v. S.B. Thomas, Inc. (2d Cir.1987) (emotional distress under 42 U.S.C.A. § 1981). See Chapter 3, B., supra. See generally, 1 Modern Workers Compensation, Part 3 Exclusivity (2004).

B. WHO ARE THIRD PARTIES

The exclusivity provision of workers' compensation legislation applies only to employers and others who may be so treated, such as insurance carriers and co-employees. Generally the rights of employees and survivors to pursue common law and statutory remedies against a "third party" whose conduct has caused or contributed to an injury or death, remain intact. Frequently issues arise with regard to who are "third parties" subject to separate actions for damages. One of the most troublesome groups, is that of co-employees. A majority of jurisdictions, either on the basis of statute or judicial decision, have extended the employer's immunity to co-employees. A minority of jurisdictions view co-employees as "third persons" outside of the immunity enjoyed by the employer.

It is difficult to generalize about who are third parties; however, third parties have from time to time been found among the following: physicians, product manufacturers, co-employees (including possibly corporate officers, directors, or stockholders), supervisory employees, compensation carriers and their safety inspectors, unions and their safety inspectors, governmental entities, owners and occupiers of land, etc. See chapter 3, supra. See generally, 1 Modern Workers Compensation, Chapter 103 Remedies Against Third Persons (2004).

C. THIRD PARTY ACTIONS AGAINST THE EMPLOYER

Questions of contribution and indemnity may arise when third parties attempt to recover over against the employers of injured or killed employees. Most jurisdictions deny a third party the right to contribution from an employer whose negligence has played a part in an employee's harm, because of the general common law rule that there can only be contribution from one who is liable to the plaintiff. The exclusivity provision of workers' compensation legislation relieves the employer of tort liability for injuries or deaths falling within the coverage formula; thus, generally employers cannot be the subjects of contribution actions. Third party indemnity actions present a problem for all workers' compensation jurisdictions. Prof. Larson describes this issue as an evenly-balanced controversy in workers' compensation law. Larson, "Third Party Action Over Against Workers' Compensation Employer," 1982 Duke L.J. 483, 484. Despite the exclusivity provisions in workers' compensation acts, and despite the necessity of inquiries directed at fault in non-contractual indemnity situations, the possibility of employer liability certainly exists under substantive indemnity law. See Lockheed Aircraft Corp. v. United States (1983). Additionally, in appropriate cases, indemnity may be obtained from an employer on the basis of an express or implied agreement, or on the basis of a separate and independent duty owed by the employer to the third person. See Carneiro v. Alfred B. King Co. (1975).

D. DEFENSES OF THIRD PARTIES

Normally third parties who are defendants in actions brought by employees, employers, or insurance carriers, may employ any defenses which could be utilized against the employee. Thus, regardless of whether or not the action is one for damages on the part of the employee, or a subrogation action brought by an employer or insurer, the employee's negligence or the statute of limitations may be used as defenses. Since the action, even in subrogation cases, is that of the employee, the contributory fault of an employer, may not generally be raised as a defense. Mermigis v. Servicemaster Industries, Inc. (1989) (jury not allowed to consider employer negligence in order to reduce award). See Baker v. Traders & General Insurance Co. (10th Cir.1952). See generally, 1 Modern Workers Compensation § 103:55 Third-party defenses-employee negligence (2004).

E. SUBROGATION

It is difficult to generalize about subrogation rights and procedures, but almost all jurisdictions have subrogation statutes that affect workers' compensation cases. The common-law background of subrogation arose out of duties that are no longer popular. See Seavey, "Liability to Master for Negligent Harm to Servant," 1956 Wash. U.L.Q. 309. There appears to be a common-law basis for subrogation in some compensation cases. See Federal Marine Terminals, Inc. v. Burnside Shipping Co. (1969). A variety of statutory approaches may be found. Some statutes grant employees priority in actions against third parties, and if the employee fails to take advantage of the priority, then the subrogee may maintain the action. Other statutes provide the employer or carrier with priority to proceed against third parties. Still other statutes grant no priority and allow both to proceed against third parties independently or jointly. A few jurisdictions deny subrogation rights altogether, while others bestow all rights upon the subrogee.

The central policy issue to be found in the subrogation area centers on the conflict between the desire for full and adequate compensation, and the potential problem of double recovery if subrogation is not allowed. Additional policy issues involve the following: the possibility of workers' compensation payments inuring to the benefit of a wrongdoer; the desire to impose liability on a third party at fault; and the need for a third party to indemnify those who have been required to pay workers' compensation benefits. See generally, 1 Modern Workers Compensation § 103:45 Assessment/subrogation of claim to compensation payor (2004).

F. UNINSURED MOTORIST INSURANCE AND NO–FAULT INSURANCE

Special problems have been created by the off-set provisions contained in uninsured motorist and no-fault insurance policies when claims also involve workers' compensation benefits. No uniform solution to these problems has been found, and each state's insurance statutes and public policy must be examined.

Where there is uninsured motorist insurance, some courts have held the off-set provisions invalid or void as being contrary to public policy because the insurance provision reduces effective coverage below that required by statute. Often legislation is enacted to alter this result. See generally, Mountain States Mutual Cas. Co. v. Vigil (Ct.App.1996); see also National Union Fire Ins. Co. v. Figaratto (1996). Other courts have held that insurance contracts are valid which allow insurers to reduce uninsured motorist liability by the amount of workers' compensation paid. Ullman v. Wolverine Ins. Co. (1970). In those states which allow the off-set for workers' compensation, there are divided authorities on the issue of whether reduction should be made from an insured's total damages or from the amount of insurer liability under the insurance policy; see, e.g., Waggaman v. Northwestern Security Ins. Co. (1971);

American Ins. Co. v. Tutt (1974); Michigan Mutual Liability Co. v. Mesner (1966). See generally, 1 Modern Workers Compensation § 103:41 No-fault insurance; § 103:42 Uninsured motorist claims (2004).

No-fault insurance creates a similar off-set problem when a workers' compensation claim is involved. See, e.g., Neel v. State (Utah 1995). It can be argued that the exclusive remedy provision in the workers' compensation act precludes any recovery of no-fault benefits regardless of statutes that would require workers' compensation benefits to be off-set. On the other hand, the exclusive remedy provision does not bar receipt of no-fault benefits and due process and equal protection are not violated. Mathis v. Interstate Motor Freight System (1980). In jurisdictions where reduction or off-set is allowed, no-fault coverage should be recoverable only to the extent that damages exceed workers' compensation benefits received by an injured worker.

CHAPTER 11

FUTURE OF WORKERS' COMPENSATION

A. THE NATIONAL COMMISSION ON STATE WORKMEN'S COMPENSATION LAWS

The Occupational Safety and Health Act of 1970, (29 U.S.C.A. § 651 et seq.) Section 27, established a National Commission on State Workmen's Compensation Laws and authorized "an effective study and objective evaluation of state workmen's compensation laws in order to determine if such laws provide an adequate, prompt, and equitable system of compensation for injury or death arising out of or in the course of employment." Section 27(a)(2). The National Commission submitted its report to the President and Congress on July 31, 1972, in which it made 84 recommendations for minimum state standards. The report indicated that 19 of its proposed state standards were "essential," and that the states should comply with these by July 1, 1975, or else congressional action should be taken in the form of a national minimum standards law. The National Commission found five major objectives for modern workers' compensation programs:

(1) Broad coverage of employees and work-related injuries and diseases;

(2) Substantial protection against interruption of income;

(3) Provision of sufficient medical care and rehabilitation services;

(4) Encouragement of safety; and

(5) An effective system for delivery of benefits and services.

Some of the National Commission's recommended "essential" elements of workers' compensation laws were:

(1) Compulsory coverage;

(2) No Occupational or Numerical Exemptions to coverage;

(3) Full coverage of work-related diseases;

(4) Full medical and physical rehabilitation services without arbitrary limits;

(5) Employee's choice of jurisdiction for filing interstate claims;

(6) Adequate weekly cash benefits for temporary total, permanent total, and death cases; and

(7) No arbitrary limits on duration or sum of benefits.

To date the 19 "essential" recommendations of the National Commission have not been adopted by any state, but many states have used the recommendations as a basis for the improvement of their particular workers' compensation acts. In 1976, an Inter–Agency Workers' Compensation Task Force reported in its findings that there was a need to reform state workers' compensation programs. The recommendations of both the National Commission and the Task Force have been used as a basis for a proposed National Workers' Compensation Standards Act.

The Council of State Governments took the 84 recommendations and incorporated them into a Model Act (as revised). This effort brought about some modifications in state workers' compensation laws.

The International Association of Industrial Accident Boards (IAIABC) studies workers' compensation issues and makes recommendations for legislative changes. Its website address is: http://www.iaiabc.org.

B. NATIONAL WORKERS' COMPENSATION STANDARDS ACT PROPOSALS

Neither the National Commission nor the Inter–Agency Task Force (later merged with the Division of State Workers' Compensation Standards within the Department of Labor's Office of Workers' Compensation Programs) recommended the replacement of state workers' compensation laws with an overall federal program, but both emphasized the overall need to reform state programs. As a result of these studies, several bills have been introduced in Congress from time to time to set federal "minimum standards" for all state workers' compensation systems with one overall federal program. For example, Senate Bill 420 was introduced in the 96th Congress in an effort to create the "National Workers' Compensation Standards Act of 1979." There has never been sufficient political support for these proposals in Congress.

C. ALLOCATION OF FUTURE ECONOMIC AND SOCIAL BURDENS FOR INDUSTRIAL ACCIDENTS AND DISEASES

Despite the many justifiable criticisms of state workers' compensation laws, these acts will probably continue to serve as the chief vehicles for compensating workers for employment related injuries and deaths. The Report of the National Commission on State Workmen's Compensation laws indicates that workers' compensation is preferable to tort actions because of the fact that: (1) in many cases both employee and employer fault and causation produce industrial accidents; (2) the tort process is expensive, lengthy, and uncertain in nature with an assurance of no compensation to some victims; and (3) the tort system contains an inherent deterrence to rehabilitation.

The National Commission also indicated that presently it would be impracticable and unbeneficial to attempt to disassemble the present workers' compensation system and place its various branches under other social programs. The report further noted that it is unlikely that acceptable medical program alternatives to workers' compensation with regard to medical care will be established in the foreseeable future. Furthermore, the report observed that no other delivery system is more effective than workers' compensation. In summary, the conclusion of the National Commission was to the effect that workers' compensation systems, with recommended changes, should continue. See Report of the National Commission on State Workmen's Compensation Laws, pp. 119–121 (1972).

It is certainly likely that in the future there will be federal and state social programs which, to some extent, may overlap with workers' compensation. Every effort should be made to avoid a duplication of benefits and to insure the coordination of complementary systems. See 9 Larson §§ 156.01–157.05 (2004).

It is possible that tort reform in the future will look to the workers' compensation model for guidance, particularly in the areas of medical malpractice and catastrophic injuries.

There is definitely a trend toward managed health care in workers' compensation programs throughout the states. See Hashimoto, The Future Role of Managed Care and Capitation in Workers' Compensation, 22 Am. J.L. & Med. 233 (1996). The insurance industry has debated genetic testing as a part of various insurance plans, including workers' compensation, but to date the political environment has not been receptive to these ideas. For comparisons of state law changes, see generally, 3 Modern Workers Compensation, Chapter 321 Statutory Comparison Table (2004).

PART 3

EMPLOYEE PROTECTION LEGISLATION

CHAPTER 12

UNEMPLOYMENT COMPENSATION

A. BACKGROUND

In 1935, an unemployment insurance system was established in order to provide economic security for workers during periods of temporary unemployment. The original system was created by Title IX of the Social Security Act of 1935. In 1939, the tax provisions of Title IX became the Federal Unemployment Tax Act, under the Internal Revenue Code. Today the Social Security Act, the Federal Unemployment Tax Act, and numerous amendments to these acts provide the statutory basis for federal unemployment compensation programs in the United States. Constitutional challenges to the system have met with little success. Chas. C. Steward Machine Co. v. Davis (1937); Carmichael v. Southern Coal and Coke Co. (1937); W.H.H. Chamberlin v. Andrews (1936). Recent constitutional challenges have generally been unsuccessful. See McKay v. Horn (1981). This is not to say that the unemployment insurance system is free from all constitutional problems. For example, payment or nonpayment of compensation during labor disputes creates a federal preemption question under the Supremacy Clause; see Nash v. Florida Industrial Commission (1967). First Amendment rights can also pose problems. Frazee v. Illinois Dept. of Employment Security (1989).

The principal federal statutes comprising the basis of the unemployment insurance system today are: the Federal Unemployment Tax Act (I.R.C. §§ 3301–3311); the Social Security Act, Titles III, IX, and XII; 5 U.S.C.A. §§ 8501–8508, 8521–8525; the Wagner–Peyser Act; the Social Security Amendments of 1960; the Manpower Development and Training Act of 1962; the Federal State Extended Unemployment Compensation Act of 1970; the Employment Security Amendments of 1970; the Disaster Relief Act of 1970; the Emergency Unemployment Compensation Act of 1971; the Disaster Relief Act of 1974; the Trade Act of 1974; the Emergency Unemployment Compensation Act of 1974; the Emergency Jobs and Unemployment Assistance Act of 1974, as amended; the Emergency Compensation and Special Unemployment Assistance Act of 1975; the Unemployment Compensation Act Amendments of 1976; the Emergency Unemployment Compensation Act of 1977; the Omnibus Reconciliation Act of 1980; the Omnibus Budget Reconciliation Act of 1981; the Tax Equity and Fiscal Responsibility Act of 1982; the Social Security Amendments of 1983; the Omnibus Budget Reconciliation Acts of 1987 and 1990; the Emergency Unemployment Compensation Act of 1991; the Unemployment Compensation Amendments of 1993; the Personal Responsibility and Work Opportunity Reconciliation Act of 1996; the Balanced Budget Act of 1997; the Taxpayer Relief Act of 1997; and Unemployment Assistance for 9/11/01 Victims. In addition to the foregoing, each state, the District of Columbia, Puerto Rico, and the Virgin Islands have separate unemployment compensation laws.

The unemployment insurance system relies on cooperative federal-state programs. Federal laws provide general guidelines, standards, and requirements, with administration left to the states under their particular unemployment legislation.

The unemployment compensation system is generally funded by unemployment insurance taxes or "contributions" imposed upon employers. The federal taxes are generally applied to the costs of administration, while the state taxes provide trust funds for the payment of benefits. Federal taxes are paid into a Federal Unemployment Trust Fund from which administrative costs and the federal share of extended benefits are paid. The Fund is also used to establish a Federal Unemployment Account from which the states can borrow if their state trust funds become depleted. Unemployment taxes should not be confused with the separate Social Security taxes imposed by the federal government, or with the separate disability benefits taxes imposed by some states. It should be noted that unemployment benefits are taxable as ordinary income.

The U.S. Department of Labor maintains a useful website at: http://www.dol.gov.

B. FEDERAL UNEMPLOYMENT INSURANCE PROGRAMS

1. REGULAR STATE PROGRAMS

a. Overview

The principal vehicle for providing weekly unemployment benefits is referred to as the regular state program. Subject to federal guidelines, the states determine: (1) qualifying requirements; (2) amounts of benefits; (3) duration; and (4) grounds for disqualification.

While state unemployment compensation laws can vary, ordinarily qualification requires a demonstration of: employment by an employer subject to the unemployment tax of a particular jurisdiction, and employment during a "base period" (a recent 12 month period); and generally one must have been employed in more than one quarter.

Payments usually take the form of weekly benefits. The weekly amount is calculated on the basis of a particular jurisdiction's formula. Commonly an employee's average weekly wage provides the basis for the weekly benefit amount, and this average amount is determined by dividing one's high quarter wages by the 13 weeks in a quarter; one-half of the result is the weekly benefit amount paid to the worker. There may be a waiting period prior to the initial payment of benefits. In some jurisdictions this may be referred to as the "waiting week;" however, not all jurisdictions impose an unemployment period of one week prior to the payment of compensation. Normally, claimants have a "benefit year" of a designated 52 weeks within which to receive or "draw out" all compensation entitlements.

The duration of unemployment compensation benefits varies with the particular jurisdiction; however, the vast majority of jurisdictions determine duration on the basis of the length of employment or the amount earned (variable duration approach). The longer the length or the greater the amount, the more weeks of benefits one can receive. A minority of jurisdictions consider an employee's work history to be irrelevant, and all claimants who qualify for benefits are treated in the same manner; i.e., each uniformly receives the same number of weeks of benefits on the theory that benefits should be tied to that period of time necessary to secure new employment (uniform duration approach).

Workers are denied compensation benefits if certain grounds for disqualification exist. Unemployment compensation policy dictates payment only to those employees who have lost their jobs through no fault on their part. In all jurisdictions an employee is disqualified from benefits if the worker: (1) voluntarily quits employment without good cause; or (2) is discharged for employment related misconduct. Additionally, disqualification can occur at any time if a claimant or benefit recipient refuses to accept suitable employment without good cause. Finally, in order for benefits to continue, a claimant must: (1) register for employment with the jurisdiction's Employment Service; (2) be able to work; (3) be available for work; and (4) seek work on one's own.

b. Procedures and Appeals

Representatives of the state employment agencies, who may be called deputies or claims examiners, make initial findings of fact (usually on the basis of interviews) which lead to a grant or a denial of unemployment compensation benefits. The appellate rights of a dissatisfied claimant are generally guaranteed by Title III of the Social Security Act, Section 303(a), which requires administration by the states in a manner "reasonably calculated to insure full payment of unemployment benefits when due," and which requires an "opportunity for a fair hearing before an impartial tribunal for all individuals whose claims for unemployment are denied." See Graves v. Meystrik (1977). It should be noted that employers have appellate rights as well, and they frequently exercise these rights because an employer's unemployment experience rating affects the amounts that an employer is required to contribute. Appellate procedures vary from state to state, but all jurisdictions allow access to the state judicial system for appellate review, once administrative remedies have been exhausted (usually after a hearing before an appeals tribunal whose decision may or may not be then reviewed by a board or some other state administrative body). A state administrative practice of permitting the automatic suspension of benefit payments upon the filing of an appeal by an employer was enjoined by the Supreme Court. California Department of Human Resources Development v. Java (1971). See Jenkins v. Bowling (7th Cir.1982).

c. *Extended and Supplemental Benefits*

In recent times, certain amendments have provided extended, supplemental or special unemployment benefits, thus increasing unemployment compensation for many unemployed persons in the United States. The Federal–State Extended Benefits Program pays "exhaustees" (individuals who have exhausted their regular program entitlements) further unemployment compensation, with the costs shared equally by the federal and state governments. The Omnibus Budget Reconciliation Act of 1981, repealed the national "on" and "off" triggering indicators which automatically regulated the extended benefits program. The Federal Supplemental Compensation Act of 1982 made additional unemployment benefits available in states experiencing periods of "higher unemployment;" these benefits are funded out of general federal revenues. The Social Security Amendments of 1983 extended the Federal Supplemental Compensation program. More recent federal acts have made similar adjustments.

2.   FEDERAL EMPLOYEES AND EX–SERVICEMEN

In 1956, unemployment compensation coverage was extended to federal employees. The state law of the jurisdiction in which a claimant worked as a federal employee usually determines an employee's eligibility. This eligibility may also be determined by the law of the state in which a claimant subsequently worked in privately covered employment, or by the law of the state in which a claimant resides at the time of the filing of the claim. The amount of benefits is determined by state law. The conditions and eligibility requirements for compensation are also governed by state law, but findings of fact provided by the employing federal agency with regard to federal employment, wages, and the reasons for separation (which have been made under U.S. Department of Labor procedures) are binding upon the states.

In 1958, unemployment compensation coverage was extended to ex-servicemen. The state law of the jurisdiction in which a claimant first files an unemployment compensation claim which establishes a benefit year after the claimant's most recent separation from active duty, determines eligibility. A U.S. Department of Labor schedule prescribes applicable wages for benefit purposes. These are based upon a claimant's pay grade at the time of one's latest discharge or release from federal service. If a claimant is eligible for certain Veterans Administration benefits (subsistence or educational), the claimant is not entitled to unemployment compensation during these periods of eligibility.

3. DISASTER UNEMPLOYMENT ASSISTANCE

Those employees who suffer unemployment as a result of major disasters are entitled to unemployment benefit assistance. This program is now generally known as the Disaster Relief and Emergency Assistance (DREA) program. The President makes disaster area declarations. The states generally administer the payment of benefits, and these are strictly derived from federal revenues. Individual benefits are payable for the period of unemployment caused by the disaster, or until suitable reemployment is obtained, but in no event longer than the prescribed disaster assistance period.

4. TRADE ADJUSTMENT ASSISTANCE

Direct assistance is provided to employees who find themselves unemployed because of foreign competition. These benefits are provided only to those employees whose terminations are the result of foreign imports. These imports must be a substantial cause of actual or threatened termination. Assistance is paid out of federal revenues and is generally administered by the states. This assistance takes the form of weekly benefits, training allowances, relocation allowances, and job search allowances.

C. STATE FINANCED PROGRAMS

1. EXTENDED AND ADDITIONAL BENEFITS

A few states have enacted supplemental unemployment programs. These programs are financed completely by the particular jurisdiction, and they are usually aimed at providing extended benefits during high unemployment periods. California, Connecticut, and Puerto Rico have state extended benefit programs. Hawaii has enacted an Additional Unemployment Compensation Benefits Law that provides benefits for unemployment resulting from disasters.

2. UNEMPLOYMENT COMPENSATION DISABILITY BENEFITS

Six jurisdictions in the United States have enacted special disability benefit programs to assist workers who are ineligible for either unemployment compensation or workers' compensation. Workers' compensation generally excludes disabilities arising out of nonwork-related diseases or injuries; benefits are not payable through unemployment insurance programs to disabled workers because the ability to work is a condition of eligibility. California, Hawaii, New Jersey, New York, Rhode Island, and Puerto Rico have special unemployment disability benefit programs that fill the gap between workers' compensation and unemployment compensation laws. A branch of the particular jurisdiction's labor agency administers the program. Contribution by employers to state funds, private insurance, or self-insurance finance the programs. Some states make distinctions between the employed and the unemployed in their benefit formulas, while other jurisdictions do not.

CHAPTER 13

FAIR LABOR STANDARDS ACT

A. INTRODUCTION

The federal attempt to regulate the wages and hours of employees began in 1892 with the passage of the Eight–Hour Law. Later, the Supreme Court in Hammer v. Dagenhart (1918), held that Congress could not properly exercise its power under the Commerce Clause to prohibit the shipment of goods produced by child labor in interstate commerce. The Fair Labor Standards Act of 1938, 29 U.S.C.A. § 201 et seq. (hereinafter referred to as "FLSA") was enacted to regulate wages and hours (set minimum wage and overtime requirements) and child labor. The FLSA was upheld as constitutional in United States v. Darby (1941), in which the Hammer v. Dagenhart case, supra, was overruled. Over the years Congress has amended the FLSA and added major and minor acts to the federal wage-hour laws. The Equal Pay Act of 1963 was an important amendment to the FLSA; it generally prohibits sex-based wage discrimination by requiring equal pay for equal work regardless of sex. The Congressional extension of wage and hour coverage to public schools and hospitals was upheld as constitutional in Maryland v. Wirtz (1968), but this decision was overruled in National League of Cities v. Usery (1976). In this latter case, the Supreme Court held that the attempted Congressional regulation of wages and hours of employees of state and local governments constituted an unconstitutional infringement on state sovereignty. Constitutional issues again reached the Supreme Court in Garcia v. San

Antonio Metro. Transit Authority (1985), in which a divided court upheld the application of the FLSA to state and local governments, and overruled National League of Cities v. Usery. Congress passed the Fair Labor Standards Amendments of 1985 in order to lessen the impact of Garcia by authorizing the use of compensatory time in the place of overtime for state and local government employees.

The FLSA may be applied to a nonprofit religious organization that derives income largely from commercial business, despite constitutional challenges based upon the First Amendment. Tony and Susan Alamo Foundation v. Secretary of Labor (1985).

The Fair Labor Standards Amendments of 1989 created a "training wage" for eligible employees under 19 years of age at rates less than the minimum wage. The Small Business Job Protection Act of 1996 increased the minimum wage, and it replaced the "training wage" with an "opportunity wage."

Today the FLSA, as amended, provides compensation standards and regulation in four basic areas: (1) minimum wages; (2) overtime compensation; (3) sex-based wage discrimination (equal pay for equal work); and (4) child labor. The FLSA, as amended, is liberally construed by the courts, and, with certain exceptions, it applies generally to interstate commerce and industry. Other federal acts apply compensation standards to federally financed public works contracts (Davis–Bacon Act), government service contracts (Service Contract Act), and government supply contracts (Walsh–Healey Public Contracts Act). See generally, U.S. Department of Labor websites: http://www.dol.gov/asp/programs/guide/dbra.htm; http://www.dol.gov/asp/programs/guide/sca.htm; and http://www.dol.gov/asp/programs/guide/walshh.htm. Some states have enacted higher compensation standards than those existing under federal law. These higher state standards are not superseded or preempted, and the federal standards cannot be used to excuse noncompliance with the higher state ones. If employees are covered by both federal and state compensation standards, then the stricter federal or state standards are applicable.

B. STANDARDS AND REQUIREMENTS

1. MINIMUM WAGE

Congress changes the minimum wage rate from time to time, and as of September 1, 1997, the FLSA established the minimum hourly rate for all covered employees at $5.15. This means, for example, that employees who are paid on a monthly basis and who are working 40 hour weeks, must be paid at least $892.67 per month; employees who are paid semi-monthly must be paid $446.33; employees who are paid weekly must be paid $206.00 per week. The foregoing are monthly, semi-monthly, and weekly average standards; the FLSA does not require an employer to pay these amounts each period, but the average standards must be met (based upon 8 hour work days; 40 hour work weeks; and 2,080 work hours in a year).

It must always be remembered that the workweek is the longest unit of time over which wages can be averaged in order to determine whether the minimum wage has been paid. This does not mean that all employees must be paid solely on an hourly rate basis; they can be paid on a salary, commission, or piecework basis that is monthly, semi-monthly, or weekly, but the minimum hourly rate must be received by them. If employees are paid solely on an hourly rate basis, then the minimum hourly rate must be met.

Problems sometime arise because certain deductions may be legally made from an employee's wages. Wages must be paid in cash or "facilities furnished," and thus the reasonable costs of board, lodging or other facilities can be used in meeting minimum wage requirements. Payment in scrip, tokens, coupons, etc., is prohibited. Gifts, talent fees, discretionary bonuses, and certain other payments are excluded from wage calculations. The application of the minimum wage to particular employees requires detailed research, because of the complexity and exceptions contained in the FLSA and related wage and hour laws. See generally, U.S. Department of Labor website: http://www.dol.gov/asp/programs/guide/minwage.htm.

2. OVERTIME COMPENSATION

The federal wage and hour laws do not limit the number of hours that an employee can work in a workweek, but the employee must be paid time and one-half the employee's regular rate of pay for each hour worked over 40 in a workweek. It should be noted that an employee's regular rate of pay can be higher than the minimum hourly rate set by law for these purposes. The workweek is the longest period over which earnings may be averaged in arriving at an employee's regular hourly rate of pay. For example, if an employee works 45 hours in one week and 35 in the next week, the employee must be paid overtime for five hours in the first week, despite the fact that the employee's hourly average over two weeks is 40 hours per week. Time lost on the job must be made up in the same workweek, or else overtime must be paid for all hours subsequently worked over 40 in any other workweek. Overtime exceptions and exemptions exist that must be researched in particular cases.

Many disputes arise because employers and employees fail to agree on what activities are to be considered "working time." For example, time spent on call may or may not be considered as working time. The Portal-to-Portal Act of 1947, excludes preliminary and postliminary activities from working time not otherwise compensable by contract, custom, or practice. Premium pay can also create overtime calculation difficulties. This is pay received in excess of basic straight-time wages, and it can take the form of holiday pay, contracted overtime, gifts, bonuses, sick pay, etc. If premium pay is considered to be part of an employee's regular earnings, then FLSA overtime is increased, otherwise premium pay may be offset against the statutory overtime pay.

It should be noted that effective August 23, 2004, new overtime regulations promulgated by the U.S. Department of Labor changed the overtime rules for white collar workers. See 29 C.F.R. Part 542 Defining and Delimiting the Exemptions for Executive, Administrative, Professional, Outside Sales and Computer Employees. These workers who earn more than $100,000.00 per year are automatically exempt from overtime pay requirements under the changes. Further, a white collar employee must be paid overtime unless the worker meets three tests: (1) the worker is paid a set salary and not hourly; (2) the salary is at least $455.00 per week, or $23,600.00 per year; and (3) the worker's job qualifies as administrative, professional, or executive. These changes are the first in over 50 years in this area, and they are controversial. Labor unions have opposed the changes, while employers have generally supported them. One of the reasons for the changes has been the marked increase in overtime lawsuits brought by employees in the past 5 years. Employers are hopeful that the changes will reduce overtime litigation.

3.　SEX–BASED WAGE DISCRIMINATION

The Equal Pay Act of 1963 amended the minimum wage provisions of the FLSA, and prohibited wage discrimination based upon sex. The provisions require equal pay for equal work for men and women doing equal work on jobs requiring equal skill, effort and responsibility and that are performed under similar working conditions. Minimum, overtime, and premium wages for men and women must be equal if the work is equal, and the wages of one sex cannot be lowered in order to comply with the law. Exceptions are allowed for: (1) seniority systems; (2) merit systems; (3) systems measuring earnings by quantity or quality of production; and (4) factors other than sex. The act prohibits sex-based wage discrimination only in "any establishment" operated by an employer. The act does not cover discriminatory rates as between an employer's two or more legitimate "establishments." It should be noted that wage differences authorized by the Equal Pay Act are valid pay practices for the purposes of the Civil Rights Act of 1964, Title VII; however, it is possible for sex-based discrimination involving pay practices, beyond the reach of the Equal Pay Act, to be remedied under Title VII. In order for equal pay coverage to exist, an employee generally must be covered by the FLSA minimum wage provisions. It should also be pointed out that amendments in 1972, placed executive, administrative, and professional employees within equal pay coverage. See Ch.20, B., infra.

4. CHILD LABOR

The FLSA prohibits "oppressive child labor" in commerce or in the production of goods for commerce. There is a "hot goods" ban that prohibits the interstate shipment of goods from establishments that have employed oppressive child labor. Enterprise coverage is used to prohibit the use of oppressive child labor, regardless of whether the work of children has an interstate impact or is purely local in nature. The FLSA defines "oppressive child labor" through the use of age restrictions. Essentially, minors under 14 cannot be employed, except in agriculture; minors 14 to 16 can work limited hours outside of their school hours in a limited class of jobs; and minors 16 to 18 cannot be employed in certain hazardous occupations. Employers generally obtain age or permit certificates for each minor in accordance with Department of Labor regulations and state guidelines. See generally, U.S. Department of Labor website: http://www.dol.gov/asp/programs/guide/childbr.htm.

C. COVERAGES

Compensation standards have been imposed by Congress through the exercise of its powers to regulate interstate commerce and through it powers to control federal government contracts and federally financed projects. All geographical areas under the jurisdiction of the United States, including possessions and leased bases in foreign countries, are subject to the FLSA. Two forms of coverage are provided by the FLSA: (1) "enterprise" coverage; and (2) "individual employee" coverage. Enterprise coverage generally exists if an employer has two or more workers engaged in interstate commerce, or in the production of goods for interstate commerce, while meeting a requirement of business volume. If enterprise coverage exists, then all employees of the enterprise are covered. Individual employee coverage can exist even if an employer's business does not qualify for enterprise coverage. An individual employee can be covered if the employee is engaged in commerce or in the production of goods for commerce, or is employed in a closely related process or occupation directly essential to the production of goods. The FLSA contains a number of exemptions based upon the type of industry or the type of employee. Once FLSA coverage is found to exist, the minimum wage, overtime, equal pay and child labor provisions are applicable, unless a specific exemption governs.

In those situations in which government contract laws impose compensation standards, the particular transaction and the appropriate federal act must be considered. For example, the Walsh–Healey Act imposes employee compensation standards through the terms and conditions of federal government supply contracts.

D. ENFORCEMENT AND REMEDIES

The administration and enforcement of federal compensation standards primarily rests with the U.S. Department of Labor, Employment Standards Administration. The Wage and Hour Division performs inspections and investigations, makes compliance determinations, and issues rules and regulations. The Equal Employment Opportunity Commission is now charged with the enforcement of the equal pay provisions.

The Secretary of Labor is authorized to file suit on behalf of employees to collect wages and overtime, plus liquidated damages in an equal amount. The Secretary is also empowered to file suits enjoining or restraining employer violations; the Secretary can also seek civil contempt citations against employers for continued violations of decrees. It should be noted that a "clearly erroneous" standard of review is to be used by courts of appeal in reviewing the application of an exemption to the FLSA. Icicle Seafoods, Inc. v. Worthington (1986). The U.S. Department of Justice can prosecute wilful violators in criminal proceedings. Employees are authorized to file suit for reinstatement, back wages, liquidated damages in an equal amount, reasonable attorney's fees, and costs. A three year statute of limitations exists for wilful violations, while a two year statute exists for other violations. McLaughlin v. Richland Shoe Co. (1988) (definition of "willful" in connection with 3 year statute of limitations). It should be noted that employees generally do not have the right to release employers for less than the full amounts owing or to waive their rights to compensation. See D.A. Schulte, Inc. v. Gangi (1946); Brooklyn Savings Bank v. O'Neil (1945).

CHAPTER 14

OCCUPATIONAL SAFETY AND HEALTH ACT

A. BACKGROUND AND SCOPE

In 1970, Congress enacted the Occupational Safety and Health Act, 29 U.S.C.A. § 651 et seq., for the purpose of assuring as far as possible that safe and healthful working conditions exist for all workers in the United States. The basic act has withstood constitutional challenge; Atlas Roofing Co. v. OSHRC (1977); but some procedural difficulties have been encountered. See Marshall v. Barlow's, Inc. (1978). The act extends geographically to all areas under U.S. jurisdiction, including territories, possessions, and the outer continental shelves. The act provides coverage and applies to all employers engaged in a business that affects interstate commerce, and the act's jurisdictional scope has been broadly construed. See Usery v. Lacy (1980). State and local governments are excluded from coverage. Federal employees are not covered, but special safety and health programs are required by Executive Order 12196. See 29 C.F.R. Part 1960.

Essentially, the act imposes a twofold obligation upon all employers: (1) there is a "general duty" clause requiring employers to furnish a workplace free from recognized hazards that are likely to cause serious injury or death to workers, and (2) there are safety and health standards that employers must meet. Employers are required by the act to keep records of accidents, illnesses, deaths, and particular hazards. The posting of OSHA information and citations for violations are also required under the act. Finally, employers are required to make reports to OSHA.

Of importance to both employers and employees is OSHA's Hazard Communication Program. 29 C.F.R. § 1926.59. The purpose of this program is to give employers and employees vital information about chemical hazards through product container labeling and dissemination of "material safety data sheets." Some states have enacted "right to know" legislation that may be preempted by OSHA unless the particular state is operating under an approved plan.

Several federal agencies administer and enforce the act. Safety and health standards are usually recommended on the basis of research by the National Institute for Occupational Safety and Health, and they fall under the responsibility of the Secretary of Health and Human Services. The Occupational Safety and Health Administration (OSHA) of the U.S. Department of Labor promulgates and enforces standards. An independent agency, the Occupational Safety and Health Review Commission adjudicates contested cases through the use of administrative law judges. Judicial review of commission decisions rests with the federal circuit courts of appeal.

The act provides that the states may assume responsibility for workplace safety and health by adopting a plan of standards and enforcement that is at least as effective as the federal one. See generally, Gade v. National Solid Wastes Management Ass'n. (1992). All state plans must receive approval from the Occupational Safety and Health Administration. Upon approval, the states are entitled to enforce their own laws. A minority of states have adopted these plans.

It should be kept in mind that no private rights of action are created against employers for violation of standards under the act. See Russell v. Bartley (1974). Citations and standards, however, can have a significant impact on private damage actions. The safety and health standards can be evidence of an employer's standard of care in tort actions. See Donovan v. General Motors (1985) (standard of care issue); Schroeder v. C.F. Braun & Co. (1974). See also, Hines v. Brandon Steel Decks, Inc. (1989) (use of OSHA reports as evidence in civil trial).

Public criticism of the entire program has emerged in recent years, especially in the area of costs to employers versus effectiveness. See e.g., Barstow and Bergman, Death on the Job, Slaps on the Wrist, New York Times, Jan. 10, 2003, page 1.

B.　STANDARDS AND VARIANCES

There are three types of safety and health standards, and two types of variances that come into play under the act. First of all, there are interim or "start-up" standards based upon existing federal and national consensus standards. The existing or already established federal standards originate from the Service Contract Act, the Longshore and Harbor Workers' Compensation Act, the Construction Safety Act, and the Walsh–Healey Act. The consensus standards originate from national standards organizations such as the American National Standards Institute, the National Fire Protection Association, and the American Society for Testing and Materials. Consensus standards also originate from federal procedures permitting consideration of opposing views or from designated standards of the Secretary of Labor after consultation with particular federal agencies.

A second type of standard is called a permanent standard. Permanent standards are designed to replace or supplement the interim ones, and they generally come into being after advisory committee recommendation, publication in the Federal Register, receipt of comment by interested parties, and public hearing. The Secretary of Labor then makes a permanent standard determination.

The third type of safety and health standard is called a temporary emergency standard, which the Secretary of Labor establishes when the Secretary determines that new safety and health findings demonstrate that employees are exposed to grave dangers.

All of the three foregoing types of safety and health standards are subject to judicial review by the U.S. Circuit Courts of Appeal upon petition by any person affected by the standard, within 60 days of a standard being set. The development and promulgation of safety and health standards can be the subject of serious judicial scrutiny. See Industrial Union Department, AFL–CIO v. American Petroleum Institute (1980).

An employer may obtain either a permanent or a temporary variance from the safety and health standards in certain circumstances. A permanent variance is obtained after application and a showing that an employer's working conditions, practices, methods, etc. are as safe and healthful as those provided by the standards. Applications are filed with the Assistant Secretary of Labor for Occupational Safety and Health. Temporary variances may be obtained from the Secretary of Labor if an employer can demonstrate either that necessary equipment or personnel are not immediately available or that the construction or alteration of required facilities or controls cannot be completed by a standard's effective date. Economic hardship is not a consideration in these determinations, and temporary variances are only good for a limited time period.

C. ENFORCEMENT AND PROCEDURES

The enforcement of the act usually involves OSHA inspections, and citations of employers for: (1) breach of the general duty obligation; (2) breach of specific safety and health standards; or (3) failure to keep records, make reports, or post notices required by the act.

Upon the presentation of appropriate credentials, OSHA inspectors are authorized to enter without delay and at reasonable times an employer's premises. These investigations are to occur at reasonable times, within reasonable limits, and be conducted in a reasonable manner. OSHA inspectors are entitled to private interviews with employers, owners, agents, employees or operators. If an OSHA inspector is denied entry, a search warrant may be obtained from a U.S. District Court by the Solicitor of Labor. The probable cause requirements are less stringent than those in criminal cases. See Marshall v. Barlow's, Inc., supra. Ex parte warrants are obtainable under OSHA regulations. It should be noted that it is unlawful to discriminate against employees or to discharge them for OSHA inspection requests, testimony in OSHA inspection requests, testimony in OSHA proceedings, or for the exercise of any rights under the act.

When a violation is discovered, a written citation, proposed penalty, and correction date are furnished to the employer. Citations may be contested, and in such cases, administrative law judges are assigned by the Occupational Safety and Health Review Commission, to conduct hearings. The commission may or may not grant review of an administrative law judge's decision; commission review is not a matter of right. If commission review is not undertaken, then the judge's decision becomes the final order of the commission 30 days after receipt. In any event once a decision is final, it may be appealed by any aggrieved party to the appropriate U.S. Circuit Court of Appeals within 60 days.

Civil and criminal penalties exist for various violations. Penalties are usually accessed in a monetary on a per day per violation basis, and criminal fines, along with imprisonment, are allowed. In cases involving civil penalties, it is important, as a matter of practice, to distinguish between serious and nonserious violations. Serious violations require that a penalty be proposed. In nonserious violation cases, penalties are rarely proposed. It should be noted that employers can be cited by OSHA and still be subject to prosecution without violating the ban on double jeopardy. See Herman v. S.A. Healy (1997); Hudson v. United States (1997).

The Secretary of Labor is further empowered by the act to obtain temporary restraining orders shutting down business operations that create imminent dangers of death or serious injury. This procedure is available when imminent dangers cannot be eliminated through regular OSHA enforcement procedures.

The U.S. Department of Labor maintains a useful website at: http://www.dol.gov/asp/programs/guide/osha.htm.

CHAPTER 15

FEDERAL BLACK LUNG BENEFITS LEGISLATION

A. BACKGROUND AND SCOPE

The Federal Coal Mine Health and Safety Act of 1969, 30 U.S.C.A. § 801 et seq., was enacted in an effort to provide standards for safety and health for coal mines in the United States. It also provided compensation benefits for coal miners and their dependents, or survivors, when a miner's disability or death was the result of pneumoconiosis, otherwise known as "black lung," a chronic dust disease of the lungs, which is more fully defined in the act. This act has been the subject of several important amendments: the Black Lung Benefits Act of 1972; the Black Lung Benefits Reform Act of 1977; the Black Lung Benefits Review Act of 1977; the Black Lung Benefits Revenue Act of 1981; the Black Lung Benefits Amendments of 1981 and the Consolidated Omnibus Budget Reconciliation Act of 1985. The constitutionality of federal black lung legislation was upheld in Usery v. Turner Elkhorn Mining Co. (1976). See Pauley v. Bethenergy Mines, Inc. (1991) (upholding rebuttal regulations).

The original federal black lung legislation attempted to place the responsibility for compensation and medical expenses on responsible mine operators whose identities could be determined, but the federal government assumed these obligations when no responsible mine operator could be determined. Various devices have been employed by the federal government to insure the payment of black lung benefits.

Reforms in 1977, created a Black Lung Disability Trust Fund which is administered jointly by the Secretaries of Labor, Treasury, and Health and Human Services. This fund is financed primarily by excise taxes on mined coal. The Black Lung Disability Trust Fund has suffered from a chronic lack of funding, and this resulted in amendments in 1981 aimed at preserving the fund through increased excise taxes and through benefit limitations. From 1974 through 1996, over $10.7 billion in black lung payments were made to claimants.

Originally, claims were processed by the Social Security Administration; however, the Department of Labor has assumed this responsibility. This was logical, in light of the fact that the Department of Labor is the responsible agency for mining health and safety. Claims filed up to July 1, 1973, continued to be under the Social Security Administration's jurisdiction, but claims filed after July 1, 1973, are administered by the Department of Labor. The Black Lung Benefits Reform Act of 1977, broadened entitlement and provided review for some previously denied claims, either by the Social Security Administration or the Department of Labor. Current claims procedures are set forth in detail in 20 C.F.R. § 410.101 et seq. and in 20 C.F.R. § 718.1 et seq. See 20 C.F.R. Parts 722, 725, 726 & 727. See generally, U.S. Department of Labor website: http://www.dol.gov/asp/programs/guide/blklung.htm.

B. ELIGIBILITY AND BENEFITS

Monthly cash benefits are payable under the federal black lung program to past and present coal miners who are totally disabled as a result of pneumoconiosis; a miner's compensation increases if there are dependents. Additionally, in miner death cases, widows, children, surviving divorced wives, parents, brothers and sisters may receive benefits. If a widow was entitled to benefits at the time of her death, her children may receive benefits.

The basic benefit for a disabled coal miner is equal to 37½ percent of the monthly pay of a federal employee in the Grade of GS–2, step 1, who is totally disabled. A surviving widow is paid the same benefit. Any single surviving child would receive the same benefit that a surviving widow would have received. Single surviving children are entitled to a full widow's benefit, if a widow dies while receiving benefits. Miner's benefits and the benefits of dependents are increased based upon the number of dependents. Benefits are reduced by state workers' compensation, unemployment compensation, state disability insurance, or excess earnings under the Social Security Act.

In order to be eligible for benefits under the federal black lung program, a coverage formula must be met. See Mullins Coal Co. v. Director (1987). The formula requires: (1) a "miner," who is (2) "totally disabled due to pneumoconiosis." In order to qualify as a "miner," a person must have worked as an employee in a coal mine whether underground or above ground, performing functions in extracting the coal or preparing the coal so extracted. The definition of "miner" has undergone several statutory changes since the original act, and in 1977, it was expanded to provide coverage for self-employed miners, and certain others in the coal mine construction and transportation industries. See Baker v. United States Steel Corp. (1989) (liberal construction given to the term "miner"). Once "miner" status is established, a claimant must prove total disability due to pneumoconiosis. In proving total disability due to pneumoconiosis, claimants traditionally enjoyed the assistance of certain rebuttable and irrebuttable presumptions. The 1981 amendments effectively eliminated some presumptions, however, two important ones remain: (1) a miner with pneumoconiosis who was exposed for 10 or more years is rebuttably presumed to have pneumoconiosis that arose out of employment; and (2) a miner with complicated pneumoconiosis receives an irrebuttable presumption of the necessary total disability, or in death cases, that death was due to the pneumoconiosis; or additionally in death cases that total disability from pneumoconiosis existed at the time of death. See generally, Pittston Coal Group v. Sebben (1988).

The 1981 amendments also addressed the issue of proof and provided that after the effective date of the 1981 amendments, the Secretary of Labor need not accept a radiologist's interpretation of chest x-rays, and could consider second interpretations. Furthermore, the Secretary need not accept as binding the affidavits of interested persons who are eligible for benefits in death cases.

C. PROCEDURES

Claims for black lung benefits may be filed at certain offices of the Department of Labor, Social Security district offices, or Foreign Service offices of the United States by mail or presentation. The Department of Labor's Office of Workers' Compensation supervises the claims procedures, and once a claim has been forwarded to them, a deputy commissioner conducts an initial investigation which is designed to determine a claimant's eligibility for benefits, and if a responsible operator exists.

Deputy commissioner decisions in contested cases are assigned to Administrative Law Judges for formal hearings in accordance with the Administrative Procedure Act. See Pyro Mining Co. v. Slaton (1989). Appeals from these hearings are lodged with the Benefits Review Board, which may enter a final decision or remand the case either to the Administrative Law Judge or to the deputy commissioner. Final decisions of the Benefits Review Board may be appealed to the U.S. Circuit

Court of Appeals in the circuit where the miner was last employed.

D. MINING SAFETY AND HEALTH

The Federal Mine Safety Act of 1997, 30 U.S.C.A. § 801 et seq., protects persons working on mine properties. The Mine Safety and Health Administration (MSHA) administers the Act. Responsibility is placed upon employers for miners' safety and health. Regular inspections are required for both underground and surface mines. Miners' training requirements have been established, and dangerous mines can be closed. The Act prescribes penalties for health and safety violations, and specific health and safety regulations cover mining hazards. See generally, U.S. Department of Labor website: http://www.dol.gov/asp/programs/guide/msha.htm.

CHAPTER 16

SOCIAL SECURITY

A. INTRODUCTION

The federal Social Security system began in 1935 in an effort to provide limited retirement or death benefits for workers in commerce and industry. Since 1935, the system has greatly expanded, and benefits have increased dramatically.

Historically significant changes occurred as follows: in 1954, coverage became almost universal; in 1956, disability insurance benefits were added; in 1958, disability eligibility was liberalized, and benefits were added for dependents of disability insurance recipients; in 1961, early but reduced retirement was permitted for men at age 62; in 1965, medicare benefits were added; in 1972, automatic cost-of-living-adjustments (COLA) were added to the benefit system; in 1977, substantial increases in tax rates were enacted to cover projected long term deficits; and in 1981, short term deficits were financed by interfund borrowing.

Amendments in 1983 resulted in the taxation of certain social security benefits for the first time; called for the normal retirement age to be gradually changed from 65 to 67; established mandatory coverage for employees of nonprofit organizations; resulted in some federal workers being covered by social security rather than by civil service; established deferred compensation plan taxation for social security purposes; prohibited states from terminating coverage of state and local government employees; altered cost-of-living-adjustment computation methods; and eliminated several gender-based distinctions previously made by the social security laws. The Disability Reform Act of 1984 changed the standard of review for terminating disability benefits and, among other changes, provided for the evaluation of pain. Technical amendments were passed in 1986 and 1987. Catastrophic health care coverage and financing was enacted under the Medicare Catastrophic Coverage Act of 1988; however, Congress voted to repeal this Act in 1989. The Omnibus Budget Reconciliation Act of 1990, the Omnibus Budget Reconciliation Act of 1993, the Social Security Domestic Employment Reform Act of 1994, the Social Security Independence and Program Improvements Act of 1994, the Contract with America Advancement Act of 1996, Omnibus Consolidated and Emergency Supplemental Appropriations Act, 1999, Foster Care Independence Act of 1999, Ticket to Work and Work Incentives Independence Act of 1999, Medicare Prescription Drug Improvement and Modernization Act of 2003, and Social Security Protection Act of 2003, have added other changes in policies.

Today, the Social Security system contains the following benefit programs: (1) Retirement and survivors benefits (Old–Age and Survivors Insurance—OASI); (2) Disability benefits (Disability Insurance—DI); (3) Medicare benefits (Hospitalization Insurance—HI; a separate Medicare Medical Insurance (MMI) program requires enrollment and premium payments); and (4) Supplemental Security Income benefits (SSI). With the exception of state and local governments, and certain nonprofit organizations, coverage is generally mandatory; election of coverage is permitted, however, for these groups.

For the most part, Social Security benefits are financed by taxes or "contributions" collected from employers, employees, and self-employed persons who work in employments covered by Social Security. The Federal Insurance Contributions Act (FICA) which falls within the Internal Revenue Code, governs taxation and collection. In 2004, the Social Security tax rate (combined OASDI and HI 2004 FICA withholding) on wages was 7.65 percent (6.2 percent plus 1.45 percent each for Medicare (Part A—Hospital Insurance)) for employees. Employers paid an equal rate, and this established a total rate of 15.3 percent. The self-employment rate was 12.4 percent for OASDI and 2.9 percent for Medicare (15.3 percent total). The maximum OASDI wage base for 2004 was $87,900. There was no limit on the Medicare wage tax portion. These collected taxes pay for retirement, survivors, disability, and hospital insurance benefits. In the case of certain persons, however, hospital insurance benefits are paid from the general revenues of the United States, and it should also be noted that supplementary medical insurance benefits are generally financed through the collection of monthly premiums. The general revenues of the United States pay for supplemental security income benefits.

Three basic trust funds hold Social Security contributions: (1) the Old–Age and Survivors Insurance Trust Fund; (2) the Disability Insurance Trust Fund; and (3) the Hospital Insurance Trust Fund (this fund also receives general revenues in order to pay benefits to uninsured persons 65 and older). The Supplementary Medical Insurance Trust Fund receives premium collections and general revenues that have been appropriated for the fund. A Board of Trustees, consisting of the Secretaries of Health and Human Services, Treasury, and Labor, hold these funds, and amounts not currently needed are invested in federal securities that bear interest.

The Department of Health and Human Services, through its Social Security Administration, basically administers the retirement, survivors, disability, hospital and medical insurance, and supplemental security income programs. Other public assistance and welfare services programs are financed separately, and they are generally administered by the states in cooperation with the federal government; these include: aid to needy families with children; medical assistance, maternal and child-health services; crippled children services; child support and welfare services; food stamps; and energy assistance.

The Department of Health and Human Services maintains websites at: http://www.hhs.gov and http://www.ssa.gov.

B.   RETIREMENT AND SURVIVORS INSURANCE (OASI)

1.   ELIGIBILITY FOR OASI

Eligibility for retirement and survivors benefits depends upon the "insured status" of an employee. Generally, an employee's insured status is established by the number of "quarters of coverage" that have been earned in work covered by Social Security. A worker and family can become "fully insured" with as little as 31 quarters (eight years) of work. The requisite age and quarters of coverage can vary. 20 C.F.R. § 404.115 (chart of age and quarters). If a worker is "currently insured," benefits can be paid to survivors upon the worker's death; six quarters of coverage in the 13 quarters preceding death gives rise to this "currently insured status." OASI benefits are conditioned upon the attainment of retirement age or death. Full OASI benefits are payable at age 65; reduced benefits are available at 62. The 1983 amendments will gradually increase the retirement age to 67. Other OASI benefits have age eligibility variations. OASI benefits are in the form of monthly benefit payments.

2.   OASI BENEFIT CALCULATIONS

The past earnings of covered workers generally determine the benefit levels which are to be paid to retired employees, disabled workers, dependents and survivors. Four basic concepts govern benefit calculations: (1) computation years; (2) index earnings; (3) average indexed monthly earnings (AIME); and (4) primary insurance amount (PIA). The "computation years" is essentially the number of years worked in employment covered by Social Security. The "index earnings" represents the earnings of each year which have been converted to reflect increases in wage levels over the years; this indexing creates an earnings record. The "average indexed monthly earnings" (AIME) is the result of having divided the total indexed earnings by the number of months in the "computation years." Finally, a "primary insurance amount" (PIA) or basic benefit level is obtained by applying a percentage formula to the AIME. All benefit levels are subject to periodic cost-of-living-adjustments (COLA).

3. OASI BENEFITS

The figure which provides the basis for almost all benefit amounts is the primary insurance amount (PIA). Lump sum death benefits are fixed; special benefits are sometimes paid without reference to the PIA. The OASI types of benefits payable and the percentage of the primary insurance amount (PIA) receivable in for retirees, disabled workers, dependents and survivors are generally as follows:

(1) *Full retirement*—100% of PIA (eligible at age 65); reduced benefits available at 62.

(2) *Widowed spouses*—100% of PIA (eligible at age 65); reduced benefits available at 60.

(3) *Spouses*—50% of the PIA (eligible at age 65 or younger if caring for a disabled child, or child under 16); reduced benefits available at 62.

(4) *Divorced spouses*—50% of PIA (eligible on the same basis as spouses, supra, but 10 years of marriage also required).

(5) *Children*—50% of PIA (eligible until age 18 if a child of a retired or deceased insured employee; eligible while attending full-time elementary or secondary school).

(6) *Surviving children*—75% of PIA (eligible on the same basis as children, supra).

(7) *Parents*—82½% of PIA if one parent entitled; 75% of PIA if more than one parent entitled.

(8) *Maximum family benefits*—175% of PIA.

(9) *Lump sum death benefit*—$255 payment to survivors (not a percent of PIA).

(10) *Transitionally insured benefits*—Not a percent of PIA (eligible if over 65 with insufficient quarters of coverage).

(11) *Special age 72*—Not a percent of PIA (eligible if over 72 with insufficient quarters of coverage to permit retiree benefits; must not receive public assistance).

(12) *Special minimum*—Not a percent of PIA (eligible are workers with low average earnings).

(13) *Currently insured*—OASDI benefits (eligible if survivor of worker not fully insured so long as deceased employee worked at least 6 of the 13 quarters in covered employment preceding death).

It should be noted that there can be reduction in all benefits based upon a beneficiary's annual earnings. See 20 C.F.R. Subpart E. This reduction can vary, but generally all benefits are charged on the basis of $1.00 of excess earnings for each $1.00 of monthly benefits. In 1996, Congress enacted changes that will gradually increase the annual exempt amount for beneficiaries ages 65 to 69. Self employment at age 70 and thereafter is exempt.

C. DISABILITY INSURANCE (DI)

1. ELIGIBILITY

In general, the test for disability benefit eligibility employs the same "insured status" concept used by OASI, supra. Disability eligibility requires that an employee be both: (1) "fully insured" under OASI; and (2) "disability insured." The disability insured requirement is met if a worker has 20 quarters of coverage in the 40 quarters immediately preceding disability. A waiting period of 5 months exists before these benefits can be paid. At age 65, disability benefits cease, and regular full retirement benefits are paid. In making eligibility determinations, "disability" is generally defined as the inability to engage in gainful activity by reason of any medically determinable physical or mental impairment that can be expected to last at least 12 continuous months or to result in death. Social Security disability benefits are generally offset by any other disability benefits.

2. DI BENEFITS

Generally, there are five fundamental types of disability insurance benefits:

(1) *Disabled worker*—100% of PIA (eligible 5 months after disability if fully insured under OASI and disability insured).

(2) *Disabled surviving spouse*—100% of PIA (eligible at age 60; benefits available at age 50, if disabled).

(3) *Disabled surviving divorced spouse*—50% of PIA (eligible at age 60; benefits available at age 50 if disabled).

(4) *Disabled child*—50% of PIA (eligible at age 18).

(5) *Disabled surviving child*—75% of PIA (eligible at age 18).

It must be pointed out that the Disability Insurance Trust Fund only pays benefits to disabled workers and their dependents. The benefits payable to "disabled surviving spouses" and "disabled surviving children" are paid from the Old–Age and Survivors Insurance Trust Fund. The 1980 amendments provided for the review and assessment of eligibility every three years with the exception of cases of permanent disability. This policy generated a great deal of controversy and litigation, and resulted in the Disability Reform Act of 1984.

3.   DI EVALUATION

There is a stepped sequential approach to disability determinations. 20 C.F.R. § 404.1520 (20 C.F.R. § 416.920 for supplemental security income disability determinations). The claimant must initially demonstrate physical and/or mental impairments that are severe and meet the duration requirements. There is a five-step evaluation that asks and answers certain key questions. Favorable disability determinations for claimants can be made at steps three and five. (1) Is the claimant working in a substantial gainful activity; if so, then no disability will be found regardless of medical condition or age, education and work experience. (2) Does the claimant have a severe impairment; if there is no impairment or combination of impairments that significantly limit physical or mental ability, then no disability will be found. If a severe impairment(s) does exist, then the following question is necessary. (3) Does the claimant's impairment or impairments meet or equal the "listings," contained in 20 C.F.R. Part 404, Subpart P, Appendix 1, containing specific medical criteria; if so, then a finding of disability will be made without considering age, education and work experience. (4) If a claimant does not meet the "listings," then inquiry is made whether the claimant's impairment(s) prevents the claimant from performing past relevant work. A review of residual functional capacity and the physical and mental demands of past work are evaluated at this point. If the claimant is found able to perform past relevant work, then a finding of no disability will be made. (5) If the claimant cannot perform past relevant work because of severe impairment(s), then the burden shifts to the agency to prove the claimant capable of performing other gainful employment. The question of residual functional capacity to perform other work is therefore evaluated, considering the age, education and past work experience of the claimant. At this point, vocational-expert testimony or Medical–Vocational Guidelines contained in 20 C.F.R. Part 404, Subpart P, Appendix 2 (commonly known as the "Grids") may be used to aid in the ultimate determination of disability. See Bowen v. Yuckert (1987) ("severity regulation" upheld); Heckler v. Campbell (1983) (medical-vocational guidelines are valid).

It should be noted that a constitutional tort challenge to the continuing disability review program was made in Schweiker v. Chilicky (1988), but the Court rejected the cause of action by a narrow margin.

It should also be noted that claims under the Americans with Disabilities Act (ADA) are not automatically barred by the receipt of social security disability benefits. See Tranker v. Figgie International (1998).

D. MEDICARE–HOSPITAL INSURANCE (HI) AND SUPPLEMENTARY MEDICAL INSURANCE (SMI)

Certain disabled and aged persons are entitled to the benefits of a national health insurance program called Medicare. Most persons over 65 are eligible automatically; if not eligible, coverage can be purchased for an annual premium. There are two basic medicare programs: (1) Part A, Hospital Insurance (HI), which is fundamentally financed through special payroll taxes similar to FICA taxes, and which are held in the Hospital Insurance Trust Fund; and (2) Part B, Medicare Medical Insurance (MMI), which is fundamentally financed through individual medical premiums and general revenues of the United States, and which are held in the Supplementary Medical Insurance Trust Fund. Both Part A and Part B benefit programs contain cost-sharing measures, usually in the form of coinsurance and deductibles. The Health Care Financing Administration (HCFA) administers both programs. Part A (HI) payments are generally tied to "benefit periods." If a patient has not been hospitalized for 60 consecutive days, a benefit period is available; there are no limits on the number of benefit periods that patients can have during their lifetime, except for inpatient psychiatric hospital services. Each benefit period under Part A pays for: (1) inpatient hospital care (subject to 90 days of coverage and other limitations); (2) extended care services up to 100 days during each benefit period; (3) home health services; and (4) in lieu of certain other benefits, hospice care, subject to limitation periods. Part B (MMI) was designed as a voluntary program that essentially pays 80% of reasonable charges for doctors, osteopaths, chiropractors, psychiatrists, independent therapists, and most medical, outpatient, and laboratory services that Part A does not cover. The elderly and disabled pay only portions of program premiums and the difference is paid by the federal government from general revenues.

E.　SUPPLEMENTAL SECURITY INCOME (SSI)

The Supplemental Security Income (SSI) program provides financial assistance to U.S. citizens and lawfully admitted aliens who meet income and resource criteria. They must be aged, blind, or disabled. The SSI program provides a "floor of income" for these persons, and it is financed by general tax revenues. SSI benefits are paid monthly to persons who are: (1) age 65 or older; or (2) blind; or (3) disabled. Generally, these persons must be U.S. citizens or lawful residents of the 50 states, the District of Columbia or the Northern Mariana Islands. "Federal Benefit Rates" (FBR) help determine the eligibility of individuals and couples. These rates are increased periodically and the FBR is employed on a per month basis in order to compare the income and resource criteria in an effort to determine eligibility. The periodic redetermination of eligibility is required for all recipients. The receipt of Social Security insurance benefits does not necessarily disqualify persons from receiving SSI benefits, but Social Security insurance benefits are included in the income determinations that must be made before SSI benefits can be paid.

F. PROCEDURE

The claims procedure for most Social Security benefits under retirement, survivors, disability, medicare insurance programs and under the supplemental security income program, is initiated on special forms provided by the Social Security Administration. These claim forms are usually filed with a local Social Security office which makes an initial determination of eligibility. If there is a dispute, the claimant or the claimant's representative must request a reconsideration of the initial decision. A claimant who is dissatisfied with a reconsideration decision is entitled to a hearing before an administrative law judge. The administrative law judge's decision becomes final unless Appeals Council review is requested within 60 days of receipt by the claimant, or unless the Appeals Council decides to review the decision on its own motion. An expedited appeals process may be requested in certain instances. Denials of review or decisions of the Appeals Council can be appealed within 60 days to the U.S. District Courts. Attorney's fees are permitted for the representation of claimants. Furthermore in some cases the claimant may be entitled to an additional award of attorney's fees under the Equal Access to Justice Act ("EAJA"), 28 U.S.C.A. § 2412(b).

CHAPTER 17

FEDERAL AND STATE ANTI-DISCRIMINATION LAWS IN GENERAL

A. FEDERAL LAWS

Federal and state laws provide workers with significant safeguards against discrimination in the workplace. The First, Fifth, Thirteenth, and Fourteenth Amendments to the U.S. Constitution, together with the Commerce Clause, form the foundation for most federal anti-discrimination measures affecting employment. Three of the Reconstruction Civil Rights Acts passed in the aftermath of the Civil War—42 U.S.C.A. §§ 1981, 1983, and 1985(3)—are still useful, to differing degrees, in challenging particular kinds of discrimination by state, local, or private employers.

Title VII of the Civil Rights Act of 1964 is the most broadly based and influential federal statute prohibiting discrimination in employment. Its prohibitions on discrimination based on race, color, sex, religion or national origin extend to all "terms, conditions or privileges" of employment. Section 703(a)(1), 42 U.S.C.A. § 2000e–2(a)(1). The federal courts have construed this language quite broadly to embrace any benefit actually conferred or burden actually imposed in the workplace, whether or not provided for by contract. See, e.g., Hishon v. King & Spalding (1984) (right to be considered for law firm partnership). The concept embraces such intangible aspects of employment as workplace assignments, environment, and even mentoring opportunities as well as more tangible problems like refusals to hire or promote, unequal pay or discriminatory discharge. Decisions interpreting Title VII have frequently served as interpretive models for the Age Discrimination in Employment Act of 1967 ("ADEA") and other statutes, including the Reconstruction Civil Rights Acts. See Western Air Lines, Inc. v. Criswell (1985) (ADEA).

Title VII was amended by the Civil Rights Act of 1991. The principal stated purposes of the Act were to "provide appropriate remedies for intentional discrimination and unlawful harassment in the workplace"; to "confirm statutory authority and provide statutory guidelines for the adjudication of disparate impact suits under Title VII...."; and to "respond to recent decisions of the Supreme Court by expanding the scope of relevant civil rights statutes....". Civil Rights Act of 1991, Pub.L. 102–166, §§ 3(1), (3), and (4), 105 Stat. 1071.

In addition to Title VII and the Reconstruction Civil Rights Acts, the federal laws, rules, regulations, and remedies affecting employment discrimination include: the Equal Pay Act of 1963 ("EPA"); ADEA; the Civil Rights Act of 1964; Title IX, Education Amendments of 1972, banning sex discrimination in federally funded education programs; the Civil Rights Attorney's Fees Awards Act of 1976; the Rehabilitation Act of 1973 ("RHA") and Americans with Disabilities Act of 1990 ("ADA"), prohibiting disability discrimination; the Immigration Reform and Control Act of 1986, or "IRCA"; the Civil Rights Act of 1968, Title I; the Intergovernmental Personnel Act of 1970; the Vietnam Era Veterans Readjustment Act of 1974; the Age Discrimination Act of 1975; the Foreign Boycott Laws (Export Administration Act of 1969, as amended); the Labor Management Relations Act; Executive Order 11246 (Government Contractors and Subcontractors); and Executive Order 11141 (Age Discrimination). Summaries of the more important federal anti-discrimination laws are provided in Chapters 18, 19 and 20. For a fuller treatment of these protections, see Lewis and Norman, Civil Rights Law and Practice (Thomson/West 2004), and Lewis and Norman, Employment Discrimination Law and Practice (2d ed. Thomson/West 2004).

Title VII's broad sweep distinguishes it from statutes, like the EPA, that prohibit employment discrimination solely with respect to one term or condition of employment, like compensation. Further, the Title VII prohibitions on race, color, sex, religious and national origin discrimination set it apart from single-focus employment-related statutes that ban only sex discrimination (EPA and Title IX); age discrimination (ADEA); race, ancestry and possibly national origin discrimination (42 U.S.C.A. § 1981); or disability discrimination (the RHA or ADA).

B. STATE LAWS

Most of the states have enacted anti-discrimination statutes that supplement the remedies available under federal law by extending protection to persons not federally protected or, in some cases, adding grounds of prohibited discrimination or supplementary remedies. For the most part, state laws prohibiting employment discrimination are called "Fair Employment Practices" laws. But Michigan has a Civil Rights Act; California has a Fair Employment and Housing Act; New Mexico has a Human Rights Act; and New York's employment discrimination prohibitions are part of its Executive Law. The federal laws, standards, and programs do not generally preempt these state efforts unless a state law purports to permit conduct that would be federally prohibited or would in practice undermine the enforcement of a federal law.

The state legislation usually forbids discrimination based upon race, religion, color, ancestry, national origin, sex, age, or marital status. Still, there is considerable variation in prohibited grounds. Alabama, for example, has very little in the way of fair employment laws regulating private employment, while California has enacted laws specifically covering race, age, sex, national origin, religious, arrest record, and blindness discrimination. California also regulates equal pay, pregnancy benefits, and employee records, as well as the employment uses of lie detector tests and voice stress analyzers. A growing minority of states prohibit discrimination on the basis of sexual orientation, a ground Congress has declined to protect but recurrently reconsiders.

CHAPTER 18

TITLE VII OF THE 1964 CIVIL RIGHTS ACT, AS AMENDED THROUGH 1991

A. SCOPE AND COVERAGE

1. PROTECTION FOR INDIVIDUALS

Title VII's principal provisions defining unlawful employment practices, contained in § 703, extend protection to any "individual," whether or not an employee. This is somewhat curious because the statute contains a separate, if singularly unilluminating definition of employee: "any individual employed by an employer." Relying on § 703's broad protection of "any individual," courts have had no difficulty according plaintiff status and standing on former employees as well as applicants. Further, they have sometimes even recognized claims on behalf of persons who fall outside any common-law understanding of the employee-employer relationship, provided the circumstances satisfy an "economic realities" test that protects those in a position to suffer the kind of discrimination Title VII was designed to prevent. The key factor in the inquiry is the employer's right to control the means and manner of the plaintiff's performance of his work. Occasionally, however, a court will rely on the "employee" definition to deny protection to persons, mainly independent contractors, who do not satisfy the common law's test for employee status, the "totality of the working relationship." For example, employees working for independent contractors are not generally considered employees of the other contracting party.

Relying on the statutory language "any individual," courts have permitted plaintiffs to sue for harm respecting employment with third parties. These courts reason that while the Title VII defendant must be a defined "employer," the plaintiff need not be an "employee" but instead is referred to in the statute as a "person aggrieved." (For the same reason, the statute applies to defendant labor unions and employment agencies, which may have no direct employment relationship with a plaintiff.)

By contrast, the § 704 protection against retaliation for opposing unlawful employment practices or participating in proceedings to protest them extends to "employees or applicants for employment." The Supreme Court has agreed with the overwhelming view of the circuit courts that, despite the possible implication that "employees" refers only to those currently working, former employees also enjoy protection from retaliation. Robinson v. Shell Oil Co. (1997).

2. EMPLOYERS GOVERNED BY TITLE VII/ADEA

Title VII applies to employers, employment agencies, apprenticeship programs and labor organizations whose activities affect interstate commerce. There are very few categorical exclusions from the definition of "employer" in either Title VII or ADEA. Title VII expressly exempts private membership clubs exempt from taxation under the Internal Revenue Code and Indian tribes. ADEA contains neither such exemption in express terms, but Indian tribes have been exempted by judicial construction. By far the most significant exclusion is numerical: an employer is covered by Title VII only if it has 15 or more employees, and by ADEA only if it has 20 or more employees, for each working day in 20 or more calendar weeks in the current or prior calendar year. Persons holding an employment relationship with the employer during a calendar week (usually manifested by presence on the payroll) are counted regardless of how many of them actually worked or received compensation on any particular working day in that week.

Courts have wrestled with whether to aggregate for coverage purposes the number of employees employed by affiliated enterprises, for example by subjecting a parent corporation to potential liability for the conduct of a subsidiary; whether to consider all of an employer's employees when the alleged unlawful employment practice is confined to a discrete operating location; whether to impose liability on a successor employer after a sale of the business or bankruptcy; whether a government-appointed receiver is a Title VII "employer" of employees of a failed financial institution; whether a contractor is liable for a subcontractor's unlawful employment practice; whether a nonprofit organization qualifies as an "employer"; and whether an employment agency or union meets the statutory "employer" definition even when it has fewer than 15 employees. These and other coverage questions are capably discussed in detail in several standard works.

Unions may be liable as labor organizations representing employees in collective bargaining without regard to the number of employees represented, but are liable in their capacity as "employer" only if they satisfy the employer definition, including the requirement of at least 15 employees under Title VII.

Answering an increasingly important question in an economy depending heavily on temporary employees referred through employment agencies, federal courts have permitted such employees to recover under Title VII from the firms to which they are assigned, provided that firm exercises sufficient control over the means and manner of their performance or interferes with any employment relation they have established with the referring agency. An EEOC Guidance explains that both temporary staffing firms and their clients may be jointly liable for unlawful discrimination if both have the right to control the worker and each meets the statutory minimum number of employees. And according to the EEOC, employees who are assigned jobs in welfare-to-work programs are also protected by federal discrimination statutes in the same way as other workers.

States, their political subdivisions, and agencies of each are also employers under Title VII. The constitutionality of applying Title VII to state defendants, and their amenability to suit in federal court is settled. Even before Garcia v. San Antonio Metropolitan Transit Authority (1985) determined that the Tenth Amendment does not supersede Congress' Commerce Clause authority to regulate the wages and hours of state employees, the Supreme Court had held in Fitzpatrick v. Bitzer (1976) that Title VII's grounding in § 5 of the Fourteenth Amendment empowered Congress to override the Eleventh Amendment barrier to state liability in federal court.

The federal government and its agencies are not defined "employers," but special provisions in each statute mandate that personnel actions affecting most federal employees be made free from discrimination based on any of the grounds those statutes address. Title VII generally does not apply to uniformed members of the armed services because of the *Feres* non-justiciability doctrine. The Supreme Court has not decided whether a soldier in a state National Guard may sue under Title VII, and the circuits are split on the issue.

Both Title VII and ADEA define a covered "employer" to include any "agent" of an employer. At a minimum, this definition makes the employer as an entity liable for the acts of subordinates by means of respondeat superior. The circuits that have confronted the issue have uniformly concluded, however, that a supervisor is not such an "agent" who can be subjected to personal liability. The argument favoring individual liability is arguably slightly stronger now that the 1991 Civil Rights Act affords, in cases of intentional discrimination, elements of relief (namely compensatory and punitive damages) that individual defendants may provide. Nevertheless, the provisions of that Act that add damages liability do not refer to individual liability. Further, the retention of a fifteen-employee threshold for employer liability suggests the continuing Congressional reluctance to impose liability on small entities, and therefore presumably also individual employees. Where supervisory employees are held subject to Title VII their liability has been limited to conduct deemed to have been undertaken in their official capacities and where they exercised independent authority or were unmistakably acting as "agent" of the employer.

3. AMERICAN CORPORATIONS' EMPLOYEES WORKING ABROAD; "FOREIGN" EMPLOYERS' PERSONNEL IN U.S. AND OVERSEAS; AND NATIONAL ORIGIN, ALIENAGE AND ANCESTRY DISCRIMINATION UNDER TITLE VII, IRCA, AND 42 U.S.C.A. § 1981

Discrimination on any ground against an *alien* (for this purpose, someone who has not yet attained full American citizenship) working *outside* the United States for either an American or non-U.S. company is not prohibited by either Title VII or ADEA. This results from an exemption to Title VII and a restriction in the ADEA's definition of "employee." Somewhat more difficult questions concern the statutory protection available to citizen employees of American companies stationed overseas and to the American-and overseas-based employees of foreign enterprises.

Unlike the ADEA, which was amended in 1984 to apply to the overseas work of American corporations and American-controlled foreign corporations, Title VII initially had no language specifically extending its application to work performed for the more than 2000 U.S. firms operating more than 21,000 foreign subsidiaries abroad. These include U.S. citizens who work overseas for an American employer on a long-term basis, those who maintain their American residency during temporary assignments overseas, and American-based employees who routinely travel outside U.S. territorial limits in the course of their employment. If given a choice, the plaintiff would usually find it more advantageous to litigate in the United States under U.S. employment discrimination law than to litigate overseas under foreign law, as the foreign tribunals customarily place far greater limits on discovery (particularly depositions) and relief (especially injunctions directing reinstatement and punitive damages). The Supreme Court, revivifying a nineteenth-century presumption against extraterritorial application of American statutes absent express statutory direction, limited Title VII's scope to unlawful employment practices arising in connection with work performed in the United States. The Civil Rights Act of 1991 overturns that decision by defining most covered employees to include U.S. citizens "with respect to employment in a foreign country."

This protection for U.S. citizens is now coextensive with that earlier provided by the ADEA. The 1991 Act subjects to Title VII jurisdiction not only U.S. corporations but also those foreign corporations "controlled" by American employers, and it appears to provide dual defendants in this situation by presuming that unlawful employment practices of the controlled foreign affiliate are engaged in by the controlling (American) employer as well. But it exempts conduct that would cause any employer to violate the national law of the foreign workplace. This exemption is not triggered simply because the type of discrimination in question (e.g., gender or religious) is permitted by foreign law; rather, that law must affirmatively prohibit the particular employer conduct (e.g., hiring a woman as a driver in Saudi Arabia) that compliance with Title VII would otherwise require the employer to permit. But the foreign "law" that would be violated if ADEA were respected may include a collective bargaining agreement with a foreign labor union.

Truly foreign corporations—those not "controlled" by a U.S. business—are not subject to Title VII with respect to work *outside* the United States. U.S. citizens working abroad meet the amended § 701 definition of "employee," and firms chartered in other nations are not excluded from the definition of "employer." To relieve foreign corporations of liability with respect to foreign work, therefore, Congress in 1991 had to specifically provide that the basic prohibitions of the Title do not apply "with respect to the foreign operations of an employer that is a foreign person."

If the employer is not shielded by a treaty authorizing discrimination in the selection of executives on the basis of citizenship, the more than half a million American-based employees of foreign corporations may rely on Title VII and ADEA. But those statutes may not afford them protection against some of the more common forms of discrimination they may encounter. In the first place, although Title VII prohibits national origin discrimination, it does not reach discrimination based on alienage status (i.e., noncitizenship), which is dealt with by § 1981 and the Immigration Reform and Control Act of 1986 ("IRCA") or ancestry (i.e., ethnic or physiognomic characteristic transcending national borders, e.g., against Arabs or Jews), covered by § 1981. Title VII therefore will not avail a plaintiff whose employer, whether U.S. or foreign, excludes applicants solely because they lack U.S. citizenship or belong to a distinct cultural subgroup.

Further, although Title VII and IRCA prohibit discrimination on the basis of national origin, evidence that the plaintiff's compatriots are as well as or better represented in such an employer's workforce than others can defeat a claim that a U.S. citizenship requirement is in fact a smokescreen for intentional discrimination based on national origin. It may be, however, that neutral practice has the effect of discriminating on the basis of national origin; and if that is the case, a plaintiff excluded as a result of that practice may be able to state a prima facie national origin claim notwithstanding the fair or favorable treatment of her group.

Since 1988, limited protection against discrimination in hiring because of alienage, i.e. citizenship status, is separately provided to lawfully admitted aliens, and a few others, by IRCA. But unlike the IRCA protection against national origin, which extends to "any individual," the protection against alienage discrimination applies only to a rather narrowly defined "protected individual" who is well on the way to achieving full U.S. citizenship or has been granted refugee or asylum status. Correlatively, IRCA imposes fines and imprisonment on employers who knowingly hire or employ undocumented persons or fail to check their authorization to work— in other words, it requires employers to discriminate against those aliens.

A charge of discrimination under IRCA may be filed within 180 days after the occurrence of a violation before a U.S. Justice Department Office of Special Counsel for Immigration–Related Unfair Employment Practices. The Special Counsel has 120 days within which to investigate and determine whether there is reasonable cause to believe the charge is true and whether to file a complaint with a specially trained administrative law judge designated by the Attorney General. If the Special Counsel does not file such a complaint, the charging party may do so directly within 90 days after receiving notice to that effect from the Special Counsel. If the administrative law judge finds a violation after hearing, the employer may be ordered to hire the charging party with or without back pay, to pay attorney fees, and to pay civil penalties of amounts that vary with the number of persons discriminated against and the number of prior offenses. An anti-duplication provision is designed to ensure that national origin discrimination claims may be brought only before EEOC, if the complainant proceeds under Title VII, or to the Justice Department, if the complainant proceeds under IRCA, but not both. Protection against retaliation is also provided, as is judicial review in the United States court of appeals for the circuit in which the violation allegedly occurred or where the employer resides or transacts business. A March, 2000 report by the Special Counsel's office reported that in the thirteen years of its existence, it had processed over 6,000 complaints, but had collected a mere $2.1 million in back pay and had levied less than $1.8 million in civil penalties.

It has been contended that the fact that an alien is neither lawfully admitted for permanent U.S. residence within the meaning of IRCA nor authorized by law to work does not deprive him of capacity to sue and receive remedies under Title VII for the kinds of discrimination that are prohibited by that statute. This follows not only from the fact that Title VII defines "employees" broadly as "individuals" employed by an employer but also from a negative implication of its alien exemption clause, which precludes application of the statute to the employment of aliens *outside* the United States. The problem is that alien victims of the kinds of discrimination Title VII bans will often as a practical matter be ineligible for important Title VII remedies. If reinstatement would require the employer to violate IRCA, Title VII's mixed-motive or after-acquired evidence doctrines would probably preclude a reinstatement order. A worker's undocumented status may also affect her eligibility for or the appropriate amount of back or front pay, since she may be "unavailable" for work after termination—either literally (e.g., out of the country) or legally, because of IRCA. Recent Fourth Circuit decisions go further, holding that undocumented aliens working in violation of IRCA have no failure to hire claim under Title VII. But EEOC takes the position that the plaintiff's undocumented status has no effect on the availability of injunctive relief or other more appropriate damages, and precludes the ordinary presumption favoring reinstatement or instatement only if the worker is unable to satisfy IRCA's verification requirements within a reasonable period of time and limits back pay only where the worker is unavailable in the sense of "being out of the company." The Commission does recognize that the worker's unauthorized status may form the basis for limited remedies in a mixed motives or after-acquired evidence case. A claim alleging private employer alienage discrimination under 42 U.S.C.A. § 1981 has been held not to offend IRCA even though the plaintiff was an unauthorized alien where the court deemed him not to be complaining of discrimination because of his unauthorized status.

Discrimination against aliens in general is not, absent adverse impact, treated as discrimination on the basis of any particular national origin, and is therefore not condemned by Title VII. There is sauce for the gander, however, even though the goose gets none: discrimination *against* U.S. citizens, in favor of citizens of a particular nation, does amount to prohibited national origin discrimination under Title VII as well as IRCA. The rationale may be that only in the latter situation can it be said with some confidence that the discrimination relates to a particular national origin—putting aside the dubious assumption that U.S. citizenship corresponds to any particular national origin. Title VII protection from this "anti-American" discrimination based on national origin is limited, however, by treaty exemptions designed to give foreign companies operating in the United States a free hand in selecting their own citizens for executive positions.

The U.S.–Japanese Treaty of Friendship, Commerce and Navigation, for example, authorizes "companies of either party," such as a Japanese-chartered employer, "to engage, within the territories of the other Party ... executive personnel ... of their choice." A U.S.-chartered American subsidiary of a foreign corporation will ordinarily not be deemed a company of the signatory entitled to this exemption. But in a case where the foreign parent admitted that it dictated the American subsidiary's discriminatory discharges of executives, the subsidiary was allowed to assert the parent's treaty rights. These treaties have in other respects been construed narrowly, though, so as to permit only discrimination based on citizenship and not, for example, based on race, sex or age. Nevertheless, they have been read to permit citizenship discrimination even when it has a statistical adverse impact on the basis of national origin. This happens, for example, where the executives preferred by the treaty hail from a homogeneous ethnic population, so that all or virtually all those preferred by virtue of their citizenship also share the same national origin. Thus while companies of signatory countries are, despite these treaties, subject to liability, in their executive hiring and firing, for *intentional* discrimination based on national origin (but not citizenship), they cannot be liable for a citizenship-preference practice that merely has a disproportionate adverse impact on a particular national origin. Courts have reached this result in order to avoid indirect nullification of the guest company's treaty right to discriminate in favor of its own country's citizens.

4. PURELY OR PARTLY RELIGIOUS EMPLOYERS: COVERAGE, EXEMPTIONS, DEFENSES

Religious organizations are also viewed as Title VII "employers," and as such may be subject to a specially defined duty not to discriminate on that ground. But they are specifically permitted to make certain employment decisions on the basis of religion. A welter of related and somewhat overlapping statutory and constitutional provisions afford different kinds of covered employers exemptions from or exceptions to liability for religious discrimination. In addition, the special prohibition on religious discrimination—subsuming the ordinary imperative not to discriminate and a duty to make "reasonable accommodation" to an employee's religious beliefs and practices—is subject to the general affirmative defense that permits an employer to discriminate under circumstances where the exclusion is a "bona fide occupational qualification." The nature of the two-part prima facie prohibition on religious discrimination is discussed below. The exemptions, exceptions and BFOQ defense for religious and other employers will be treated here.

a. *Overview: Discrimination Because of Religion*

The § 702 exemption, strictly limited to pervasively religious institutions like churches, missions and seminaries, declares Title VII inapplicable with respect to the employment "of individuals of a particular religion" in any of its activities, for any position. It does not exempt from regulation for sex, race, national origin (or age) discrimination. Section 702 has been upheld against the objection that it unconstitutionally "establishes" the institutions it protects, at least with respect to their nonprofitmaking activities. Corporation of Presiding Bishop v. Amos (1987).

Section 703(e)(2) excludes from the definition of "unlawful employment practice" the hiring of employees of a particular religion by educational institutions insufficiently religious to qualify for the § 702 exemption but that are (a) substantially owned, supported, controlled or managed by a particular religion or (b) direct their curriculum "toward the propagation of" a particular religion.

If the ground alleged is sex, race, national origin, or age— where, that is, the foregoing statutory exemptions will not avail the employer—it may invoke a Free Exercise or Establishment Clause (excessive government entanglement) override of Title VII or ADEA regulation. These may succeed where the position (e.g., minister) or duties (e.g., teacher of theology, church music director) in question lie close to the religious core of the institution, or perhaps where the reason for discharge relates to malperformance of subsidiary religious duties.

b. *Prima Facie Prohibitions*

If no statutory or constitutional exemption applies, one turns to the prima facie case. Section 703(a)(1), amplified by the 701(j) definition of "religion", raises two questions:

(1) Has the employer drawn a distinction because of "religion"? And has it disparately treated the plaintiff "because of" religion, or rather imposed a neutral practice, not specifically targeted to religion, that has adverse impact on plaintiff's particular religion? If the latter, the practice may be defended as justified by job relatedness and business necessity.

(2) Even if an employer has made no hostile discrimination, has it breached the separate 701(j) duty to accommodate:

(a) "Reasonable accommodation" need not fully meet the needs of an employee's religious belief or practice, or be costless to the employee, and the employer need not accept the particular accommodation proposed by employee; and

(b) A reasonable accommodation works "undue hardship" and is thus not legally mandated if it requires an employer to incur more than de minimis cost.

So diluted, § 701(j) does not violate the Establishment Clause.

c. BFOQ Defense

In a refusal to hire case, if statutory exemptions and constitutional overrides fail, and plaintiff establishes a prima facie case of disparate treatment because of religion, an employer still has the BFOQ defense of § 703(e)(1). As restrictively construed by International Union, UAW v. Johnson Controls (1991), an employer must show that its religious exclusion relates to the "essence" of its business and that all or substantially all persons of the excluded faiths could not fulfill the requirements of the job in question.

5. "PURELY" RELIGIOUS ORGANIZATIONS

In general, the more thoroughly "religious" the employer, the more widely it is insulated from liability with respect to terms and conditions of employment and even wholly sectarian activities. This discussion will identify those employers in descending degree of religiosity, and hence insulation.

First, any pervasively "religious" employer—paradigmatically a church, mission, seminary or one of their branches or subunits—is exempt by virtue of § 702(a) from liability for religious discrimination. This section exempts a "religious corporation, association, educational institution, or society" from Title VII "with respect to the employment of individuals of a particular religion to perform work connected with the carrying on" of any of the institution's "activities." But the exemption has been widely interpreted not to ban discrimination based on race, gender, or national origin, with important exceptions.

For the most part, only churches or institutions owned or partly owned by them have qualified for the § 702 exemption. The determination whether an organization, including an educational institution, is eligible for its sweeping protection hinges on whether "the corporation's purpose and character are primarily religious." That question, in turn, is answered on a case-by-case basis, with the court weighing "[a]ll significant religious and secular characteristics." A nondenominational school that was established under a will requiring all trustees and teachers to be Protestants and that began classes with daily prayer but whose purpose, curriculum, and activities had evolved over the years from primarily religious to predominantly secular and most of whose students were not Protestant was held to reflect "a primarily secular rather than a primarily religious orientation" and hence held ineligible for the exemption.

The § 702 exemption extends to any of the religious employer's activities, secular or sectarian, and applies regardless of the particular term and condition of employment involved. A 1972 amendment to § 702 deleted the word "religious" that had appeared before "activities" in the original 1964 legislation, and so the exemption has since been understood to shield a covered institution from liability for religious discrimination even with respect to its secular activities, provided those are non-profitmaking. It has nevertheless withstood challenge as an unconstitutional establishment of religion. The Court in *Amos* reasoned that § 702, by lifting what would otherwise be government regulation of religion, merely permits the religious organization to advance its own religion and does not result in the government itself advancing a particular religion.

The distinctions among the grounds on which Title VII bans discrimination, the § 702 exemption, and a separate, nonstatutory overriding defense based on the First Amendment are pointed up by a recent case in which a parochial school's married librarian was terminated for being pregnant by someone other than her husband. Even though the employer decision to fire the plaintiff was driven by its religious beliefs, it appeared that the discrimination was on the ground of pregnancy and therefore, in Title VII terms, because of sex rather than religion. Accordingly, the court ruled that the § 702 defense was not available. But if it turned out that the real reason for termination was her adultery rather than her pregnancy, the ground of discrimination would be sex-neutral and therefore not prohibited by Title VII. (Then there would be no Title VII violation even if the adultery ground were not tantamount to religious discrimination—that is, even if the defendant could not avail itself of the § 702 exemption from liability for discrimination because of religion.) Moreover, the court added that ultimately the First Amendment might halt the action in any event if the proceedings, or a judgment of liability, were determined to interfere unduly with the church school's free exercise of religion.

An overlapping defense based on the religion clauses of the First Amendment is available to truly "religious" institutions, educational or not, where litigation raises the spectre of excessive government monitoring of religious decisionmaking or matters of doctrine. Where a university's canon law department was governed by the Vatican, for instance, the claim of a faculty member in that department who alleged sexually discriminatory tenure denial was rejected, wholly apart from § 702(a), because the court decided it lacked competence to review competing opinions about materially religious subjects in published articles. Both the Free Exercise and Establishment Clauses would be violated by scrutiny under Title VII that would "impair a religious institution's choice of those who teach its doctrine and participate in church governance."

6. RELIGIOUSLY AFFILIATED EDUCATIONAL INSTITUTIONS

Because relatively few organizations are sufficiently religious to qualify for the broad exemption from Title VII afforded by § 702, Congress added a limited exception from liability designed to benefit religiously affiliated schools.

Under § 703(e)(2) of Title VII, an *educational* institution not qualifying as sufficiently religious to be exempt under § 702(a) but which is substantially supported or directed by a particular religion, or has a religiously oriented curriculum, may "hire and employ" persons of the particular religion with which it is affiliated. Section 702(a), it will be remembered, provides that Title VII "shall not apply" to the "purely" religious institutions it protects. By contrast, § 703(e)(2) more modestly states that it is not an "unlawful employment practice" for an "educational institution or institution of learning to hire and employ employees of a particular religion" if that employer is "in whole or in substantial part, owned, supported, controlled, or managed by a particular religion" (hereinafter, the "structure clause") or maintains a curriculum "directed toward the propagation of a particular religion" (the "curriculum clause").

It is only somewhat easier for a religiously affiliated educational institution to qualify for the more limited § 703(e)(2) hiring immunity than for a religious organization or school to qualify for the broader exemption under § 702. One court, for example, declined to decide whether the defendant university qualified for the § 703(e)(2) exemption even though it had a long history as a Jesuit institution, until 1970 had only Jesuit trustees, still required that more than one-third of the trustees and the President be Jesuit, and enrolled students of predominantly Catholic background. It further appears that to qualify under the curriculum clause it is not enough that a school require religious education courses, schedule prayers and services, and employ Protestant teachers for principally secular subjects. The courts have consistently held that the § 703(e)(2) exception to the definition of an unlawful employment practice by a religiously affiliated school, like the § 702 exemption from Title VII for a religious organization, does not shield the defendant from Title VII liability when the institution discriminates against an employee or applicant (say one who seeks a secular job like science teacher or custodian of a seminary or university) on some basis *other* than religion— sex, race, national origin, or retaliation.

ADEA has no express exemption for religious or religiously affiliated institutions. But because ADEA's substantive prohibitions are derived *in haec verba* from Title VII, courts have crafted an immunity from age discrimination liability of the same scope, and with the same limitations, for religious organizations that meet the § 702 (or, apparently, § 703(e)(2)) requirements.

7.   ALL EMPLOYERS, RELIGIOUS OR NOT: THE "BFOQ" AFFIRMATIVE DEFENSE

Under § 703(e)(1), *any* employer, even one wholly sectarian, may "hire and employ" (a labor organization may "admit or employ" in apprenticeship or retraining programs) on the basis of religion where religion is a "bona fide occupational qualification ['BFOQ'] reasonably necessary to the normal operation" of the enterprise. The principal discussion of the BFOQ defense, as it applies to express gender and national origin discrimination, is set forth in Chapter 3 immediately following. The discussion here will be confined to its role in defending against express discrimination based on religion.

Section 703(e)(1) has the same textual limitation to hiring as does Section 703(e)(2). Accordingly, the BFOQ affirmative defense protects employers from liability only for certain religiously discriminatory hiring decisions; it does not excuse discrimination concerning subsequent terms and conditions of employment like compensation, promotion, discipline, harassment or discharge.

Moreover, the Supreme Court's decision in International Union, United Auto. Workers v. Johnson Controls (1991) confirms the narrowness of the BFOQ exception—in any context, i.e., gender or national origin as well as religion. The bare language of § 703(e)(1) would appear satisfied if an employer can show that a refusal to hire based on religion, sex, or national origin is reasonably necessary to the normal operation of the defendant's overall "enterprise." As a textual matter, that is, the employer need not show that the exclusion on those grounds is conducive to the sound performance of the particular plaintiff's job, only that it will further general business goals. Nor does the text of the BFOQ defense suggest that the discriminatory job qualification must relate to the heart of employer's business, only to its "normal operation." Yet the Court has concluded that to prevent the exception from virtually eliminating an applicant's protection against these forms of express discrimination, the employer must show that its discriminatory rule bears a "high correlation" to the plaintiff's ability to perform the job in question *and* relates to the "essence" or "central mission" of the employer's business. Relying on *Johnson Controls*, an appellate court has denied the BFOQ defense to schools that insisted on hiring Protestant teachers to maintain a Protestant "presence" assertedly important to their general educational operations. E.E.O.C. v. Kamehameha Schools/Bishop Estate (9th Cir. 1993).

8. CONSTITUTIONAL PROBLEMS SURROUNDING REGULATION OF RELIGIOUS DISCRIMINATION

Subjecting a religiously based institution to Title VII regulation (and hence to the administrative scrutiny of EEOC and indirect regulation by the courts) for discrimination on grounds other than religion has survived most challenges based on the Free Exercise Clause. The critical inquiry under that clause concerns the impact of statutory regulation on the institution's exercise of its sincerely held religious beliefs. Because of the statutory exemptions, the statutory regulation will not extend to employment practices motivated or compelled by the religious beliefs of the employer or its affiliated church. Accordingly, although defense of an employment discrimination charge may have substantial adverse impact on a church or other religious institution, the administrative proceeding or action should have slight or no impact on the religious practices or beliefs of its adherents. Any such incidental impact has been held outweighed by the government's "compelling" interest in ending employment discrimination.

Where, however, the challenged employment practice relates to a staff member who occupies the functional status of clergy within the employer's denominational structure or belief system, courts have construed Title VII, the ADA, and the ADEA not to reach the practice in order to avoid transgressing the free exercise rights of the religious organization or its members.

The distinct question remains whether judicial regulation under Title VII, ADA, or ADEA that is not challenged, or survives a challenge, under §§ 702 or 703(e)(2) violates the Establishment Clause by fostering "an excessive government entanglement with religion." In N.L.R.B. v. Catholic Bishop of

Chicago (1979), where lay faculty sought to unionize under the protection of federal law, the Supreme Court construed the National Labor Relations Act as not affording jurisdiction over religiously associated organizations absent an affirmative, clearly expressed contrary intention of Congress. Yet it later intimated in dictum that the First Amendment does leave room for some degree of state intrusion into religious schools' employment practices. Subjecting a religiously affiliated organization to the full regulatory umbrella of the national laws governing employee self-organization and collective bargaining falls on the prohibited side of the line.

Lower courts have generally extended protection against employment discrimination to those teaching staff and supporting personnel of schools and seminaries who have no religious duties or whose religious duties, if any, are "easily isolated and defined" rather than pervasive. *Catholic Bishop* has been distinguished on the ground that regulation of the labor relations of parochial schools by the National Labor Relations Board under the National Labor Relations Act is far more comprehensive and ongoing than the limited inquiry required in anti-discrimination disputes. But where a terminated Catholic school teacher brought Title VII charges alleging *religious* discrimination, the religion clauses were held too implicated to permit determination by secular courts. At least one appellate opinion permitting an age discrimination action to go forward notwithstanding the entanglement objection has nevertheless expressed concern that government could become an arbiter of the truth or validity of religious beliefs when a court determines whether a religious employer's stated justification for an employment action is "implausible" or "false." While the factfinder may determine whether an employer took adverse action against the plaintiff because of a failure to fulfill religious duties, a lawful reason, or because of age, an unlawful one, the court may not question the validity or necessity of the duties themselves. Cases suggest that counsel for such religious or religiously affiliated institutions would be well advised, whenever consistent with the facts, to plead specifically that the duties at issue in an adverse disciplinary action are religious or that the action was taken for religious reasons.

The substance of the employer's Title VII duty not to discriminate because of religion—particularly the "reasonable accommodation" feature of that duty—has been distinctly diluted by judicial interpretation, perhaps to ensure that the statute, so construed, will survive First Amendment challenges.

B. TITLE VII: THE BASIC SUBSTANTIVE PROHIBITIONS

Section 703(a)(1) declares it an "unlawful employment practice" for a covered employer:

> to fail or refuse to hire or to discharge any individual, or otherwise to discriminate against any individual with respect to his compensation, terms, conditions or privileges of employment, because of such individual's race, color, religion, sex, or national origin.

Section 703(a)(2) forbids limiting the employment "opportunities" of an applicant or incumbent employee on any of the same grounds. The controversies addressed by the case law have centered on two intertwined issues. First, what employer conduct or classifications correspond to the forbidden kinds of discrimination—what, in other words, constitutes discrimination on the grounds of "race, color, religion, sex or national origin"? The answers to these questions are not always self-evident. Discrimination based on alienage status, for example, is not tantamount to the prohibited discrimination based on national origin, even though a non-U.S. citizen would not have that status unless she or an ancestor recently arrived here from another nation. Whites may sue for race discrimination, as may blacks, based on the racial animus directed against them by other blacks.

The second pervasive issue concerns the nature and degree of the nexus that must exist between prohibited employer conduct and harm to a plaintiff's employment status. When, in other words, is adverse action taken by the employer "because of" prohibited discrimination? For example, the Supreme Court has treated as prohibited gender discrimination certain forms of employer speech and action characterized by sex stereotyping; but it has simultaneously demanded evidence that the employer actually relied on the stereotype as a factor in the challenged employment decision before that decision could constitute an unlawful employment practice under Title VII. Price Waterhouse v. Hopkins (1989).

Punishing an employee for voicing views associated with women does not unlawfully discriminate against her because of her sex. For example, has held that an interviewer's questions about child-bearing and child-rearing plans, asked only of women, did not violate Title VII where the interviewer was apparently reassured by the plaintiff's answers and she could not otherwise show that her rejection was attributable to the employer's stereotypical beliefs. In this respect Title VII contrasts with some state and local antidiscrimination laws, as well as the Americans With Disabilities Act, which treat such questions as per se violations. In general, the plaintiff must show a nexus between a supervisor's occasional or sporadic slurs related to an employee's protected characteristic and a subsequent adverse employment action. Thus a supervisor's repeated directive that a Korean–American "learn to speak English" constituted circumstantial evidence of prohibited national-origin based animus but did not suffice to establish unlawful discrimination absent evidence that the employer ultimately relied on the impermissible criterion in discharging the employee.

The courts have answered the statute's definitional silence on this causation or nexus question by developing different evidentiary allocations and burdens that are deemed equivalent to proof that adverse action was imposed "because of" an employer's reliance on a prohibited characteristic. These proof modes are discussed below.

Because Title VII applies so comprehensively to employment decisions affecting millions of private employees and is therefore invoked and litigated so pervasively, decisions interpreting its conceptual framework of discrimination, and even some of its defenses, have frequently served as interpretive models for other statutes. These include not only the cognate ADEA—constructions of which have also cross-pollinated Title VII—but also the Reconstruction Acts, notably 42 U.S.C.A. §§ 1981 and 1983. For example, courts have transplanted the evolving judicial elaboration of unlawful individual disparate treatment under Title VII to both of these nineteenth century statutes, and even imported into § 1981 the explicit textual Title VII defense for bona fide seniority systems.

1. THE MEANING OF DISCRIMINATION BECAUSE OF "RACE," "COLOR," "NATIONAL ORIGIN," "RELIGION," AND "SEX"

a. Race

For the most part the Supreme Court has defined the concept of "race" in connection with actions under 42 U.S.C.A. § 1981, the 1866 statute which secures to all persons the same right to make and enforce contracts, including contracts of employment, as is enjoyed by white citizens. In one of those decisions, however, *McDonald v. Santa Fe Trail Transportation Co.* (1976), the Court held that the Title VII prohibition on race discrimination is enforceable by whites as well as blacks. And whites have been granted standing to assert discrimination based on their association with or marriage to blacks, where the court is persuaded that a black plaintiff with those associations would not have endured similar treatment. But some circuits have required in cases alleging discrimination against whites evidence of "background circumstances" tending to prove that the defendant is the "unusual employer who discriminates against the majority." In a failure to promote situation, the white or male plaintiff can meet this burden by proving that the plaintiff's qualifications were superior to those of the successful minority applicant—a showing the Supreme Court has specifically ruled is not required in the ordinary Title VII case. Direct evidence, of course, will support a reverse discrimination claim.

A particular species of race discrimination—harassment affecting the plaintiff's work environment or tangible terms of employment—is condemned on the same terms as sexual harassment. The EEOC and the courts apply the same "subjective" and "objective" standards developed in sexual harassment cases to assess claims of unlawful harassment based on race, religion or national origin. The majority's recognition in Faragher v. City of Boca Raton (1998) that the elements of actionable sexual harassment derive from earlier race and national origin decisions have also resulted in the use of the *Faragher/Burlington* standards to determine employer liability for racial or national origin harassment.

The race concept has been viewed broadly under § 1981 as well. In St. Francis College v. Al–Khazraji (1987) and Shaare Tefila Congregation v. Cobb (1987), the Court held that the § 1981 ban on race discrimination could be enforced by Arabs and Jews, respectively, if they could prove adverse treatment on the basis of their ancestry. Observing that these holdings in effect mean that whites can maintain a viable § 1981 claim against other whites, a court has concluded that a black plaintiff may maintain a Title VII claim based on alleged race discrimination by a black supervisor. And the distinct Title VII prohibition on discrimination because of "color" has supported claims by lighter-or darker-skinned blacks based on discrimination by a black employer agent with skin of a different hue. There is authority permitting proof of discrimination on a compound basis—e.g., gender and race.

b. National Origin, Including Accent Discrimination and Language Rules

Discrimination because of national origin presents special difficulties because it is relatively seldom that defendants refer explicitly to the particular country of origin of the plaintiff or his ancestors. One example we saw above, an employer rule requiring citizenship as a precondition to hire, is an example. Because citizenship as such is not a forbidden ground of discrimination, the rule might violate Title VII if but only if in operation it has disproportionate adverse impact on persons of an identifiable national origin. Similarly, ethnic slurs more commonly stain an individual's ancestry (e.g., slurs pertaining to Arabs, Jews, or persons hailing from Asia, Africa, Central or South America, Mexico, or Puerto Rico), another basis of discrimination not forbidden by Title VII, than her particular national origin. In addition, employer practices or rules based on language characteristics will usually also be neutral on their face. They therefore could violate Title VII only if applied in ways that are designed to injure or that have disproportionate adverse impact on persons of a particular national origin.

Two language problems of this kind have surfaced in the cases—discrimination based on foreign accent, and "speak-

English-only" rules. Several circuit courts have considered discrimination because of accent, where the adverse employer action is typically meted out ad hoc, rather than pursuant to an across-the-board rule. Consequently, the decisions evaluate the evidence in these cases under the theory of individual disparate treatment, rather than disproportionate adverse impact. The leading case, Fragante v. City and County of Honolulu (9th Cir.1989), relied on an EEOC Guideline in assuming without deciding that proof of discrimination based on foreign accent establishes a prima facie case of discrimination based on national origin. But it upheld the employer's bona fide occupational qualification defense, writing that an adverse employment decision taken because of accent is lawful only when the accent "interferes materially with job performance." Nevertheless, because accent and national origin "are obviously inextricably intertwined in many cases," the Court cautioned that a "searching look" is demanded to ensure that employer assertions about a candidate's poor communications skills are not used as a cover or pretext for national origin discrimination.

EEOC charges alleging discrimination the basis of English-only rules quintupled in the four-year period from 1996 to 2000. The few appellate opinions on the issue treat English-only rules as neutral employer practices that are subject to evaluation on the theory of disproportionate adverse impact because of their potential adverse effect on non-English speakers as well as bilinguals. Even if the rule is limited to certain times, the EEOC guideline cited above gives it the same prima facie effect and says it must be "justified by business necessity." Moreover, failure to give employees advance notification of the required circumstances and consequences of violation will be considered "evidence of" national origin discrimination.

The part of this guideline that specifies a business necessity defense would appear to be of no current import. Title VII itself, as amended by the Civil Rights Act of 1991, requires the employer, once a prima facie case of disproportionate adverse impact is made, to "demonstrate that the challenged practice is job related for the position in question *and* consistent with business necessity." While there will continue to be great uncertainty about the content of "business necessity" under the new statute, it is clear that neutral practices will now also have to be justified as "job related for the position in question," a requirement absent from the EEOC Guideline. See Chapter 3 for a fuller discussion of the concepts of "business necessity" and "job relatedness."

The currently significant issue raised by the guideline is its presumption that an English-only rule has adverse impact in all circumstances, particularly as applied to bilingual employees. This presumption, if accepted, establishes the plaintiff's prima facie case, thereby casting on the employer the burden of justification.

Subsequently, however, the Ninth Circuit rejected the EEOC Guideline in *Garcia v. Spun Steak Co.* (9th Cir.1993). In *Spun Steak* the court insisted that adverse impact must be proved and not merely presumed. But the scope of *Spun Steak* as applied to varying employer rules is uncertain. For example, there the court found that the employer's English-only rule had no disproportionate adverse impact because the plaintiff, being bilingual, could readily comply without jeopardizing his employment. Further, the *Spun Steak* policy was justified as a business necessity because it facilitated worker safety on a production line. That defense might not be available where a similar rule is applied to office personnel or to off-duty inter-employee conversations.

Another circuit has held that an English-only rule challenged by Spanish-speaking employees cannot constitute unlawful disparate treatment absent evidence that English speakers were permitted to speak in languages other than English. A related contention is that a policy of *permitting* employees to speak their native foreign language on the job may violate the right of English speakers to be free from discrimination based on national origin.

c. *Discrimination Based on Gender*

Whereas the problem with national origin discrimination is that it is often not relied on expressly, the definitional problem with many permutations of sex discrimination frequently is that sex, while an explicit part of an employer's decision or rule, is not the sole factor. For example, the employer's rule in Phillips v. Martin Marietta Corp. (1971), disqualified from employment women, though not men, with pre-school-aged children. The rule, then, excluded only women, but not all women. The question was whether this was the kind of express discrimination on the basis of sex that would require the greatest level of employer justification. The Supreme Court found express discrimination, holding that the rule impermissibly created "one hiring policy for women and another for men." It was no defense that the policy discriminated not because of sex alone but because of a compound "sex-plus"—with the plus factor here being the early stages of motherhood.

Although Title VII does not expressly prohibit employers from using marital status to make employment distinctions, the logic of *Martin Marietta* and decisions of other federal courts and the EEOC demonstrate that such distinctions may constitute unlawful discrimination if sex is one of the factors the employer took into account when making such distinctions. For example, it is unlawful sex discrimination to reject applicants or fail to promote employees who are married women, but not married men.

An important lesson for plaintiff's counsel in sex-plus disparate treatment cases is that a plaintiff, in a marital status case, must produce evidence of a similarly situated comparator group. See Fisher v. Vassar College (2d Cir.1995) (the absence of any comparison between married males and married females rendered plaintiff's proffered statistics of unlawful gender-based discrimination meaningless); Bryant v. International Schools Services (3d Cir.1982) (plaintiffs failed to show that married women were treated differently from similarly situated males).

Since only women become pregnant, it might seem that a distinction on the basis of pregnancy would be tantamount to express or facial discrimination because of gender. That result might clearly have been expected after *Martin Marietta*, which seemingly would have considered it irrelevant that pregnancy discrimination also draws a distinction on the basis of the "plus" characteristic of pregnancy. The Supreme Court held otherwise, however, in General Electric Co. v. Gilbert (1976), when it concluded that a pregnancy exclusion from an otherwise comprehensive disability insurance plan did not discriminate against women because it distinguished on a "gender-neutral" basis between pregnant women and non-pregnant persons. Congress legislatively overruled this result in the Pregnancy Discrimination Act of 1978.

Relying on the *Gilbert* reasoning, employers also contended that pension plan provisions requiring greater contributions by female employees, or awarding them lesser retirement benefits despite their equal contributions, are geared to the neutral factor of greater average female longevity rather than to gender. The Supreme Court, however, has invalidated plans that require women to make greater contributions or that award them lesser benefits. These decisions have revolutionized the employer-sponsored pension industry, forcing many insurers to offer plans featuring gender-neutral annuity assumptions.

Lower courts have long held, with substantial unanimity, that discrimination because of one's sexual orientation does not amount to gender discrimination prohibited by Title VII. These courts have relied heavily on the repeated failure in Congress of bills that would have prohibited sexual orientation discrimination. For these courts, unless an anti-homosexual policy is disparately enforced in favor of or against members of a particular gender, the employer rule is simply not on the basis of gender. Efforts to circumvent this barrier, either by proceeding on a disparate impact theory or by asserting that a campaign of anti-homosexual hostility amounted to unlawful environmental harassment based on gender, have also generally failed. For example, an anti-homosexual practice, gender-neutral on its face and neutrally applied, may nevertheless result in disproportionately greater exclusion of male homosexuals (as will be the case, if, for example, they are more readily identifiable) and might therefore be said to discriminate because of gender. But since the impetus for the discrimination is anti-homosexual rather than anti-male animus, the circuit opinions accordingly conclude that recognizing the impact theory would amount to an end-run around the Congressional purpose not to forbid discrimination based on sexual orientation. By contrast, disparate enforcement of an anti-homosexual policy in favor of or against members of a particular gender would presumably violate the statute. Despite the absence of national protection, numerous state and local laws provide protection from this type of employment discrimination.

Relying on Price Waterhouse v. Hopkins (1989), several circuits have permitted plaintiffs to proceed where they alleged they were discriminated against because they failed to meet certain gender stereotypes. In *Price Waterhouse,* the Supreme Court held that a woman who was denied partnership in an accounting firm because she did not match a sex stereotype—her appearance and behavior were considered too masculine—had an actionable claim under Title VII. In Nichols v. Azteca Restaurant Enterprises (9th Cir.2001), for example, the Ninth Circuit applied the same principle in holding that a male employee was entitled to redress under Title VII because his employer (through its employees) discriminated against him for not comporting with the employer's stereotypical notion of how a man should behave.

Rules prohibiting the employment of spouses in the same office, department or plant of one company have been viewed as neutral on their face, actionable only if they are disparately enforced against members of a particular gender or if they have the statistical effect of disproportionately adversely impacting wives or husbands. A no-dating rule is likewise neutral on its face and could violate Title VII only if disparately enforced or disproportionately impacting.

Grooming and dress code regulations that on their face pertain only to one gender—men must have short hair, for example—have nevertheless been judicially assessed as neutral rather than as a form of express disparate treatment. See Willingham v. Macon Telegraph Publishing Co. (5th Cir.1975) (en banc).

The same approach has disadvantaged women with respect to regulations governing attire and grooming. Even when the employer's rule specifically imposes more demanding clothing and coiffure requirements on one gender than the other, the tendency has been for the courts to assert that the employer has one omnibus grooming regime that naturally has distinctive variations to account for gender differences. In a variation on this theme, courts will observe that the employer has *some* grooming standard for each gender and will treat that standard as the common, neutral employer practice. The fact that the employer imposes different, or more stringent, or differentially applied dress or grooming requirements on its employees of different genders is usually just ignored or minimized. Plaintiffs have also been compelled to litigate no-beard rules within the framework of disproportionate adverse impact rather than disparate treatment. The consequence of these decisions is that employers are far more easily able to justify such rules as a matter of business necessity or job relatedness than they would be if the rules were classified as discriminating facially on the basis of gender.

The general judicial rejection of women's gender discrimination complaints about harsher grooming or clothing requirements represents an exception to the Supreme Court's general recognition that employer practices driven by sex stereotyping unlawfully discriminate because of gender.

There are a number of other frequently litigated issues that wrestle with the question when grounds of discrimination that correlate differentially or exclusively with one gender amount to the prohibited discrimination "because of sex." Most of these are specially treated by Title VII or related statutes and are considered below.

d. *Sexual Harassment*

(1) Scope and Requirements

Early decisions doubted whether a supervisor's imposition of adverse terms and conditions of employment on a subordinate employee for resisting the superior's sexual advances constituted discrimination "because of sex" even where the superior and subordinate were of different genders. After all, these cases reasoned, the selection of a "target" would usually not be based on the factor of gender alone, except perhaps if the superior targeted *all* subordinate employees of the opposite gender. That is, there would usually be a "plus" factor in the superior employee's calculus, usually the target's relative attractiveness or vulnerability to the superior. Subsequently, however, the Supreme Court has appeared to assume that, as in *Martin Marietta*, the target's gender need not be the sole motivating factor in the superior's advance in order for the subsequent reprisal to be actionable. The court held in Meritor Savings Bank, FSB v. Vinson (1986) that it is sufficient if gender is a "but-for" cause of the advance. This of course would be the case in the most commonly charged sexual harassment scenario, an advance by a heterosexual directed toward a person of the opposite gender.

Nevertheless, the requirement that the discrimination be based on and directed against a particular gender, and not merely against sexual behavior attributable to persons of either gender, has some continuing significance in the law governing harassment. It undercuts claims based on antihomosexual harassment unless the discrimination is limited to homosexuals of one gender, e.g., lesbians, or there is evidence that homosexuality by an employee of a different gender would be tolerated. It apparently also exempts from Title VII scrutiny sexual advances or reprisals made by a bisexual supervisor, who by hypothesis would not usually be selecting a target because of the target's particular gender. Yet claims have been upheld based on nonsexually oriented "equal opportunity harassment" of both men and women where the evidence supports the conclusion that the harasser would not have sought to demean either victim except for their respective genders. By the same token, where a male supervisor's nonsexual but gender-based harassing conduct is in fact directed only against women, it is no defense to conjecture that men might find the supervisor's conduct equally offensive.

Same-sex harassment is actionable when a male harasses another male (or a female harasses another female) not because of the harassee's sexual orientation but because of the harassee's gender. As the EEOC's Compliance Manual asserts, "the crucial inquiry is whether the harasser treats ... members ... of one sex differently from members of the other sex." A unanimous Supreme Court recently endorsed this reasoning in Oncale v. Sundowner Offshore Services, Inc. (1998). The victim's gender must be a "but-for" factor in the harassment. Thus, workplace harassment does not automatically constitute sex discrimination "merely because the words used have sexual content or connotations." This evidentiary minimum is exactly, and only, what the Supreme Court in *Meritor* required in the classic case of opposite gender heterosexual harassment. Thus, conduct motivated by the harasser's homosexual interest in the harassee (rather than by the plaintiff-harassee's own sexual orientation) falls on the actionable side of the line because such conduct would not occur unless the victim were of a particular gender. By contrast, same-sex harassment inspired by the particular victim's prudishness, shyness or apparent relative vulnerability to sexually tinged teasing or taunting would generally not be actionable if the particular harasser would for the same reasons harass members of the other gender, too. *But see Nichols v. Azteca Restaurant Enterprises* (9th Cir.2001).

The Court in *Oncale* identified several ways that a same-sex harassee can prove that he was targeted "because of" his gender. The most direct way of course is to prove that men and women were treated differently. In single gender workplaces, like the offshore drilling platform in *Oncale*, this type of evidence is impossible to produce. Alternatively, a plaintiff can proffer credible evidence that the harasser is gay or lesbian; courts can reasonably assume that such a harasser would not sexually harass members of the other sex. A third approach, useful in cases factually similar to *Oncale*, is to prove that the harassee was harassed "in such sex-specific and derogatory terms" as to make it clear that the harasser is motivated by a general animus toward persons of plaintiff's gender. Sometimes a combination of two or more approaches is necessary to survive a summary judgment motion. It should be noted that the third approach requires the plaintiff to adduce evidence of the specific nature of the allegedly derogatory comments and to carefully avoid any admission that the harassment was on the basis of sexual orientation. *Rene v. MGM Grand Hotel, Inc.* (9th Cir.2001).

Same-race racial harassment has also been found to be actionable after *Oncale.* In *Ross v. Douglas County* (8th Cir. 2000), the defendant argued that a black supervisor could not have had the racial animus required to support a hostile work environment claim brought by a black subordinate. The Court, relying on *Oncale,* summarily rejected this contention, stating "we have no doubt that, as a matter of law, a black male could discriminate against another black male 'because of such individual's race.' "The court opined that racial epithets could have been made to please the white superior or they may have been intended to create a negative and distressing environment for the plaintiff; however, whatever the motive, the court recognized that "the only reason" that the plaintiff "was called a 'nigger' was because he was black—that [the harasser] was also black does not alter this."

The same "because of sex" requirement will also usually defeat the typical claim of sexual favoritism, in which a plaintiff denied a job or benefit alleges that another employee was hired or promoted because he or she participated in a consensual romantic relationship with a supervisory or managerial agent of the employer. In that situation both women and men are disadvantaged for a reason other than, or in addition to, their gender, viz., they were not the object of the agent's sexual interest. Thus in these settings the "gender-plus" liability avoidance persists, despite the Supreme Court's repudiation of it in *Phillips* and *Meritor*. If, however, an employee is coerced into sexual participation as a condition of receiving a job benefit, other employees of the same gender could prevail with a variant on the standard sexual harassment theme if they could prove that sexual favors were demanded generally as the "quid pro quo" for advancement.

Ultimately the judicial rationale for relieving employers of liability based on sexual orientation and sexual favoritism discrimination is extra-textual. It rests instead on a judicial perception about the underlying or motivating purposes of Title VII: to free applicants and employees from the imposition of adverse (thus excluding sexual favoritism discrimination) working conditions on the basis of the very few characteristics protected by Title VII (thus excluding sexual orientation discrimination).

Courts have also been cautious before deciding that sexual harassment constitutes unlawful gender discrimination because in some cases the alleged harasser's proposition or advance may have been invited or received as welcome. Any sexual harassment plaintiff must therefore show that she or he subjectively perceived a proposition or advance as "unwelcome." This requires first a showing that there was in fact a sexual advance. On this question Congress has balanced the scales against the defendant by approving the admission of evidence of past similar conduct by the alleged harasser. An amendment to the Federal Rules of Evidence, applicable to trials commencing on or after December 1, 1994, eases the plaintiff's proof on this issue in those harassment cases that are "predicated on a party's alleged commission of conduct constituting an offense of sexual assault." In such cases, F.R.E. 415 provides that "evidence of that party's commission of another offense or offenses of sexual assault ... is admissible and may be considered as provided in Rule 413 ... of these rules." In turn, Rule 413, which authorizes the use of such evidence in criminal cases, provides that evidence concerning a defendant's prior sexual assault "may be considered for its bearing on any matter to which it is relevant." Further, Congress has directed that Rule 413 itself "shall not be construed to limit the admission or consideration of evidence under any other rule." The last quoted provision seems strikingly at odds with explicit legislative history which reflects Congress' understanding that Rule 415 simply creates an exception, in cases involving sex offenses, to Rule 404(b)'s exclusion of evidence of other crimes or acts that are offered to prove character and current action conforming thereto. But textually Rules 415 and 413 taken together override all other rules of evidence that ordinarily might result in the exclusion of such evidence—for example, where the prejudicial effect of the evidence outweighs its probative value, or where the evidence is introduced in the form of hearsay (not eligible for one of the usual hearsay exceptions), or where it is admissible only in the form of reputation or opinion testimony.

If there was an advance, its welcomeness vel non is determined by a subjective test. Until recently, sufficient evidence of the plaintiff's off-hours conduct and attitudes has sufficed to refute her assertion that workplace harassment was unwelcome. An employer may attempt to overcome a showing that an actionable level of interference was unwelcome with evidence about the plaintiff's past sexual conduct, "fantasies," or failure to object to sexual advances. But recent decisions caution against equating participation in off-duty sex-related activities with acquiescence to sexual advances on the job. For example, evidence that the plaintiff had posed nude for a magazine did not negate her evidence that she did not welcome the employer's sexual advances in the workplace. Indeed even a plaintiff's "vulgar and unladylike" language and behavior on the job did not negate her showing that she did not welcome the crude sexual epithets, sexually insulting messages, and offensive demonstrative conduct (including urination and self-exposure) directed at her by her male co-workers. On this issue it was important to the court that the plaintiff plainly resented their conduct and complained of it repeatedly to her supervisor.

Federal Rule of Evidence 412(b)(2), applicable to trials commencing after December 1, 1994, may rule out all but the most probative evidence of the *plaintiff's* prior sexual behavior. Rule 412 provides that in a civil action, "evidence offered to prove the sexual behavior or sexual predisposition of any alleged victim is admissible if ... its probative value *substantially* outweighs the danger of harm to any victim and of unfair prejudice to any party." The FRE 412 amendment tilts the scales against admissibility in three respects, as compared to standard probative value-prejudicial impact balancing under FRE 403. First, it reverses the presumptive weighting, by requiring the proponent to justify admissibility rather than requiring the opponent to justify exclusion. Second, the prerequisites for admissibility are more stringent, because the value of the proffered evidence must "substantially" outweigh the specified dangers. Third, harm to the victim must be explicitly placed on the exclusion side of the balance, in addition to party prejudice.

This alteration of the rules' usual neutrality in weighing probative value against prejudice suggests that evidence of consensual sexual conduct in a plaintiff's prior or even contemporaneous private life will seldom be admissible. The amendment casts doubt on the likelihood that a court would admit evidence of plaintiff's response to or initiation of sexual jokes, sexually tinged language, or erotic pictorial displays in the workplace, which may be regarded as tangential to her receptivity to an unconsented touching or sexual proposition. Indeed it may lead to the exclusion of evidence of plaintiff's consensual sexual relationships with co-employees, including even the alleged harasser.

Of course the potential inadmissibility of any such evidence would not necessarily prevent the employer from pursuing these topics in discovery. But the amendment to the evidence rules should strengthen a plaintiff's motion for a protective order designed to eliminate or limit inquiry into her past or contemporaneous sexual habits or history where the court is persuaded that the evidence is unlikely to be admitted at trial and is being sought principally to embarrass or intimidate.

(2) "Quid Pro Quo" or "Tangible Terms" Harassment

Title VII is violated when submission to an employer's sexual demands is expressly made the "quid pro quo" of gaining a job, promotion, continued employment, pay increase, work assignment or other economic job benefit, or of avoiding demotion, diminished compensation, a disadvantageous transfer, or formal discipline or discharge. The Court in Burlington Industries v. Ellerth (1998), stated that a tangible employment action "constitutes a significant change in employment status, such as hiring, firing, failing to promote, reassignment with significantly different responsibilities, or a decision causing a significant change in benefits." EEOC's Guidelines assert that quid pro quo harassment also occurs when submission to unwelcome sexual advances or conduct is "implicitly" made a term of condition of the target's employment and made the basis for an employment decision. Relying on the Guidelines, a circuit opinion has held that "quid pro quo sexual harassment occurs whenever an individual explicitly or implicitly conditions a job, a job benefit, or the absence of a job detriment, upon an employee's acceptance of sexual conduct." However, a victim need not provide evidence of a direct and express sexual demand to make a claim under the "tangible employment action" analysis. "A supervisor may simply intimate that a subordinate's career prospects will suffer if she does not submit to his advances, with the hope of concealing his harassment if his statements are repeated to a third party."

The Ninth Circuit has adopted a per se rule that "a supervisor's intertwining of a request for the performance of sexual favors with a discussion of actual or potential job benefits or detriments in a single conversation constitutes quid pro quo harassment." Nichols v. Frank (9th Cir.1994). On this theory, quid pro quo discrimination may occur even though, by submitting to the superior's sexual demands, the employee suffers no tangible economic loss. More recently, however, where a harassing superior officer of the employer did not carry out threats to adversely alter the plaintiff's tangible terms of employment despite her refusal to submit, the Supreme Court and the circuit courts have treated the discrimination as an instance of a hostile work environment, limiting the "quid pro quo" classification to situations in which the threat is consummated. This suggests that the Court might analyze "submission" scenarios as non-quid pro quo, unless perhaps the employer agent does adversely alter the target's terms of employment despite her submission.

In sum, the "quid pro quo" or "tangible terms" sexual harassment plaintiff must prove that (1) he or she encountered verbal, visual or physical propositions or advances of a sexual nature; (2) the harassment was based on her or his gender, and not, for example, sexual orientation; (3) she or he experienced the propositions or advances as subjectively unwelcome; and (4) the harassment was perpetrated by a supervisor, manager or other high-ranking agent of the employer who had the authority to and did in fact give the plaintiff a tangible employment benefit for submitting, or imposed a tangible detriment for resisting, the proposition or advance.

Since *Burlington*, an appellate decision has held that merely assigning extra work to the plaintiff was not sufficiently "tangible" to impute automatic, vicarious liability to an employer. Reinhold v. Commonwealth of Virginia (4th Cir.1998). But another has held that forcing the plaintiff to give up her office and her secretary was a tangible adverse action. Durham Life Ins. Co v. Evans (3d Cir.1999). The Court in *Ellerth* defined a tangible employment action as one that "constitutes a significant change in employment status ... such as hiring, firing, failing to promote, reassignment with significantly different responsibilities, or a decision causing a significant change in benefits." In most cases, but not always, "a tangible employment action ... inflicts direct economic harm."

Resolving a circuit split, the Supreme Court has held that an employer may ordinarily assert the *Faragher/Burlington* affirmative defense to a constructive discharge resulting from a supervisor's hostile and abusive environmental harassment. The defense would be precluded only if, as a part of or following that harassment, the constructive discharge were precipitated by an official company act that imposed a tangible detriment on the plaintiff, such as a severe demotion, extreme pay decrease, or humiliating transfer. The Court stressed, however, that as with other uses of the defense, the employer must establish by a preponderance of the evidence both that it exercised reasonable care to prevent and promptly correct the harassing behavior and that the plaintiff unreasonably failed to take advantage of employer-provided preventive or corrective opportunities or failed to mitigate harm. Pennsylvania State Police v. Suders (2004).

Where harassment is recognized as tangible, the available remedies would include back pay representing the economic loss of a lost job or promotion; injunctive relief directing the award of any lost position; emotional distress and, for a willful or reckless violation, punitive damages, with the sum of both types of damages capped at $50,000 to $300,000 depending on the number of persons employed by the defendant; and attorney fees and costs.

(3) EMPLOYER LIABILITY FOR QUID PRO QUO (TANGIBLE TERMS) DISCRIMINATION

Because only supervisors or managers can alter such tangible terms of employment, and they are clothed by the employer with at least apparent authority to do so, a finding of quid pro quo harassment results, as with most other violations of Title VII, in automatic or "strict" liability of the employer. Dictum in companion cases decided by the Supreme Court in June 1998 confirms that the employer is not only vicariously but strictly or "automatically" liable without more for quid pro quo harassment by a supervisor or other employer agent who has the means to and does in fact alter the plaintiff's tangible terms and conditions of employment. Strict liability means that if the plaintiff demonstrates that her obtaining a tangible job benefit or avoiding a tangible job detriment turned on her compliance or noncompliance with an unwelcome sexual advance, and the employer agent carried out such a promise or threat, the employer, even if it was unaware of the harassment, will have no affirmative defense. In a "tangible terms" case, the Court reasons, "there is assurance the injury could not have been inflicted absent the agency relation" between the supervisor and a defendant employer.

Evidence of an adequate anti-harassment policy and prompt and effective remedial action may still be admissible in tangible benefit cases on the issue of punitive damages. Under 42 U.S.C.A. § 1981a(b)(1), and the Supreme Court's decision in Kolstad v. American Dental Association (1999), a party may recover punitive damages if his employer engaged in intentional discrimination "with malice or with reckless indifference to the federally protected rights of an aggrieved individual." The terms "malice" and "reckless indifference" refer to the employer's knowledge that it may be violating federal law, not its awareness that it is engaging in discrimination. Thus, the employer must perceive some risk that its actions violate federal law in order to be liable for punitive damages. In a case involving vicarious liability, the plaintiff must also establish a basis for imputing liability to the employer by showing that the employee who discriminated against him was a manager, acting within the scope of his employment. An employer may escape punitive damages liability for its manager's acts, however, if it can demonstrate a good faith attempt to establish and enforce an antidiscrimination policy. According to *Kolstad*, "an employer may not be vicariously liable [for punitive damages] for the discriminatory employment decisions of managerial agents where these decisions are contrary to the employer's 'good faith efforts to comply with Title VII.'" Such good faith efforts, if proven, demonstrate that the employer itself did not act in reckless disregard of federally protected rights, thus making it inappropriate to punish the employer for its manager's contravention of its established policies.

(4) "Hostile Environment" Discrimination

Suppose the victim is subjected to worsened working conditions or other "environmental" harassment that affects only intangible aspects of the job? Until Title VII was amended by the Civil Rights Act of 1991, a plaintiff who could prove only an abusive or hostile work environment, without tangible detriment to her employment status, could recover no monetary relief. There was thus little incentive to sue under Title VII for environmental sexual harassment, unaccompanied by termination, demotion, or other adverse action resulting in a reduction or loss of pay or benefits. But Section 102 of the Civil Rights Act of 1991 authorized compensatory and, if appropriate, punitive damages, for all intentional forms of unlawful discrimination, including harassment. (Punitive damages are not available against government employers). These damages are capped in amounts that vary with the number of employees employed by the defendant.

In *Meritor* and *Oncale* the Supreme Court reaffirmed its traditional broad interpretation of covered "terms and conditions of employment," holding that harassment is actionable, even if it does not affect a tangible term of employment, provided it is sufficiently severe or pervasive to create a hostile or abusive working environment. The "hostile environment" label defines all actionable sexual harassment claims other than "quid pro quo." Thus it includes situations in which the harasser is (a) a co-worker, customer or subordinate without authority to reward or punish with tangible job benefits or detriments; (b) a supervisor whose conduct consists of unwanted verbal or physical sexually oriented advances (or of speech or conduct demeaning to the abilities or status of women), unaccompanied by a tangible job detriment, as in *Faragher*; or (c) a supervisor who threatens but does not fulfill a threat respecting the target's tangible terms of employment, as in *Burlington*. The Court explains that labeling a harasser's conduct as "hostile environment" rather than "quid pro quo" means that the plaintiff will have to show more aggravated or persistent conduct to prove sex discrimination violating Title VII, but does not by itself control whether the employer is liable for that conduct.

The "hostile environment" sexual harassment plaintiff must prove that (1) she or he encountered verbal, visual or physical propositions, advances, insults or invasions of person; (2) those propositions or insults were based on her or his gender, as distinct from, for example, her or his sexual orientation; (3) he or she experienced the alleged harasser's conduct as *subjectively* unwelcome; (4) the harassment was of sufficient nature and magnitude (e.g., on one hand, a one-time flagrant physical assault or intimate touching, or, on the other, ongoing, relatively frequent or continual physical or verbal propositions, advances, or insults) to have created an *objectively* intimidating, hostile, offensive, or abusive work environment of a kind that would have unreasonably interfered with the work performance, working conditions, or general well being of a reasonable person in her position; and (5) the harassment was perpetrated either by a supervisor, manager or high-ranking agent of the employer, or by a co-worker, subordinate, customer or other business invitee in circumstances that fasten liability on the employer under general principles of agency law.

The plaintiff's most formidable obstacle here is usually establishing the objectively hostile or abusive work environment, element (4). Whether conduct reaches a level of unreasonable interference with the employee's ability to work, or creates a sufficiently intimidating work environment, "should be evaluated from the objective standpoint of a 'reasonable person.'" Thus a "normal" level of workplace obscenity, isolated sexual suggestiveness or propositions, and even some single instances of unwelcome touching, may not amount to unreasonable interference. And although the terminology "sexual harassment" implies that the harassment must be sexual in nature, the Court in *Oncale* explained that the "harassing conduct need not be motivated by sexual desire to support an inference of discrimination on the basis of sex."

The circuit courts are still sorting out whether the "person" from whose standpoint reasonableness should be assessed is the genderless prototype of torts litigation (the "reasonable man") or a reasonable victim—usually, in this context, a woman. The EEOC blurs this division in its Policy Guidance, advocating a "reasonable person" standard but adding that in applying that standard the factfinder "should consider the victim's perspective and not stereotyped notions of acceptable behavior." The Supreme Court in Harris v. Forklift Systems (1993) described the required environment as one "that a reasonable person would find hostile or abusive...." Subsequently, in *Oncale*, the Court characterized that requirement as meaning "that the objective severity of harassment should be judged from the perspective of a reasonable person in the plaintiff's position, considering 'all the circumstances.'" It is submitted that neither of these statements unequivocally indicates that the "position" or "circumstances" of the plaintiff that may permissibly be considered include his or her race or gender, although one circuit so concludes.

The Supreme Court has upheld a "hostile environment" claim when workplace intimidation, ridicule and insult are "sufficiently severe or pervasive to alter the conditions of the victim's environment *and* create an abusive working environment." The plaintiff suffered a series of gender-related insults and unwanted sexual innuendos. Because in totality this conduct may have been sufficient to create an abusive work environment from the standpoint of a hypothetical reasonable person, the Court held that the plaintiff was not required to show that it seriously affected her psychological well-being. The Court located the required level of injury somewhere "between making actionable any conduct that is merely offensive and requiring the conduct to cause a tangible psychological injury." Psychological harm is just another, nonessential factor relevant to the issue of abusiveness. A plaintiff can meet the *Harris* threshold without showing that the harassment affected her psychologically, diminished her work performance, or caused her to quit or even want to quit her job.

Justice O'Connor's opinion for the *Harris* majority emphasizes that when the defendant's conduct consists entirely of epithets or sexual innuendo, those must be sufficiently severe or pervasive "to create an objectively hostile or abusive work environment," one that a "reasonable person would find hostile or abusive." (In addition, the victim must "subjectively perceive the environment to be abusive.") The opinion does little more than identify a number of unweighted, nonexhaustive factors relevant to the objective question of an "abusive" or "hostile" work environment: the nature of the discriminatory conduct, i.e., whether it is merely offensive or also physically threatening or humiliating; the conduct's frequency and severity; and whether it unreasonably interfered with the plaintiff's work performance. None of these is identified as indispensable or even preeminent, and this leads the EEOC to conclude that none is.

Justice Ginsburg, concurring, opined that the inquiry should "center, dominantly, on whether the discriminatory conduct has interfered with the plaintiff's work performance." For her this would mean that the plaintiff need show only that the defendant's conduct made it more difficult for her to do her job, and not that the plaintiff's productivity actually declined. Several court of appeals decisions appear to hold just that: a supervisor's sexual innuendo and banter was actionable because it was unwelcome and made it more difficult for plaintiff to do her job, even though it was not of sufficient severity to prevent her from timely meeting her work obligations. But the *Harris* majority did not hold that a showing that the plaintiff's job has been made more difficult suffices. On the other hand, interference with the plaintiff's work performance is not essential to the required demonstration of hostility or abusiveness. It is enough if the offensive conduct is shown, through the totality of the circumstances, to create, cumulatively or in the aggregate, an abusive work environment, or even just that it adversely affected plaintiff's daily working conditions.

Because no bright line separates merely vulgar banter (usually lawful) from a consistently hostile or severely abusive environment (usually unlawful), some circuits confide the pervasiveness and severity questions to a jury, so long as the district judge is satisfied that the harasser's comments or conducts were "because of sex." Others, however, consider actionable harassment a question of law and accordingly reserve decision on the sufficiency of severity and pervasiveness for the district courts or for themselves.

Where environmental harassment is severe and obvious, as with intensive physical sexual abuse, assault, or rape, the limitations period begins to run immediately. But where such conduct is so severe as to disable a plaintiff from taking the steps necessary to prosecute a claim, equitable tolling may extend the duration of the period.

(5) EMPLOYER LIABILITY FOR PROHIBITED HOSTILE ENVIRONMENT HARASSMENT BY SUPERVISORS AND CO-WORKERS

The plaintiff will ordinarily receive no remedy for sexually harassing conduct of the "hostile environment type" unless the employer as an entity is liable for that conduct. This is because most of the federal appellate circuits addressing the question have held that supervisors, managers and most high officials of a covered "employer" cannot be held individually liable, even though the statute defines a covered "employer" to include "any agent of" that employer. So the requirements of employer liability for environmental harassment are critical.

While recognizing that a supervisor's sexually harassing conduct is probably a "frolic and detour" outside the scope of his authority, the Supreme Court has nevertheless held that an employer "is subject to vicarious liability to a victimized employee for an actionable hostile environment created by a supervisor with immediate (or successively higher) authority over the employee." As observed above, where the supervisor's harassment culminates in a tangible employment detriment to the victim—where it is "quid pro quo"—employer liability is not only vicarious but strict. Thus, there is no employer defense where actionable harassment of the tangible type results in an actual or even constructive discharge. Pennsylvania State Police v. Suders (2004). But where the supervisor does not impose a tangible employment detriment for nonsubmission to a sexual demand—in, that is, an "intangible" or "hostile environment" case—the employer may avoid liability if by a preponderance of the evidence it carries *both* elements of the following affirmative defense: "(a) that the employer exercised reasonable care to prevent and correct promptly any sexually harassing behavior, and (b) that the plaintiff employee unreasonably failed to take advantage of any corrective opportunities provided by the employer or to avoid harm otherwise." Faragher v. City of Boca Raton (1998). Burlington Indus. v. Ellerth (1998).

This test expands employer liability for unlawful hostile environment harassment by supervisors or other high officials. Applied literally, an employer avoids liability for otherwise actionable supervisory harassment only when it exercised reasonable care to "prevent" and "correct" unlawful environmental harassment *and* when the plaintiff unreasonably failed to use available employer-provided channels of complaint or other remedies. To show that it took "reasonable care to prevent" under prong (a), and to meet prong (b)—that the plaintiff "unreasonably" failed to utilize corrective opportunities—the employer must typically prove that it had in place a policy that specifically condemned sexual harassment and that it maintained an internal effective complaints procedure with reasonable reporting procedures, including a mechanism that assured victims a means of bypassing the alleged harasser to register a complaint, and that was widely disseminated among employees, and adequately enforced (with appropriate training of managers) in a climate that did not discourage complaints. But because alleged victims will usually take advantage of such policies and procedures, the defense would frequently founder on this second prong. Unreasonable failure to invoke the employer's procedures has been widely found where plaintiffs waited to report the harassment or failed to report ongoing harassment altogether because they fear retaliation or were uncertain allegations would be held confidential, especially where employers' anti-harassment policies contain express anti-retaliation provisions. Indeed, employers may be at risk in honoring complainants' requests for strict confidentiality, since doing so impedes full investigation which in turn may prevent them from taking the prompt and appropriate corrective action required by *Burlington/Faragher* to satisfy the affirmative defense. Gallagher v. Delaney (2d Cir.1998). It has even been held that an employee cannot maintain a work environment claim if she coupled an internal complaint with a request for confidentiality, at least absent evidence of the kind of egregious harassment that would predictably lead to serious physical or psychological harm if the employer does not act. Torres v. Pisano (2d Cir.1997). And the employer will be able to show plaintiff's noncompliance under prong (b) if her complaint, although timely, does not provide notice that the agent's offensive conduct was of sexual or perhaps gender-based nature.

But there may be considerably more flexibility as to when the employee must complain where harassment has been extreme. In the statute of limitations context, equitable tolling may extend the time in which plaintiff may comply with prerequisites to suit where the harassment is so severe as to be disabling. This concept might easily be transplanted to enable a plaintiff to resist the employer's evidence that she unreasonably failed timely to invoke an available internal complaints procedure.

While a literal application of the two-pronged defense often prevents even explicit, fair and fairly enforced internal grievance procedures from avoiding liability altogether, employers still have an incentive to adopt them. Such procedures will encourage internal complaints, thereby enhancing the employer's ability to take prompt corrective action that will limit its exposure for emotional distress, punitive damages and attorney fees. And a complete avoidance of liability for supervisory environmental harassment is still possible, even when the plaintiff invokes a complaints procedure and a court applies the literal reading of the compound affirmative defense, for the plaintiff must still carry her prima facie burden of showing a sufficiently severe or hostile environment. The Court hinted in *Faragher* itself that it intended to continue to insist on palpable harm to the plaintiff's work environment, observing that the *Harris* standards for judging actionable interference "are sufficiently demanding to ensure that Title VII does not become a 'general civility code.'"

In dictum in *Faragher* the Court confirmed the "negligence" standard widely used by most circuit courts and EEOC to determine employer liability for actionable environmental harassment by a plaintiff's co-worker (or subordinate or customer). This negligence standard has been carried forward in post-*Burlington/Faragher* circuit decisions. Because a co-worker, subordinate or customer cannot independently adversely alter the plaintiff's tangible terms of employment, the underlying violation here is of the "hostile environment" rather than "quid pro quo" variety. It is even clearer with co-worker as with supervisory environmental harassment that the harasser is not acting on behalf of the employer or carrying out its business. In those cases, therefore, the circuit courts, with the Supreme Court's apparent approval, are unanimous that the employer will be liable only if it actually knew or should have known of the co-worker's (or subordinate's or customer's or supplier's) unlawful harassment and failed to take prompt and effective corrective action. In co-worker or subordinate cases, then, the employer can assure its nonliability by its own unilateral action.

A key question that arises then is whether the harasser is a supervisor or a co-worker. If the harasser is only a co-worker, then the burden is on the plaintiff to prove that the employer was negligent, i.e., that the employer knew or should have known of the harassment yet the employer failed to take prompt corrective action. But if the harasser is a supervisor, the burden is on the defendant to establish the two-pronged *Burlington/Faragher* affirmative defense. A confused Eleventh Circuit panel decision illustrates the difference. In Coates v. Sundor Brands, Incorporated (11th Cir.1999), the per curiam opinion analyzes the case as involving co-worker harassment; it employs the standard negligence framework under which the employee has the burden of showing that the employer knew or should have known of the harassment yet failed to react timely and appropriately. However, in a special concurrence, one judge applies the *Burlington/Faragher* framework for supervisory harassment (but apparently mistakenly places the burden on the plaintiff to disprove the two-pronged affirmative defense). It is not clear in the opinion whether the court carefully considered the status of the harasser. But the characterization of the harasser is critical at summary judgment or post-trial: summary judgment or judgment as a matter of law is uncommon when the moving party has the burden at trial as would the defendant-employer in a supervisory environmental harassment case that turns on the *Burington/Faragher* affirmative defense.

Although the circuits have articulated various formulations for identifying supervisory status, a central question is whether the harasser had the authority to affect the terms and conditions of the harassee's work environment. The Tenth

Circuit has limited the term "supervisor" to those persons having actual and immediate authority over the plaintiff. In Harrison v. Eddy Potash, Inc. (10th Cir.1998), the court rejected both an "alter ego" and apparent authority jury instruction requested by the plaintiff. The court relied on *Burlington*, and stated that employer liability cannot be grounded on a theory that a supervisor was an alter ego of the employer. The court further stated that to be a supervisor, the person must have actual authority; the false impression of authority is not sufficient. Only the misuse of actual authority can create employer liability.

Employers have asserted rights to indemnity or contribution with respect to supervisory conduct that has resulted in employer liability. But the Supreme Court has held that no such right is provided by Title VII itself or at common law. Claims by supervisors disciplined for violating their employer's anti-sexual harassment policy have generally not fared well, most courts reasoning that the employer must enjoy reasonable latitude to conduct a vigorous internal examination without risking additional charges of sexual harassment. Thus even a hostile, unprofessional and abusive employer investigation of sexual harassment charges ultimately determined to be unfounded could not support a separate sexual harassment claim by the exonerated suspect.

On the other hand, unsuccessful sexual harassment charges in litigation have spawned defamation suits by the alleged harasser against accusers and against employers who placed stock in the charges and took unilateral corrective action. In one case, the Virginia Supreme Court upheld a verdict against the plaintiff's female subordinate, rejecting her contention that sexual harassment is an "inherently subjective concept" that as such represents a pure expression of opinion absolutely protected by the First Amendment. Defamation suits have been defeated by the employers' assertion of a conditional privilege which arises where the recipient of an alleged defamatory statement has an important interest that is advanced by frank communication. But another plaintiff, who was fired in the wake of allegations of sexual harassment by two female employees, failed to survive summary judgment for want of sufficient evidence of the "actual malice" Texas law required to recover for defamation. At most, the court found, the employer may have been hasty or mistaken, but there was no evidence that it took that action for any ulterior motive reflecting animus against the plaintiff. And a discharged executive failed to prove a violation of ERISA in connection with his loss of severance benefits even though his conduct, although violative of company policy, was too sporadic to violate Title VII.

(6) First Amendment Implications of Imposing Liability for Environmentally Harassing Speech

It seems even clearer after *Harris* that speech alone may violate Title VII. That is to say, sexually offensive, demeaning or obscene speech or pictorial displays may alone adversely alter the conditions of the plaintiff's employment. Few courts have addressed the constitutional problems that arise where the supervisor's or co-worker's allegedly harassing "conduct" consists entirely of speech or symbolic speech. When that is so, federal or state regulation in the form of mandated procedures and judicial sanctions implicates the First Amendment. The situation is aggravated by the reality that employers have an incentive to over regulate the speech of their employees by taking the "prompt and effective corrective action" that the courts have held will absolve them of liability for the sins of co-workers and sometimes even supervisors.

Two features of emerging harassment law fuel that incentive. First, as the *Harris* language underscores, the contours of the violation are vague. Generally courts have found that a plaintiff states a prima facie case under Title VII when the environment is pervasively disrespectful to women or minorities. Similarly, sexual propositions in the workplace can create a hostile environment. The only guidance given employers is that, "verbal conduct of a sexual nature [that] has the purpose or effect of unreasonably interfering with an individual's work performance or creating an intimidating, hostile, or offensive work environment" is harassment. Moreover, the existence of a hostile environment is determined by a totality of the circumstances test. The employer is uncertain as to whether a hostile environment exists until the court makes that determination.

Second, an effective policy and procedure against sexual harassment may avoid employer liability for harassment by subordinate employees and for environmental harassment by supervisors. Accordingly, when, as will frequently be the case, the employer is in doubt, it has the incentive, in order to avoid the vagaries of liability for uncertain workplace speech and pictorial displays, to over regulate and over punish. Nevertheless, fired managers have generally had difficulty persuading courts that their discipline or discharge as the result of an internal investigation violates federal or state law. Still, while an employer may discipline supervisors for engaging in sexual harassment, it may not discipline them for their speech or conduct in participating in an investigation of that harassment.

e. The Special Statutory Concept of "Religion"

Employers not qualifying for immunity from liability for religious discrimination under § 702 or § 703(e)(2), or for the BFOQ defense with respect to religiously-based hiring decisions are subject to a special affirmative obligation somewhat distinct from the normal duty not to discriminate. Section 703(a)(1) forbids an employer from discriminating because of "religion"; and § 701(j), added in 1972, in turn defines "religion" to include "all aspects of religious observance and practice as well as belief, unless an employer demonstrates that he is unable to reasonably accommodate to an employee's ... religious observance or practice without undue hardship."

At the threshold, when does an employer rule discriminate because of "religion"? A circuit court has assumed that an employer rule excluding all but "Protestants" (no particular denomination required) and preferring "Jesuits" (members of a Catholic order) does draw a distinction based on religion. Pime v. Loyola Univ. of Chicago (7th Cir.1986). The panel rejected the approach suggested by a concurring judge who argued that rejection of the Jewish plaintiff was not on an unlawful ground. Judge Posner wrote that plaintiff's rejection because he was not a Jesuit was *not* tantamount to a rejection for not being a Catholic, since a non-Jesuit Catholic would also have been denied the job. Implicitly Posner's position was that adverse distinctions drawn on the basis of being or not being Jesuit are not actionable, while those relating to Catholicism are, even though only Catholics can be Jesuit. This position could be rephrased as an argument that discrimination on the basis of "religion-plus" (being Catholic *plus* being a Jesuit) is not prima facie unlawful while discrimination on the basis of religion alone is. As such, it seems discredited by the Supreme Court's rejection in *Phillips* of the employer's assertion that its rule was not unlawful sex discrimination because it excluded not women alone but only those who shared the "plus" factor of having pre-school-aged children.

On facts that sharpened the distinction between a religion and one of its orders, a later panel of the Seventh Circuit grappled with a Catholic plaintiff's claim that she was denied employment by another university because of sex and the school's Jesuit preference policy. The court rejected her claims, finding that she was denied an academic appointment not because of her gender but because her views did not conform to Catholic doctrine. Maguire v. Marquette Univ. (7th Cir.1987). But if that were so, and if "religion" includes "all aspects of religious ... belief," why was she not held to have been discriminated against on the basis of religion, as she apparently claimed? Did the court perhaps place a sub rosa interpretive gloss on the statute to the effect that a defendant may lawfully discriminate against a Catholic on the basis of non-adherence to Catholic belief?

Employees may assert various theories of religious discrimination, including disparate treatment, religious harassment, and failure to accommodate. To prove a claim under the disparate treatment theory, the prima facie case and evidentiary burdens of an employee alleging religious discrimination mirror those of an employee alleging race or sex discrimination. Accordingly, the courts apply the familiar burden-shifting framework of *McDonnell Douglas*. The plaintiff must demonstrate that she (1) is a member of a protected class, (2) was qualified and rejected for the position she sought, and (3) nonmembers of the protected class were treated more favorably. Harassment on the basis of religion similarly tracks the now-familiar sexual or racial harassment cases.

More typically, the religious discrimination plaintiff complains of a particular employer practice that burdens the practice of his religion. The prima facie case consists of evidence that an employer practice conflicts with the employee's exercise of a sincerely held religious belief, that the employee has put the employer on notice of the conflict, and the employer has nevertheless imposed an employment detriment. The employer then defends by showing either that it fulfilled its obligation to reasonably accommodate or that any accommodation of the plaintiff's religious needs would work an undue hardship. But two Supreme Court decisions have greatly eased the resulting employer obligation to reasonably accommodate the religious practice.

In Ansonia Bd. of Education v. Philbrook (1986), the Court suggested that if an employer's schedule conflicts with the plaintiff's religious need to refrain from secular employment on holy days, the employer could ordinarily satisfy its accommodation obligation by offering the employee additional unpaid leave rather than affording additional paid leave. In particular, the employer was not required to accept the plaintiff's proffered fuller accommodation if the employer's own accommodation is "reasonable." (Contrast the far more substantial duty to accommodate disabilities under the ADA of 1990).

Second, Trans World Airlines, Inc. v. Hardison (1977) held that an employer's reasonable accommodation, even as alleviated by *Ansonia*, works "undue hardship" whenever it results "in more than a *de minimis* cost." An accommodation that requires the employer to hire an additional worker in order to permit the plaintiff to observe his religion every Saturday works undue hardship. So do accommodations that permit a religious observer to skip assignments that would have to be picked up by others, or that allow the observer to work less than others, even if he reimburses the employer for the resulting additional costs. Largely because the duty to accommodate has thus been substantially diluted by judicial construction, § 701(j) has survived challenge under the First Amendment's Establishment Clause.

f. *Wage Discrimination and the Equal Pay Act*

The Equal Pay Act of 1963, 29 U.S.C.A. § 206(d) ("EPA") prohibits only sex-based pay differentials for "equal work," defined to mean jobs involving substantially the same skill, effort, and responsibility. EPA also contains four listed affirmative defenses to a claim of unequal pay for equal work.

The "Bennett Amendment" to Title VII, the last sentence of § 703(h), attempts to harmonize the two statutes' treatment of sex-based wage discrimination. It provides that a successful affirmative defense to an EPA claim does double duty as a defense to liability under Title VII. Lower courts are divided, however, on the converse question, whether EPA liability automatically means Title VII liability as well.

On the other hand, intentional sex-based wage discrimination may violate Title VII even if no member of the opposite sex performs "equal work" within the meaning of EPA. But the related "comparable worth" theory has generally been rejected. An employer does not violate Title VII merely by observing market norms that result in its paying more for male-dominated jobs than for female-dominated jobs that have similar value to the employer but would not be considered "equal" under EPA. Nor can the Equal Pay Act be used to assert a claim for equal benefits based on the alleged "comparable worth" of male-and female-dominated jobs when those jobs do not entail the substantially equal skill, effort and responsibility that EPA claims require. See Chapter 7 for a fuller discussion of the theory of comparable worth.

Even without explicit authorizing text in EPA, the circuit courts have held unlawful employer retaliation against employees for asserting an EPA claim or protesting an EPA violation.

2. PARTICULAR PRACTICES GIVEN SPECIAL STATUTORY TREATMENT

a. Restrictions Relative to Pregnancy and Abortion

The Pregnancy Discrimination Act of 1978, or "PDA," added to Title VII a new § 701(k). This amendment defines the sex discrimination prohibited by § 703 to include distinctions "on the basis of pregnancy, childbirth or related medical conditions." The PDA, in other words, effectively equates pregnancy discrimination with discrimination "because of sex" within the meaning of § 703. Refusing to hire or firing someone because she is pregnant therefore violates § 703, and such a violation is a form of facial or express gender discrimination, defensible only if the employer establishes a BFOQ. The PDA thus accomplishes the objective that principally motivated its enactment, overturning the Court's conclusion in General Electric Co. v. Gilbert (1976) that discrimination based on pregnancy is not based on gender.

The PDA does not require an employer to provide leaves or benefits for pregnancy that it does not provide to male employees for "comparable" conditions; as the Court wrote in California Federal Savings & Loan Ass'n v. Guerra (1987), the amendment's dominant principle is nondiscrimination, rather than preference. PDA does not even require an employer to provide *any* leaves or benefits for pregnancy if it treats similar disabilities the same. For the same reason, the Act does not require more indulgence for absence or tardiness occasioned by pregnancy than for absences or tardiness attributable to any other ailment or medical condition.

On the other hand, as *Guerra* held, the Act does not preempt state legislation that preferentially treats pregnant employees by affirmatively requiring employers to offer leave benefits to pregnancy-disabled employees that the employer does not offer to others. The Court has since explained that the state statute in question was not preempted because it "was not inconsistent with the purposes of the . . . [PDA] and did not require an act that was unlawful under Title VII." Similarly, an employer is not forbidden from offering greater health insurance benefits for pregnancy than for other medical conditions as a matter of contract. On the other hand, an employer may not give female parents child care leaves, keyed to childbirth rather than to pregnancy disability, if fathers are denied leave under similar circumstances.

There are some tensions and apparent contradictions in the patchwork of holdings under the PDA. How, for example, could *Guerra* affirm that the PDA enacts a nondiscrimination principle but then sustain state-mandated preferential employer treatment of pregnancy-related disabilities as not inconsistent with PDA's purposes? Why should a woman asserting a PDA violation be relieved of showing that a man received better treatment, if PDA enshrines only a principle of nondiscrimination? If, on the other hand, PDA contemplates preferential handling of pregnancy, why have EEOC and lower courts limited the permissible preference to periods of actual physical disability, and not to subsequent child-rearing leaves? The answers reside in the awkward construction of PDA's text and the history antedating its enactment.

Where the plaintiff simply produces evidence that the adverse action was based on pregnancy, and the employer fails to offer comparative evidence involving the disabilities of other employees, the first clause of the PDA has supported the per se equation of distinctions based on pregnancy with discrimination "because of sex." In effect this was the path the Supreme Court followed in *International Union, U.A.W. v. Johnson Controls* (1991), where an employer rule denying women jobs in positions where they would encounter special levels of lead was applied only to fertile, not all women. Finally, the permission for employers to accord pregnancy preferential treatment that is inferable from the first clause is sharply circumscribed. *Guerra* is reasonably clear that PDA does not mandate such treatment, and so does not require an employer to afford reasonable accommodation to pregnancy by offering *any* leaves, benefits or relaxed work assignments that it does not offer to employees with other disabilities.

Although the legislative history of PDA focused on the health and medical requirements of female employees, a majority of the Court has held that the amendment also prohibits employer-sponsored health insurance provisions that exclude spousal pregnancies and thereby offer male employees inferior total coverage than their female co-workers. PDA also proscribes discriminating against an employee for undergoing an abortion, either by terminating her employment or, apparently, denying her sick leave available for other medical disabilities. But PDA explicitly relieves employers from subsidizing abortions through health insurance benefits, except in cases of "medical complications" or "where the life of the mother would be endangered if the fetus were carried to term."

Courts are still exploring the full reaches of the medical conditions related to pregnancy with respect to which the PDA applies. In *International Union, U.A.W. v. Johnson Controls* (1991), the Supreme Court held prima facie violative of PDA employer policies precluding fertile women from holding certain jobs in which their fetuses would be exposed to workplace environment health risks. Employers justified these rules as necessary to protect employees' fetuses or offspring from health risks, or to protect the employer from tort liability in the event employees' fetuses or children suffered injury that could be traced to the workplace.

While PDA thus does not compel employers covered by Title VII to afford maternity leaves or benefits not provided for other disabilities, the Family & Medical Leave Act of 1993 requires employers with 50 or more employees to permit eligible employees, female and male alike, to take up to twelve weeks of unpaid leave per year after the birth or adoption of a child, as well as for serious health emergencies affecting the employee or his close relatives.

b. Fetal Vulnerability Rules

Because the fetal vulnerability rules are prima facie subject to PDA, they must be treated as a form of express gender discrimination that can survive scrutiny only if they pass muster under the BFOQ defense. That, however, is unlikely under traditional BFOQ standards, since protection of employees' offspring would not normally be essential to the operation of an employer's business. In order to uphold these rules as a matter of public policy or personal morality, courts sometimes modified the BFOQ requirements or permitted the policies to be defended as though they were neutral practices. EEOC also took the position that, even though the discrimination resulting from fetal protection policies is expressly gender based, employers should not be restricted to the BFOQ defense but should be permitted to justify those policies under the somewhat less stringent standard of "business necessity."

The Supreme Court in *Johnson Controls* definitively rejected these end-runs around the PDA, ruling that fetal protection policies exclude fertile women from employment opportunities on the basis of gender and are accordingly defensible only as BFOQs. Further, the Court stringently applied the BFOQ defense. In attempting to prove that fertile employees lacked essential job qualifications, employers had sought to justify their exclusion by invoking protection of the fetus. The Court held that the safety of an employee's fetus, as distinct from the safety of plant visitors or customers, is not essential to the operation of the employer's business in the sense meant by the BFOQ defense. Perhaps the broadest significance of *Johnson Controls* is its explication of dual requirements for any BFOQ. Not only must the employer's gender-, religion-or national origin-based exclusion substantially relate to the plaintiff's ability to perform her particular job; it must also go to the "essence" or "central mission" of the employer's business.

c. *Seniority Systems*

Two neutral practices are singled out for special treatment by the text of Title VII. Section 703(h) provides that "notwithstanding any other provision" of Title VII, an employer does not commit an unlawful employment practice by imposing different terms or conditions of employment pursuant to a bona fide seniority or merit system. The employer is immune from liability even if the effect or impact of these systems falls more heavily on the plaintiff's protected group. Judicial construction of these provisions, however, has afforded far greater protection for seniority and merit systems than for professionally developed ability tests.

Unless the plaintiff is able to prove that a seniority system was initially adopted or maintained with a specific discriminatory purpose, and is thus not "bona fide," a seniority system cannot be the basis of employer liability. And such a system is lawful even though it was first *adopted* after the enactment of Title VII. Absent proof of discriminatory purpose by the employer and union in adopting or maintaining such a system, § 703(h) insulates a bona fide seniority system from being declared an unlawful employment practice notwithstanding that it perpetuates underlying hiring, assignment or promotion discrimination that took place before or even after the effective date of Title VII. Thus, a bona fide system may not be dismantled wholesale by declaratory judgment or injunction. But where other, primary unlawful employment practices are proved—hiring, assignment, or promotion discrimination, for example—courts have the remedial authority in effect to adjust the system's seniority ladder incrementally by awarding retroactive seniority for bidding or other competitive purposes to proven victims of discrimination.

A system will not forfeit its status as bona fide merely because it has the effect of disproportionately "locking in" minority employees to lower paying or less skilled positions—for example, by discouraging them from transferring to better jobs in separate bargaining units where they might forfeit accumulated seniority with the company. The mere impact of the system does not, standing alone, demonstrate the requisite discriminatory purpose. Factors in assessing a system's bona fides include whether it discourages different protected groups equally from transferring between units; whether, if the seniority units are in separate bargaining units, the bargaining unit structure is rational and conforms to industry practice; whether the system has its "genesis" in prohibited discrimination; and whether subsequent negotiations that have maintained the system were tainted by unlawful motivation.

The Court has broadly interpreted the kinds of collectively bargained arrangements that qualify as "seniority systems" entitled to the special protection of § 703(h). For example, a requirement that an employee work for a specified time *before* entering the permanent employees' seniority ladder has itself was held to constitute part of a protected seniority system. On occasion, however, a plaintiff has succeeded in sidestepping § 703(h) by framing a challenge to an employer decision that is related to but distinct from the functioning of a seniority system.

The seniority system defense is bolstered in procedural ways as well. First, even though the structure and text of § 703(h) appear to create a true affirmative defense, the employer does not have to persuade the court that the system is bona fide. The employer is well advised to plead the defense affirmatively in its answer. But in response to a plaintiff's prima facie evidence that a facially neutral system had disproportionate adverse impact, the employer need only prove that the personnel decision in question was made pursuant to that system. To overcome the defense, the *plaintiff* must then prove by a preponderance of the evidence that the system is *not* bona fide. Second, the Supreme Court has held that trial court determinations about the adopters' intent—the ultimate issue on the bona fides of a seniority system—are unmixed findings of fact, reversible under Federal Rule of Civil Procedure 52(a) only if "clearly erroneous."

The Supreme Court's decision in Lorance v. AT & T Technologies (1989), held that the limitations period for a claim attacking the bona fides of a seniority system runs from the date a system is adopted, even if the plaintiff could not then have anticipated harm from the system or for that matter first became employed thereafter. Section 112 of the Civil Rights Act of 1991 overruled *Lorance* by providing statute of limitations accrual dates later than the original adoption of an intentionally discriminatory, collectively bargained seniority system. Where applicable, the limitations period on such a claim will now begin to run only when the plaintiff became subject to the system's challenged provision or, later still, when that provision was first applied to the plaintiff. This change aids attacks on seniority systems, but only on those that discriminate intentionally; the legislation leaves undisturbed the Court's holdings that a system's mere adverse effect on a group is immune from Title VII challenge.

d. *Professionally Developed Ability Tests*

Section 703(h) permits employers to act upon the results of a "professionally developed ability test." But in sharp contrast to the great deference shown seniority systems, the judicial protection accorded these tests has been inconsistent. In many cases it has proven even *more* difficult for an employer to defend the adverse impact of a paper-and-pencil test than to avoid liability for other neutral practices. This is because, soon after Title VII became effective, the EEOC issued "guidelines" on employee selection procedures that require employers to conduct highly technical and demanding "validation" studies of ability tests to demonstrate that they reliably pinpoint desired employee traits essential to a particular job. The Supreme Court's deferral to those guidelines in Albemarle Paper Co. v. Moody (1975) required employers to incur considerable expense in validation efforts before they could safely hinge employment decisions on the results of tests having significant differential adverse impact.

Lower courts have since somewhat eased validation requirements, holding that employers need not slavishly adhere to the difficult and complex EEOC guidelines. Instead employers may defend more generally with evidence that tests are "predictive of or significantly correlated with important elements of work behavior ... relevant to the job ... for which candidates are being evaluated." Contreras v. City of Los Angeles (9th Cir.1981). Nevertheless, even this version of the validation defense places a considerably greater burden on an employer than merely producing evidence that "a challenged practice serves, in a significant way," one of many possible "legitimate employment goals."

By its terms the Civil Rights Act of 1991, in an effort to restore the rigor of the defense, requires employers to justify the adverse impact of a particularly identified neutral practice by demonstrating the practice to be "job related for the position in question and consistent with business necessity." If the courts should abandon the relaxed scrutiny delineated by *Contreras* and hold professionally developed ability tests either to the new statutory standard or to strict compliance with the EEOC guidelines, employers would once again find it considerably more difficult to justify those tests than § 703(h) apparently intended. The 1991 amendments do not address validation standards in particular, but add a prohibition against the practice known as "race norming." The Act makes it unlawful in selecting, referring, or promoting employees to adjust or use different cutoff scores or otherwise alter test results because of race, color, religion, sex or national origin.

The Civil Rights Act of 1991 specifically forbids employers to use the employment related test in a way that would expand employment opportunities for minorities. Such tests have long been held unlawful when they disproportionately screen out applicants or employees on the basis of race, sex, religion or national origin and the employer cannot justify their use through a job-relatedness or business necessity defense. As a remedy for such violations, courts sometimes ordered employers not to fill vacancies on a rank-order basis but instead to fill them from among candidates with examination scores that fell within specified "bands" or ranges, in order to minimize the differential impact. The new legislation does not directly attack this judicial remedy, and indeed one section specifically reaffirms "court-ordered remedies, affirmative action, or conciliation agreements, that are in accordance with the law." Yet it adds a provision that makes it an unlawful employment practice for an employer itself "to adjust the scores of, use different cutoff scores for, or otherwise alter the results of, employment related tests" on any of the prohibited grounds of discrimination. Apparently, then, it is now specifically unlawful for an employer to do directly what a court may order it to do in order to offset the discriminatory effects of an employment related test.

3. RETALIATION

To protect employees who seek to vindicate their rights under § 703, a separate provision, § 704(a), broadly prohibits retaliation. Two basic species of conduct are protected: (1) participation in any administrative or judicial investigation, proceeding, or hearing to enforce Title VII rights; and (2) less formal, but good faith opposition to practices that an employee reasonably believes to be prohibited by the Act.

Once conduct is characterized as protected, the prima facie case is straightforward. The plaintiff must produce evidence of (1) her voluntary or involuntary participation in proceedings authorized by Title VII, or her opposition to what she reasonably and in good faith believes is one or more *apparently* prohibited practices (the practice opposed must be one "made an unlawful employment practice by" Title VII, although the plaintiff may prevail even if the employer was not in fact violating the statute); (2) her employer's awareness of her protected participation or opposition; (3) an adverse employment action thereafter; and (4) a causal connection between the adverse employment action and the protected opposition or participation. Evidence that the adverse action was taken shortly after the protected participation or opposition fortifies or perhaps suffices to show the required causal link; the passage of several years between the protected conduct and the act of alleged retaliation may defeat the inference of retaliatory motive; but the passage of a substantial period of time does not conclusively refute the possibility of the required causation. A plaintiff creates a jury question on causation with evidence, including circumstantial evidence, that the employer was aware of the protected activity or expression at the time it took the adverse action; and temporal proximity between the protected activity and the adverse action may permit the jury to find the required causal link.

In Clark County Sch. Dist. v. Breeden (2001), the Court carefully re-reviewed the timing of the protected conduct and the adverse job action and found that although the plaintiff was transferred one month after the decisionmaker learned of the filing of the lawsuit, plaintiff failed to satisfy the temporal nexus because the decisionmaker had discussed the possibility of transfer before she had knowledge of the suit. Plaintiff rebutted this evidence in her appellate reply brief with evidence that the decisionmaker knew of the filing of the EEOC charge, but the Court stressed the twenty month lapse of time between the charge and the transfer. "The cases that accept mere temporal proximity between an employer's knowledge of protected activity and an adverse employment action as sufficient evidence of causality to establish a prima facie case uniformly hold that the temporal proximity must be 'very close'.... Action taken (as here) 20 months later suggests, by itself, no causality at all."

Once the employee satisfies her prima facie burden, the resulting presumption of retaliation must be rebutted by the employer by producing evidence of a legitimate nondiscriminatory reason for the adverse employment action. If the employer meets this burden, the presumption of retaliation disappears, and the plaintiff must present evidence sufficient to prove to the fact finder that the reason proffered by the employer was a pretext for unlawful retaliation. Section 703(m), the "mixed motives" provision that relieves an employer of retroactive relief when it demonstrates that it would have taken the same action apart from an unlawful ground, includes among such grounds only "race, color, religion, sex, or national origin," with no mention of retaliation. Nevertheless, as discussed below, an employer may mount a mixed-motive defense to retaliation on the terms provided by § 703(m) or under pre-existing law.

The "opposition" right has been subject to a number of fact-sensitive qualifications, developed case by case, concerning the lawfulness or reasonableness of the manner and means of opposition. In McDonnell Douglas Corp. v. Green (1973), the Supreme Court wrote that employers are not required to "absolve" employees who engage in "unlawful activity against it." Employee protests that constitute both opposition to practices made unlawful by Title VII as well as violations of established, legitimate work rules have posed especially difficult problems. The linchpin is the "reasonableness" of the opposition; the law protects employees in the filing of formal charges of discrimination as well as in the making of informal protests of discrimination, "including making complaints to management, writing critical letters to customers, protesting against discrimination by industry or society in general, and expressing support of co-workers who have filed formal charges." But not all forms of protest are protected by Title VII's prohibition on retaliation. For instance, Title VII "does not constitute a license for employees to engage in physical violence in order to protest discrimination." When a court adjudges an employee's manner of opposition to have gone beyond what is necessary for effective protest—when, for example, she gratuitously embarrasses a superior—employee discipline will likely be upheld. Some circuits locate this principle in the prima facie case, the first step in the burden-shifting under *McDonnell Douglas*. For example, in Laughlin v. Metropolitan Washington Airports Authority (4th Cir.1998), the Fourth Circuit held "as a matter of law," that the plaintiff "did not engage in protected oppositional activity and, therefore, did not establish a prima facie case of retaliatory discharge." Other courts have treated unreasonable opposition activities as the employer's legitimate nondiscriminatory reason for the adverse employment action.

By contrast, the "participation" protection, designed to assure free access to the administrative and judicial bodies empowered to investigate and adjudicate Title VII violations, is virtually unlimited in scope. Just as an "opposing" plaintiff's underlying informal complaint need not have been in fact well founded under § 703 to support a claim of unlawful retaliation under § 704, so a "participating" plaintiff need not have prevailed in the proceeding initiated by her formal charge or lawsuit. Indeed it has been held that an employer's unilateral view that an employee lied in the EEOC charge documents cannot justify retaliatory action against him. In

Clover v. Total System Services, Inc. (11th Cir.1999) the Eleventh Circuit announced a seemingly broad standard for the activity constituting protected "participation." Plaintiff's responses to questions directed at her during an employer internal investigation prompted by a co-employee's filing of a charge with EEOC was recognized as participation "in any manner in an investigation ... under this subchapter." However, the Eleventh Circuit also held that participation in an employer's internal investigation that is prompted only by internal complaints and not an EEOC charge is not protected activity. EEOC v. Total System Services, Inc. (11th Cir.2000).

A plaintiff asserting that he was retaliated against for having filed an EEOC charge generally need not file a distinct retaliation charge with EEOC or otherwise exhaust administrative remedies before suing for retaliation in federal court. Such retaliation is actionable even if it occurs after dismissal of the plaintiff's EEOC charge. At least one circuit reads a reasonableness requirement into the participation clause as well as the opposition clause.

Section 704 in terms protects only "employees or applicants," unlike § 703's embrace of "any individual." Most courts that have considered the question have nevertheless concluded that even a former employee may maintain a claim of retaliation, and even for post-employment conduct. The classic example would be negative references of blacklisting by a former employer advising a prospective employer that she had filed an EEOC charge against it. The Supreme Court has now confirmed that former employees do enjoy protection against retaliation. But the retaliation against the ex-employee must usually impair an existing or subsequent prospective employment relationship.

Retaliation charges may be based on the manner in which an employer defends a charge or complaint of discrimination.

Employer investigations of sexual or racial harassment undertaken to claim the affirmative defense authorized by *Faragher* and *Burlington* may also be "an investigation ... under this subchapter" in which participants are protected from retaliation. Similarly, the "after-acquired evidence" doctrine that limits a plaintiff's relief when an employer discovers after-the-fact information that would have led it to terminate the plaintiff on lawful grounds encourages employers to investigate plaintiff misconduct that occurred during employment after a charge or complaint has been filed.

Despite language in § 704 that appears to limit protection to those who have opposed or participated personally, the Sixth Circuit has upheld the legal sufficiency of a retaliation claim by an employee whose co-employee protested on his behalf, EEOC v. Ohio Edison Co. (6th Cir.1993) and the Eighth Circuit has upheld a retaliation claim brought by a husband who supported his wife's wage discrimination suit. Broadus v. OK Industries, Inc. (8th Cir.2001). In any event, the plaintiff may state a claim for retaliation based on his own association with members of racial minorities, Maynard v. City of San Jose (9th Cir.1994), women or because he was required by his employer to discriminate against others. Moyo v. Gomez (9th Cir.1994). Courts are divided over the standing of plaintiffs to complain of retaliation based on discrimination practiced against other employees with whom the plaintiffs are associated or wish to associate.

In the past several years the circuits have more critically scrutinized the element of a material adverse employment action. It seems clear that the adverse employment action necessary to support a retaliation claim is not equivalent to the tangible employment action (which inflicts direct economic harm and must involve an official act by the company) necessary to support a quid-pro-quo sexual harassment claim. There are, however, no bright line rules, and the courts must assess in each case if plaintiff suffered a material adverse change in the terms or conditions of employment. The decisions range from an apparent insistence that pay itself be diminished to the suggestion at the other extreme that a transfer to a higher paying position could in certain circumstances constitute unlawful retaliation. It is widely accepted that purely lateral transfers do not constitute an adverse employment action; if, however, the court perceives the transfer as equivalent to a demotion, the court will find actionable retaliation. The circuits are split on whether negative employment evaluations alone can support a claim of retaliation. In general, EEOC interprets the relevant statutory language as prohibiting any adverse treatment that rises above petty slights or trivial annoyances. The degree of harm, EEOC believes, goes to the issue of damages, not liability. But in the circuit opinions, it is difficult to discern any clear line dividing employer actions deemed sufficiently adverse and those that are not. In the majority of the circuits, adverse employment actions are not, however, merely limited to ultimate employment decisions, and retaliatory harassment or co-worker hostility may, if sufficiently severe, support a retaliation claim.

Most circuits treat the "mixed motive" provisions of § 107 of the Civil Rights Act of 1991 as inapplicable to retaliation, with the consequence that a retaliation plaintiff may have no remedy whatsoever. These opinions note that on its face § 107 amends only § 703, the main Title VII discrimination prohibition, and not § 704. Consequently, in these circuits, an employer shown to have acted against the plaintiff in part from a retaliatory motive can avoid liability altogether—even for prospective relief and attorney's fees—if it can carry the burden of demonstrating that it would have imposed the same employment detriment for one or more lawful reasons.

4. CONSTRUCTIVE DISCHARGE

Closely related to but distinguishable from environmental harassment and retaliation is the doctrine of constructive discharge. In essence, the claim avails an employee whose departure is in form voluntary but who in fact was virtually compelled to quit as the result of discriminatory job terms or harassment extreme in significance, duration or offensiveness. The consequence of establishing the claim is a broader remedy: the plaintiff who succeeds will be eligible for an order directing reinstatement as well as available monetary relief.

At a minimum the claim requires the standard showing that the plaintiff's involuntary resignation was caused by differential, unwelcome and intolerable treatment unlawful because based on her race, sex, religion, national origin or age. Evidence that the plaintiff would have resigned for independent personal reasons or work-related reasons unconnected with substantial, aggravated discrimination breaks the causal connection and therefore defeats the constructive discharge claim. This is akin to the same-decision showing which, under *Price Waterhouse*, sufficed to avoid employer liability altogether and today, under the Civil Rights Act of 1991, still limits available relief. The date of the forced resignation triggers the running of the applicable 180–or 300–day administrative charge filing period.

The element that has generated the most litigation centers on the reasonableness of the employee's decision to quit in relation to particular unlawful employer conduct. The decisions are uniform that an employee has been constructively discharged when the termination results from intolerable working conditions that the employer created with the specific intent of forcing the employee to resign. Some circuits have considered evidence of subjective intent, or of "aggravating circumstances," indispensable to constructive discharge. The

Supreme Court, however, in formally approving the doctrine for the first time, has recently articulated a purely "objective" formulation previously endorsed by other circuits: the plaintiff must prove working conditions so intolerable that a reasonable person would have felt compelled to resign. Pennsylvania State Police v. Suders (2004). The Court specifically observed that this standard for constructive discharge is more stringent than what is required to prove a case of hostile racial or sexual environmental harassment: a showing of offending behavior sufficiently severe or pervasive to alter the victim's employment conditions and create an abusive working environment. The plaintiff who alleges that constructive discharge resulted from the creation of a hostile environment must therefore make both those showings. Because the employer conduct that gives rise to colorable claims of constructive discharge is usually extreme or persistent, those claims are often joined with companion claims under state law for such torts as outrage or intentional infliction of emotional distress.

Most acts of discrimination are such that a "reasonable" employee should stay on the job; oppose the employer practice informally or by filing a charge; and trust in the efficacy of the separate § 704 protection against retaliation. Classic instances include wage discrimination, nonpromotion, or assignment to less attractive or lucrative (but not intolerably demeaning) positions. At the other end of the spectrum, where the prospects of proving constructive discharge are much improved, lie the "aggravating circumstances" sometimes required to meet the objective test of "intolerable" working conditions. These include subjecting the plaintiff to repeated slurs, assigning him especially demeaning work for unlawful discriminatory reasons, or subjecting him to egregious, unrelenting, and unremedied harassment. Sexual harassment in particular has served as a predicate for constructive discharge but is not necessarily sufficiently severe to meet a particular circuit's test. In one decision, an employee who was subjected to shift changes, public berating, and demeaning job assignments for reporting apparent sexual harassment directed against a co-employee established constructive discharge, even though the retaliation lasted only three weeks. Rupp v. Purolator (10th Cir.1994). On occasion, "objective test" courts have dispensed with the necessity of aggravating circumstances, ruling that a "single non-trivial incident of discrimination" may suffice to make resignation reasonable. Between the polar extremes are situations where the plaintiff is subjected to "unreasonably exacting standards of job performance"; one court announced a virtual presumption that an employee with this complaint cannot reasonably resign, or else the courts would be undermining employer insistence on high standards.

The employee must therefore make a critical decision, usually without benefit of counsel, concerning how to respond to varied employer actions. If racial slurs are so offensive or repeated that an employee who quit over them would later be deemed by a court to have acted reasonably, the employee could safely quit or take the lesser measure of remaining on the job and demanding an apology. If he keeps working but his demand leads to his discharge, he might well have a claim for retaliation in violation of § 704. But if he overestimates the seriousness or offensiveness of the employer's discrimination and quits, he may find that his only remedy is back pay from the time of the underlying discrimination until the date of his "voluntary" termination.

Employers in constructive discharge cases growing out of sexual harassment may invoke the *Burlington/Faragher* two–pronged defense unless the employee quit because of the implications of a tangible adverse term or condition of employment. *Suders* (2004). That is, the employer may avoid liability if by a preponderance of the evidence it carries *both* elements of the following affirmative defense: "(a) that the employer exercised reasonable care to prevent and correct promptly any sexually harassing behavior, and (b) that the plaintiff employee unreasonably failed to take advantage of any corrective opportunities provided by the employer or to avoid harm otherwise."

5. UNION LIABILITY

Labor unions are not excluded from the general definition of "employer," and consequently may be liable for violations of § 703(a) on the same terms as any other employer. In addition, § 703(c) declares distinct unlawful practices applicable to labor organizations alone. One, found in § 703(c)(3), is to "cause or attempt to cause an employer" to discriminate in violation of § 703. Another, declared by § 703(c)(2), is to rely on prohibited grounds in segregating or classifying union members or applicants, or in failing to refer individuals for employment, so as to deprive them of employment opportunities. Finally, wholly apart from any effect on employment opportunities, labor organizations are prohibited by § 703(c)(1) from excluding applicants from membership or otherwise discriminating against them. Construing this last prohibition quite broadly, the Supreme Court has held that a union commits an unlawful employment practice by refusing to file race-bias grievances presented by black members, even when it does so in order to avoid antagonizing the employer and in turn to improve its chances of success on other collective bargaining issues, and even though the percentage of all types of grievances filed on behalf of black members is proportional to their representation in the union. Courts typically find that a union violates Title VII when it breaches it duty to provide fair representation on the basis of race, color, religion, sex, or national origin.

Unions may also be liable for retaliation under § 704. For example, a union that refused to process race discrimination grievances under a collective bargaining contract whenever the would-be grievant had a charge pending against the union with a state or federal antidiscrimination agency was found to have violated Title VII. Liability attached even though the union processed other grievances as fairly for black as for white members and claimed that its policy was compelled by the employer. Johnson v. Palma (7th Cir.1992).

Whether an international can be held liable for the acts of a local depends on whether the local was acting as an agent for the international. Common law agency principles determine whether such a relationship exists. If the local engages in illegal conduct in furtherance of its role as an agent of the international, the international will be liable for the local's actions. However, if the local exercises considerable autonomy in conducting its affairs, it cannot be regarded as an agent of the international, and the international accordingly cannot be held liable under an agency theory for the local's actions.

CHAPTER 19

TITLE VII MODES OF PROOF, ADMINISTRATIVE PROCEDURES, AND REMEDIES

The most critical and frequently litigated questions under Title VII concern the theories on which liability may be predicated and the corresponding modes of proof. In general, there are two generic forms of employer conduct actionable under Title VII. First, there are a variety of forms of intentional discrimination or "disparate treatment"; a broad legislative and social consensus supports imposing liability on employers when such conduct can be proved. More controversial is employer liability for "neutral," that is facially nondiscriminatory, work practices that have greater adverse statistical impact on members of the plaintiff's protected group than on others. Liability imposed in such circumstances is denoted by the terms "disproportionate adverse impact" or "disparate impact." Distinct proof modes have been developed to provide guidance to judges and juries in determining liability under each of these theories. Each mode presents its own conceptual and practical difficulties, and these in turn have generated a burgeoning body of judicial decisions. It should be noted that particular employer practices may implicate two or more modes of proof.

A. INDIVIDUAL DISPARATE TREATMENT— "DIRECT" EVIDENCE

1. IN GENERAL

The most obvious way of showing an unlawful employment practice is to offer "evidence that can be interpreted as an acknowledgment of discriminatory intent by the defendant or its agents." Troupe v. May Dep't Stores Co. (7th Cir.1994). Examples include epithets or slurs uttered by an authorized agent of the employer, a decisionmaker's admission that he would or did act against the plaintiff because of his or her protected characteristic, or, even more clearly, an employer policy framed squarely in terms of race, sex, religion, or national origin. When produced, such "direct" evidence will without more ordinarily suffice to show that an adverse employment condition, or limitation on an employment opportunity, was imposed "because of" the plaintiff's protected group characteristic—that is discrimination is presumed from the admission of evidence deemed "direct." Circuit opinions sometimes define direct evidence as evidence that, if believed, would prove the existence of the fact without inferences or presumption. Others subscribe to an "animus" position that deems any kind of evidence "direct" if it is tied to, that is directly reflects, the alleged discriminatory animus. This approach is hospitable to circumstantial evidence, but excludes evidence of "stray" remarks not sufficiently tied to the challenged decision as to shed light on the employer agent's intention in making it. Still other circuits, the "animus plus" courts, have insisted not just on evidence of animus but also that the statements reflecting the animus bear squarely on the contested employment decision. Under any of these formulations, it appears that statements weakly proved or inherently ambiguous cannot be considered "direct" for the purpose of relieving a plaintiff from proving the elements of inferential, *McDonnell Douglas* proof.

Even if courts refuse to characterize particular evidence as direct, the same evidence may sometimes fortify the inferential *McDonnell Douglas* prima facie case. Moreover, the Supreme Court's decision, discussed below, in *Desert Palace v. Costa* (2003) reduces the significance of the "direct"/"indirect" classification by allowing a plaintiff to cast the burden of the "mixed-motive" showing on a defendant regardless of the nature of a plaintiff's prima facie case.

Despite the remaining importance of the question, there remains rampant disagreement and confusion in the appellate decisions concerning what prima facie evidence is "direct." It is even sometimes difficult to determine whether an employer policy may be said to discriminate expressly or facially on the basis of race, color, sex, religion or national origin. In the notorious *Gilbert* decision that prompted Congress to spank the Court by enacting the Pregnancy Discrimination Act of 1978, the Court held that an employer rule that denied disability benefits for pregnancy but no other physical conditions did not discriminate "because of gender" within the meaning of § 703. General Elec. Co. v. Gilbert (1976). The rule, the Court explained, treated pregnant women differently, relative to benefits, not only from men but also from nonpregnant women. The rule therefore did not draw a distinction on the basis of gender, even though its sting was felt only by women.

By the same reasoning, the practice of excluding fertile women from working in areas where they will encounter sufficient lead exposure to endanger a fetus or potential fetus might be conceived of as not predicated on gender: it, too, treats fertile women differently not only from all men but also from nonfertile women. Yet the Supreme Court, evidently chastened by the legislative overruling of the result in *Gilbert*, viewed such a practice as expressly gender discriminatory, observing that the adverse effects of the practice fell 100% on women. International Union, UAW v. Johnson Controls, Inc. (1991). Similarly, an employer or union requirement that a new applicant be related by blood or marriage to an existing employee or union member, while neutral in form, may result in the absolute exclusion of members of a protected group that historically was systematically excluded through intentional discrimination. Such practices have been viewed on occasion as instances of express, egregious discrimination. In other words, practices that are formally neutral may be analyzed as intentional disparate treatment when their adverse impact is not merely substantial but absolute, or put otherwise, when they correlate to a very high degree with exclusion of a group protected by Title VII.

Unsurprisingly, outside the realm of policies that discriminate by their clear terms on the basis of a protected characteristic, cases presenting smoking-gun exemplars of "direct," "express" or "facial" evidence are relative rarities. Three decades after the effective date of Title VII employers are familiar with the requirements and penalties of the statute and consequently more apt to comply or better skilled in disguising noncompliance. In Price Waterhouse v. Hopkins (1989) (plurality opinion and opinion of O'Connor, J.), the Supreme Court has treated employers' agents' statements reflecting stereotypical views of women as direct evidence of gender discrimination, even when the views expressed bear somewhat tangentially on the plaintiff's capacity to perform the core elements of the position.

Justice O'Connor's concurring opinion sets out three prerequisites for employer speech to constitute "direct" evidence: the remarks must be by the applicable decision maker, be related to the decision process, and not "stray." In practice, however, this standard gives rise to multiple, interrelated issues. At a minimum, for plaintiff's evidence to be deemed "direct"—thus enabling her to avoid the difficult evidentiary requirements of the inferential *McDonnell Douglas*/*St. Mary's* mode of proof—the statements she relies on must have been made by the person who made the adverse employment decision of which she complains, by someone with power to make effective recommendations to that decisionmaker, or by someone in the control group to which that decisionmaker belongs. Second, the content of the statement or statements, together with the context in which they were made, must suggest to the trier of fact that the decisionmaker in fact relied on the bias those statements reflect in making the decision in question. For this reason statements made by or to the decisionmaker in connection with the making of the decision at issue are treated as far more probative of prohibited discrimination than those made by the decisionmaker or others at times remote or on matters unrelated to the employment decision plaintiff is challenging. And evidence of the bias of a subordinate is relevant where the ultimate decisionmaker is not insulated from the subordinate's influence.

There remains considerable uncertainty about how to differentiate those gender-or age-related comments or conduct that amount to "direct" evidence of discrimination and therefore, standing alone, create a prima facie case, from merely "isolated" incidents or "stray" remarks. Even though slurs and stereotypes are sometimes treated as "direct" evidence of discriminatory intent, their real meaning or purpose may be equivocal. The frequent ambiguity of language and intent lends support to Judge Posner's observation that perhaps the "only true direct evidence of intent that will ever be available" consists of outright litigation admissions or policies that discriminate by their own terms on grounds prohibited by the statute. Troupe v. May Dep't Stores (7th Cir.1994).

Even if such comments are accepted as "direct" evidence of discrimination, the plaintiff may also have to prove that the attitudes they reflect played at least a motivating part in the employment decision under challenge. Discrimination "in the air," that is, must be brought to ground, lest Title VII be used as a mechanism for controlling pure thought or speech. To do so the plaintiff must show first that a discriminatory attitude was to some degree actually relied on by the relevant decision-maker. In one decision, for example, Chief Judge Posner wrote for a panel, "Discrimination is not preference or aversion; it is acting on the preference or aversion." EEOC v. Consolidated Serv. Systems (7th Cir.1993). For this reason, he concluded, an employer who would prefer to exclude members of national origin groups other than his own does not violate Title VII even if the employment practice in question (there, word-of-mouth hiring) brings about that result, so long as the practice is motivated only by other reasons, e.g., efficiency. Similarly, a statement attributable to management or even a sign on the employer's premises expressing a disinclination to hire members of a protected group probably does not by itself violate Title VII, although it would violate the fair employment laws of some states and municipalities. Of course, to bring a prejudicial statement to actionable territory the plaintiff must also show that the difference in treatment adversely affected a term or condition of the plaintiff's employment.

The tendency of appellate court decisions to strain against labeling evidence "direct" may be moderated by a Supreme Court decision that should substantially aid plaintiffs in surviving motions for summary judgment or judgment as a matter of law in cases presenting evidence of slurs or other derogatory references to the abilities or characteristics of the members of plaintiff's protected group. In Reeves v. Sanderson Plumbing Products, Inc. (2000), the Court, in reversing an appellate court's grant of judgment as a matter of law pursuant to Federal Rule of Civil Procedure 50, wrote that the lower court impermissibly supplanted the jury's judgment about the weight of the evidence. In particular, it criticized the appellate court for failing to draw all reasonable inferences in plaintiff's favor on the question of whether the slur utterer was the actual decisionmaker and for discounting the decisionmaker's age-related comments on the ground that they were not made directly in the context of plaintiff's termination.

Even more than *Reeves*, the Supreme Court's decision in Desert Palace v. Costa (2003), should ultimately reduce the debates over whether to classify evidence of discrimination as "direct" or "indirect." The Court held that regardless of whether a plaintiff used "direct" or "indirect" evidence to demonstrate prima facie that the employer relied in part on an unlawful reason, a Title VII plaintiff may obtain an instruction requiring the defendant to persuade that it would have made the same employment decision for an independent lawful reason. *Desert Palace* thus treats as immaterial the purported direct-indirect distinction in deciding the very issue for which the distinction was principally devised and used. Accordingly, whatever the pre-*Desert Palace* definitions of "direct" evidence, plaintiffs can now impose the same-decision limited defense on defendants in mixed-motive cases either by establishing the *McDonnell Douglas* prima facie case and persuading the fact finder that defendant's legitimate nondiscriminatory reasons are unworthy of credence, or by demonstrating through other evidence that a discriminatory reason more likely than not motivated the defendant in imposing the adverse term or condition of employment. On the one hand, therefore, plaintiff may not be compelled to invoke the *McDonnell Douglas* proof mode and presumption; but on the other, if she does, she suffers no legal disadvantage relative to the plaintiff who has proceeded with evidence heretofore labeled as "direct."

2. THE "BFOQ" AFFIRMATIVE DEFENSE

Section 703(e)(1) affords an employer its only defense to policies or work rules that expressly or facially discriminate in hiring; and the defense is available only to discrimination on the basis of gender, religion or national origin. It authorizes the employer to "hire and employ," and a labor organization or joint labor management committee to "admit or employ" to membership or apprenticeship or retraining programs, on the basis of gender, religion or national origin, when that group status is a "bona fide occupational qualification ['BFOQ'] reasonably necessary to the normal operation" of the enterprise. It does not excuse discrimination in post-hire terms and conditions of employment—compensation, promotion, discipline, harassment or discharge. See EEOC v. Fremont Christian School (9th Cir.1986). Nor does it defend against any discrimination on the basis of race. ADEA contains a similarly worded BFOQ defense, and the Court has construed the corresponding provisions of the two statutes virtually identically. See, e.g., Western Air Lines, Inc. v. Criswell (1985).

As its text would suggest, BFOQ is a true affirmative defense which the employer therefore has the burden of pleading and proving by a preponderance of the evidence. Still, the language of § 703(e)(1) would appear satisfied if an employer could show that a refusal to hire based on religion, sex, or national origin is reasonably necessary to the normal operation of the defendant's overall business. Yet in order to prevent the exception from virtually eliminating an applicant's protection against these forms of express discrimination, the Supreme Court has required the employer to show that its discriminatory rule relates to a trait that goes to the "essence" of the enterprise, *and* that the rule bears a "high correlation" to the plaintiff's ability to perform her particular job. *Johnson Controls.*

The two basic elements of the defense derive from a pair of decisions of the former Fifth Circuit, Diaz v. Pan American World Airways, Inc. (5th Cir.1971) and Weeks v. Southern Bell Telephone & Telegraph Company (5th Cir.1969). *Diaz* insisted that the job qualification or employee trait for which the employer's practice or policy screens must be closely related to the "essence" of the business. Thus the psychological reassurance or sexual titillation ostensibly afforded airline passengers by a requirement that flight attendants be female could not justify the exclusion of males once the court defined the essence of the business as safe transportation rather than maximum profit. And employers may not define the essence of their business as maximizing profit, because then customer preference—often the embodiment of the very kind of accumulated prejudice or stereotype Title VII seeks to overcome—could be invoked to justify a vast range of expressly discriminatory rules. Fernandez v. Wynn Oil Co. (9th Cir.1981).

Weeks added the second layer. Even if an exclusion of members of a particular protected group is designed to enhance execution of a function critical to the business, the employer's evidence must demonstrate that "all or substantially all" members of the excluded group lack the required trait and would therefore be unable adequately to perform the job in question. The defense would therefore still work for the positions of sperm donor and wet nurse. But the *Weeks* test will doom many BFOQ defenses rooted in the assertion that only members of a particular gender have the strength or endurance required by the job.

An early Supreme Court decision, still good law on its extreme facts, upheld the exclusion of women from contact positions as guards in unusually dangerous maximum security prisons in Alabama, even though the state failed to offer evidence that substantially all of the women who would seek those jobs would be incapable of maintaining order and safety.

The Court merely hypothesized that women guards would be attacked because they were women—skipping over the fact that *all* guards in the Alabama maximum security system were targets simply because they were despised authority symbols. Dothard v. Rawlinson (1977).

But the Court's decision in *Johnson Controls* confirmed the narrowness of the BFOQ defense. The employer's rule barred all still-fertile women of any age, marital status, or child-bearing inclination from holding a job in which they would likely be exposed to levels of lead that endangered the health of a fetus they might be carrying. Relying on the "occupational" limitation in § 703(e)(1), the Court concluded that the defense fails unless the employer demonstrates objectively that the exclusion is not only "reasonably necessary" to the "normal operation" of the "particular" business but also relates to "job-related skills and aptitudes." The Court rejected the defense because, so far as the record revealed, "Fertile women ... participate in the manufacture of batteries as efficiently as anyone else." Distinguishing *Dothard*, the Court wrote that third-party safety concerns had figured in the BFOQ analysis there only because inmate safety "went to the core of the employee's job performance"—something demonstrably not the case with batterymaking.

Johnson Controls also restricted the employer's option to skirt *Weeks* by showing only that some, rather than "substantially all" members of the excluded group lack traits essential to the job and business when it is "impracticable" to ascertain the other members of the group who do. When the two BFOQ requirements, refined by *Johnson Controls*, are combined, the defendant faces a formidable task: "An employer must direct its concerns about a woman's ability to perform her job safely and efficiently to those aspects of the woman's job-related activities that fall within the 'essence' of the particular business."

Given the stringency of the BFOQ defense, its principal remaining utility may lie in resisting claims of age discrimination, especially where an employee's deteriorating physical capabilities correlate strongly with aging and would impair safe hands-on performance. See Usery v. Tamiami Trail Tours, Inc. (5th Cir.1976). It is unlikely that the BFOQ defense could justify a slur, as opposed to an employer policy. Lower courts have, however, upheld relaxed applications of the defense to accommodate a legitimate business need to assure customer privacy. Healey v. Southwood Psychiatric Hosp. (3d Cir.1996). Moreover, EEOC guidelines relax the rules where employers have an interest in the gender-authenticity of such employees as actresses, actors, strippers, and food and drink servers at restaurants or bars where a primary job and business function is the projection of a sexually provocative display. See 29 C.F.R. § 1604.2 (1979) (actors and actresses). Finally, the Supreme Court has dispensed altogether with the necessity of a BFOQ showing to justify otherwise permissible "benign," "voluntary" employer affirmative action programs favoring women. Johnson v. Transportation Agency (1987).

B. INDIVIDUAL DISPARATE TREATMENT— INFERENTIAL PROOF

1. IN GENERAL

Because direct evidence of intent has been so rarely accepted, courts have recognized alternative ways of establishing unlawful discrimination. Circumstantial evidence may be classified into three types which, alone or in reinforcing combination, may suffice to show intentional discrimination forbidden by Title VII.

First there is suspicious timing, ambiguous statements, or other behavior toward or comments directed at other employees in the protected group from which an inference of discriminatory intent might be drawn.

Second is evidence, statistical or anecdotal, that persons outside the plaintiff's protected group, otherwise similarly situated to the plaintiff, were treated differently with respect to the relevant terms and conditions of employment. This of course is the essence of disparate treatment, but plaintiffs should take care that their "comparator" is in fact similarly situated from the standpoint of status or conduct. In one appellate decision, the court in effect viewed the Hispanic plaintiff laid off in a force reduction as a member of a (white) racial group, rather than as representing a particular national origin. Accordingly, it compared him not to non-Hispanics, who fared well in the force reduction, but to African–American employees, none of whom was terminated. Jackson v. E.J. Brach Corp. (7th Cir.1999). A pair of contemporaneous circuit decisions illustrate through comparator evidence the unlawfulness of differential race-based job assignments—in one case driven by actual customer preference, in the other by stereotypical assumptions about managerial effectiveness. Ferrill v. Parker Group, Inc. (11th Cir.1999); Johnson v. Zema Sys. Corp. (7th Cir.1999).

The third, or "pretext" mode, is perhaps most easily understood as an even more indirect way of showing the second, or "comparative" mode. This method of proving "individual disparate treatment" owes its origin to McDonnell Douglas Corp. v. Green (1973), and was later elaborated in several other Supreme Court decisions culminating in Texas Dep't of Community Affairs v. Burdine (1981), and St. Mary's Honor Ctr. v. Hicks (1993). The plaintiff makes a *McDonnell Douglas prima facie* showing in a failure to hire case—and thereby survives a Federal Rule of Civil Procedure 41(b) involuntary dismissal motion, or, in the jury trials authorized by the Civil Rights Act of 1991, a Rule 50(a)(1) motion for judgment as a matter of law at the close of her case in chief—by offering evidence that she (1) belongs to a protected group; (2) applied for or continued to desire the position in question; (3) met minimum uniform qualifications to receive or retain the position at the time of the adverse action; and (4) was rejected, and thereafter the employer continued to receive applications from persons having the complainant's qualifications. This evidence, the Court has explained, eliminates several of the most common nondiscriminatory reasons for the plaintiff's failure to be hired (or other rejection, nonpromotion, discipline or discharge) and thus makes it more likely that the employer's real reason, or one of them, was a status protected by Title VII. In brief, when a qualified employee who is a member of a racial minority traditionally victimized by workplace discrimination is not hired for a vacant job, the failure to hire alone suffices to raise an inference of discrimination, which the employer must then rebut by producing evidence of a legitimate, nondiscriminatory reason.

The elements, as the Court in *McDonnell Douglas* noted, are flexibly adapted to the facts of a given case. For example, the first of the numbered prima facie elements is *pro forma*—anyone, even a white male, can claim protected group status by contrasting himself in racial, religious, national origin, or gender terms to the group he claims was preferred. Further, an employee complaining of promotion denial need not show element (2), that she applied for the higher position, if it was the employer's routine practice to offer promotions to persons with her seniority and position. Loyd v. Phillips Bros., Inc. (7th Cir.1994). In general, however, courts read *McDonnell Douglas* to require a plaintiff to allege that she applied for a specific position for which she was rejected, rather than merely asserting that from time to time she requested promotion at large. Dotson v. Delta Consol. Industries, Inc. (8th Cir.2001). But a number of circuits have relieved plaintiffs of submitting a formal application for a particular position where the position was not posted, there was no formal application mechanism, and the employee had no knowledge of the position or applied informally for a specific position in a manner endorsed by the employer. The third element, qualifications for the position sought, has the greatest practical importance, as it eliminates the most common nondiscriminatory reason for rejection where an application for hire or promotion has been made. The Court has now declared relatively clearly that this showing refers to minimal or absolute rather than relative or comparative qualifications. Patterson v. McLean Credit Union (1989). The final element, sometimes relaxed or waived by lower courts, is evidence that the employer, after rejecting the plaintiff, continued to seek applicants with her general qualifications and/or selected a person from outside her protected group. In rehiring cases, the plaintiff need not show that he was identically situated with others of a different race who were initially terminated or who resigned at the same time; it suffices that the plaintiff's former position was filled by a member of a different race or simply that he was qualified for the new job for which he was rejected. Talley v. Bravo Pitino Restaurant, Ltd. (6th Cir.1995); Richardson v. Leeds Police Dep't (11th Cir.1995).

Accepting the Supreme Court's invitation to modify the basic template for differing circumstances, the circuit courts have adapted the *McDonnell Douglas* failure-to-hire elements to meet the realities of claims alleging unlawful discharge, promotion, discipline, and unequal pay. In an age discrimination case, the Court itself held unanimously that a terminated plaintiff need not invariably show that he was replaced by someone outside the protected class—there, someone younger than 40—so long as he was replaced by someone sufficiently younger as to generate a plausible inference that age was a determinative factor. O'Connor v. Consolidated Coin Caterers

Corp. (1996). This is consistent with the approach *McDonnell Douglas* itself took in failure-to-hire situations, where the Court never described element (4)—the employer continued to seek applications from qualified persons after plaintiff's rejection—as requiring evidence that the employer hired, or by implication replaced plaintiff with, someone outside plaintiff's protected class. Such a requirement would preclude otherwise meritorious claims by a woman or minority deemed too feminist or assertive, provided their replacement was another woman or minority member; it would also doom claims against employers who replace the plaintiff with another member of her group solely in order to avoid the consequences of threatened or actual litigation.

Circuit courts have followed suit, generally listing the required prima facie elements in a termination case as follows: (1) plaintiff belongs to a protected class (a requirement that can be met under the right circumstances by anyone, even a white male); (2) plaintiff possessed the absolute, or minimum uniformly required qualifications for the job she held; (3) despite those qualifications, she was discharged; and (4) the job was not eliminated after the discharge. Significantly, element (4) does not require the plaintiff, except perhaps a nonwhite plaintiff alleging race discrimination, to show that her job was filled by a person outside her protected group. Thus, the termination plaintiff usually satisfies element (4) simply by producing evidence that the employer had a continuing need for someone to perform the plaintiff's work, or, even more clearly, that the employer in fact filled plaintiff's former position, but not necessarily with someone from another protected class.

On the other hand, in cases where an employer alleges and the court agrees that plaintiff's termination was part of a classic, true reduction in force ("RIF"), i.e., where the plaintiff was not replaced, "it would make no sense to require a

plaintiff to show the position from which she had been terminated 'remained open'." One circuit modifies plaintiff's burden in that situation by substituting for the "remain open"
requirement a showing that similarly situated employees not
members of plaintiff's protected class were treated more favorably. Bellaver v. Quanex Corp. (7th Cir.2000) (part of alternative holding). A plaintiff might carry that burden, in turn,
with evidence that a non-protected class member was given
plaintiff's work or a purportedly "riffed" non-protected class
member was moved to another job with the employer. Thorn
v. Sundstrand Aerospace Corp. (7th Cir.2000). But a replacement employee's work performance following a RIF is irrelevant to the critical question whether management had an
economic or unlawful discriminatory motive at the time of
terminating the plaintiff. Cullen v. Olin Corp. (7th Cir.1999).

   In failure to promote cases, the circuit opinions more often
insist than in termination cases that plaintiff prove as part of
the prima facie case that the successful promotee is not a
member of plaintiff's protected class. Typical formulations of
the prima facie elements require plaintiff to adduce evidence
that (1) he is a protected group member; (2) he was qualified
and applied for the promotion; (3) he was then rejected despite
those qualifications; and (4) equally or less qualified employees, not members of plaintiff's protected class, were promoted.
Some opinions purport to trace the requirement that the
promotee be outside plaintiff's protected group to the Supreme Court's opinion in *McDonnell Douglas*; in fact, as at
least one court has noted, the High Court's actual language
merely demands evidence that after the rejection, "the position remained open and the employer continued to seek applicants from persons of complainant's qualifications." *McDonnell Douglas*. Recognizing this, a minority of the circuits
treating the question streamline the prima facie promotion
denial case, requiring evidence only that the plaintiff be a

protected group member, an unsuccessful applicant for a position for which he was qualified, and thereafter the employer continued to seek applicants. Mauro v. Southern New England Telecommunications, Inc. (2d Cir.2000) (citing Brown v. Coach Stores, Inc. (2d Cir.1998)).

The Title VII prima facie case of sex-based wage or salary discrimination is in most circuits more exacting than the required counterpart demonstration under the Equal Pay Act. Like the EPA plaintiff, the Title VII plaintiff must show that she is paid less for performing substantially comparable work to that performed by one or more members of the opposite gender. That showing suffices for a form of strict prima facie liability under EPA. In a Title VII action, however, the plaintiff must also offer at least inferential evidence, per *McDonnell Douglas*, that the salary shortfall is a product of the employer's intentional discrimination against her because of her or his gender. Thus she must first show, as under EPA, that (1) she is a member of a protected class and (2) that she was paid less than non-members of that class for work requiring substantially the same skill, effort and responsibility. Then she must also show, to establish a claim under Title VII, that the underpayment occurred under circumstances raising an inference of discrimination.

Claims of disparate treatment in discipline present fewer complications. The plaintiff must show prima facie that (1) he belongs to a class protected by Title VII; (2) that he was qualified for the job he holds or held; and (3) that a similarly situated employee engaged in identical or similar misconduct but received lesser or no discipline.

If the plaintiff establishes the prima facie case, a judicially created presumption declares the resulting inference of discrimination conclusive unless the defendant offers evidence that it had one or more "legitimate, nondiscriminatory reasons" for an employment decision. *McDonnell Douglas*. The defendant must set forth this reason "clearly" and through "admissible evidence." *Burdine*. Moreover, the reason must relate to what the defendant knew and relied on at the time of the challenged decision.

The preliminary question whether plaintiff established a *prima facie* case loses all significance once defendant presents its proof. Put otherwise, the definition of the prima facie case merely aids the court in determining whether to grant a defendant's motion for judgment as a matter of law under FRCP 50(a) at the close of plaintiff's case (or "directed verdict" as it is still known in most state courts). Once both sides rest, the trier of fact must evaluate all admitted evidence, including but not limited to the plaintiff's *prima facie* evidence, to decide if plaintiff has carried the ultimate burden of demonstrating intentional discrimination. Thus jury instructions in an age discrimination case that in effect permitted the jurors to find that age was a determining factor in the plaintiff's termination if they believed his prima facie evidence that younger employees were treated more favorably during a reduction in force have been held harmfully prejudicial to the employer. Seman v. Coplay Cement Co. (3d Cir.1994). A trial judge's ultimate determination about discriminatory intent—whether shown through direct or indirect evidence—is one of fact and may therefore be overturned on appeal only if "clearly erroneous." Anderson v. City of Bessemer (1985); Federal Rule of Civil Procedure 52(a).

Traditionally, most courts have viewed as "legitimate" virtually any reason the employer shows it relied on that can be distinguished from the five group characteristics protected by statute and from the few "proxy" factors that perfectly correspond with one of those groups. Thus, personality conflicts between the plaintiff and a supervisor, or management's genuine perception, accurate or not, that a plaintiff is adversarial, are classic "legitimate, nondiscriminatory reasons" that will absolve the employer of liability unless plaintiff proves them to have been offered as a pretext for unlawful discrimination. This view is evidently driven by deference to the employer's superior knowledge of its own productivity, safety and efficiency requirements. See Hazen Paper Co. v. Biggins (1993).

Although the opinion in *McDonnell Douglas* suggested that the employer need only "articulate" a legitimate, nondiscriminatory reason, perhaps simply in an argument or brief, the Court definitively determined in *Burdine* that the employer's burden, while not onerous, may be discharged only through evidence that clearly explains its proffered reason or reasons. But the Court has insisted that the defendant's burden is one of production only and that the burden of persuading about intentional discrimination resides with the plaintiff throughout. Accordingly, like the presumptions described in Federal Rule of Evidence 301, the *McDonnell Douglas* presumption of unlawful discriminatory motive that arises from a successful prima facie case disappears and has no further force in the litigation if the employer discharges its relatively modest burden of producing evidence of a legitimate, nondiscriminatory reason for the challenged employment action—the bubble bursts.

A plaintiff can nevertheless prevail on rebuttal. To do so the plaintiff must persuade the court that the defendant's purported legitimate reason is a smokescreen or "pretext" for intentional discrimination. It bears emphasis, however, that the plaintiff does not encounter this burden until after the defendant has produced evidence of one or more specific legitimate nondiscriminatory reasons. Thus, in making the prima facie case, the plaintiff need only show that she possessed the base, minimum qualifications the employer uniformly required for attaining or retaining a job. She need not do more at that stage of the case—for example, rebut employer assertions that she engaged in misconduct or possessed qualifications equal to or superior to the employee retained or selected in her stead. Such a requirement would, in effect, prematurely demand that she prove that the employer's reason is pretextual before the employer is called on clearly to identify, through evidence, its legitimate nondiscriminatory reason. That, in turn, would prematurely force the plaintiff to turn to the ultimate issue in the case, intentional discrimination.

The Court had written that the plaintiff could make the pretext showing, by the standard preponderance of the evidence quantum, in either of two generic ways: by demonstrating through plaintiff's own affirmative evidence, *including* that previously adduced prima facie, that the employer, in reaching its decision, explicitly relied on plaintiff's protected group status, rather than on its proffered legitimate reason; or, less directly, simply by convincing the judge or jury that the proffered reason is an implausible explanation for the challenged decision. *Burdine*; *Aikens*. The Supreme Court held, in St. Mary's Honor Ctr. v. Hicks (1993), that the latter showing merely permits but does not mandate a judgment for the plaintiff. In jury-triable intentional discrimination cases authorized by the Civil Rights Act of 1991, therefore, the jury should be charged accordingly. But the Court reaffirmed that evidence of the falsity of the employer's proffered legitimate reason could suffice for liability. Thus the court rejected a "pretext-plus" rule that had evolved in some of the circuit courts which had required plaintiffs to prove discriminatory intent not only by establishing the falsity of the employer's explanation but also through affirmative independent evidence.

The Supreme Court, in perhaps its most significant employment discrimination opinion in decades, has resolved the post-*St. Mary's* debate favorably to plaintiffs, consistent with the approach taken by the majority of the circuit courts. In Reeves v. Sanderson Plumbing Products, Inc. (2000), a case under the Age Discrimination in Employment Act ("ADEA"), the Court, taking note of the differing *St. Mary's* passages, wrote that the jury may find the ultimate fact of discrimination on a prohibited ground simply from (1) evidence establishing a prima facie case, coupled with (2) "sufficient" evidence that the employer's asserted legitimate nondiscriminatory explanation is false. The Court considered this approach consistent with general evidence law: "the factfinder is entitled to consider a party's dishonesty about a material fact as 'affirmative evidence of guilt' "; and once the employer's asserted reason is rejected, unlawful discrimination "may well be the most likely alternative explanation."

As long as plaintiff's counsel substantially impeaches or contradicts defendant-favorable evidence, a court should not consider that evidence in determining whether to uphold a plaintiff's verdict. In effect *Reeves* not only affirms the approach of most of the lower courts that uncorroborated evidence of the decisionmaker does not warrant judgment as a matter of law in the face of plaintiff's contradicting evidence; it rules the same way when plaintiff's evidence merely impeaches the decisionmaker's statement of legitimate, nondiscriminatory reasons.

Judgment as a matter of law should accordingly now be granted only in the presumably rare case that a court—considering all of the plaintiff's evidence and the uncontradicted, unimpeached evidence favoring the defendant—determines that a jury could not rationally find (or, after verdict, could not have rationally found) by a preponderance of that evidence the ultimate fact of unlawful race, sex, religious, national origin, or age discrimination. In such a case, however, judgment for defendant is warranted even if the jury reasonably believes the plaintiff's prima facie case and the falsity of the employer's stated legitimate, nondiscriminatory reason.

It seems apparent from the *Reeves* opinion that the Supreme Court intends these rules to apply to cases under Title VII, not just to cases under ADEA. Citing and adopting the approach taken by the courts of appeals, the Court assumed arguendo that the Title VII, *McDonnell Douglas* evidentiary framework for cases based on "circumstantial," as opposed to "direct" evidence, as that framework was elaborated in *St. Mary's*, was "fully applicable" to the ADEA case at hand. This conclusion follows logically as well. The Court repeated its statement from Hazen Paper Co. v. Biggins (1993), that in ADEA actions, the plaintiff must show that his age played not just a role but had a "determinative influence" on the outcome of the employer's decisionmaking process. In Title VII cases, by contrast, the statute as amended in 1991 provides that a plaintiff need only prove that race, sex, religion or national origin was a "motivating" factor in the employer's decision. It is therefore to be expected that Title VII plaintiffs should be able to survive Rule 56 summary judgment motions and Rule 50 motions for judgment as a matter of law at least as readily as ADEA plaintiffs will be able to under the standards announced in *Reeves*.

In the wake of *Reeves*, however, the lower Federal courts still differ as to the quantum of evidence a plaintiff must adduce to get to the jury, or to uphold a jury verdict post-trial. Few read *Reeves* literally to permit a plaintiff to survive summary or trial judgment merely because a defense witness testifying to a legitimate nondiscriminatory reason is impeached by minimal or doubtful evidence or by equivocal cross examination.

Because under *St. Mary's* as elucidated by *Reeves* the fact finder will continue to be permitted to infer unlawful age discrimination in most cases where the "legitimate nondiscriminatory reason" proffered by the employer is disbelieved, one may imagine a fairly complex, sequential series of decisions to be made by the judge, or instructions to be followed by the jury, in post–1991 Act intentional discrimination actions. First, in rare cases the trial judge must at the close of defendant's case grant the plaintiff judgment as a matter of law under FRCP 50(a)(1). This would happen only if any rational jury would have to find by a preponderance the existence of the facts constituting the plaintiff's prima facie case and the defendant failed even to produce evidence recognized as a nondiscriminatory reason for the challenged action.

Second, far more commonly, the judge at the close of all the evidence may, at the employer's request, have to charge the members of the jury that if the plaintiff has persuaded them not to believe the evidence the employer produced about a purported legitimate nondiscriminatory reason, they nevertheless *need not* conclude that the employer relied on that reason as a pretext for unlawful discrimination.

Third, the judge may also have to charge, at plaintiff's request, that the jury members *may* find unlawful pretext, and hence the ultimate fact of intentional discrimination, based solely on their disbelief of defendant's proffered legitimate reason, together with the prima facie evidence earlier presented by plaintiff during her case in chief, even absent other more "direct" or "affirmative" evidence of unlawful pretext. *Reeves* supports this position:

"In appropriate circumstances, the trier of fact can reasonably infer from the falsity of the explanation that the employer is dissembling to cover up a discriminatory purpose. Such an inference is consistent with the general principle of evidence law that the factfinder is entitled to consider a party's dishonesty about a material fact as "affirmative evidence of guilt. "... Moreover, once the employer's justification has been eliminated, discrimination may well be the most likely alternative explanation, especially since the em-

ployer is in the best position to put forth the actual reason
for its decision."

Reeves v. Sanderson Plumbing Prods., Inc. (2000).

Some circuits have held, however, that it is not reversible
error, and indeed is preferable, not to give pretext instructions
at all. Two instructions have been found sufficient: first,
defendant failed to hire plaintiff; and second, plaintiff's race
was a motivating factor in defendant's decision. Moore v.
Robertson Fire Protection Dist. (8th Cir.2001). Under these
instructions, the Eighth Circuit found that a jury is free to
consider evidence of pretext.

It should be remembered that even after *St. Mary*'s a
plaintiff *may* prevail on pretext by buttressing its case about
the falsity of the employer's stated reason with more direct or
affirmative evidence that the employer relied on a group
characteristic prohibited by statute. Alternatively, such evidence may suffice by itself to show intentional discrimination,
as it does in the cases of "express" or "facial" discrimination—e.g., cases involving slurs by employer agents or explicit
employer prohibitions against the hire or placement of members of a particular protected group.

On the other hand, a plaintiff's demonstration in a nonpromotion case that he was in fact the most qualified applicant is not necessarily tantamount to a showing that the
employer understood or agreed with that assessment and
promoted another as a pretext for discrimination. The employer's explanation, in other words, may be erroneous in fact but
sincerely believed by the decision-maker and therefore nonpretextual in the sense intended by *St. Mary's*. An employer's
decision may be subjective, mistaken, unwise, erroneous, or
reflect a misjudging of relevant credentials, without necessarily being motivated by a consideration prohibited by Title VII
or ADEA. For example, only if a disparity between the creden-

tials of the plaintiff and a comparator "jump off the page and slap you in the face" and thus warrant a jury's conclusion that the employer based its decision on something other than qualifications can employer error furnish the foundation for liability. Deines v. Texas Dep't of Protective and Regulatory Servs. (5th Cir.1999).

A standard legitimate nondiscriminatory reason is that plaintiff violated a customary work rule of the employer. The decisions outline a number of specific ways in which a plaintiff may show such a reason pretextual. First, a plaintiff may persuade a jury that she did not violate the rule in question if the testimony about many of her alleged deficiencies does not accurately reflect the work situation. Of course evidence that the plaintiff did not in fact violate the rule does not preclude the possibility that the employer honestly believed she did, but nevertheless has been held to preclude summary judgment; more clearly still, summary judgment is improper if a plaintiff who concededly did violate a work rule offers evidence that other employees outside her protected class were not similarly disciplined for committing a similar infraction. Evidence that the decisionmaker herself engaged in the same policy violation as the plaintiff is "especially compelling" evidence of pretext. Ross v. Rhodes Furniture, Inc. (11th Cir.1998).

McDonnell Douglas, in describing the variety of evidence the plaintiff may use to rebut a proffered legitimate, nondiscriminatory reason, makes clear that the individual disparate treatment plaintiff who sues alone may fortify the inference of discrimination arising from his use of direct or indirect evidence with anecdotal evidence that one or more similarly situated members of his protected group experienced discriminatory treatment at the hands of the same employer. Statistical evidence of the adverse differential treatment of the plaintiff's group may also fortify the case of the solo disparate treatment plaintiff. Testimony of prior discriminatory acts against members of plaintiff's protected group by the particular employer agent alleged to have discriminated against plaintiff is particularly probative of that agent's state of mind. Of course the assertedly comparable evidence must reflect discrimination under similar circumstances to be admissible on the question whether the particular plaintiff was also the victim of unlawful discrimination.

It should be stressed that all these modes of intentional discrimination are designed to ferret out and penalize only employer conduct that adversely differentiates on the basis of one or more of Title VII's prohibited grounds; they are not designed to assure workplace norms or mores that are fair in other respects. Thus any reason for the employer's challenged decision deemed not "because of" race, gender, religion or national origin (or a proxy for one of those grounds) is likely to be viewed as legitimate, even if the trier of fact also considers that reason unfair, unreasonable or unenlightened. In particular, courts express great reluctance to substitute their own judgment for the standards of proficiency or competence assertedly relied on by academic employers. This question must be sharply distinguished, however, from the question whether the academic employer actually relied on the standards it professed to follow; *St. Mary's* implicitly leaves that question for the jury.

2. THE PROBLEM OF "MIXED MOTIVES"

The classic evidentiary structure erected by *McDonnell Douglas* and *Burdine*, while furnishing a workable matrix for inferentially ferreting out intentional discrimination, does not fully come to grips with the complexities of many cases because it assumes that an employer's motivation was grounded *entirely* on a prohibited reason *or* a legitimate one. In fact, employers commonly advance more than one asserted legitimate reason for a challenged employment decision, and courts often conclude that an employer relied on one or more of those reasons as well as a reason condemned by Title VII.

In Price Waterhouse v. Hopkins (1989), a Supreme Court plurality concluded that when an employer undertakes a challenged employment decision for more than one reason, and the reason that is unlawful under Title VII is a "motivating," or "substantial motivating" factor in the employer's decision, liability will attach unless the employer can prove by a preponderance of the evidence that it would have reached the same decision for one or more independent, lawful reasons. The plurality rejected the dissenters' suggestion that an employer should also be nonliable if the court finds such an independent reason existed at the time of the challenged decision, regardless of whether the employer relied on it. The plurality insisted that the employer, to be relieved of liability, must have *acted* on the basis of a lawful reason, of which it necessarily had knowledge.

If an employer carries that persuasion burden, the plurality wrote, it should be found not to have committed an unlawful employment practice, despite the evidence of partial unlawful motive. If on the other hand the employer cannot carry by a preponderance of the evidence the "same-decision" showing, it will be liable. Indeed, even a plaintiff using evidence of indirect disparate treatment who fails its burden of persuading that a lawful reason proffered by the employer at trial is a pretext for prohibited discrimination (see the *McDonnell Douglas/Burdine/St. Mary's Honor Ctr.* mode of proof discussed above) can still prevail under *Price Waterhouse* by showing another employer motive that was unlawful and motivated the challenged decision.

A critical fifth vote for giving the employer the burden of persuasion on this "same decision" issue was cast by Justice

O'Connor. She, however, would have imposed that burden only where the plaintiff proffers "direct evidence" that the discriminatory factor played a substantial role in the employer's decision. (O'Connor, J., concurring).

Much has been written about the *Price Waterhouse* decision. Observers differ on whether affording the employer an escape from liability when it makes the "same-decision" showing but saddling it with the persuasion burden on that question, a development favorable to plaintiffs or defendants.

Section 107 of the Civil Rights Act of 1991, codified as new Title VII Section 703 (m) declares that an unlawful employment practice is established when the plaintiff demonstrates that employer reliance on protected group status was a "motivating factor" for "any" employment practice, "even though other factors also motivated the practice." The language requiring a "motivating" factor, derived from *Price Waterhouse*, evolved in the legislative process from the less stringent "contributing." The resulting linguistic connotation, against the background of existing appellate jurisprudence about mixed motive, suggests that at least this change should marginally improve the litigation prospects of defendant employers. The "motivating" requirement appears less burdensome than the counterpart demonstration of a "determinative" factor that has evolved in cases under the ADEA.

In 2003, the Supreme Court resolved a long-standing circuit split arising from Justice O'Connor's crucial fifth vote in *Price Waterhouse*: whether a plaintiff could establish a violation under Section 703(m), in mixed-motive cases, and therefore receive the limited remedies afforded by Section 706(g)(2)(B), when her evidence that race, sex, religion, or national origin was a motivating factor in the employer's decision was solely circumstantial, that is within the *McDonnell–Douglas* inferential proof scheme. In Desert Palace, Inc. v. Costa (2003), a

unanimous court concluded that after the 1991 amendments
to Title VII, the plaintiff need not offer "direct" evidence—
only persuasive evidence, direct or indirect—that race, sex,
religion, or national origin was a motivating factor in an
employer's adverse employment decision in order to obtain a
"mixed-motive" or "same-decision" instruction requiring the
employer to demonstrate that it would have made the same
employment decision wholly apart from its consideration of
one of those unlawful grounds. As a practical matter, the vast
majority of intentional discrimination cases involve mixed
motives: the plaintiff must prove the employer acted, at least
in part, for an unlawful reason, and employers respond to the
plaintiff's prima facie case by offering evidence of one or more
"legitimate nondiscriminatory reasons" for their action. So it
is critically important in the great bulk of Title VII cases to
know whether plaintiffs can prevail, and if so what remedies
they may receive, where the evidence shows both lawful and
unlawful reasons.

Before *Desert Palace*, the circuits, other than the Ninth, had
held Title VII plaintiffs could not establish a violation under
Section 703(m), in mixed-motive cases, and therefore could
not receive the limited remedies afforded by Section
706(g)(2)(B), unless their evidence that race, sex, religion, or
national origin was a motivating factor in the employer's
decision was "direct." Then they had reduced the categories of
evidence they considered "direct" almost to the vanishing
point. In practice, therefore, it was the rare plaintiff who could
obtain an instruction placing the burden of persuasion concerning the same-decision issue on the defendant.

But the Supreme Court, speaking through Justice Thomas,
concluded that the words of Section 703(m) were unambiguous; that the section "does not mention, much less require,
that a plaintiff make a heightened showing through direct
evidence;" and accordingly that Congress abrogated the "di-

rect evidence" requirement of Justice O'Connor's *Price Water-house* concurrence. Congress did define the quantum of evidence a plaintiff must develop to show a partial, unlawful motivating factor (and the quantum of evidence a defendant must produce to make a same-decision showing) by providing in a different section of the 1991 Act that "demonstrates," as used in Sections 703(m) and 706(g), means meeting "the burdens of production and persuasion." But it did not define the nature of the evidence plaintiff must use to show an unlawful motivating factor—the showing that establishes a violation under Section 703(m) and triggers the production and persuasion burden the defendant must carry with respect to the same-decision issue if it wishes to avail itself of the limited affirmative defense of Section 706(g)(2)(B). For that purpose, the Court observed, circumstantial evidence not only suffices but may be more persuasive than direct evidence.

So long as a plaintiff presents sufficient evidence for a "reasonable jury" to find by a preponderance that race, sex, religion or national origin was a motivating factor (which in most circuits means "played some part") in the challenged employment decision, the plaintiff is eligible to establish a violation pursuant to Section 703(m) and is entitled to the same-decision instruction imposing the persuasion burden on defendant respecting the limited affirmative defense of Section 706(g)(2)(B)—even, apparently, over the defendant's objection. This should mean that virtually every plaintiff bringing the most common type of Title VII intentional discrimination or individual disparate treatment claim who has enough evidence to survive a FRCP 50(a) motion for judgment as a matter of law should be able to obtain that same-decision instruction. And the Court makes it somewhat easier to survive that motion by citing approvingly its decision in Reeves v. Sanderson Plumbing Products, Inc. (2000). There the Court warned lower federal courts ruling on FRCP 50(a) motions to credit the testimony of employment discrimination plaintiffs, whether impeached or unimpeached, contradicted or uncontradicted, and not to take into account testimony favoring employers unless it is both uncontradicted and unimpeached. In practice, therefore, so long as a Title VII plaintiff's case survives summary judgment and is capably tried, it should usually get to the jury and the jury will at plaintiff's or defendant's option hear a "same-decision" instruction placing a burden of persuasion on the defendant.

To be faithful to the new statutory scheme, a district court's complete instructions should inform jurors that they need not consider whether the employer has carried its burden by a preponderance on the same-decision issue unless and until they have concluded that the plaintiff has carried her burden of showing by a preponderance that race, sex, religion or national origin was a motivating factor underlying the challenged employment practice. But of course therein lies the potential for jury confusion that could redound to the benefit of plaintiff. Some jurors, hearing that a defendant bears, or may bear, a burden of persuasion on one issue (about "same decision"), may not understand or remember that the plaintiff bears a burden of persuasion on another, preliminary issue (about whether an unlawful ground was a "motivating" factor in the employer's decision). In any event, *Desert Palace* enhances the chances for the typical one-on-one intentional discrimination Title VII plaintiff to prevail, at least for prospective relief and attorney's fees, even where the defendant can carry its same-decision burden.

To avoid monetary liability, the employer must demonstrate "that it would have taken the same action in the absence of the impermissible motivating factor"—even if there is evidence that at the time of the adverse employment action the employer knew that the employee had disobeyed work rules or lied. Section 107(b) (amending Title VII § 706(g), 42 U.S.C.A. § 2000e–5(g) (1972)); Stacks v. Southwestern Bell Yellow

Pages, Inc. (8th Cir.1994). The Act codifies the *Price Water-house* view that the required employer "demonstration," once triggered, extends to the burden of persuasion as well as production on this question. Section 104 (adding subsection 701(m) to Title VII, 42 U.S.C.A. § 2000e–m).

In fact the legislation goes somewhat beyond the *Price Waterhouse* plurality in providing that even the defendant who makes the required demonstration is relieved only of mone-tary liability. If unlawful discrimination was a "motivating" factor in the challenged employment decision, the employer has committed a law violation remediable by prospective relief and attorney's fees. Section 107(b)(3) (adding paragraph (2)(B) to § 706(g) of Title VII, 42 U.S.C.A. § 2000e–5(g)).

The addition to Title VII of Sections 703(m) and 706(g)(2)(B), and, in contrast, their omission from the ADEA, is significant in practice. First, thanks to Section 703(m), the plaintiff's ultimate burden in establishing Title VII liability is only to demonstrate that an unlawful ground motivated, rath-er than determined, the imposition of an employment detri-ment or denial of an employment benefit. Second, correlative-ly, where the Title VII plaintiff attempts to meet this burden through the indirect *McDonnell Douglas* formula, judges rul-ing on summary judgment and FRCP 50 motions will apply the *St. Mary's* requirements for "pretext" less stringently than in similar litigation under ADEA. Third, a Title VII plaintiff who takes the *McDonnell Douglas* path and presents evidence sufficient under *St. Mary's* to survive a Rule 50 motion at the close of all the evidence will, like the Title VII plaintiff who uses "direct" evidence, be entitled to a Section 703(m) instruction imposing on the employer the burden of demonstrating that it would have reached the same decision independent of the unlawful reason. It is not at all clear that the counterpart ADEA plaintiff who presents only indirect evidence of age discrimination is eligible for such an instruction under *Price Waterhouse.* Fourth, under Section 706(g)(2)(B), the Title VII defendant who carries the "same-decision" showing is nevertheless liable and subject to limited declaratory and injunctive relief and attorney's fees; the ADEA defendant who carries that showing per *Price Waterhouse* is relieved of liability altogether.

3.   "AFTER–ACQUIRED EVIDENCE": A LIMITATION OF EMPLOYER LIABILITY

Suppose an the employer can produce evidence it discovered during a post-termination investigation or litigation of a legitimate nondiscriminatory reason that would have induced it to take the same action against the plaintiff had the facts come to light before the adverse action. Should it be relieved of liability altogether, enjoy a limitation on liability, or be subject to full relief?

In McKennon v. Nashville Banner Publ'g Co. (1995), the Court steered a middle course among these alternatives. To capitalize on employee misconduct discovered only after the employer discriminatorily imposed an employment detriment, the employer bears the burden of proving "that the wrongdoing was of such severity that the employee *in fact would* have been *terminated* on those grounds alone if the employer had known of it at the time of the discharge." *McKennon* (emphases added). It appears from this standard that it is unnecessary for the court to agree with the employer's assessment that the employee's misconduct is "serious" or "pervasive" as long as the employer can prove that under its established rules, applied without discrimination, it would have discharged the employee had it known of such conduct when it occurred.

Still, the employer demonstration of such misconduct serves only to limit liability, not as a complete defense. The Supreme

Court observed that under ADEA as well as Title VII, remedies serve the twin objectives of deterring violations and compensating past injuries. The plaintiff advances those objectives, the Court wrote, by demonstrating the employer's discrimination. Allowing after-acquired evidence to serve as a complete bar to liability would unjustifiably undermine the statutes' remedial goals. In reaching this conclusion, the Supreme Court specifically distinguished mixed-motive situations; after-acquired evidence does not even figure in the decisional calculus until the factfinder has determined that the employer's sole or motivating basis for the challenged employment decision was unlawful (and that the employer would not have reached the same decision independent of its pure or partial unlawful motivation). *McKennon.*

But the Court was equally insistent that the employer's wrongdoing could not simply be disregarded in the formulation of an appropriate remedy. In this connection the Court read ADEA's authorization of legal or equitable relief as a mandate for the trial court to take the employee's wrongdoing into account as a way of recognizing the significant managerial prerogatives that ADEA, like Title VII, preserves to the employer. While acknowledging that the relevant equitable considerations will vary from case to case, the Court nevertheless concluded that here, and as a general rule in cases of this type, neither reinstatement nor front pay is an appropriate remedy. It would be both inequitable and pointless to order the reinstatement of someone the employer would have terminated, and will terminate, in any event and upon lawful grounds.

Declining to formulate an across-the-board back pay rule, the Court concluded that the "beginning point" in the trial court's formulation of a monetary remedy should be calculation of back pay from the date of the unlawful discharge to the date the new information was discovered. Unlike the "mixed-motive" employer who establishes that it would have taken the challenged action at the time even absent reliance on a motivating factor forbidden by Title VII, the employer who carries the persuasion burden on after-acquired evidence will almost surely sustain some monetary liability, even if that liability terminates as of the date of discovery of employee wrongdoing. This is because after-acquired evidence presupposes that the employer committed an unlawful employment practice; the tardily discovered legitimate reason was not any part of its motivation when it demoted or terminated the plaintiff.

In principle, the line drawn by the Court for back pay—presumptively available before but not after the date of the employer's discovery of the information that would have led to termination independent of the unlawful employment practice—should apply to ADEA "liquidated" damages and Title VII compensatory and punitive damages as well. As the Court wrote about back pay, an absolute rule barring these remedies "would undermine the ADEA's objective of forcing employers to consider and examine their motivations, and of penalizing them for employment decisions that spring from age discrimination." On this reasoning, only "extraordinary equitable circumstances" would defeat claims under Title VII for compensatory, punitive damages or both through that date of discovery. Neither type of damages would constrain significant managerial prerogatives or discretions, the sole equitable consideration the Court identified as a reason for restricting plaintiff's recovery.

The EEOC and at least one circuit court have since opined that Title VII compensatory and punitive damages and ADEA liquidated damages are available notwithstanding after-acquired evidence. Russell v. Microdyne (4th Cir.1995). Further, EEOC does not view the *McKennon* concern of protecting the employer's interest in severing the employment relationship as a warrant to place a time limit on compensatory damages for emotional harm. Rather, the after-acquired showing limits only those out-of-pocket losses that are analogous to back pay. Nor does EEOC see in *McKennon* a ban or limitation on punitive damages, provided the plaintiff proves the employer's malice or reckless indifference.

The after-acquired evidence defense has practical potency well beyond its limitation on relief. Defense counsel will routinely pursue discovery on the issue, which should raise the costs to plaintiff and intimidate some serious wrongdoers. And at trial even defendants who fail in their burden of proving misconduct so serious as to warrant discharge may nevertheless succeed in damaging the plaintiff's credibility, with a consequent loss of jury sympathy and potential reduction of compensatory and punitive awards. Plaintiffs may counter these tactics with motions to limit discovery, or with motions *in limine* to exclude misconduct evidence unless the employer makes a threshold showing that under established policies or practices it would have fired employees for the misconduct in question.

Now that the Supreme Court has recognized after-acquired evidence as a factor that lessens relief, trial judges in Title VII jury actions will have to issue still another set of instructions on top of the many already required in even the simplest cases of individual disparate treatment. Presumably these would be the last in the series, following any required instructions on mixed motive. For example, the jury might be charged that if it finds the employer would have made the challenged decision for lawful reasons independent of other, unlawful reasons that the jury finds the employer also took into account, the employer is presumptively liable only for prospective relief and attorney's fees under the Civil Rights Act of 1991's modification of *Price Waterhouse*. If, however, the jury also finds after-acquired evidence of employee misconduct sufficiently serious that the employer would have terminated the plaintiff upon discovery during the plaintiff's employment, the court would not order the plaintiff reinstated either. The only potential relief remaining in that situation would be a declaratory judgment, an injunction, or nominal damages, and perhaps attorney's fees to the extent of the plaintiff's limited success.

C. SYSTEMIC DISPARATE TREATMENT

Intentional discriminatory treatment may also be demonstrated in the aggregate. "Systemic disparate treatment" proof depends primarily upon statistical evidence of gross disparities between the actual and expected representation of the plaintiff's group in one or more levels of an employer's workforce. According to the underlying theory, articulated in International Brotherhood of Teamsters v. United States (1977), an employer that does not routinely discriminate should over time achieve within its employee complement an incidence of protected group representation not significantly less than the group's representation in an available pool of qualified applicants.

Systemic disparate treatment, the residue of a number of individually discriminatory decisions, is evidenced by a significant workforce underrepresentation of a protected group relative to the incidence one would expect based on its members' interest, availability and qualifications. Unlike the impact case, it is predicated on a showing of intentional discrimination. Further, the systemic treatment case is typically brought by several joined plaintiffs or a plaintiff class, and endeavors to prove that the defendant, as the result of an unspecified variety of policies, practices, and individual decisions by employer agents, discriminated against members of the protected group in general. In the systemic treatment case all members of the protected group denied hire or promotion to the job level during the period when the protected group was found to be grossly underrepresented are presumptively entitled to remedies, regardless of which particular employer policies or decisions by employer agents led to their rejection. Franks v. Bowman Transp. Co. (1976). By contrast, relief in the "impact" case is limited to those plaintiffs, sometimes as few as one, who suffered an employment detriment as the result of a particular practice shown to have had disproportionate adverse impact on the plaintiff's group.

Occasionally, an employer's policy will on its face draw a distinction on the basis of a prohibited characteristic; a group of plaintiffs suing as a class or joined under Federal Rule 20 could then establish systemic disparate treatment on the basis of the policy alone. More typically, the plaintiffs will offer statistical evidence in an attempt to show a raw, substantial underrepresentation of their protected group relative to the numbers of their members that might have been expected had the employer hired or promoted randomly. This prima facie statistical case of systemic disparate treatment compares the employer's actual or "observed" number of protected group members hired for or promoted to the job in question against a hypothetical number of protected group members that an employer who hired or promoted randomly might have been "expected" to select. The theoretical underpinning of statistically-premised judicial findings of systemic disparate treatment is that, "absent explanation, it is ordinarily to be expected that nondiscriminatory hiring practices will in time result in a work force more or less representative of the racial and ethnic composition of the" relevant pool. *Teamsters.* Although anecdotal evidence of instances of individual disparate treatment certainly fortifies the inference of systemic disparate treatment raised by statistical disparities, it has been held that statistical disparities alone may prove intentional discrimination, at least where the disparities are gross. E.E.O.C. v. O & G Spring and Wire Forms Specialty Co. (7th Cir.1994).

In undertaking a showing of gross underrepresentation of the protected group the plaintiff must take care to calculate the "expected" number by reference to the relevant pool from which the selection will be made; and that pool must be refined to account for the minimum qualifications, including geographic proximity, requisite for the job in question. In an order that ascends with the complexity of the skill level at issue, this pool may range from general population or workforce statistics within an actual or feasible recruiting zone, to a nationwide pool of candidates with the key educational or experience credentials. In the case of promotions that the employer has historically made exclusively or primarily from within, the pool would consist of lower-level employees in the employer's own workforce who meet the base requirements for promotion. Statistical analyses may also compare employees who are competing against one another to be retained notwithstanding a reduction in force, but in such cases comparisons of protected group members with others must be strictly limited to the pool of persons evaluated by the same decisionmaker. Smith v. Xerox Corp. (2d Cir.1999).

Defining the pool from which the expected percentage of minority representation should be calculated is often keenly contested. While protected group representation in a recruiting-zone population or local workforce may suffice where the jobs in question are largely unskilled, *Teamsters*, or from the percentage of protected group members employed by other area employers for jobs that are moderately skilled, the fair measurement of disparities in highly skilled positions demands refinement not just for availability and interest but, above all, for specialized qualifications. Courts have on occasion dispensed with refined evidence of the characteristics of the pool from which applicants are drawn when the disparities presented are extreme. The classic example is where the protected group in question constitutes what has been termed the "inexorable zero"—no representation at all in the employer's workforce.

Whatever comparison is used, plaintiff must establish a statistically significant "gross" disparity between observed and expected protected group representation. The magnitude of this disparity must be sufficient to show that discrimination was an employer's routine operating procedure such that relief should be granted to the entire underrepresented class. This generally requires expert testimony concerning the statistical technique of binomial distribution and its key measure, standard deviation. The actual and expected numbers of protected group members, together with the total number of persons hired for or promoted to the job during the liability period alleged in the complaint, are fed into the binomial distribution formula, which is designed to gauge the degree to which an "underrepresentation" departs from hypothetical "random" or "chance" hiring or promotion. Statisticians have conventionally ruled out chance as the likely cause of a negative deviation from the norm when the formula shows that the observed number falls more than 1.95 standard deviations below the expected number; this convention holds that there is then less than a 5% chance that the underrepresentation is itself the result of chance. Apparently determined to avoid "false positives"—implicating an innocent employer—the Supreme Court has written somewhat vaguely that unlawful discrimination may be suspected as the cause of an underrepresentation only "if the difference between the expected value and the observed number is 'greater than two or three [negative] standard deviations' "—a level at which statisticians would exclude chance as the explanation with overwhelming confidence. *Hazelwood*.

It is because the law requires an underrepresentation of this magnitude that a court may rely solely on statistical evidence to indict an employer for systemic disparate treatment discrimination in violation of § 703(a) without running afoul of a distinct provision of Title VII, § 703(j). Section 703(j) provides that Title VII shall not be:

"interpreted to require any employer to grant preferential treatment ... because of race, color, religion, sex, or national origin ... on account of an imbalance which may exist with respect to the total number or percentage of persons of any race, color, religion, sex or national origin employed by any employer ... in comparison with the total number or percentage of persons of such race, color, religion, sex, or national origin in any community ... or in the available work force in any community."

The Court in *Teamsters* could plausibly deny that holding an employer liable for systemic treatment discrimination upon proof of a gross statistical underrepresentation was tantamount to a requirement, condemned by § 703(j), "that a work force *mirror* the general population." *Teamsters* (emphasis added). Many employee complements will fail to mirror the protected group's percentage in a surrounding population or work force without falling short *enough* to violate the "two or three standard deviation" test or therefore to violate § 703(a).

A more sophisticated statistical technique, multiple regression analysis, will usually be required to establish the requisite disparity when variations in the particular term and condition of employment at issue—for example, compensation—are explainable by reference to a large number of factors. Regression analysis has also been held mandatory when the employer's measure of which employees will receive a scarce benefit—say, performance evaluations used to decide who will be retained during a reduction in force—are a product of multiple causes. Smith v. Xerox Corp. (2d Cir.1999). The Court has indicated, however, that a plaintiff's multiple regression analysis need not eliminate all potential nondiscriminatory explanations of disparity, only the most significant. Bazemore v. Friday (1986). But even if a multiple regression analysis is not undertaken and the plaintiff relies merely on a standard deviation of two or more, the statistical evidence, if proven reliable, is relevant to rule out chance, and this ruling out of chance is "an important step in the plaintiffs' proof, even if it was not a single leap from the starting line to the finish line." Adams v. Ameritech Services, Inc. (7th Cir.2000).

Once the plaintiff group adduces express or statistical evidence of systemic disparate treatment, the employer has an opportunity to offer what *Teamsters* termed a nondiscriminatory "explanation" by way of rebuttal. Absent a defense, liability will be deemed established and the case moves to a second, bifurcated remedy phase. The employer's principal defense in these cases is to present evidence that casts doubt on the logical, statistical, or legal probative value of plaintiff's evidence. For example, an employer may avoid the force of evidence of disparity by showing infirmities in the plaintiff-defined pool that exaggerate the availability of qualified members of the protected group; by challenging the validity of the statistical conclusions drawn by plaintiff's expert, including objections to insufficient sample size; or by demonstrating (as will seldom be the case twenty-five years after the effective date of the Act) that a protected group's underrepresentation is attributable largely to then-lawful, even if discriminatory, hiring that took place before the employer became subject to Title VII.

In the alternative, the employer may affirmatively present counter-comparative statistics. A more restrictively refined availability pool, for example, may generate negative disparities of a magnitude (less than two or three standard deviations) that judges will deem insignificant to alter the status quo and impose liability on an employer. Indeed, the employer may refute the existence of any negative disparity by offering data suggesting that it hired or promoted a *greater* number of protected group members than their availability in the employer-advocated pool would predict: in that instance, the standard deviation would be positive. Most powerfully, an employer that has maintained records differentiating its applicants by race, national origin or gender may be able to offer "applicant flow" statistics to establish that it hired at least as great a percentage of protected group members as of others. *Hazelwood*. Such evidence tends to show the particular defendant's comparative treatment of actual members of the protected group and others who had the requisite interest to offer themselves for hire or promotion. Applicant flow evidence is therefore generally credited with greater probative value than standard deviation evidence drawn from the number of hires or promotions that might theoretically have been expected based on protected group availability in an appropriately defined pool of persons none of whom may have actually sought employment with the defendant.

In the face of a showing of gross underrepresentation of the protected group, as evidenced by substantially unimpeached standard deviation data, applicant flow data could nevertheless point in favor of the employer. When the employer treated fairly or even favorably a relatively small number of protected group members applied. But why did so few protected group members apply, given their significant representation in the underlying pool? One possibility is a self-selected lack of interest in the particular employment, despite presumptive minimum qualifications and availability. That argument appears to have lesser force when the court views the statistical underrepresentation as overwhelming, and particularly when there are no protected group members in the job in question.

Another explanation of underapplication by the protected group is a well-developed, notorious employer reputation for discrimination against the group in question, a reputation so extreme as to render it "futile" for a member of that group to apply. If the plaintiffs can prove that more protected group members would have applied during the period of the alleged discrimination but for the employer's discriminatory practices, they may persuade a court to disregard or discount the employer's applicant flow evidence. An employer unable to impeach or counter a finding of gross statistical underrepresentation must nevertheless be permitted to attempt to offer some other nondiscriminatory "explanation" for the disparity. *Teamsters*. A controversial defense accepted by some courts is that, relative to others, the particular protected group lacked interest in or qualifications for the job in question. A highly publicized Seventh Circuit decision so held with respect to women seeking positions as commissioned salespersons. E.E.O.C. v. Sears, Roebuck & Co. (7th Cir.1988). The court seemed to consider it irrelevant whether, assuming the validity of the key fact findings, the relative lack of interest in or qualifications to hold those positions was "inherent" in women or a product of stereotyping long rooted in American history or culture.

An employer may also explain an unimpeached, prima facie gross statistical underrepresentation by offering evidence that one of its own neutral practices had disproportionate adverse impact on the protected group. This puts the employer in the odd position of becoming its own accuser, since such a practice may independently give rise to Title VII liability even without proof of discriminatory intent. In effect, the employer argues that an unlawful employment practice (a facially neutral test or experience requirement that disproportionately affects the protected group) explains the significant bottom-line under-representation of the protected group in the job level for which the test or experience requirement screens. Courts before the 1991 Civil Rights Act that permitted employers to defend a gross underrepresentation by pointing to such a neutral practice required them to bear the burden of persuasion on the neutral practice justification. Griffin v. Carlin (11th Cir. 1985) By undertaking this showing the employer may limit its liability to those members of the protected group who were personally affected by the neutral practice. Even if the employer cannot persuade the trier of fact that the neutral practice that caused the systemic underrepresentation was justified, the employer will be exposed only to back pay liability for an unlawful neutral practice, and not for the compensatory and punitive damages available since 1991 for intentional discrimination. Better yet for the employer, the court may conclude that the neutral practice which accounts for an underrepresentation is justified because "job related for the position in question and consistent with business necessity" within the meaning of § 703(k)(1)(A)(i), added by § 105(a) of the Civil Rights Act of 1991; then the employer would not be liable to anyone for anything.

It is unclear whether these decisions will survive an amendment to Title VII, also added by § 105(a) of the Civil Rights Act of 1991, that provides: "A demonstration that an employment practice is required by business necessity may not be used as a defense against a claim of intentional discrimination under this title." Title VII, § 703(k)(2). At a minimum this provision confirms the Supreme Court's position in International Union, UAW v. Johnson Controls, Inc. (1991), that a facially discriminatory practice may be excused, if at all, only under the stringent BFOQ defense, and not merely by a showing of job relatedness and business necessity. Read broadly, however, the new § 703(k)(2) could also be applied to cases where the prima facie evidence of intentional discrimination consists of gross statistical disparities sufficient to establish systemic disparate treatment of the plaintiff class. If so, Section 703(k)(2) would appear to deny the employer the last-chance defense discussed in *Griffin*.

The sounder view, however, is that new Section 703(k)(2) should be limited to the context that gave rise to its enactment: individual-plaintiff express or facial evidence, as contrasted to statistically proven systemic disparate treatment. Part of the fundamental underpinning of the systemic disparate treatment theory is that an employer should not be exposed to classwide liability if it has a nondiscriminatory explanation for the gross statistical underrepresentation of the plaintiff's protected group. A neutral practice that the employer can prove was the real cause of a systemic disparity proven by the plaintiff is precisely such a nondiscriminatory explanation. While the employer who can carry that explanation should still have to defend the adverse impact of its neutral practice on specific protected group members disadvantaged by it, it should not face the more far-reaching liability to every member of that group who was denied a job or promotion during the period of systemic underrepresentation.

D. THE RELIEF STAGE OF THE BIFURCATED SYSTEMIC DISPARATE TREATMENT ACTION

Systemic treatment trials are conducted in distinct liability and remedial phases. First, from evidence of a facially discriminatory policy, from statistics alone, from anecdotal evidence, or some combination of the above, the court determines whether the employer has intentionally discriminated against

the plaintiff's protected group. If so, individual members of
the plaintiff class who reapply (or, in certain cases, apply for
the first time) for a position or promotion at this stage of the
action may thus become eligible to receive the full panoply of
all otherwise appropriate Title VII remedies: not only declaratory and injunctive relief but reinstatement, back pay, retroactive seniority and, since the violation involves intentional
discrimination, the capped compensatory and punitive damages made available by the Civil Rights Act of 1991.

The Supreme Court has substantially eased the individual
plaintiff's burden of demonstrating entitlement to relief at the
remedy stage of the systemic treatment case. Even if the
prima facie case consists only of statistical evidence, that
evidence, if believed by the factfinder and not successfully
rebutted with a nondiscriminatory explanation, gives rise to a
presumption that each plaintiff who unsuccessfully sought
hire, promotion, or retention during the established liability
period was rejected because of his or her protected group
status. Franks v. Bowman Transp. Co. (1976). So long as the
individual applied for the position in question during the
established liability period, she need not even produce evidence of her minimum qualifications. Proof of a broad-based
policy of unlawful discrimination, in other words, generates
"reasonable grounds to infer that individual hiring decisions
were made in pursuit of the discriminatory policy and to
require the employer to come forth with evidence dispelling
that inference." *Teamsters*. Although the prima facie case does
not "conclusively demonstrate that all of the employer's decisions were part of the proven discriminatory pattern and
practice," it creates "a greater likelihood that any single
decision was a component of the overall pattern."

The employer is now a "proven wrongdoer," and must bear
the burden of showing nondiscriminatory reasons for rejecting
any individual plaintiff. But individual plaintiffs have been

denied this automatic inference at the relief stage, and required to prove the *McDonnell Douglas* elements (especially that they were qualified at the time they were denied a position), where the classwide finding of liability is the product of a settlement and consent decree, rather than trial. Reynolds v. Roberts (11th Cir.2000). And it has been suggested that even after trial the inference of discrimination as to each individual should not be drawn where the evidence of classwide liability, instead of showing that the plaintiffs' protected group was absolutely excluded from the positions at issue, revealed that significant numbers of plaintiffs' group obtained (and unlawfully were denied) those positions.

To rebut the presumption, the employer may avoid liability to individual plaintiffs or plaintiff class members by persuading a court that they were not in fact victims of discrimination. For example, the employer may demonstrate that there were no vacancies in the pertinent position at the time a particular class member applied, that the plaintiff lacked minimum qualifications that the employer insisted upon at the time of the plaintiff's rejection, or that a successful applicant was better qualified. *Franks* (1976); *Teamsters*. Even class members who did not apply for a position during the proven liability period may sometimes receive individual relief; but they carry the heavy burden of persuading that it was futile for them to apply because of an employer's notorious reputation for egregious discrimination against their protected group and that they would have applied otherwise. *Teamsters*. It does not suffice for nonapplicants to show only that they are interested in obtaining a job at the time of judgment; discriminatees may be awarded retroactive seniority for the period they would have accrued seniority had the employer not discriminated, so the job available through court order may be far more attractive than it was originally. Further, they, unlike "applicant" plaintiff class members, bear the burden of showing their own minimum qualifications at the time that, but for futility, they prove they would have applied.

E. HOW THE INDIVIDUAL AND SYSTEMIC DISPARATE TREATMENT CASES INTERRELATE

Given the relative ease of establishing a prima facie case of individual disparate treatment under *McDonnell Douglas/Burdine,* and the expense and difficulty of gathering and analyzing the data necessary to establish a case of systemic disparate treatment, solo plaintiffs usually proceed with "direct" or inferential evidence alone. Nevertheless, there is a complementary relationship between evidence of individual and systemic disparate treatment. A well financed individual plaintiff may fortify the individual disparate treatment case with evidence of statistically discriminatory patterns. Similarly, a plaintiff class may, and as a practical matter is well advised, to bolster a case of systemic discriminatory treatment with anecdotal evidence of discrimination against its individual members. The advocate should bear in mind that statistical systemic treatment evidence merely suggests that the employer routinely discriminated, but by itself does not suggest how. Counsel may fill the gap for skeptical judges by offering "direct" or inferential evidence that individual plaintiffs were discriminatorily treated. In both *Teamsters* and *Hazelwood* the Supreme Court observed that the plaintiffs had breathed life in the statistical evidence by offering evidence of individual disparate treatment.

On the other hand, the failure of a systemic treatment class action—or of the government plaintiff equivalent, a "pattern or practice" action by the U.S. Attorney General under Section 707—does not imply lack of merit to the individual disparate treatment case of any particular member of the plaintiff class. Cooper v. Federal Reserve Bank of Richmond (1984) Nor does that failure negate the employer's potential liability to an individual member of a plaintiff class for harm caused by a neutral employment practice. A given practice may disproportionately adversely impact those members of the plaintiff group who encounter it even though the group as a whole fares well at the "bottom line" of all policies, practices and decisions by employer agents. Connecticut v. Teal (1982).

F. NEUTRAL PRACTICES WITH DISPROPORTIONATE ADVERSE IMPACT

The federal courts have at times struggled to clarify the evidentiary frameworks for proving individual and systemic disparate treatment, but there has been no real question that such intentional conduct constitutes unlawful discrimination. By contrast, neutral employer practices that in operation fall with disproportionate adverse impact on the plaintiff's protected group have proven far more troublesome.

Initially a strong judicial consensus emerged that Congress intended to eradicate such practices on much the same terms as intentional acts of discrimination. Writing for a unanimous Court in Griggs v. Duke Power Co. (1971), Chief Justice Burger wrote that practices fair in form but discriminatory in effect may violate Title VII even though the employer's motivation in adopting the practice is neutral or benign. The early cases developing this theory considered the lawfulness of "objective" (really, specific or concrete or readily identifiable) employer practices such as educational requirements or standardized aptitude or psychological tests. The classic example is a labor union's requirement that an applicant for membership had to be sponsored by one of the existing members, all of whom were white. When none of the 30 members admitted under this policy during a six-year period were African–American or Hispanic, the plaintiff had proven prima facie that this "neutral" practice had a disproportionate adverse impact on members of the protected group. E.E.O.C. v. Steamship Clerks Union, Local 1066 (1st Cir. 1995).

Occasionally, however, disproportionate adverse impact analysis was applied to a "subjective" employer process such as the unstructured evaluation of black employees by white foremen. Rowe v. General Motors Corp. (5th Cir.1972). The Supreme Court approved the use of impact analysis to scrutinize these "subjective" promotion decisions, Watson v. Fort Worth Bank and Trust (1988), a decision not addressed and therefore apparently left undisturbed by the Civil Rights Act of 1991. Even a single employer practice—for example, a one-time layoff—may trigger disproportionate adverse impact analysis; the practice need not be a repeated or customary method of operation to be subject to impact scrutiny. Council 31, Am. Fed'n of State, County and Mun. Employees v. Ward (7th Cir.1992). Yet even after the 1991 Act, there are decisions ruling out the use of disparate impact proof when, in the court's view, the plaintiff fails to specify a particular aspect of an employer's subjective decisionmaking process that is allegedly responsible for an underrepresentation of the plaintiff class. And a court has held that an employer's reliance on interviews to screen subjectively for such traits as empathy and caring in the selection of social workers does not in and of itself reflect gender bias, even if those traits are disproportionately evident in women, because one may assume the traits are present in all candidates for the position of social worker. Scott v. Parkview Mem'l Hosp. (7th Cir.1999).

In Connecticut v. Teal (1982), the Supreme Court clarified that a single component of an employer's multi-stage selection process may have unlawfully discriminatory adverse impact on the particular protected group members it screens out even if the protected group as a whole fares better than a non-minority group in the overall process. The Court explained that the "principal focus" of Title VII is "the protection of the individual employee," rather than of minority groups. It rooted the disproportionate adverse impact theory in the language of § 703(a)(2): even though a plaintiff is not "discriminated against" in the disparate treatment sense intended by § 703(a)(1), neutral practices may, in the language of § 703(a)(2), "deprive or tend to deprive ... [the] individual of employment opportunities." Section 703(a)(2) is accordingly not concerned solely with how the plaintiff's group fares at the statistical "bottom line" of jobs or promotions, but also with "limitations" or "classifications" that deprive individual members of that group of the chance to advance. In sum, a racially balanced workforce—even one that results from affirmative action in favor of the plaintiff's protected group—does not immunize an employer from liability for a specific act of discrimination, whether intentional or neutral.

How to measure whether an employer's neutral practice has a "disproportionate" adverse impact on a protected group is a question that is addressed only vaguely by the Court's cases and remains unresolved by the 1991 Act. Some courts have adopted as a measure of disproportion the "eighty percent rule" from EEOC's Uniform Guidelines on Employee Selection Procedures. Smith v. Xerox Corp. (2d Cir.1999); In Re Employment Discrimination Litigation Against The State of Alabama (11th Cir.1999). These provide that a protected group's selection rate which is less than 80 percent of the rate for the group with the greatest success will be regarded by the Commission for enforcement purposes as evidence of adverse impact. 29 C.F.R. § 1607.4.

But the 80% rule has come under increasing attack from academic and court critics alike. It does not take sample size into account and thus may fail to detect statistically significant adverse impact on large samples, and its comparison of group pass rates may not measure the magnitude (as opposed to mere statistical significance) of a disparity as well as other techniques. David C. Baldus & James W. L. Cole, Statistical Proof of Discrimination (1989). Justice O'Connor, writing for a plurality in Watson v. Fort Worth Bank & Trust (1988), observed that EEOC's 80% test, while perhaps appropriate as a rough administrative guide for allocating agency prosecutorial resources, was not binding on judges. Insisting that the plaintiff should have to produce evidence that the challenged practice had a "significantly discriminatory impact," Justice O'Connor alluded to the need for a more rigorous and reliable measure of intergroup disparity. Justice O'Connor hinted that a better measure of whether a practice has legally and not just statistically significant adverse impact is the binomial distribution analysis approved by the Court for cases of systemic disparate treatment.

A year later, a majority of the court in Wards Cove Packing Co. v. Atonio (1989), appeared to agree with this approach when it required a prima facie demonstration that the challenged practice has a "significantly disparate impact" on the protected group. Further, the Court in *Wards Cove* appeared to demand prima facie evidence virtually indistinguishable from the statistical showing it had required for systemic *treatment* cases. Consistent with the Court's concerns, circuit decisions, too, have approved or even required standard deviation analysis or multiple regression analysis. These developments leave a lingering question. Why would a plaintiff undertake an impact challenge to a neutral practice—a proof mode the Court devised in *Griggs* precisely as an alternative to proof of intentional discrimination—if she must develop the same data and proffer the same expert statistical testimony that a class must adduce when it undertakes to show across-the-board intentional discrimination?

But several decisions emphasize that regardless of the particular measure of the magnitude of disparate impact created by an employer's neutral practice, the disparity will have no significance unless it is based on a fair and logical comparison. Thus, "what the plaintiff must attempt to do is show that there is a legally significant disparity between (a) the racial composition, caused by the challenged employment practice, of the pool of those enjoying a job or benefit; and (b) the racial composition of the qualified applicant pool." In re Employment Discrimination Litigation Against The State of Alabama (11th Cir.1999). These decisions reject the probative value of disparities derived from populations that fail to reflect the employment realities of the relevant applicant pool or employer practice.

The Court, in *Wards Cove*, cautioned the judiciary against too readily accepting a plaintiff's proposed lesser discriminatory alternative. The alternative must be "equally effective" as the employer's chosen practice, and "cost or other burdens" are "relevant in determining whether they would be equally as effective." The Court added that if a plaintiff could demonstrate the existence of a less discriminatory alternative so defined, in essence it would be showing that the employer's reliance on its original, challenged practice would be a "pretext" for discrimination. By thus implying that impact proof ultimately shows an employer's state of mind that is prohibited in any event by individual or systemic treatment evidence, the Court leaves us to wonder about the independent utility of the impact case so resoundingly supported by the unanimous decision in *Griggs* less than two decades before.

The Civil Rights Act of 1991 attempted to overrule significant aspects of the *Wards Cove* decision—just how effectively remains to be seen. As we consider the specifics, it is important to keep in mind that *Wards Cove* enfeebled group attacks on neutral practices by altering preexisting understandings about the three major phases of the disparate impact case: (1) plaintiff's prima facie evidence that a particular employment practice caused a specified disproportionate adverse impact on plaintiff's group; (2) the nature and quantum of the employer's defense to disproportionate impact; and (3) the plaintiff's rebuttal that an alternative practice would have largely, rather than perfectly, served the employer's legitimate goals, with lesser adverse impact on the group.

The legislation unequivocally declares that the employer's justification to a prima facie case is an affirmative defense on which the employer must persuade as well as produce evidence. In most other respects, though, the Act reflects Congress' inability to reach a unitary understanding about any of the three previously declared stages of the disproportionate adverse impact case. It fails to clarify the magnitude of the required prima facie case of disproportionate impact; it procedurally complicates the prima facie showing by requiring that the plaintiff ordinarily disentangle the effects of bundled employer practices; it declares that the defense consists of separate elements of job relatedness and business necessity, but offers only a calculatedly ambiguous understanding of what business necessity means; and it carries forward the seemingly unworkable *Wards Cove* innovation that the employer may avoid liability by adopting an alternative practice, perhaps even at the eleventh hour in the middle of a trial. On balance, therefore, the legislation falls well short of restoring the impact case to its pre-*Wards Cove* state.

The central provision, § 703(k)(1)(A), declares that an impact-based unlawful employment practice is proved when:

(i) a complaining party demonstrates that a respondent uses a particular employment practice that causes a disparate impact on the basis of race, color, religion, sex, or national origin and the respondent fails to demonstrate that the challenged practice is job related for the position in question and consistent with business necessity; or

(ii) the complaining party makes the demonstration described in subparagraph (C) with respect to an alternative employment practice and the respondent refuses to adopt such alternative employment practice.

The legislation sheds no light on the required magnitude of prima facie differential impact. In the hands of a Court that has proven resolutely hostile to borderline Title VII evidentiary showings, the legislative void on this question may well be filled by restrictive new mathematical requirements that could be justified on the authority of *Watson* and *Wards Cove*, which in this respect remain untouched.

Wards Cove, again furnishing a majority for a proposition that a plurality had endorsed in *Watson*, also required the plaintiff to isolate the single practice among several that produces an alleged adverse impact. *Wards Cove*. New § 701(k)(1)(B)(i) relieves the plaintiff who is attempting to demonstrate adverse impact under § 703(k)(1)(A)(i) from having to disentangle bundled practices, but only if she can "demonstrate" (again a burden of persuasion as well as production) "that the elements of a respondent's decisionmaking process [a 'process' is apparently a package of 'practices'] are not capable of separation for analysis." Section 105(a) (adding Title VII § 703(k)(1)(B)(i)). Otherwise she must show that "each particular challenged employment practice causes a disparate impact." These provisions invite satellite litigation over the extent to which the plaintiff has taken advantage of discovery and the employer has forthrightly responded. Employer initiated motions on the issue are more than a remote possibility.

A related provision, § 703(k)(1)(B)(ii), is apparently intended to apply when the plaintiff has been allowed, by virtue of § 703(*l*), to attack an entire selection process without demonstrating the adverse impact of each particular component practice. Subdivision (ii) relieves the employer of showing the business necessity of any particular practice that *it* can demonstrate does not cause a disparate impact on plaintiff's group. In tandem, subdivisions (i) and (ii) of § 703(k)(1)(B) seem to assume that sometimes the employer will be able to disentangle the effects of bundled practices even after the plaintiff has satisfied the court that, after discovery, she cannot.

Once the plaintiff demonstrates that a specific practice causes a disparate impact (of still unquantified magnitude), the employer must, after the effective date of the 1991 Act, "demonstrate that the challenged practice is job-related for the position in question and consistent with business necessity." Section 105(a) (adding Title VII § 703(k)(1)(A)(i), 42 U.S.C.A. § 2000e–2(k)(1)(A)(i)) (emphasis added). Further, the obligation to "demonstrate" these elements imposes on the employer, as was generally held before *Wards Cove*, the burden of persuasion on this defense. The net result is that the text of the legislatively overhauled impact defense closely resembles the two-pronged *Diaz/Weeks* BFOQ defense to an expressly discriminatory policy after *Johnson Controls*. The employer bears the compound burden of showing that a neutral practice is necessary for the business (probably a less demanding showing than the *Diaz* "essence of the business" requirement) and is keyed to the particular occupation it screens for (although only "related" to that job, a showing considerably less demanding than the required *Weeks* proof that "all or substantially all" protected group members could not perform it). It is true that requiring the employer to link its practice to requirements of the job, and not just to unspecified "legitimate goals" of the business as a whole, seems to place the plaintiff in a somewhat better posture than she was in after *Wards Cove*. But what do job-relatedness and business necessity now mean? Congress tell us in a preliminary provision on legislative purpose, Section 3, that it seeks to codify those concepts as they were defined by *Griggs* and in subsequent Supreme Court disparate impact decisions before *Wards Cove*. In an unusual attempt to control the judicial interpretive process in advance, Congress adds in § 105(b) that only one specified interpretive memorandum may be "relied upon in any way as legislative history in construing or applying . . . any provision of this Act that relates to *Wards Cove*—Business necessity/cumulation/alternate business practice." Unfortunately, the referenced memorandum, dated October 25, 1991, rather unhelpfully repeats virtually verbatim Section 3's statement that the business necessity and job relatedness concepts in the Act are akin to those developed by the Supreme Court before *Wards Cove*.

Leaving the definition of the defense for decision by the federal bench could result in a formulation markedly less stringent than the consensus approach of the intermediate appellate courts during the years preceding *Wards Cove*. There is even some possibility that the Supreme Court will return to a definition that approximates the lax *Wards Cove* standard: whether the challenged practice serves to some unspecified degree unspecified general business goals. The Court's latitude to do so arises from the opposing directions, pointed to by its pre-*Wards Cove* decisions, the new benchmark mandated by the 1991 Act.

Two decisions subsequent to the 1991 Act, in reaching different conclusions about the validity of a no-beard rule, illustrate how application of the new job relatedness and business necessity defense may vary depending upon the requirements of the job. *Fitzpatrick v. City of Atlanta* (11th Cir.1993) (fire department beard ban for black males upheld); *Bradley v. Pizzaco of Neb., Inc.* (8th Cir.1993) (no beard rule for pizza delivery men struck down).

Before *Wards Cove*, the plaintiff could rebut the employer's defense of business justification by establishing that an alternative practice would serve the employer's job-related needs with less discriminatory impact on the protected group. Albemarle Paper Co. v. Moody (1975). *Wards Cove* tightened the concept by insisting that the plaintiff's identified alternative be "equally" effective as the employer's chosen practice, cautioning that the "cost or other burdens of proposed alternative selection devices are relevant" in making that determination. (Quoting *Watson*). It so concluded even though cost defenses ordinarily have not avoided Title VII violations predicated on disparate treatment. International Union, UAW v. Johnson Controls (1991).

The Act responds to the *Wards Cove* requirement that an alternative practice be "equally effective" by returning to "the law as it existed on June 4, 1989, [the day before the *Wards Cove* decision] with respect to the concept of 'alternative employment practice.' " Section 105(a) (adding subparagraph (k)(1)(C) to § 703 of Title VII, 42 U.S.C.A. § 2000e–2). Of course this still leaves the possibility that the courts will continue to adhere to the *Wards Cove* insistence on equal effectiveness, with its focus on avoiding additional cost to the employer, because that notion had earlier surfaced in the plurality opinion in *Watson*. In any event, even if the Act is construed to allow the plaintiff to rebut with a less effective, somewhat more expensive alternative, it is doubtful that the Court will read it to require an employer to bear as much additional expense as the Americans With Disabilities Act requires employers to bear in making "reasonable accommodations" to individuals with disabilities.

Finally, even if the plaintiff meets whatever new standards the Court may demand for demonstrating a less discriminatory alternative, the rebuttal may ultimately fail because the Act also carries forward another innovation of *Wards Cove* that first surfaced in *Watson*: there will be no law violation unless in addition "the respondent refuses to adopt such alternative employment practice." Section 105(a)(ii) (adding subsection (k)(1)(A)(ii) to § 703 of Title VII, 42 U.S.C.A. § 2000e–2). Section 703(k)(1)(A)(ii) provides that an unlawful employment practice is established if the plaintiff "makes the demonstration described in subparagraph (C) with respect to an alternative employment practice [the subparagraph that returns to the pre-*Wards Cove* law] *and* the respondent refuses to adopt such alternative practice."

When must such a refusal take place to pin liability on the employer under this provision? "Respondent" and "complaining party" rather than "defendant" and "plaintiff" are the words used here, which might suggest that the employer's last chance to trump a showing of violation is during state, local or EEOC proceedings rather than at trial. But the section in which the refusal-to-adopt provision is found prescribes for the entire "title" how to establish an "unlawful employment practice" based on disparate impact. This implies that an employer may defeat the plaintiff's newly relaxed showing of a lesser discriminatory alternative as late as the latter stages of a trial on the merits. That construction is supported by the present-tense verbs in Section 703(k)(1)(A)(ii): the violation is established if the respondent "refuses to adopt" an alternative practice, but that happens only after the complaining party "makes the demonstration" of such a practice. A "demonstration," in turn, probably cannot be made until judicial trial; "demonstrates" is defined by new § 701(m) to refer to satisfying burdens of production and persuasion.

If a Supreme Court majority holds that a last-minute employer adoption of the plaintiff's proffered alternative avoids all liability (because, in the words of the Act, there would then be no "unlawful employment practice"), the named plaintiffs, who successfully attacked the employer's original practice through all three phases of the impact case, will be deprived of any relief and, in turn, eligibility for attorney's fees. Although protected group members who work for that employer will enjoy the benefits of the adopted lesser discriminatory practice in futuro, what incentive would prospective plaintiffs have to sue (or prospective plaintiffs' counsel to take the case)? The problem is particularly acute because in the end Congress failed to overturn Supreme Court decisions approving of defendants' procedural maneuvers that avoid or diminish their liability for attorney's fees to prevailing plaintiffs.

In sum, the Civil Rights Act of 1991 reflects Congressional equivocation about the group protection theory advanced by the disproportionate adverse impact mode of proof. Although it describes a defensive standard likely to be somewhat more rigorous than that declared by *Wards Cove*, it leaves the prima facie case vulnerable not only to ad hoc statistical requirements but also to unrealistic trial court conclusions that discovery devices suffice to enable the plaintiff to disentangle the effects of compound employer practices. More clearly still, the Act fails in the end to restore the pre-*Wards Cove* status of the plaintiff's rebuttal, by affording the employer a last-ditch means of avoiding liability altogether.

G. ADMINISTRATIVE PREREQUISITES AND PROCEDURES

1. IN GENERAL

Title VII sets out federal and state agency prerequisites to suit. In general, the private sector applicant or employee need only comply with two such prerequisites: (1) timely filing of a charge with the U.S. Equal Employment Opportunity Commission ("EEOC"), either in the first instance or, in the majority of states that have parallel state or local antidiscrimination legislation and agencies, after filing with those agencies; and (2) timely filing of a federal or state court action within 90 days after receipt from EEOC of a "notice of right to sue." Failure to follow the specified procedures and meet the charge-filing and suit-commencement deadlines usually results in dismissal of the administrative charge or ensuing judicial action.

Although 1972 amendments to Title VII gave EEOC the right to seek judicial relief in the first instance, most judicial action takes the form of private suits in federal district court. The path to court is strewn with a series of intricate and time-consuming administrative procedures at the state and federal levels. These requirements are designed to give state or local antidiscrimination agencies and EEOC opportunities to obtain voluntary resolution of discrimination disputes, as well as to promote federal-state comity.

The complainant must first file a written charge with the EEOC, "sufficiently precise to identify the parties and to describe generally the action or practice complained of." In addition, however, the statute requires "deferral" to a state or local agency where local law prohibits the unlawful employment practice alleged and establishes an agency with authority to grant or seek relief concerning that practice. In the few states that do not have such fair employment practices legislation and enforcement agencies, or where the local law does not provide its authority jurisdiction over a particular violation, a charge must be filed with EEOC within 180 days of an alleged unlawful employment practice. In the great majority of states that do have such laws and agencies, the charge must be filed with EEOC within the earlier of 300 days of the alleged violation, or 30 days after the charging party receives "notice that the state or local antidiscrimination agency has terminated" proceedings under state or local law. But unless it dismisses a charge earlier, this state or local "deferral" agency must be given 60 days in which to attempt to resolve the dispute before EEOC may proceed. This latter requirement suggests not only that the state filing must precede a filing with EEOC, but also, by subtracting 60 from 300, that the charge must ordinarily be filed with the state or local "deferral" agency within 240 days of the alleged unlawful employment practice. However, a state or local filing later than 240 but still within 300 days of the alleged unlawful practice will be considered timely if the state or local agency terminates its proceedings before day 300. Moreover, the plaintiff gets the benefit of the 300–day period for filing with EEOC, and may use the 240–day "plus" schedule approved by *Mohasco* for filing with the state or local agency, even if the latter filing is untimely under the state or local antidiscrimination law to which the EEOC is deferring. These time constraints apply, however, even if the plaintiff seeks only declaratory relief.

It should be noted that the foregoing time limitations specified by statute refer to filing directly "with" the state or local agency and then "with" EEOC. In fact, informal administrative agreements between EEOC and many state and local deferral agencies, now sanctioned by case law, have altered these requirement so that a filing with one can constitute a filing with the other; the EEOC filing may even precede the local one. For example, the state or local administrative filing will be considered adequate even where the complainant has filed a charge only or initially with EEOC, if EEOC itself refers the charge to the local agency and suspends its proceedings for the required 60 days or until local proceedings terminate. Conversely, a "worksharing" agreement may specify that where the complainant files first with a state or local agency, that agency becomes EEOC's agent for receiving the charge even if it never forwards the charge to EEOC.

Where a state or local agency waives the right to process the charge initially, or to proceed if the charge is filed more than a specified time after the occurrence of the alleged unlawful employment practice, the circuit courts have extended the Supreme Court's approval of work-sharing agreements by holding that the state's waiver is a "termination" of state or local proceedings that authorizes the EEOC to begin its investigation without waiting 60 days. In such a jurisdiction the complainant need never file with a state or local agency and need file a charge with EEOC only within 300 days of the alleged unlawful employment practice, instead of the 240 days that would govern if there were no work-sharing agreement. The state or local agency may retain jurisdiction, however, to process the charge thereafter if it chooses.

In brief, although § 706 appears to require that the state or local filing precede the filing of a charge with EEOC, it is apparent from the Court's approval of deferral and work-sharing agreements that in practice EEOC is often the first, and sometimes the only agency to investigate and conciliate charges, even in deferral states. Nevertheless, where the state or local agency has made a prior determination, the statute directs EEOC to give its findings "substantial weight" in determining whether there is reasonable cause to support the charge. Nevertheless, it is not a prerequisite to suit that EEOC find reasonable cause to believe the Act violated, and even an EEOC determination to the contrary will not bar suit in court.

The 180–day or 300–day charge-filing deadline periods are triggered only when the alleged unlawful employment practice is complete and when the applicant or employee knows or should know of the facts that support a claim under the statute. For this purpose the date of an alleged unlawful employment practice is usually the date on which the complaining applicant or employee should be aware of the consequences and unlawfulness of employer conduct, not when those consequences become manifest. This approach can cut both ways: starting the charge-filing clock well before a termination is consummated or stopping the clock from running until, after termination, the employee learns the facts that suggest the termination was unlawful. Pursuing a grievance under a collective bargaining agreement will not toll the time to file a charge with EEOC. But the 180–day and 300–day EEOC charge-filing deadlines, although critical, are not technically jurisdictional. Rather they are procedural preconditions to suit, analogous to statutes of limitations, and thus may be waived, estopped, or equitably tolled.

For example, the following facts illustrate both the accrual date definition problem and the doctrine of equitable tolling. A law firm employee asserted a claim of discriminatory dismissal in her EEOC charge, later amending that charge to complain of a subsequent failure to rehire. These claims would have been untimely under the applicable 300–day charge-filing period if they accrued on the date of her dismissal. But the plaintiff claimed in addition that the firm had actively misled her about the reason for termination, misrepresenting that there was insufficient work for her to do when in fact there was. The court held that under the "discovery" rule, which marks the running of a claim when the plaintiff learns of an injury, both claims were barred. Plaintiff knew of the termination when it occurred, making her dismissal claim untimely, and the failure to re-hire claim was therefore simply an amendment to an untimely charge. By contrast, if her claim of misrepresentation proved well founded, the court held, the plaintiff could benefit from equitable tolling. It explained that active deception will toll the running of the charge-filing period until the facts that would support a charging party's allegations become apparent or should be apparent to a person having a reasonably prudent regard for her rights.

Tolling does not necessarily require positive misconduct on the part of the employer. Some courts have equitably tolled the 300–day EEOC filing deadline when an unrepresented claimant receives misleading advice about filing from a state deferral agency, even when the advice is only ambiguous rather than false. But equitable tolling will not save the untimely filing of a claimant who simply waits until others similarly situated complete a successful challenge to the policy affecting them all. Further, there is no general doctrine that allegations of constructive discharge will equitably toll the relevant deadlines.

2. CONTINUING VIOLATIONS

The judicially created continuing violations doctrine aids attacks on discriminatory acts that occurred "outside," that is, before the beginning of, the applicable Title VII charge-filing deadline. Because that deadline is 180 or at most 300 days, but the Act permits back pay to accrue as far back as two years (i.e., roughly 730 days) before the filing of an EEOC charge, Congress may have envisioned continuing remediable violations that existed prior to the running of the period. But the courts have generally limited the employer's liability to discriminatory acts that occur within the charge-filing period. Adverse *effects* of pre-period discriminatory conduct do not ordinarily revive the statute on that conduct even when those effects are felt within the period. United Air Lines, Inc. v. Evans (1977). Ordinarily the "present consequence of a one-time violation" does not extend the period, and so the EEOC charge must be filed within 300 (or 180) days of that discrete act. See EEOC v. Westinghouse Electric Corp. (3d Cir.1983).

The relatively permissive use of the doctrine under the Equal Pay Act is explained by the fact that the sole EPA violation, discrimination in compensation, is an ongoing practice. Title VII, by contrast, also reaches a variety of employer decisions that may be deemed complete at one moment in time. For example, the Supreme Court, rejecting a simple "last day of work" rule, held that a college professor's claim of discriminatory discharge accrued when he was notified of the employer's decision to deny him tenure, not later when his appeals or grievances were denied or his contract expired. Delaware State College v. Ricks (1980). It is clear, however, that some Title VII violations are subject to the continuing violations doctrine. In Bazemore v. Friday (1986), plaintiffs challenged a public employer's pay system as racially discriminatory. The employer argued that the statute's charge filing period should run from the dates it adopted and first applied the system. But the Court held that "[e]ach week's pay check that delivers less to a black than to a similarly situated white is a wrong actionable under Title VII." And the Court also observed that even where the doctrine is inapplicable, *evidence* of past, out-of-time discrimination may be admissible because it "might in some circumstances support the inference that such discrimination continued [into the 180-day or 300-day charge-filing period], particularly where relevant aspects of the decisionmaking process had undergone little change."

Aside from salary discrimination, continuing violations have been found respecting some ongoing denials of promotion and racial or sexual harassment that consists not of one dramatic or "discrete" episode but of a series of less aggravated acts that in the aggregate alter the plaintiff's conditions of employment or create a hostile or abusive work environment. Provided, therefore, that at least one alleged act of harassment occurred within the charge-filing period, courts will admit related evidence, antedating the beginning of that period, that constitutes part of the same general pattern of conduct. The Supreme Court has recently approved a generous continuing violation approach to environmental, or non–"discrete," sexual (or racial) harassment, upholding the timeliness of an entire claim provided any one incident forming part of the pattern occurred within the applicable charge–filing period. *National R.R. Passenger Corporation v. Morgan* (2002).

The Civil Rights Act of 1991 has made resort to the continuing violation doctrine unnecessary with respect to Title VII violations caused by the unlawful adverse impact of unlawful, non-bona fide seniority systems. Overruling a Supreme Court decision, the Act provides that such violations occur not only when the system is adopted, but subsequently when a person is injured by it. Section 706(e)(2). This provision illustrates that claims alleging that an employer's neutral practice has unlawful discriminatory impact do not even accrue until the plaintiff's protected group experiences adverse effects and the plaintiff herself is denied an employment benefit through the implementation of that practice.

It is often difficult to distinguish between an ongoing unlawful practice and the delayed consequence of a single discriminatory act that took place more than 180 or 300 days before an EEOC charge was filed. The circuits are split, for example, on when the limitations period begins to run on challenges to hiring lists compiled from discriminatory test results. Compare Bouman v. Block (9th Cir.1991) with Bronze Shields, Inc.

v. New Jersey Dep't of Civil Serv. (3d Cir.1981). While a challenge to a subjective employment evaluation has been held timely if filed within a limitations period running from the date the evaluation resulted in adverse effect, another court deems the limitations period triggered by a denial of training, not the subsequent layoff resulting from the lack of training. See, respectively, Johnson v. General Electric (1st Cir.1988) and Hamilton v. Komatsu Dresser Indus., Inc. (7th Cir.1992).

3. CHARGE–FILING PROCEDURE

Within the 180–or 300–day period described above, a charge may be filed either by an aggrieved individual or a commissioner of EEOC. It need only be in writing, be subscribed to by oath or affirmation, and contain such information and be in such form as the Commission by regulation requires; and Commission regulations require only that the charge include a clear and concise statement of the facts, including the pertinent dates, constituting the alleged unlawful employment practices. Nevertheless, the complainant, to protect her ability to commence a judicial action should she remain aggrieved after the relief if any is afforded through the EEOC proceedings, must provide the defendant notice of the ground or grounds of prohibited discrimination alleged as well as the circumstances giving rise to the charge through a timely filed charge.

EEOC regulations provide that certain amendments to charges may relate back to the filing date of the original charge, and if so would be deemed timely although the amendment was not made until after the applicable 180–or 300–day deadline. Under the regulations, an amendment, to be eligible for relation back, must correct technical defects or omissions, clarify or amplify the allegations in the original charge, or add new allegations "related to or growing out of the subject matter of the original charge." The last category is naturally the most controversial, and the lower federal courts have devised a variety of formulations to gauge whether allegations in amendment meet the quoted requirement.

Regardless of who files a charge, EEOC is required to serve a notice of the charge on the respondent or respondents, setting forth the "date, place and circumstances of the alleged unlawful employment practice," within ten days after its filing. The statute protects the confidentiality of Commission proceedings by stipulating criminal penalties if a Commission employee, prior to the institution of a judicial proceeding, makes public information obtained by the Commission. This prohibition, however, does not apply to the charging party. To protect the Commission's role as a guardian of the public interest, courts have regularly invalidated private agreements, usually entered into to settle an ongoing dispute, whereby an employee or former employee agrees not to file a charge with EEOC or not to assist in an EEOC investigation.

The Agency is entitled to examine and copy evidence of any person under investigation that is "relevant to the charge under investigation." The Supreme Court has construed the statute to give the Commission administrative subpoena power to enforce its right of access to evidence in the possession of an investigated person that is relevant to a prohibited unlawful employment practice and the charge in question. The charge must meet the minimal statutory requirements before an EEOC subpoena warrants judicial enforcement, but no greater detail is required for a "pattern or practice" charge than for charges alleging individual instances of discrimination. In addition, compliance with the notice requirement is apparently a jurisdictional prerequisite to judicial enforcement of the subpoena, but the notice, like the detail concerning the objects of the subpoena, need be no more elaborate in a pattern or practice case. The Court has fortified the Commission's subpoena authority by refusing to recognize a common-law privilege for academic institutions that would have required the Commission to show particularized need for subpoenaed documents, rather than mere relevance. Similarly, the Seventh Circuit, observing that under Federal Rule of Evidence 501 state law privileges do not apply in federal litigation, has upheld on federal supremacy grounds an EEOC subpoena for a transcript of a state unemployment compensation hearing. The 300–day charge-filing deadline does not serve as a temporal limit on the scope of EEOC's subpoena, which may reach records dating from three years or more before the alleged unlawful employment practice. While no statute of limitations applies to an EEOC pattern or practice suit, employers have on rare occasions successfully argued laches.

Recognizing the Agency's public function, the Supreme Court has declined to limit the EEOC's ability, after investigation, to seek judicial enforcement in its own name to the 180–day period in which it alone, to the exclusion of a private party, may file suit. Occidental Life Ins. Co. v. EEOC (1977). But a circuit court has held that once private parties have initiated litigation by requesting right to sue notices from the Agency and filing a civil complaint based on the events described in their EEOC charges, EEOC, whatever its independent power to file suit in its own name, may no longer continue to investigate. EEOC v. Hearst Corp. (5th Cir.1997).

Although Title VII provides that the EEOC "shall make an investigation" of a charge filed, it does not prescribe the manner for doing so. "The nature and extent of an EEOC investigation into a discrimination claim is a matter within the discretion of that agency." Because the nature and extent of the investigation are discretionary, a plaintiff does not have a "clear right" to a writ of mandamus to force the EEOC to pursue an investigation.

4. FROM EEOC TO FEDERAL OR STATE COURT

The EEOC investigation ultimately arrives at one of two basic conclusions. After investigation, the Agency may find "reasonable cause" to believe that the Act has been violated, and must then undertake conciliation. Alternatively, EEOC may find "no reasonable cause" and issue a notice of dismissal. 42 U.S.C.A. § 2000e–5. In either event, a complainant is entitled upon demand to receive a "right-to-sue" letter from EEOC no later than 180 days after the effective date of the filing of a charge with the agency. Since EEOC frequently takes years to process charges, the question has arisen how long a prospective Title VII plaintiff may wait beyond 180 days before demanding a right-to-sue letter. Courts have occasionally barred Title VII actions in these circumstances on grounds of laches, when a delay of several years in demanding a suit letter was deemed unreasonable and caused tangible prejudice to the defendant. An appellate court has recently reached the opposite conclusion under ADEA, reasoning that laches cannot be a bar under a federal statute that contains a statute of limitations. Miller v. Maxwell's International Inc. (9th Cir.1993). On the other hand, if EEOC is willing to issue the right to sue notice before the end of its 180–day period of presumptive exclusive jurisdiction, the plaintiff may proceed to court, provided she files within 90 days of receiving the notice. Sims v. Trus Joist MacMillan (11th Cir.1994).

Title VII affords plaintiffs a liberal federal venue choice among the districts where the alleged unlawful employment practice occurred; where records pertaining to the practice are maintained; or where the plaintiff allegedly would have worked but for the unlawful practice. Title VII § 706(f)(3), 42 U.S.C.A. § 2000e–5(f)(3). When the prospective defendant cannot be "found" in any of the above districts, the statute provides as a default the district where it has its principal office. The text also indicates that each of these districts is a suitable place for the action to be transferred under 28 U.S.C.A. §§ 1404 and 1406. It has been held that in considering a motion for transfer under Title VII, the court should apply the same considerations of party and witness convenience that ordinarily apply under those sections, rejecting the argument that the special Title VII venue choices are intended to give plaintiff the last word on forum selection. Ross v. Buckeye Cellulose Corp. (11th Cir.1993).

Although the vast majority of Title VII actions are brought in federal court, state courts have concurrent jurisdiction. Yellow Freight v. Donnelly (1990). A complainant who wishes to sue in either state or federal court must commence an action by filing a complaint within 90 days after receipt of the EEOC "right-to-sue" letter or notice of dismissal. That deadline is generally strictly enforced, although it, like the administrative charge-filing deadline, is apparently amenable to equitable tolling, estoppel, or waiver. See Baldwin County Welcome Center v. Brown (1984). Related actions under the Reconstruction Civil Rights Acts, notably § 1981, may be commenced even before Title VII charges have been administratively processed; but the limitations periods and administrative deadlines of the respective statutes must be satisfied independently. Johnson v. Railway Express Agency, Inc. (1975).

The right to bring a judicial lawsuit does not turn on EEOC's evaluation of the probable merits of a charge. The judicial action may be commenced even if EEOC concludes that there is no reasonable cause to believe that the employer has violated Title VII. *McDonnell Douglas*. The case may proceed even if EEOC believes that an employer offer of settlement affords the charging party full relief. An EEOC determination of no reasonable cause to believe that race discrimination allegations are true may be admissible under the public record exception to the hearsay rule in a private action for employment discrimination. Barfield v. Orange County (11th Cir.1990). Similarly, an EEOC or state agency determination that there is reasonable cause is also admissible, at least in bench trials. Heyne v. Caruso (9th Cir.1995); Gilchrist v. Jim Slemons Imports (9th Cir.1986). But see Walker v. NationsBank (11th Cir.1995). In any event, the agency's determination of "reasonable cause" or "no reasonable cause" will be given only such weight at trial as the federal court believes it deserves. If EEOC certifies to the court that a case initiated by a private party is of "general public importance," it may intervene as of right in the proceeding. Section 706(f)(1), 42 U.S.C.A. § 2000e–5(f)(1).

Title VII also provides that a district court may appoint counsel "[u]pon application by the complainant and in such circumstances as the court may deem just." The circuits are split on the issue of whether a court order denying the appointment of counsel is immediately appealable under the collateral order exception to the "final decision" rule of 28 U.S.C.A. § 1291.

5. ARBITRATION

Until 1991, it was settled that a putative plaintiff's resort to a grievance or arbitration procedure, prosecuted by her union, would not bar her later judicial action under Title VII, even after an unfavorable arbitral disposition. That was the message of Alexander v. Gardner–Denver Co. (1974). Today, however, the judicial avenue of redress may be altogether foreclosed to an uncertain number of potential plaintiffs who, individually or perhaps even through their union's agreement in collective bargaining, have agreed to arbitrate claims of employment discrimination.

This possibility was posed a 1991 decision by the Supreme Court that arose from an arbitration requirement contained in a securities exchange's rules that a brokerage house employee agreed to abide by in his application with a member firm. In Gilmer v. Interstate/Johnson Lane Corp. (1991), the Court ruled that an employee who made such an agreement could be compelled to arbitrate his statutory discrimination claim— there, under the Age Discrimination in Employment Act—by virtue of the Federal Arbitration Act ("FAA"). The Court also strongly implied, although it did not hold, that an adverse arbitration award would bar the plaintiff's subsequent ADEA action (although not a classwide enforcement action by EEOC). In so suggesting the Court distinguished *Gardner–Denver* as a case where the agreement to arbitrate (1) was collectively bargained and (2) required arbitration of claims concerning the interpretation and application of the terms of the union contract, rather than claims of statutory employment discrimination. The majority's opinion reflected some sensitivity to the risk that a union's agreement to arbitrate might effectively bargain away the statutory rights of union members.

Thus when a pre-dispute agreement to arbitrate is contained in a collectively bargained agreement, most post-*Gilmer* decisions have continued to apply *Gardner–Denver*, excusing the plaintiff from arbitrating a statutory claim and permitting him to pursue it in court, unless he agrees to arbitrate after a dispute has arisen. But the Fourth Circuit construed *Gilmer* as overriding *Gardner–Denver* even when an arbitration clause is contained in a collective agreement. It upheld arbitration under a collective bargaining agreement that specifically required the employer to comply with federal civil rights laws. The court dismissed *Gardner–Denver* as "old law" superseded by *Gilmer* and relied on changes in legal culture that have increasingly favored arbitration as a means to resolve statutory discrimination claims, including *Gilmer* itself and § 118 of Title VII, an encouragement to voluntary alternative dispute resolution added by the Civil Rights Act of 1991. The court wrote broadly that as long as an agreement to arbitrate is voluntary, it is valid whether contained in "a securities registration application, a simple employment contract, or a collective bargaining agreement."

In Wright v. Universal Maritime Service Corp. (1998), the Supreme Court declined to decide if a union-negotiated, pre-dispute waiver of a judicial forum for the resolution of federal statutory employment discrimination rights could ever be validly enforced against the individual union member. Instead it held that such a waiver was not entitled to any presumption of arbitrability and must at a minimum be clear and unmistakable. Because the collective bargaining agreement at issue did not specifically require the employer to adhere to the ADA, and the arbitration clause did not specifically refer to claims under the ADA (or any other federal employment discrimination statute), the Court's "clear statement" requirement was not met and the grievant accordingly could not be required to arbitrate as a precondition of filing suit.

The EEOC takes the position that pre-dispute agreements entered into as a condition of employment that mandate arbitration of discrimination claims are by their nature presumptively involuntary or coercive. EEOC will therefore process a charge of statutory discrimination regardless of whether the charging party's pre-dispute agreement to arbitrate is contained in an individual or collectively bargained contract. The Supreme Court resolved a circuit split by deciding that EEOC in its role as public representative is not bound by an individual employee's agreement to arbitrate when it seeks classwide injunctive relief. EEOC v. Waffle House (2002).

Outside the collective bargaining context, in the continuing absence of controlling Supreme Court guidance, federal appellate courts have incrementally extended *Gilmer* beyond ADEA by enforcing individual employees' agreements to arbitrate. The circuit decisions began by compelling arbitration, in the same securities industry setting, of claims asserted under Title VII. These courts have found that *Gilmer* can coexist with *Gardner–Denver* because the latter simply holds that an employee has not waived the right to pursue the Title VII statutory remedy merely by permitting his union to arbitrate a grievance procedure contractually agreed to and controlled by his employer and his union. By contrast, these courts have ruled, the individual employee's acquiescence in the arbitration clause, manifested by her signing a registration application such as the one that the New York Stock Exchange requires of applicants for employment with member firms, evidenced a voluntary personal commitment to arbitrate all claims related to that employment. These agreements to arbitrate statutory discrimination claims have therefore been deemed enforceable under the FAA when contained in contracts which, like most, touch interstate commerce.

Whether the federal judiciary will in the end enforce individual employees' agreements to arbitrate discrimination claims when those agreements are contained in a plaintiff's own employment contract—that is, outside the securities industry where the agreement is formally obtained by an applicant's agreement to abide by rules of an exchange of which the prospective employer is a member—may depend on the resolution of several related issues.

One threshold question that the Supreme Court has answered concerns an exception to FAA's enforcement powers contained in FAA § 1. That provision excludes from FAA's reach arbitration agreements in "contracts of employment of seamen, railroad employees, or any other class of workers engaged in foreign or interstate commerce." In line with the eleven circuit courts that embraced the narrow, "transportation-only" interpretation of § 1, the Court in Circuit City Stores v. Adams (2001), held that only employment contracts of transportation workers were exempted from FAA.

The Supreme Court has not directly disturbed the holding of *Gardner–Denver* that permits Title VII or ADEA plaintiffs to pursue their statutory discrimination claims in court after an adverse arbitration award, issued pursuant to the authority of the FAA, determines their rights under a *collective* bargaining agreement. Indeed, to harmonize *Gilmer* with the broadest implications of *Gardner–Denver*, the Court might go further still and deny even front-end enforceability under the FAA to arbitration promises contained in agreements that are collectively bargained. Even then, *non-union* employers subject to Title VII, the ADEA, and the Americans with Disabilities Act will have an incentive to "negotiate"—more realistically, at least where jobs are scarce, to insert unilaterally—agreements to arbitrate statutory discrimination claims in *individual* employment contracts. Even if *Gardner–Denver* is reaffirmed, those agreements would remain enforceable under *Gilmer* and the circuit authority that has extended it.

With the 1991 Act's addition of § 118 to Title VII, the circuits that have confronted the issue have extended *Gilmer* to enforce individual employees' agreements to arbitrate Title VII and other statutory employment discrimination claims against employers outside the securities industry. Although the Civil Rights Act of 1991 is silent about *Gilmer,* § 118 provides additional impetus for the arbitration of several kinds of statutory discrimination claims. Section 118 provides: "Where appropriate and to the extent authorized by law, the use of alternative means of dispute resolution, including settlement negotiations, conciliation, facilitation, mediation, fact-finding, mini-trials, and arbitration, is encouraged to resolve disputes arising under the Acts or provisions of Federal law amended by this title." This includes Title VII, ADEA, § 1981, and ADA. Several federal circuit courts have relied *inter alia* on § 118 in holding that claims under the ADA and Title VII may not proceed in court where the plaintiff had failed to invoke a grievance or arbitration forum contemplated by a pre-dispute agreement to arbitrate. And at least nine circuits now hold that Congress did not intend to prohibit the use of predispute arbitration agreements for resolving claims under Title VII and other statutes prohibiting employment discrimination. Some of these decisions cite the Supreme Court's directive to resolve all doubts concerning arbitrability in favor of arbitration, even when the agreement to arbitrate was made before the dispute arose and as a condition of employment.

Initially the Ninth Circuit, alone among circuits addressing the issue, held in Duffield v. Robertson Stephens & Co. (9th Cir. 1998), that the Civil Rights Act of 1991, enacted to expand employees' rights and increase the possible remedies available to civil rights plaintiffs, *precludes* such arbitration because the kind of "voluntary" alternative dispute resolution encouraged by § 118 impliedly prohibits employers from requiring their employees, as a condition of employment, to agree to arbitrate Title VII claims. Subsequently, however, in E.E.O.C. v. Luce, Forward, Hamilton & Scripps (9th Cir. 2003) (en banc), the Ninth Circuit, sitting en banc, overruled *Duffield*. It concluded that the Supreme Court's intervening decision in *Circuit City* reflected that Court's approval of a broad range of individual agreements to arbitrate Title VII claims, even including predispute arbitration agreements extracted as a condition of initial employment.

Yet some circuits, relying on the judicially crafted FAA presumption of arbitrability, have found even general language in individual employment contracts (whereby the parties agree to resolve all contract-related disputes) adequate to embrace statutory discrimination claims. On the other hand, courts have not been nearly so ready to infer a knowing, voluntary waiver of substantive statutory rights when the employer relies on a complete release of those rights contained in an ad hoc agreement entered into at the time of a termination. Perhaps the difference is that in the arbitration setting the employee is not waiving the statutory right altogether, but "merely" the judicial forum and perhaps some of the remedies that Congress provided for its vindication.

The Supreme Court may resolve the questions regarding interpretation of § 118 of Title VII and § 1 of the FAA in a number of distinct ways. It might reaffirm *Gilmer* and overrule *Gardner–Denver* by asserting that its numerous decisions facilitating arbitration, coupled with § 118, have completely sapped the vitality of its earlier decisions that denied preclusive effect to arbitration awards in actions under other labor and civil rights statutes.

The Supreme Court has not decided whether *Gardner–Denver* permits a court to entertain a Title VII claim following confirmation of an arbitral award in state court. Some circuits have denied preclusion in this situation, finding that the state court's limited scope of review did not constitute a final judgment on the merits and in any event did not involve the same "claim" as that afforded by Title VII. Ryan v. City of Shawnee (10th Cir.1993); Kirk v. Board of Educ. of Bremen Cmty. High Sch. (7th Cir.1987); Bottini v. Sadore Mgmt. Corp. (2d Cir.1985). Another circuit, however, invoked collateral estoppel or "issue preclusion" in a Title VII action after finding that the state court that had confirmed the arbitration award had ruled not just on plaintiffs' collective bargaining rights but also on the merits of their Title VII claims. Rider v. Pennsylvania (3d Cir.1988).

How does the Older Workers Benefit Protection Act (OWB-PA) coexist with *Gilmer*? Shortly after *Gilmer* was decided, commentators suggested an apparent conflict between the OWBPA and *Gilmer*, in actions arising under the ADEA. The OWBPA requires that any waiver of ADEA "rights or claims" be "knowing and voluntary." If a waiver of ADEA "rights" includes a waiver of a right to a jury trial or access to federal court, the OWBPA could be interpreted to invalidate many agreements to arbitrate exacted as a condition of initial or continued employment. But the federal courts to consider the issue have uniformly held that the OWBPA does not undermine the holding of *Gilmer*.

6. SUIT BY EEOC

The EEOC has an option other than issuing a determination of reasonable or no reasonable cause, followed by a notice of right to sue. It may initiate suit in its own name against private employers. See §§ 706(f)(1) and 707, 42 U.S.C.A. §§ 2000e–5(f)(1) and 2000e–6. EEOC's authority to bring "pattern or practice" suits on behalf of a class affected by an unlawful employment practice enables it to assert claims on behalf of large numbers of employees whose diverse claims might not withstand a typicality or representativeness attack under Federal Rule 23 in a private class action. EEOC v. Mitsubishi Motor Mfg. of America, Inc. (C.D.Ill.1998).

Unlike individual plaintiffs, the agency faces no fixed deadlines within which it must file suit. There is even authority that it may commence an action based on a charge filed by an employee whose own judicial action was dismissed as untimely. See EEOC v. Harris Chernin, Inc. (7th Cir.1993). Thus only a delay long enough to invoke the defense of laches serves as a check on EEOC's promptness in bringing suit. See Occidental Life Ins. Co. of California v. EEOC (1977).

But unlike private litigants, who need satisfy *only* charge-filing and action-commencement deadlines in order to sue, EEOC has other pre-suit responsibilities. It must notify the charged party within 10 days after it receives a charge and attempt during the administrative process to eliminate unlawful employment practices through "conference, conciliation, and persuasion." 42 U.S.C.A. § 2000e–5(b).

If EEOC files suit before one can be commenced by a private charging party, the private party is limited to intervention in EEOC's action and may not file her own. See Behlar v. Smith (8th Cir.1983). And EEOC may attempt to preserve its suit priority by rescinding a previously issued notice of right to sue before the private action is commenced. Lute v. Singer Co. (9th Cir.1982). If, however, the charging party commences an action under Title VII before EEOC does, EEOC may only exercise its statutory right to intervene. Johnson v. Nekoosa–Edwards Paper Co. (8th Cir.1977). There is authority under the ADEA, however, that EEOC may either intervene or commence an independent action even if the complainant has filed first. EEOC v. G–K–G, Inc. (7th Cir.1994).

It has been held that a person potentially affected by an action brought by EEOC must intervene to avoid being bound by a judgment against EEOC. Adams v. Proctor & Gamble Mfg. Co. (4th Cir.1983). But it is unclear whether this authority survives a Supreme Court decision holding that private plaintiffs must join such persons, who need not intervene and who remain free to attack judgments in actions in which they were not joined as parties. Martin v. Wilks (1989). A provision of the 1991 Act responds to *Wilks* by barring actions challenging employment practices authorized or commanded by litigated judgments or consent decrees if the challenger failed to intervene after receiving notice of the proceedings or was adequately represented in them by another party—e.g.,

EEOC. Section 108 (adding subsection 703(n)(1) to Title VII, 42 U.S.C.A. § 2000e–2(n)(1)).

7. PLAINTIFF JOINDER AND CLASS ACTIONS

Title VII actions in federal court are limited by statutory requirements concerning parties and allegations. The EEOC charge which forms the predicate for a Title VII action may be filed either "by or on behalf of" a person who is "aggrieved." Thus named plaintiffs who have filed charges may prosecute the action on behalf of class members in a Federal Rule 23 class action, and those class members need not themselves have filed individual EEOC or state agency charges if the class is certified. But the Supreme Court, with its 1980 decision in General Telephone Co. of Southwest v. Falcon (1982), has strictly applied the Rule 23 requirements for class certification.

Rule 23 provides that an action may be maintained as a class action if the prerequisites of Rule 23(a) are satisfied, and in addition:

(1) the prosecution of separate actions by or against individual members of the class would create a risk of (A) inconsistent or varying adjudications with respect to individual members of the class which would establish incompatible standards of conduct for the party opposing the class, or (B) adjudications with respect to individual members of the class which would as a practical matter be dispositive of the interest of other members not parties to the adjudications or substantially impair or impede their ability to protect their interests; or

(2) the party opposing the class has acted or refused to act on grounds generally applicable to the class, thereby making

appropriate final injunctive relief or corresponding declaratory relief with respect to the class as a whole; or

(3) the court finds that the questions of law or fact common to the members of the class predominate over any questions affecting only individual members, and that a class action is superior to other available methods for the fair and efficient adjudication of the controversy.

Rule 23(b)(1) creates a mandatory class and is most appropriate where there is a limited fund that must be distributed "ratably." Rule 23(b)(1) is not generally used by plaintiffs in discrimination class actions. Employment discrimination plaintiffs usually seek certification under Rule 23(b)(2) or Rule 23(b)(3).

Rule 23(b)(2) permits class certification where "the party opposing the class has acted or refused to act on grounds generally applicable to the class, thereby making appropriate final injunctive relief or corresponding declaratory relief with respect to the class as a whole." Fed. R. Civ. P. 23(b)(2). Rule 23(b)(2) creates a mandatory class with no opt-out rights, but a court may exercise discretionary authority arising from 23(d)(2) to require notice and opt-out rights, particularly when substantial monetary awards are involved. The Supreme Court has noted that "[c]ivil rights cases against parties charged with unlawful, class-based discrimination are prime examples" of Rule 23(b)(2) class actions. A Rule 23(b)(2) class should have more cohesiveness underlying the factual and legal claims of each class member than a Rule 23(b)(3) class. Certification under Rule 23(b)(2) is only appropriate where equitable relief is the predominant remedy sought. This has been interpreted to mean that certification under Rule 23(b)(2) is precluded where monetary relief is sought, unless such monetary relief is merely incidental to the requested injunctive or declaratory relief.

To qualify for certification under Rule 23(b)(3), a class must meet two requirements beyond the Rule 23(a) prerequisites: common questions must "predominate over any questions affecting only individual members"; and class resolution must be "superior to other available methods for the fair and efficient adjudication of the controversy." Fed. R. Civ. P. 23(b)(3). The Rule 23(b)(3) "predominance" inquiry focuses on the legal and factual questions surrounding each potential class member's claims and is "far more demanding" than Rule 23(a)'s commonality requirement. In order to predominate, common issues must constitute a significant part of the individual claims. Courts will generally find that individual issues predominate over common ones where it appears that the class action will devolve into a series of individual mini-trials on issues peculiar to each plaintiff. The need for some individualized proof will not necessarily preclude certification under Rule 23(b)(3). The superiority requirement is satisfied where the advantages of a class action—increased fairness and efficiency—outweigh any problems of case manageability. Considerations relevant to manageability include the potential difficulties in notifying class members of the suit, determining individual injury, calculating individual damages, and distributing damages.

Rule 23(a), applicable also to class actions under the ADA and § 1981, has the following four threshold requirements:

(1) a sufficient number of class members that ordinary joinder under Rule 20 would be impracticable ("numerosity");

(2) questions of law or fact common to the class ("commonality");

(3) claims (or, in a defendant class action, defenses) of the representative parties that are "typical" of those of the class as a whole ("typicality"); and

(4) a likelihood that the representative parties will fairly and adequately protect the interests of the class ("adequacy").

The first two requirements are usually easily met in employment discrimination class actions, which characteristically involve a plaintiff class. Numerosity is seldom a problem, with classes containing as few as 18 members having been certified. And so long as the named plaintiffs assert that disparate treatment on a prohibited ground is classwide, or that one or more neutral practices has classwide impact on a protected group, the commonality requirement is also rarely a barrier. Employment discrimination by its very nature partakes of classwide discrimination.

The third and fourth factors, typicality and adequacy, have proven most difficult to surmount. For a putative class to comply with Rule 23's requirement that the claims of the named plaintiffs be "typical" of those of the class, *Falcon* insists that in most cases the complement of named plaintiffs in a private Title VII class action include at least one representative who complains not only on the same prohibited ground of discrimination (e.g., race or sex) as the putative class, but also of each particular discriminatory practice the class proposes to attack. In a famous footnote 15, the court recognized an exception that permits certification despite diversity in the practices challenged by the representative plaintiffs and class members where those practices are the product of a common device (e.g. a test) or common decisionmaker applying the same subjective criteria. Indeed, defendants have argued that *Falcon* also demands that at least one of the named plaintiffs must have allegedly suffered the same detrimental term or condition of employment—failure to hire, unequal pay or discipline, nonpromotion, on-the-job harassment, discharge—as the members of each class or subclass sought to be represented. Thus, unless the named plaintiff or plaintiffs who originally retained class counsel happen to embody all the characteristics of the putative class members, share all their same grievances and suffer their same injuries, *Falcon* effectively compels class counsel to try to assemble a wider group of named plaintiffs. Then some, but not all of the wider group can individually assert that they, as applicants or employees, were aggrieved by the particular employment practices, and affected in the same terms and conditions of employment, as other members of the class.

Falcon has had at least two distinct consequences. First, by effectively requiring the formation of a large and diverse plaintiff group, it has more sharply put into focus the ethical concerns associated with the solicitation of additional named plaintiffs. The Court has been rather lenient about permitting plaintiff class counsel, directly or through the original clients, to encourage others similarly situated to join the named plaintiff group, particularly when the class action is serving a "private attorney general" function in combating race discrimination. But there are limits to solicitation even after *Falcon*. For example, the Eleventh Circuit vacated two class communications and a certification order because plaintiffs' counsel's efforts to communicate with class members caused serious irreparable injury to the defendant.

Second, defendants have been resourceful in responding to the larger named plaintiff complements that *Falcon* in effect compels. *Falcon* has spurred more elaborate and expensive motion practice about the propriety of class certification and limitations on precertification discovery. Defendants commonly assert, frequently with success, that the resulting diverse named plaintiff group—representing, for example, applicants, employees, and former employees; subordinates and superiors; unsuccessful test takers and victims of discriminatory discipline; women sexually harassed, and those suffering unequal pay; persons discharged, and persons not promoted—is rife with internal conflicts, so that, in Rule 23's terms, the named plaintiffs are not fairly "representative" of the class members whose fate will ride with them if the class is certified. To alleviate such conflicts, plaintiffs or district courts have sometimes proposed that the class be subdivided into "subclasses" that one or more of the named plaintiffs can fairly represent. On occasion, however, the result of forming subclasses is that each is fewer than the approximately 30 or so that the courts have generally required before a plaintiff group is sufficiently numerous to warrant class action certification. In this way a defendant's Rule 23 objections snowball: a challenge to typicality generates a challenge to adequacy that in turn generates a challenge to numerosity. By their nature these challenges invite early consideration of the merits of the class members' claims, although the court is formally prohibited from considering those merits in determining whether to certify.

A December 1, 1998 amendment to Rule 23 of the Federal Rules of Civil Procedure overturns the result of a Supreme Court decision that had denied plaintiffs interlocutory review of decisions denying class certification. The new provision permits an appeal within 10 days of a district court's decision granting or denying certification or decertifying a previously certified class. The court of appeals' discretion to grant or deny permission to appeal should help prevent the new rule from becoming a delaying tactic in the case of employer appeals from decisions granting certification.

Sections 706(f)(1) and 707(e) of Title VII authorize the EEOC to initiate a civil suit on behalf of victims of discrimination and to bring a pattern or practice suit against private employers that engage in systemic discrimination. A district court has addressed whether and how EEOC can bring a pattern or practice case of sexual harassment, inherently problematic due to the subjective elements of the prima facie case. The court employed a bifurcated liability phase, focusing in part one on a pattern or practice of the existence of a hostile environment of sexual harassment that the employer had notice of and was negligent in not preventing or correcting it. The second phase, the individual relief phase, incorporates the *Meritor* subjective standard that the complained-of conduct was unwelcome and that it affected the work environment of the individual.

Where, as is unusual in an employment discrimination action, injunctive relief is unavailable and certification is therefore not possible under Rule 23(b)(2), there is authority permitting certification under Rule 23(b)(3) where the plaintiffs can satisfy the court that issues common to class members predominate over those affecting only individuals, and that a class action is a more efficient means of proceeding than multiple actions or Rule 20 joinder. However, plaintiffs seeking to certify disparate treatment class actions under the inferential proof mode of *McDonnell Douglas* may face significant certification problems. Defendants can defeat such claims by articulating a nondiscriminatory, nonpretextual reason for the adverse employment action—an inquiry that courts view as highly individualized. Moreover, claims for emotional distress and punitive damages are also highly variable from plaintiff to plaintiff, also undercutting the commonality and typicality necessary for certification.

ADEA suits are not subject to Rule 23. Instead, these "collective actions" are governed under § 216 of the Fair Labor Standards Act. There are some substantial differences between the ADEA class action and a Rule 23 class action. First, the only prerequisite for a § 216 action is that all putative class members must be "similarly situated." This is, of course, a fact-based inquiry, but courts have held that the standard is lower than that imposed by Rule 23(a). Second, all ADEA § 216 actions are opt-in actions; that is no potential plaintiff is part of the collective action unless that plaintiff affirmatively consents in writing to be part of the action. Third, plaintiffs who do opt-in to an ADEA collective action are granted full party status.

The rejection on the merits of class claims of systemic treatment does not bar the claims of individual class members alleging disparate treatment. *McDonnell Douglas/Burdine*. Moreover, when a court denies class action certification, the claims of individual class members who have not filed a charge with EEOC or commenced a judicial action may still be timely. This is because the filing of a class action has been held to toll, until the denial of certification, both the 90–day period for filing suit and the applicable deadline (180 or 300 days) for filing a charge with EEOC. Even when a class was decertified because no class representative had standing to assert the claim subsequently brought by individual plaintiffs, those plaintiffs have been allowed to "piggyback" on the timely filed EEOC charges of the class action plaintiffs. But rejection of class claims on the merits has preclusive effect under federal common law in subsequent actions asserting the same pattern claims. And the pendency of a class action in which class status was denied or a class decertified does not toll the charge-filing or action-commencement deadlines for class members who bring a subsequent *class* action—otherwise there would be "endless rounds of litigation ... over the adequacy of successive named plaintiffs to serve as class representatives."

A "single-filing" rule recognized by most federal circuits outside the class action context permits plaintiffs who have not filed their own EEOC charge, or in some circuits, plaintiffs who have filed an invalid charge, to piggyback on a charge or charges filed by coplaintiffs. The plaintiffs are relieved of filing their own valid charges if the claims of all parties are based on a common employer practice or practices during the same rough time frame and the filed charge or charges timely and adequately alerted the employer to the alleged illegality of all the practices ultimately challenged in court. It is not a prerequisite to single filing that the foundation claim allege class-wide discrimination. The rule has also been applied to permit the plaintiff who has not filed an EEOC charge to intervene in an action brought by the plaintiff who has, or to join that action as co-plaintiff after an unsuccessful attempt at intervention.

Another requirement, that the action be brought "against the respondent named in the charge," has sometimes been construed to authorize jurisdiction over a successor employer or even over a defendant improperly named, or not formally named in the charge at all, if its identity is sufficiently revealed in the substance of the charge or if that employer is closely related to a named respondent. In some circuits the civil action has even been allowed to reach defendants not likely to have received notice of the original EEOC charge if the agency's investigation, reasonably confined to the facts alleged in the charge, would have focused on them.

8. RELATION OF FEDERAL LAWSUIT TO EEOC INVESTIGATION

Since the EEOC charge is the necessary foundation for a Title VII action, the issues that may be litigated in federal court will be tied to some degree to the contents of the charge. But recognizing that EEOC charges are often drafted by unrepresented employees ill-equipped to craft them with care, courts following the leading case of Sanchez v. Standard Brands, Inc. (5th Cir.1970) have permitted Title VII plaintiffs to try claims "like or related to allegations contained in the charge and growing out of such allegations during the pendency of the case before the Commission."

The widespread adoption of the *Sanchez* rule puts a premium on defendants' efforts to limit the scope of EEOC proceedings. Generalizations about the meaning of "like or related" are particularly hazardous. But it may be ventured that allegations in a Title VII judicial complaint that add a new ground of discrimination (race or sex, for instance) are less likely to be entertained than are allegations that touch on additional terms or conditions of employment or implicate other potential plaintiffs in different departments or divisions. Even then, plaintiffs whose administrative charges complained of adverse treatment respecting limited terms and conditions of employment will be permitted to target in court only those other terms and conditions of employment that EEOC could reasonably have been expected to investigate based on the charge. The Seventh Circuit appears to be moving to an alternative, and apparently stricter, standard: whether the claims in the judicial action are "fairly encompassed" within or "implied" by the charge the plaintiff filed with EEOC. E.g. Vela v. Village of Sauk Village (7th Cir.2000). Decisions applying the new standard have precluded allegations by the same plaintiff on the same prohibited ground of discrimination that attack different terms and conditions of employment or implicate different individuals from those targeted by the EEOC charge. At least where the additional practices sought to be challenged in court are plausibly asserted to arise out of the practices cited in the EEOC charge, it would appear that this standard bars the litigation of claims that would be heard under the *Sanchez* "like or related" test.

An especially liberal application of the charge-filing requirement generally permits a plaintiff to press a retaliation claim under § 704, without first filing a separate EEOC charge of retaliation, where that claim grows out of a properly and timely filed predicate charge of discrimination under § 703. But that liberality is usually extended only when the underlying charge of primary discrimination was itself administratively exhausted and timely, or added by an amendment to the original charge that the court permits to relate back to the original. Some circuits have limited the federal court's ancillary jurisdiction in such cases to charges of alleged retaliation occurring after, and not before, the filing of the underlying charge; this position is consistent with the applicable EEOC regulations, discussed above, that require the filing of an original charge within the applicable 180–or 300–day period after a claim accrues.

9.   EMPLOYER RECORDKEEPING REQUIREMENTS

Pursuant to Section 709(c), EEOC has promulgated regulations requiring employers to maintain records pertinent to a wide range of employment decisions. These require employers to retain all personnel records for six months after they are created and, when a charge is filed, to retain all records relevant to that charge "until final disposition of the charge or action." 29 C.F.R. § 1602.14 (1994). In employment discrimination actions, the employer has custody of virtually all records critical to resolution of the disputed claim; hence in the reported decisions it is the employer that allegedly violated the Title VII recordkeeping requirements.

But judicial enforcement of employer recordkeeping violations has generally been conspicuously lenient. Sometimes the courts of appeals that have found employers to have destroyed documents in violation of the EEOC regulation give the plaintiff the benefit of a "presumption that the destroyed documents would have bolstered her case." See, e.g., Favors v. Fisher (8th Cir.1994). But then they may either assume or conclude that the presumption was "overcome"—the evidence for which may simply be an innocent explanation by an authorized employer agent, coupled with his assertion that he had not been instructed to preserve records in accordance with the government regulation. And sanctions have typically been mild: requiring the defendant to bear the costs of record reconstruction; limiting its production of evidence on the matters reflected in the destroyed documents; or invoking the presumption that the records would have supported plaintiff's case. See EEOC v. Jacksonville Shipyards, Inc. (M.D.Fla. 1988).

H.   TITLE VII REMEDIES

1.   REINSTATEMENT AND BACK PAY

The range of judicial remedial authority is prescribed by § 706(g). This section provides for injunctions and "such affirmative action as may be appropriate," including orders directing reinstatement or hire, back pay, and other equitable relief. It also "limits" a defendant's back pay liability retrospectively to no earlier than two years before the filing of a charge with EEOC. "Limits" is placed in quotation marks because the statute's deadlines for filing a charge with EEOC are only 180 days, in the handful of states that do not have their own local antidiscrimination laws and agencies, or 300 days in the majority of states that do. Thus in effect the 2–year "limit" on back pay authorizes its award *earlier* than the "trigger" date that starts the running of Title VII's administrative charge-filing deadlines.

Prevailing plaintiffs are routinely awarded injunctions against ongoing violations, and, where disparate treatment has been proved, reinstatement or, if there is no position available at the time of judgment, priority in filling vacancies. As with the systemic disparate treatment case, discussed above, reinstatement may be denied, however, where the discriminatee, although qualified when unlawfully rejected, is no longer qualified for the position in question at the time of judgment.

Back pay is also awarded almost as a matter of course. This is because, as the Supreme Court has explained, back pay serves both of the Act's remedial goals: to restore discrimination victims to the approximate status they would have enjoyed absent discrimination (the "make whole" purpose), and to deter employer violations. Accordingly, the Court, while recognizing that federal judges enjoy some discretion to withhold any Title VII remedy in particular circumstances, held in Albemarle Paper Co. v. Moody (1975) that back pay may be denied only for unusual reasons which, if applied generally, would not impede those remedial objectives. For example, the "neutral practice/disproportionate adverse impact" case dispenses with evidence of discriminatory intent, and a general good faith exception to back pay liability would therefore seriously erode the advantages of that mode of proof. The Court has consequently rejected such an exception. It has also suggested that the ordinary Eleventh Amendment immunity of states from federal court monetary awards is overridden in Title VII actions because Congress enacted the statute in at least partial reliance on its powers under the Fourteenth Amendment to enforce the Equal Protection Clause. It has not directly decided, however, if Congress exceeded those powers in enacting the state liability provisions of Title VII.

Back pay is defined as the total compensation the employee would have earned absent the unlawful conduct, reduced by any compensation the employee actually received and any additional amount the employee would have received through reasonable efforts to mitigate the damages. It is awarded only for a period in which plaintiff is "available and willing to accept substantially equivalent employment," with periods of disability usually excluded from the award. The employer bears the burden of proof on the issue of mitigation, which is itself a jury issue. An employer's "unconditional" offer of reinstatement that is refused by the plaintiff ends the defendant's ongoing responsibility for back pay.

Rejected applicants seeking back pay are not required to prove they would have been hired absent the unlawful discrimination. But any plaintiff seeking back pay must have made reasonable efforts to mitigate her losses. Back pay awards are reduced by amounts the plaintiff earned, or with reasonable diligence could have earned, since the date of a discharge or failure or refusal to hire; but a failure to mitigate may not absolutely forfeit the right to recovery for back pay. In those courts where an employer is relieved of the burden to prove there was comparable work available after it proves that the employee made no reasonable efforts to seek subsequent work, the employee must prove that comparable compensation was not available to save any part of a back pay award. Several circuits have held that self-employment is an acceptable form of mitigation for this purpose. The back pay clock should stop when "the sting" of discriminatory conduct has ended. There is considerable division in the circuit opinions as to whether "collateral sources" of income may be deducted from the back pay award, and if so which ones.

Title VII authorizes the award of back pay to a date as early as two years before the filing of the required EEOC charge— as distinct from the later date on which the complaint is filed in a judicial action. In states without their own anti-discrimination laws and agencies, EEOC may immediately assert jurisdiction over a plaintiff's initial charge; and any charging party may demand a notice of right to sue from EEOC after it has exercised that jurisdiction for 180 days. Even in the majority of states, where the charging party must, at least in theory, exhaust administrative remedies before state or local "deferral" agencies, the plaintiff may be able to invoke EEOC's jurisdiction promptly if the state or local agency waives its right to proceed either in the individual case or by a "work-sharing" agreement with EEOC. And at the outside the plaintiff has 300 days from the latest alleged unlawful employment practice to file with EEOC, which then can be compelled to authorize suit 180 days later. Thus as a practical matter most Title VII judicial actions will be commenced well before two years have expired after the filing of the EEOC charge. The two-year back pay accrual rule nevertheless permits back pay for violations that occurred up to two years before that charge was filed. That is to say, back pay may be recovered for "continuing violations" that began before the last event that triggers Title VII's "statute of limitations."

The 1991 Act adds compensatory and punitive damages as "legal" remedies to the Title VII plaintiff's arsenal, it does not change the "equitable" character of the pre-existing remedies like back pay or restoration of lost pension benefits. Determination of eligibility for back pay, although virtually automatic under the *Albemarle* presumption, is therefore formally for the court, not the jury, as is the critical calculation of the back pay amount. Yet at least one circuit has held that "the issue of reasonable mitigation is ultimately a question of fact for the jury."

Front pay is a discretionary remedy granted by the court as a substitute for reinstatement if reinstatement is impossible, impracticable or inequitable. It may be the only feasible way to make a victim of discrimination whole where there is no available position in which to reinstate her, or where, as in a constructive discharge or other harassment case, reinstatement would be unsuccessful or unproductive because of the workplace hostility that either prompted the claim or resulted from its prosecution. It is awarded in an amount that estimates the total future salary, pension and other benefits the plaintiff, absent an unlawful discriminatory discharge, would have earned with the employer from date of judgment until probable loss of job or date of retirement; and prospective losses of post-retirement benefits may be measured until actuarially predicted date of death. Because it is awarded and calculated on the basis of highly speculative assumptions about the health of the business, the health of the plaintiff, and the plaintiff's future satisfactory work performance and prospects for advancement, front pay is devilishly difficult to measure. That difficulty suggests that front pay may be a form of future nonpecuniary, rather than pecuniary loss. Yet there is an irreducible element of speculation in almost every front pay award—e.g., trying to determine if the plaintiff, after termination, would have survived a subsequent reduction in force and otherwise performed well enough to resist termination—and speculation alone should not render front pay unavailable, unless it is excessive.

The lower federal courts have come to presume the front pay award appropriate where reinstatement is infeasible or ill advised. Most but not all circuit courts, in decisions before the 1991 Act, held front pay available under Title VII. The principal argument against front pay revolved around the fact that all Title VII remedies were then equitable, and some judges characterized front pay as "legal." Now that the 1991 Act adds legal remedies to the menu of relief under Title VII, the Supreme Court, in dictum, has noted the availability of front pay with approval.

Front pay leaves the incumbent in place and, beginning as of final judgment, orders the employer to pay the discriminatee an amount equivalent to what he would earn if actually reinstated. Because of the uncertain duration of the period during which the victim of discrimination would have remained employed after judgment, or at what level and pay, the front pay remedy is fraught with computational difficulties. Given its purpose to restore an injured party to the position she would have occupied absent the employer's unlawful discrimination, determining the appropriateness, duration and amount of front pay is an exercise that entails "predicting the future": such an exercise involves an attempt to determine the degree to which a plaintiff possesses qualities that would make plaintiff successful in attaining career advancement. For advancements that come simply with longevity, courts have uniformly assumed that such advancement would occur, in the absence of specific disqualifying information; on the other hand, courts will not automatically assume that a person discriminated against possesses characteristics so sterling as to receive every advancement not made illegal or logically impossible under the employer's rules.

The circuit opinions grapple with a host of circumstances governing the appropriateness and duration of front pay awards. The award will not necessarily terminate when plaintiff quits subsequent, substitute employment; on the other hand, in recognition of the duty to mitigate, the employer need only pay such a plaintiff the difference between the amount she would have received had she remained employed (or secured substantially equivalent employment) and the amount she could have continued to receive in the *lesser*-paying substitute job that she quit. Almost invariably when front pay is awarded, there are numerous considerations counseling the reduction or termination of the award, including mitigation, unclean hands, speculation about the duration of plaintiff's position or personal retention, collateral sources, and the kinds and amounts of other relief awarded for the unlawful discrimination. Because front pay awards are replacing anticipated compensation after judgment that is not yet due, they must be discounted to present value; and there are numerous other technical issues that must be faced in calculating the award. All that can be said with confidence is that purely arbitrary limits on front pay may be overturned as an abuse of the trial court's discretion. On occasion, awards of as long as 25 years have been made when that represents plaintiff's first eligibility for a full pension. Perhaps the most significant unsettled issue is whether front pay is a species of recovery that is subject to the dollar caps placed by the Civil Rights Act of 1991 on the sum of compensatory and punitive damages.

Because each species of Title VII relief before the 1991 Civil Rights Act was considered equitable, jury trials were not available unless a Title VII claim was joined with a claim for legal relief—for instance, a claim under § 1981. Although the Supreme Court strongly suggested that there was no right to jury trial under Title VII, it never actually ruled on the question. Section 102 of the Civil Rights Act of 1991, codified at 42 U.S.C.A. § 1981a, now specifically authorizes jury trials for claimants alleging intentional discrimination in actions under, among other statutes, Title VII and the Americans With Disabilities Act. In addition, there is clearly a jury trial right under § 1981, and where an action presents claims under both statutes, the right to jury trial under § 1981 may not be estopped by the prior bench trial of an equitable claim. Rather, prior jury determinations of facts reached in deciding the legal, § 1981 claims should be adopted by the trial court when it later determines any equitable claims under Title VII. But a district court has ruled that it is not precluded from granting back pay as a remedy additional to whatever damages remedies may have been awarded by the jury.

The "equity" characterization has also limited the available monetary relief under Title VII (before the 1991 amendments) to an award of back pay, precluding more generous measures such as compensation for emotional distress or punitive damages. The equitable nature of all Title VII awards before the new Act also led some courts to deny nominal damages, viewing them as compensatory in nature. While nominal damages now appear available, some courts insist that the plaintiff demand them as early as the Rule 16 pretrial order; under that view a plaintiff could not wait until after verdict, or even shortly before, to seek nominal damages as a way of obtaining at least the minimal economic recovery that may be needed to support an award of punitive damages. But prejudgment, as well as the standard post-judgment, interest is an ordinary item of compensation integrally related to back pay, routinely awarded in Title VII actions. It may even be an abuse of discretion to deny it, absent unusual reasons.

Any prevailing party, plaintiff or defendant, is of course eligible for an award of "costs" under Federal Rule of Civil Procedure 54(d). These are limited, however, to items specified by 28 U.S.C.A. § 1920: clerk and marshal fees, fees by court reporters for transcripts "necessarily obtained for use in the case"; printing disbursements and witness fees; specified docket fees; and fees for court-appointed experts and certain interpreters. Most important, "costs" as used in Rule 54(d) do *not* include the prevailing party's attorney's fees. This is consistent with the ordinary "American rule" which, absent express statutory authorization, calls for each side to pay its own attorney's fees. Section 706(k) of Title VII is one such statute. It provides that a prevailing party may recover a reasonable attorney's fee as part of "costs." And for purposes of calculating the postjudgment interest allowed by 28 U.S.C.A. § 1961 "on any money judgment in a civil case recovered in a district court," these statutorily shifted attorney's fees shall be included as part of the judgment.

Section 113 of the Act authorizes the court to include the fees of experts, without a specific cap, as part of the award of attorney's fees to prevailing Title VII plaintiffs, contrary to the thrust of two recent decisions of the Court. This change facilitates the neutral practice case as well as the case of intentional discrimination. But the Act's authorization of prospective relief, and hence attorney's fees, despite the defendant's discharge of the "same decision" burden in the intentional "mixed motive" situation, affords greater relative inducement to bring intentional discrimination claims.

2. COMPENSATORY AND PUNITIVE DAMAGES FOR TITLE VII AND AMERICANS WITH DISABILITIES ACT VIOLATIONS AFTER NOVEMBER 20, 1991

Section 102 of the Civil Rights Act of 1991, codified at 42 U.S.C.A. § 1981a, authorizes jury trials and compensatory and punitive damages for claimants alleging intentional discrimination in actions under, among other statutes, Title VII and the Americans With Disabilities Act. These remedies are "in addition to any relief authorized by" § 706(g) of Title VII, and the compensatory portion of an award "shall not include back pay, interest on back pay, or any other type of relief authorized under" § 706(g) of Title VII—in other words, the equitable relief available before the Civil Rights Act of 1991. But compensatory and punitive damages are available only if the "complaining party cannot recover under 42 U.S.C.A. § 1981." Citing applicable legislative history, however, the EEOC has interpreted the latter restriction only to bar double recovery under Title VII and § 1981, not to interfere with administrative or judicial processing of claims under either statute prior to judgment.

The Act expressly denies either form of damages—compensatory or punitive—to challengers of facially neutral practices. Title VII plaintiffs who prevail only by demonstrating the disproportionate adverse impact of neutral practices, or ADA plaintiffs who demonstrate only a failure to reasonably accommodate by an employer who "demonstrates good faith efforts," are still limited to the traditional, equitable Title VII remedies of prospective relief and back pay. Perhaps more than any other, these provisions manifest the congressional view that intentional discrimination deserves more serious legal sanctions.

Section 1981a also makes compensatory, but not punitive, damages available to plaintiffs who prosecute intentional discrimination claims successfully against a government agency or subdivision. The Supreme Court held in West v. Gibson (1999) that the EEOC may award compensatory damages to federal employees (for intentional discrimination) during the federal administrative complaints process.

Punitive damages are authorized against nongovernmental defendants who are proven to have engaged in an unlawful discriminatory practice "with malice or with reckless indifference to the federally protected rights of an aggrieved individual." Although the precise standards governing jury awards of punitive damages will require considerable case law explication by analogy to punitive damages in tort, it has already been held that, as under §§ 1981 and 1983, compensatory damages are not a prerequisite to a punitive award. This is particularly important in environmental harassment claims, as victims may not incur always compensatory damages.

Section 1981a(b)(3) places dollar caps that vary with employer size on the *sum* of compensatory and punitive damages "for each complaining party." For this purpose, compensatory damages are defined by § 1981a(b)(2) to include monetary relief for "future pecuniary losses, emotional pain, suffering, inconvenience, mental anguish, loss of enjoyment of life, and other nonpecuniary losses." These caps are set at $50,000 for businesses that employ between 15 and 100 persons; $100,000 where the employer has between 101 and 200 employees; $200,000 where the employer has between 201 and 500 employees; and $300,000 for all employers with 501 or more employees. Because these damages are "in addition to" traditional, pre-November 1991 Title VII equitable relief, complaining parties' recoveries of back pay, interest on back pay, and other relief formerly available under Title VII before the 1991 amendments are not restricted by the caps. Moreover, despite the somewhat uncertain status of front pay under the pre–1991 Act case law, EEOC considers it a type of relief previously authorized by Title VII and hence excluded from the § 1981a(b)(2) definition of compensatory damages and in turn not subject to a § 1981a(b)(3) cap. In any event, a plaintiff with a state law claim that authorizes unlimited damages may avoid the Title VII and ADA damages caps altogether, and in some circumstances may assert that claim in the same federal court action.

Two principal interpretive questions are raised about the application of these caps. First, which components of a compensatory damages award—front pay is particularly important—are subject to the caps? Second, when multiple plaintiffs join together under Federal Rule 20 or, in class form, Rule 23, do the caps limit the total recovery of the group or only of each individual member?

The Supreme Court answered the first question in Pollard v. E.I. du Pont de Nemours & Co. (2001), holding that front pay is not subject to the caps of § 1981a. Acknowledging that front pay is often awarded in lieu of reinstatement, the Court reasoned that because front pay is a remedy authorized under § 706(g), Congress did not limit the availability of such awards in § 1981a. Instead, Congress sought to expand the available remedies by permitting the recovery of compensatory and punitive damages in addition to previously available remedies, such as front pay.

With regard to the second question, in the EEOC's view, in a multiple joinder or class action situation, "each complaining employee may receive" all otherwise appropriate relief up to the full value of the pertinent cap. The employer's aggregate liability, in other words, is the sum of the total proven compensatory damages (other than past pecuniary losses) and punitive damages of all plaintiffs (the applicable cap limiting each employee's damages recovery), plus the full amount of all proven back pay, front pay, past pecuniary losses, interest, and attorney's fees. Circuit courts, disagreeing with EEOC, have held that where a single plaintiff prevails on multiple claims (for example discrimination and retaliation) under the same capped statute (e.g. Title VII, or ADA), the compensatory-cum-punitive-damages cap applies to both claims combined.

Left unanswered by the text of the damages provision and the EEOC's Damages Guidance is whether the plaintiff who joins in one action claims under both Title VII *and* ADA for distinct, independently unlawful employer practices may recover more than the applicable cap pertaining to each statute alone. Suppose for instance that an employer denies plaintiff a promotion because of his race and a few weeks later discharges him because of a disability recognized under ADA. From a substantive law standpoint, plaintiff could bring two civil actions, one based on Title VII (or Section 1981), the other on ADA. But as a practical matter he is more likely to join both claims in one action to achieve an efficient, consistent resolution of the controversy, and he will be permitted to do so by Federal Rule of Civil Procedure 18(a) and the similar joinder rules of most state courts. Indeed, although the employer conduct consists of two separate acts on two separate occasions, plaintiff might be *compelled* to join both claims in the same action under the broad transactional definition of "same claim" that the Restatement (Second) of Judgments adopts as the referent for res judicata or, as it is now known, claim preclusion.

If that plaintiff had brought separate actions, he would be eligible for the appropriately capped amount of compensatory and punitive damages in each proceeding. 42 U.S.C.A. § 1977A(b) stipulates the amount of the cap corresponding to the size of the employer; and subsections (a)(1) and (2) provide for damages up to the subsection (b) cap "in an action" under Title VII and ADA, respectively. Yet a single lawsuit combining these claims could be pigeonholed as "an action" under either Title VII or ADA, with the employer arguing accordingly that the maximum compensatory-punitive recovery is limited to the amount of the single cap pertaining to an action under either statute. This seems a strained reading that ignores the possible compulsion on plaintiffs to join in one action all related claims (flowing from the law of claim preclusion) and permits the Civil Rights Act of 1991 to undermine F.R.C.P. 18(a)'s authorization for joinder of claims. The better reading would limit plaintiff's recovery concerning the conduct violative of *Title VII* to the Title VII cap referenced in Section 1977A(a)(1), and his recovery for the conduct violative of *ADA* to the cap of the same amount referenced in Section 1977A(a)(2), subject of course to standard instructions forbidding the jury from authorizing greater damages for the combination of these unlawful employment practices than plaintiff actually suffered.

The Commission also assumes that, as with back and front pay, the complaining party has a duty to mitigate pecuniary losses, with the burden of proof on the employer to demonstrate a failure to exercise reasonable diligence. On claims for nonpecuniary loss such as emotional distress, it expects the complainant to bear the usual burdens developed by tort law concerning causation. Thus the claim "will be seriously undermined if the onset of symptoms ... preceded the discrimination"; but the fact that an unusually sensitive complainant resembles the classical "eggshell plaintiff" of tort law "will not absolve the respondent from responsibility for the greater emotional harm." Expert testimony that stress resulted from discriminatory working conditions is an adequate basis for an award, and sometimes even plaintiff's own testimony about loss of sleep, marital strain, humiliation and the like will suffice. Defense motions to compel a mental examination have not been successful, but a plaintiff alleging emotional distress damages probably waives her psychotherapist-patient privilege.

The circuit decisions are divided over whether an emotional distress award is adequately supported by plaintiff's own testimony standing alone, or whether that testimony requires corroboration by fact witnesses like family and friends, or even by medical experts.

In cases of intentional Title VII and ADA violations against non-governmental defendants, 42 U.S.C.A. § 1981a(b)(1) authorizes punitive damages where the plaintiff also shows the defendant acted with "malice or with reckless indifference to the federally protected rights of an aggrieved individual."

In Kolstad v. American Dental Association (1999), the Court held that the statutory requirements of "malice" or "reckless indifference" focus solely on the defendant's state of mind. Accordingly, while evidence of an employer's egregious conduct may enable the plaintiff to persuade a judge or jury that the defendant, through its agent or agents, acted with the requisite "malice" or "reckless indifference," Section 1981a(b)(1) "does not require a showing of egregious or outrageous discrimination independent of the employer's state of mind." Accordingly, if the employer's agents could be shown on remand to have acted with malice or reckless indifference to plaintiff's rights, and the employer shown to be responsible for their actions undertaken with that state of mind, the employer might be liable for punitive damages even if its agents' conduct could not be characterized as "egregious" or "outrageous."

The Court summarized on this point that § 1981a(a)(1) requires proof of an intentional violation to subject the defendant to the possibility of compensatory or punitive damages; § 1981a(b)(1) further qualifies the availability of punitive damages, limiting them to situations where the employer has carried out intentional discrimination with " 'malice or with reckless indifference to [the plaintiff's] federally protected rights.' "

Kolstad creates a three-part framework for determining whether an award of punitive damages is proper. First, a plaintiff must demonstrate that the employer acted with the requisite mental state, i.e., the employer must have acted with knowledge that its actions may have violated federal law. Second, the plaintiff must establish a basis for imputing liability to the employer. Third, the employer may avoid liability for punitive damages if it can show that it engaged in good faith efforts to implement an antidiscrimination policy.

Courts have particularly struggled with establishing reasonable limits on the amount of a punitive award. In general, the award should "bear some relation" to the nature of defendant's conduct and the harm it caused; and taking defendant's resources into account, it should "sting" rather than "destroy." But the EEOC takes the position that in general punitive awards under Title VII and ADA should rarely be grossly excessive, because the sum of punitive damages together with future pecuniary losses and all nonpecuniary losses must stay within the caps of § 1981a(b)(3).

The Supreme Court's Due Process limits on punitive damages, or similar state law limits, will usually only constrain punitive awards where there is no statutory cap on the plaintiff's claim like the $300,000 maximum compensatory-punitive award available under Title VII or ADA. Examples include punitive awards under state law or under § 1981, § 1983 or the other Reconstruction Acts. If the amount of a punitive damages award is reduced pursuant to these rather rarely invoked Due Process limits, it is unsettled if the question is one of law or of judicial discretion. If it is a question of law, then, notwithstanding the Seventh Amendment's "reexamination clause," the trial or appellate court may enter final judgment for the amount as reduced to comply with Due Process, without giving the plaintiff the option of a new trial. If the determination is considered discretionary, the plaintiff whose verdict has been ruled constitutionally excessive must be given the choice between a reduced verdict and a new trial so as not to violate the Seventh Amendment.

But a trial court may also conclude in its discretion that either a compensatory or punitive award is simply excessive on the evidence, and may then order a new trial unless the plaintiff agrees to remit a portion of the jury's award. When a judge exercises the discretion to reduce either a compensatory or punitive award for ordinary excessiveness, the Amendment requires that the plaintiff be afforded the option of a new trial under Federal Rule of Civil Procedure 59(a) in lieu of the court's remittitur of a portion of the jury's award. But if, by contrast, damages are reduced as the result of a defendant's successfully moving after verdict under Federal Rule 50(b) for partial summary judgment as a matter of law—for example, if the evidence was insufficient to support a reasonable jury award of *any* damages respecting a particular incident or period of time—the trial court may enter final judgment on a reduced verdict and is not required by the Seventh Amendment to grant a plaintiff's motion for new trial.

3. TAX TREATMENT OF SETTLEMENT OR JUDGMENT PROCEEDS IN EMPLOYMENT DISCRIMINATION CASES

Plaintiffs are of course more inclined to settle for less if they are persuaded that the proceeds of a settlement will not be taxed. Until August 20, 1996, when President Clinton signed the Small Business Job Protection Act of 1996, Section 104(a)(2) of the Internal Revenue Code, 26 U.S.C.A. § 104(a)(2), excluded from gross income "the amount of any *damages* received (whether by suit or agreement ...) *on account of personal injuries* or sickness.... " An elaborate and confusing jurisprudence developed separately under ADEA and Title VII concerning the extent to which various elements of recovery under those statutes could be excludable under Section 104(a)(2) as "damages" received by a taxpayer plaintiff "on account of personal injuries or sickness."

The "personal injuries or sickness" requirement was acutely raised by employment discrimination, and to a lesser degree civil rights, claims. In most such cases the plaintiff's immediate injuries, while arguably "personal," and commonly resulting in emotional distress that is sometimes medically treated, are nonphysical. In 1995 the Supreme Court held that in the typical, nonphysical situation, neither the back pay nor the liquidated damages recoverable in an action under the Age Discrimination in Employment Act could ordinarily be considered "damages" on account of "personal injuries." That decision rested uncomfortably with the Court's strong suggestion three years earlier that the back pay and emotional distress damages recoverable under Title VII, as amended by the 1991 Civil Rights Acts, would be excludable from the plaintiff's income under Section 104(a)(2). At the same time, text added to Section 104 in 1989 rendered punitive damages, available since November 1991 in Title VII actions, non-excludable in a case—like most employment discrimination and many civil rights cases—that did "not involv[e] physical injury or physical sickness." (The Supreme Court has since rejected the negative pregnant that punitive damages were excludable in cases that did involve physical injury or sickness.)

Except for the nonexcludability of punitive damages, most of this landscape was altered by a stroke of President Clinton's pen in August 1996. Two additions to the text of Section 104(a)(2) tell most of the tale:

(a) ... gross income does not include—

(2) the amount of any damages (other than punitive damages) received (whether by suit or agreement ...) on account of personal physical injuries or physical sickness;

The rest of the tale is told by an addendum to Section 104(a):

For purposes of paragraph (2), emotional distress shall not be treated as a physical injury or physical sickness. The preceding sentence shall not apply to an amount of damages not in excess of the amount paid for medical care ... attributable to emotional distress.

The English translation? The most important change, particularly for Title VII cases, is the requirement of physical injury as a precondition for exclusion under Section 104(a)(2). In the usual Title VII or ADEA case, where the employer's conduct does not result in "physical" injury or sickness, no part of any judgment or settlement for back or front pay will be eligible for exclusion under Section 104(a)(2). Second, because the first sentence of the addendum excludes emotional distress from the Section 104(a)(2) definition of "physical" injury or sickness, the part of any settlement or judgment representing recovery for the intangible harms of emotional distress will also be nonexcludable in non-physical cases. Third, however, where a civil rights (or, more rarely, employment discrimination) plaintiff does suffer some actual "physical" injury as the result of the defendant's conduct—police abuse cases may be the paradigm, with the rape and invasive touching variants of sexual harassment strong possibilities—she may exclude "any damages" (other than punitive) received in respect of those injuries. Fourth, because of the "(other than punitive damages)" language, punitive damages will now almost never be eligible for exclusion, even when they are awarded in cases of *physical* injury. It therefore may be important in non-physical injury cases where the plaintiff incurred medical expenses related to emotional distress for plaintiff to seek settlement agreements that label as "compensatory" rather than "punitive" as much of the total monetary recovery as may plausibly be so characterized consistent with the underlying facts and the allegations of any previously asserted demand letters, pleadings, and subsequent litigation documents. A recent Tax Court decision, warns, however, that an allocation negotiated by the parties will not be respected if they never bargained over the allocation before arriving at an overall settlement or if an allocation is "patently inconsistent" with the underlying claims.

The essence of these changes, as applicable to claimants under federal employment discrimination and civil rights laws, may be summarized as follows: (1) At least some "physical" (probably bodily) injury or sickness is necessary for the taxpayer to exclude from gross income *any* settlement or judgment proceeds, except the relatively minor portion representing reimbursement for medical expenses attributable to emotional distress; (2) where the settlement or judgment resolves a claim involving *some* "physical" injury or sickness, the taxpayer may exclude all back pay, front pay, or compensatory damages that are received "on account of" that injury or sickness, including *all* emotional distress damages, not just those that reimburse for medical expenses; but (3), even in cases of actual physical injury or sickness, punitive damages will not be excludable.

Even more fundamentally troublesome for plaintiffs than being placed in a higher tax bracket by a lump sum award has been the dominant judicial view that attorneys' fees must be included in their own, that is the plaintiffs', gross income, not just the attorney's, and then treated as a miscellaneous itemized deduction; that deduction is then available only to the extent it exceeds 2% of a plaintiff's adjusted gross income. Moreover, the deduction is often of limited value because it can trigger the alternative minimum tax. Congress has just overturned this double taxation of attorneys' fees prospectively, with respect to fees and costs paid after October 22, 2004, American Jobs Creation Act (H.R. 4520).

There is a more confident way to reduce a claimant's or plaintiff's tax bill if she has filed a parallel workers' compensation claim. Then a reasonable portion of the discrimination claim settlement might fairly be allocated as a settlement of the workers' compensation case. These payments, while still deductible expenses for the employer, would be considered nontaxable payments to the employee-claimant.

The threshold requirement for excludability is whether, assuming the plaintiff obtains the kind of "damages" for "personal injuries" that § 104(a)(2) makes excludable, she receives them "by suit or agreement." An appellate decision holds that the receipt by an employee of a lump sum termination payment that the company increased because of his willingness to waive all claims relating to his employment or termination, including claims related to age discrimination, could not be considered "damages," or therefore the result of a "settlement," so defined. The court reasoned that a "claim must be asserted before it can be settled; plaintiff waived all claims before asserting them. . . . " Taggi v. United States (2d Cir.1994). This ruling is apparently in some tension with Tax Court practice, the waiver procedure approved for ADEA claims by the OWBPA, as well as the expressed preference of

§ 118 of the 1991 Civil Rights Act for alternative means of dispute resolution. Its lesson to older employees in a circuit subscribing to this view and facing a reduction in force would appear to be not to enter into a valid agreement waiving ADEA rights under the terms of OWBPA, but instead to have a lawyer assert a formal charge or claim before settling with the employer. This seems an unnecessary expense and formality, since it is well established that sums paid to settle a previously asserted ADEA claim may be excludable if they meet the (now stringent) requirements of § 104(a)(2).

Employer counsel should seek to reduce the payroll tax due on settlements of statutory discrimination claims, by specifying in the settlement agreement which components of recovery are non-wage items. Likely candidates include reimbursements for medical expenses and payments allocated for future medical expenses and health insurance premiums.

I. RETROACTIVE SENIORITY FOR PROVEN VICTIMS OF DISCRIMINATION: A FIRST LOOK AT THE PROBLEM OF "REVERSE DISCRIMINATION"

More complex and controversial than the availability of back pay in Title VII actions are awards of retroactive "remedial" seniority to victorious discriminatees who secure orders directing their hire, promotion or reinstatement. These are awards of seniority that enhance the measure of employer-paid compensation or benefits. Because remedial seniority restores discriminatees to their "rightful place"—the rung on the ladder to which they likely would have climbed between the date of discrimination and date of judgment—and produces benefits that are paid by the adjudicated wrongdoer (the employer), it serves both Title VII remedial objectives, deterrence as well as compensation. Accordingly, in Franks v.

Bowman Transportation Co. (1976), the Supreme Court held that retroactive remedial seniority for those economic purposes is presumptively available on the same terms as back pay. In doing so the Court rejected the argument that § 703(h)—which insulates bona fide seniority systems from being declared unlawful, and therefore protects them from *wholesale* dismantling by injunction—also prohibits the *incremental* adjustment of places on the seniority ladder that results when judges award discriminatees fictional, retroactive seniority as a remedy for an underlying discrimination in hiring, assignment or promotions.

On the other hand, retroactive seniority also serves an alternative or additional purpose: improving the discriminatee's position relative to other employees in competing for scarce job resources like better-paying positions, more favorable hours, or, most critically, protection against demotion or layoff. Unlike seniority for benefits purposes, retroactive "competitive" seniority furthers only the goal of compensation, not employer deterrence. In *Franks*, the Court recognized that such protection is necessary to make a proven victim of discrimination whole; without it, she is vulnerable to layoff, termination or simply poorer job assignments without any of the seniority protection that she would almost surely have earned absent the employer's unlawful conduct. It therefore held, following Albemarle Paper Co. v. Moody (1975) that the "competitive" as well as the "benefits" brand of retroactive fictional seniority is presumptively available.

A year later, in International Brotherhood of Teamsters v. United States (1977), the Court also agreed that an award of retroactive seniority, because it is essential to redress proven discrimination, is also not a "preference" prohibited by § 703(j). But there, in contrast to the situation in *Franks*, immediate implementation of retroactive seniority for competitive purposes would have visited highly visible harm on incumbent employees already out on layoff: restoring the discriminatees to "their" rung on the seniority ladder would have delayed the incumbents' day of recall. On those facts the Court drew back from authorizing the automatic or immediate implementation of retroactive seniority for competitive purposes. Rather, to decide "when" and "the rate at which" discriminatees may be made whole by such awards, it directed the district courts to exercise their "qualities of mercy and practicality" in balancing several unweighted equities. These include the number of protected group and non-protected group persons interested in the scarce resource, the number of current vacancies, and the economic prospects of the industry. *Teamsters* left undisturbed the *Franks* holding that seniority for benefits purposes should be implemented presumptively, unequivocally and immediately after issuance of a judgment.

Although the Supreme Court has implied that § 706(g) provides limited discretion to "bump" an incumbent employee in order to reinstate a proven victim or "discriminatee," lower courts have displayed great reluctance to do so, even when the order protects the displaced employee's former level of compensation. They have instead sometimes awarded the discriminatee "front pay".

J. AFFIRMATIVE ACTION BY "VOLUNTARY" PROGRAMS AND JUDICIAL DECREES

"Voluntary," "benign" employer affirmative action, and reverse discriminatory remedies imposed by court order or consent decree, raise similar yet legally distinct questions of fairness as between minority and majority group employees. Strictly speaking, employer affirmative action in the form of self-imposed quotas or goals does not really implicate the judiciary's remedial authority under § 706(g) at all. An employer simply institutes racial or gender preferences, without court compulsion, typically to avoid lawsuits by the group benefitting from the preference or to preserve federal contracts that require affirmative action. Rather, such a plan is unlawful, if at all, because it operates to prefer members of defined minority or female groups or classes, rather than individuals proven to have suffered discrimination at the hands of the defendant employer. As a result, these preferences are suspect under § 703 as ordinary unlawful employment practices directed against any majority group members or males who are denied employment opportunities by the plan. The jeopardy would seem considerable because the Court has regularly emphasized that the statute seeks to protect individuals from discrimination on the basis of group characteristics, rather than groups as such, e.g. Connecticut v. Teal (1982); City of Los Angeles Dep't of Water & Power v. Manhart (1978).

But the Supreme Court, in a landmark 1979 opinion, United Steelworkers of America v. Weber (1979), that expressly elevated a supposed legislative "spirit" over statutory text, gave qualified approval to "voluntary," "benign" racial preferences. A majority held that the employer there had lawfully taken race into account in preferring black employees as a group for admission to an on-the-job training program—a preference that on its face violated the specific terms of § 703(d). The Court acknowledged that the white race of Brian Weber was the factor that resulted in his denial of the employment benefit, in apparent violation of that section.

Perhaps to ease its misgivings about approving a form of race discrimination that the text of § 703(d) expressly prohibited, the *Weber* majority listed a number of sanitizing factors to circumscribe the scope of lawful "benign" discrimination. It observed that the employer plan before it did not require white employees to be discharged and therefore did not "unnecessarily trammel" their interests; that it did not absolutely bar white employees from the skilled positions, but merely limited their numbers; and that it was a temporary measure, intended not to maintain a racial balance but to eliminate a manifest imbalance in the skilled job categories. The Court satisfied itself on these points again in Johnson v. Transportation Agency of Santa Clara County (1987), when it extended the *Weber* principle by upholding an explicit *gender* preference for *promotions*, this time in the face of the apparently plain prohibition of § 703(a).

Affirmative action plans have fared less well when challenged as violations of equal protection. For example, the Court concluded in Wygant v. Jackson Board of Education (1986) that a public employer, before instituting such a program, must have "convincing evidence" of its own prior discrimination and must employ means narrowly tailored to rectify that conduct. The collective bargaining agreement in *Wygant* required the layoff of non-minority teachers with greater seniority than minority teachers who were retained, a feature that might also have offended the *Weber* sanitizing factor of "unnecessary trammeling." In any event, the *Wygant* plurality's broader approach commanded a majority of the Court in City of Richmond v. J.A. Croson, Co. (1989), where the Court struck down a municipal program to set aside a minimum amount of subcontracting work for minority business enterprises. The Court insisted that the Equal Protection Clause is violated whenever government takes race into account unless (1) it has a compelling justification and (2) the means adopted are narrowly tailored to go only so far as that justification requires. *Croson*, then, supplies the framework for evaluating the constitutionality of a current plan.

A circuit court, taking note of the first of the *Croson* requirements, has observed that a local government will now be hard pressed to justify a race-based set-aside program unless it can offer current statistical evidence demonstrating its own prior discriminatory practices and their ongoing effects. Associated Gen. Contractors of Conn., Inc. v. New Haven, Conn. (2d Cir.1994). A common circuit reformulation of those requirements takes into account four factors: (1) the necessity for the relief and efficacy of alternative means; (2) the flexibility and duration of the relief; (3) the the fit between the plan's numerical goals and the relevant labor market; and (4) the degree to which the relief adversely affects third parties, e.g., nonminority employees or applicants. Under these strict standards, most such equal protection challenges to current plans have succeeded.

In public contracting and employment settings, it is not a sufficiently compelling justification for the government to offer a purportedly "benign" preference designed to redress general societal or historical discrimination against African–Americans; in general, race has been accepted as a lawful factor in doling out benefits only to redress the governmental unit's own prior discrimination, and only as long as and to the extent necessary to remedy the discriminatory injury the government inflicted. No formal, judicial determination of past discrimination by the governmental unit in question is necessary to show the requisite compelling governmental interest. But the evidence of such discrimination must be "strong" or "convincing."

For this purpose the defendant resisting a reverse-discrimination action may use reliable statistical evidence of the kind that establishes a prima facie case of systemic disparate treatment under Title VII—evidence reflecting a gross disparity between, on one hand, the percentage of protected group members one would "expect" to see selected based on their percentage representation in a qualified labor pool, and, on the other, the actual percentage of those persons selected. For example, one circuit court has held that the litigant defending governmental contract set asides must demonstrate a strong evidentiary basis of discrimination. Where a disparity in percentage of contracting dollars awarded to minority businesses can be explained by evidence that these businesses are smaller and are thus awarded smaller contracts, the set asides program will be found to violate equal protection. Engineering Contractors Ass'n of S. Fla., Inc. v. Metropolitan Dade County (11th Cir.1997). On the other hand, racial preference provisions not justified by sufficient evidence of such underrepresentation as is required to show a remedial necessity for the preference, or not narrowly tailored to that underrepresentation, may be no better able to survive equal protection strict scrutiny merely because they are court-ordered as part of a consent decree settling litigation.

More recently, the Supreme Court has adhered to the position articulated by Justice Lewis Powell in Regents of Univ. of Cal. v. Bakke (1978): classroom diversity is a compelling governmental interest in education and universities may use race as a factor to ensure diversity, but quotas or a fixed numerical advantage during the admissions review process is unconstitutional. In Grutter v. Bollinger (2003), in a 5–4 decision with Justice O'Connor writing for the majority, the Court upheld the University of Michigan Law School's affirmative action program. The Court ruled that colleges and universities have a compelling interest in creating a diverse student body and that they may use race as one factor, among many, to benefit minorities and enhance diversity. In a companion case, Gratz v. Bollinger (2003), the Court, 6–3, invalidated an affirmative action program for undergraduate admissions that added 20 points to the applications for minority students. The Court ruled that the undergraduate program was not sufficiently narrowly tailored to meet the strict scrutiny used for government racial classifications.

Justice O'Connor's emphasis in *Grutter* on how the existence and definition of a "compelling state interest" depends on the context, coupled with her and the concurrences' approving citations to *Croson* and the plurality opinion in *Wygant*, suggests, albeit uncertainly, the continuing vitality of those precedents in their public contracting and employment settings. Yet private employers, per the *Weber* and *Johnson* interpretations of Title VII, continue to enjoy leeway to take race and gender into account to a considerably greater degree than do government employers under *Wygant*'s limited remedial-only compelling state interest for public employment. Because the Court focused on the government's compelling interest in student diversity in the classroom, the 2003 cases cannot be generalized outside the area of education.

Within the higher education setting, public (per Equal Protection, as construed in these opinions) and private (per Title VI, the prohibitions of which the Court in *Gratz* says it apparently continues to equate with those of Equal Protection) administrators can know for sure that their plan is lawful only if it mimics the Michigan Law School's, and that their plan is unlawful if it mimics the College's. That is, the line between a permissible plan and an unlawful quota remains hazy after the majority opinions. Nevertheless, the recent decisions offer guidance in one crucial respect: a majority of the Court has made the value choice that diversity among students in a classroom is a compelling governmental interest.

Unlike "voluntary" affirmative action, judgments directing preferential treatment for a minority or gender group, issued after litigated findings of discrimination or upon the parties' consent, squarely test the limits of a court's remedial authority under § 706(g) to "order such affirmative action as may be appropriate." In the case of public employers, these judgments may also deny the disfavored racial or gender groups equal protection. The justices have been deeply divided over the equitable propriety under § 706(g) of consent judgments that

afford relief to minority group members who are not themselves proven victims of discrimination. The degree of "tram-
melling" appears important.

The strict scrutiny approach to "benign" racial preferences
reflected in the Supreme Court's recent equal protection decisions, notably *Wygant* and *Croson*, has since been applied to
employment discrimination consent decrees involving government employers. And circuit decisions have held that a preference enjoys no greater protection because it is embodied in a
judicial decree than when it is part of an employer's "voluntary" affirmative action plan. It is therefore quite likely, if not
logically compelled, that an affirmative action plan or consent
decree affecting a state or local government employer may
pass muster under Title VII's *Weber/Johnson* standards as not
constituting impermissible reverse discrimination, yet still run
afoul of the Constitution. Now the flow is beginning to run the
other way. The new "race-neutral" constitutional guideposts
seem to have heightened the circuit courts' scrutiny *under
Title VII* of government employer affirmative action and consent decrees; the previously prevailing permissiveness appears
to be waning. Indeed the Eleventh Circuit has frankly acknowledged that its "application of the *Johnson* [i.e., Title
VII] manifest imbalance test ... is informed by *Croson*'s
discussion of the necessity [under the Equal Protection
Clause] for a government entity to identify with specificity the
discrimination it seeks to remedy through race conscious
measures." In re Birmingham Reverse Discrimination Employment Litig. (11th Cir.1994). The decisions have been particularly critical of promotion preferences when they are not
narrowly tailored to remedy prior discrimination by the government defendant.

Somewhat different questions are presented by a controversial California constitutional amendment prohibiting the state
from according preferential treatment based on race or gender

in public employment, education or contracting. Proposition 209, which implemented the change, was challenged as violating equal protection by impeding the political access of minorities who could otherwise petition local government for race-preferential legislation. The Ninth Circuit has rejected the challenge, reasoning that equal protection is violated only when political access is denied in a racially discriminatory manner, and not when, as the court asserted was the case with Proposition 209, it does so neutrally by *prohibiting* legislative distinctions based on race. Moreover, "that the Constitution permits [but does not require] the rare race-based or gender-based preference hardly implies that the state cannot ban them altogether."

Similarly, by viewing Title VII as flatly prohibiting discriminatory preference for any group, the court declined to find Proposition 209 preempted by that statute; Proposition 209, that is, neither requires the kind of discriminatory preference forbidden by Title VII nor, thought the court, is inconsistent with any of its purposes. Of course this view of Title VII to some degree discounts Supreme Court voluntary affirmative action decisions like *Weber* and *Johnson* that treat the preferential advancement of minority group interests as an implicit goal of that statute.

Indeed, it is even plausible that the tail, Title VII, can wag the dog, Equal Protection, when a government employer's conduct is challenged *under the Constitution*. Put otherwise, the Court's permissive construction of Title VII as respects "benign" affirmative action might actually trump the Court's own interpretation of the demands of Equal Protection as elaborated in *Wygant*. After all, in authorizing federal courts to award monetary relief against state and local government defendants notwithstanding the Eleventh Amendment, the Supreme Court relied on the fact that Congress' authority to enact Title VII derived from § 5 of the Fourteenth Amendment. Title VII might thus be viewed as a particularized expression of the Fourteenth Amendment's mandate for the employment setting, one that arguably prevails over the more general Fourteenth Amendment understanding that governs in, say, the government contract setting of *Croson*.

After *Croson*, the Court might be inclined to overrule *Weber* itself, as one justice has urged. Indeed even an affirmative action plan valid under *Weber* might be held unlawful under § 703(m) of Title VII, as amended by the 1991 CRA. That section provides that an unlawful employment practice is "established" when race or gender is shown to be "a motivating factor ... even though other [e.g., benign, compensatory] factors motivated the practice." The preface to § 703(m), though, reads "Except as otherwise provided in this title.... "; and part of that title, § 116 of the Civil Rights Act of 1991, provides that its amendments shall not be construed to affect "court-ordered remedies, affirmative action, or conciliation agreements, that are in accordance with the law."

Does this "savings" clause protect only affirmative action plans that are "court-ordered"? It might if that compound adjective were construed to modify "affirmative action" as well as "remedies," for then only "court-ordered," as distinct from voluntary *Weber/Johnson*-type affirmative action would be saved. That would leave the Court free to overturn the rather lenient *Weber/Johnson* standards in place before the CRA of 1991. But how could "court-ordered" modify both "remedies" and "affirmative action" without also modifying "conciliation agreements," the third remedy source in the statutory list? And since conciliation agreements are understood, by their nature, not to be court ordered, then perhaps "court-ordered" modifies only the first item on the list, "remedies." Even non-court-ordered, i.e., "voluntary" affirmative action plans would then be saved, provided they are in accordance with the standards of pre-November 1991 law. EEOC has given § 116 this latter reading. Without even wrestling with the text, which it found "clear" as applied to a court-ordered consent decree, the Ninth Circuit has concluded that § 116 modifies the general prohibition of § 703(m) to uphold the continued validity of an affirmative action plan designed to comply with that decree. Officers for Justice v. Civil Serv. Comm'n of San Francisco (9th Cir.1992).

K. PROCEDURES AND REMEDIES IN AFFIRMATIVE ACTION CHALLENGES

When a white or male plaintiff challenges an employment practice as a form of intentional discrimination, the employer may assert that the practice was dictated by the provisions of a valid affirmative action plan. The Court might have treated the employer justification as a true affirmative defense, thereby casting on it burdens of both production and persuasion. Instead, it treated the plaintiff's prima facie case as resting essentially on the inferential *McDonnell Douglas* mode of proof, and accordingly held that the employer may justify simply by producing evidence that its challenged decision was made pursuant to an affirmative action plan. In contrast to the BFOQ defense to express discrimination, the employer does not have to bear the burden of persuasion in defending an expressly discriminatory individual employment decision made pursuant to a valid affirmative action plan; rather, the plaintiff must prove either that the decision was not made pursuant to the plan, or that the plan is invalid.

When race-based government action is challenged under the Equal Protection Clause, however, the Court has placed the burden on the defendant to show the affirmative action plan can survive strict scrutiny. Several circuits have identified the problems inherent in these varying burdens both Title VII and constitutional claims are pursued in the same action. This asymmetry means that an equal protection challenge to a decision based on an affirmative action plan is easier to sustain than a Title VII challenge for both a substantive reason—it is easier to show that a plan fails strict scrutiny than that it violates the *Weber/Johnson* factors—and a procedural reason—Title VII plaintiffs bear the burden of showing a plan's invalidity, whereas § 1983/equal protection defendants bear the burden of showing a plan's validity. Some courts have modified the equal protection burdens by placing on the defendant the burden of producing evidence of the plan's constitutionality, still leaving the plaintiff with the "ultimate burden of proving its unconstitutionality."

There is little consensus about the remedies appropriately awarded nonminority plaintiffs when they succeed in demonstrating the unconstitutionality of a voluntary or court-ordered affirmative action plan. A growing number of federal courts have taken the position, for example, that white plaintiffs who demonstrate that they were denied the right to compete on an equal basis because of their race are entitled to damages to the extent of any demonstrated economic loss or emotional distress, even if they fail to demonstrate that, but for the race-based preference, they would have been selected. These decisions build on the Supreme Court's decision in Northeastern Florida Chapter of the Associated General Contractors of America v. City of Jacksonville (1993), which held, in the setting of a government contract "set aside" program for minorities, that when "government erects a barrier that makes it more difficult for members of one group to obtain a benefit than it is for members of another group, a member of the former group seeking to challenge the barrier need not allege that he would have obtained the benefit but for the barrier. . . . "It is enough if the plaintiff asserts that the barrier has denied him the right to be considered or compete for the benefit in question. In this view, the equal protection violation is complete when the plaintiff cannot fairly compete. It consists of a denial of the right to compete "on a level playing field," which in itself produces the "ignominy and illegality of . . . " erecting a racial bar to promotions.

The Court's apparent retreat from the approval of consent judgments that embody group-based or quota remedies, and perhaps ultimately from voluntary employer affirmative action programs, was signaled by a different procedural development. A 5–4 majority held in Martin v. Wilks (1989), that non-minority employees who object to a consent judgment adverse to their interests are not required to intervene in a Title VII action but instead may collaterally attack the judgment in independent actions. Since the Court had several times recognized that employers are principally motivated to adopt "voluntary" affirmative action programs, or settle pending lawsuits by consent agreements, in order to avoid the costs of extended litigation, the *Wilks* decision appears designed to remove much of the incentive for these arrangements.

The Civil Rights Act of 1991 substantially overrules *Wilks* by foreclosing many collateral challenges, typically by whites or males, to employment practices adopted under the authority of litigated or consent judgments. These attacks customarily assert that the underlying judgment unlawfully provides group-based, reverse-discriminatory relief to minority or female applicants or employees, including those not shown to have suffered discrimination at the hands of the defendant employer. The Court in *Wilks*, in permitting such attacks even where attackers know about the underlying litigation but do not try to intervene, relied on the familiar due process principle that a judgment cannot bind a litigant who was not a party or privy and therefore lacked an opportunity to be heard. Under the new provision, the white or male challengers generally will be barred if they had a reasonable opportunity, after adequate notice, to raise their objections during the primary proceedings or were adequately represented in them by a similarly situated litigant.

On the other hand, this provision of the Act also makes it more difficult for the parties to the primary lawsuit—the minority or female plaintiffs and the defendant employer—to achieve assurance that a judgment in their litigation will effectively end the controversy among all relevant parties. They will have to give actual notice to identifiable incumbent employees who might be adversely affected by a proposed judgment—one, for example, that directs group-based goals or quotas for a training program, promotion, or adjustments to seniority. And when such notice is given, the Act, unlike its predecessor versions, leaves intact another of the Court's 1988 Term decisions that generally relieves intervening challengers from liability for the attorney's fees incurred by the primary parties in defending the group protection features of the proposed underlying judgment.

The difficulties faced by the primary parties are even greater with respect to contemplated relief—goals or quotas concerning hiring or, in the case of a union defendant, membership—that will affect nonminority employees who are not readily identifiable and accordingly cannot be given actual notice. In those situations the primary parties, if they seek a durable, comprehensive judgment, will have to join as additional parties persons or groups who will be deemed adequate representatives of the absentees likely to be affected by the judgment.

On balance, then, the Act makes it riskier for a putative challenger to wait to attack such a judgment until after it is entered and he is denied hire or promotion pursuant to its terms. To this degree it affords indirect support for group protection remedies in the context of completed or, in the case of a consent judgment, partial litigation. On the other hand, since challengers are unlikely to face liability for their adversaries' attorney's fees, they have no substantial financial disincentive to intervene to attack proposed group-based judgments. And in cases that involve proposed group-based hiring or membership remedies, the primary parties may still be reluctant to enter into consent judgments for fear that they cannot locate or join adequate representatives of all the absent nonincumbents, who would then remain free to attack the judgment collaterally.

In a parallel procedural decision that similarly has the potential to limit Title VII affirmative action along constitutional lines, the Second Circuit has held that employment discrimination consent decrees involving a private employer may be modified before their full implementation upon the same relaxed standards the Supreme Court has applied to decrees affecting instrumentalities of government. In such "public issues litigation not involving a governmental entity," the Second Circuit wrote, it is appropriate for a court to entertain modification or termination either for "changed circumstances or substantial attainment of the decree's objective." Patterson v. Newspaper & Mail Deliverers' Union of N.Y. (2d Cir.1993).

CHAPTER 20

OTHER FEDERAL ANTIDISCRIMINATION LAWS

A. THE CIVIL RIGHTS ACTS OF 1866, 1870, AND 1871

(42 U.S.C.A. §§ 1981, 1983, *Bivens* Claims and § 1985(3))

1. IN GENERAL

The Civil Rights Acts of 1866, 1870, and 1871 are generally referred to as the Reconstruction Civil Rights Acts, and they were originally intended to enforce the 13th and 14th Amendments in the post-Civil War era. The most frequently invoked provisions are codified at 42 U.S.C.A. §§ 1981, 1983, and 1985(3). These acts remained dormant for many years but were resurrected in the 1960's.

What is now § 1981 was first enacted in 1866 under authority of the 13th Amendment, and re-enacted in 1870, two years after ratification of the 14th Amendment. This history has spawned doctrinal schisms and jurisprudential inconsistencies. On one hand, the Supreme Court has relied on the 13th Amendment origins of § 1981 (and § 1982, its legislative companion that bars discrimination in the acquiring, holding and disposing of property) to apply these statutes to purely private defendants, at least with respect to transactions held open to the public. On the other, the court has relied on the 14th Amendment origins of § 1981 to limit its reach to violations that reflect race discrimination that is intentional in character. And while the Court has insisted that it is the intent of the enacting Congress that controls the breadth of the §§ 1981 and 1982 definitions of "race," its reliance on the 13th Amendment origins of these statutes seemingly caused it to depart from the norms of that Congress by holding the statutes to bar purely private discrimination, subject only to possible First Amendment limitations related to freedom of association.

Section 1985(3), like § 1983 and in contrast to §§ 1981 and 1982, creates no rights of its own but simply provides damages and perhaps injunctive relief for the conspiratorial deprivation of certain rights independently secured by the federal Constitution and, perhaps, other federal statutes. But when the conspiracy is among purely private actors, very few rights are protected against such deprivation, and § 1985(3) offers no protection unless the conspirators, public or private, act with a specific class-based animus or motive that goes beyond the intent requirement of §§ 1981 or 1982.

2.   SECTION 1981

Section 1981 secures equal contracting rights without regard to race. It affords "all persons" in the United States "the same right ... to make and enforce contracts ... and to the full and equal benefit of all laws ... as is enjoyed by white citizens." By its terms § 1981 reaches not just employment but a host of contracting relationships—with private schools, to name just one—not reached by Title VII of the Civil Rights Act of 1964, as amended. And § 1981, unlike Title VII, has no minimum-employee numerical threshold for employer liability; § 1981 also provides for individual liability in several circuits. Section 1981 has been interpreted to provide a civil damages remedy for racial discrimination arising from contracts of employment, even though Congress has comprehensively addressed employment discrimination much more recently in Title VII. Moreover, the Supreme Court has held, Runyon v. McCrary (1976) and reaffirmed, Patterson v. McLean Credit Union (1989) that § 1981, long assumed to reach only state action, also reaches purely private conduct.

A contract for § 1981 purposes is not necessarily the legalistic agreement that the word conjures up in one's mind. In *Patterson*, the Supreme Court impliedly acknowledged that an at-will employee may bring an action under § 1981. The Court stated that Patterson, an at-will employee, might have a cause of action against her employer for failure to promote: "the question whether a promotion claim is actionable under § 1981 depends upon whether the nature of the change in position was such that it involved the opportunity to enter into a new contract with the employer. If so, then the employer's refusal to enter the new contract is actionable under § 1981." Justice Stevens, writing separately in *Patterson*, explained that an "at-will employee ... is not merely performing an existing contract; she is constantly remaking that contract." Early federal decisions on the issue were few, and were not unanimous. The 1998 Supreme Court decision in Haddle v. Garrison (1998), wherein the Court held that an at-will employee can state a claim under § 1985(2), apparently has put this issue to rest. Every circuit to consider the issue since *Haddle* has held that at-will employees can state a claim under § 1981.

The Supreme Court has construed the language that secures to all the same contracting rights as "white citizens" to refer only to the racial (as opposed to, say, gender-based or religious) character of the prohibited discrimination, rather than to limit the class of appropriate plaintiffs to non-whites. Accordingly, while the lower courts are in agreement that the statute does not prohibit discrimination because of gender, it is also settled that whites as well as blacks may assert contract denial claims under § 1981 on the basis of race.

The Supreme Court has construed § 1981's ban on "race" discrimination to include also discrimination on the basis of ancestry. The Court has understood ancestry, in turn, to mean membership in an "ethnically and physiognomically distinctive sub-grouping." This somewhat vague formulation has generated predictable confusion among the lower federal courts. We do know that § 1981 "ancestry" does not mean national origin, religion, or alienage status as such. On the other hand, these latter characteristics are often statistically correlated with an individual's descent from a particular ancestry. For example, in one recent case, a hiring supervisor disparaged the plaintiff's Israeli background, and in particular his prior sales experience in Israel, saying "Israel doesn't count." The appellate court ruled that the jury was entitled to treat these comments not just as discrimination on the basis of national origin ... actionable under Title VII ... but also as discrimination based on the plaintiff's Israeli ancestry, and thus "race" within the meaning of § 1981. It reasoned that the Israeli population was composed primarily of members of a particular ancestry and therefore the jury might have concluded that by disparaging Israel the defendant was really, or also, discriminating against plaintiff because of his "race" ... in the nineteenth century sense defined by the Supreme Court.

Although § 1981, like Title VII, does not prohibit discrimination on the basis of alienage *per se*, a limited protection from employment discrimination on the basis of non-citizenship status is now provided by the Immigration Reform and Control Act of 1986. But aliens, like other "persons within the jurisdiction of the United States," may complain of race or ancestry and alienage, i.e. non-citizenship discrimination under § 1981, or of race, gender, religious, or national origin, but not ancestry or citizenship discrimination under Title VII.

None of the Reconstruction Civil Rights Acts reaches gender or religious discrimination as such, although discrimination on those grounds might violate Equal Protection and accordingly would be redressable under § 1983.

The federal judiciary began to place significant limitations on the utility of § 1981 in General Building Contractors Association v. Pennsylvania (1982). There the Supreme Court held that a showing of disparate impact does not suffice to prove a § 1981 employment violation, which requires instead a direct or inferential demonstration of discriminatory intent. Consistent with this ruling, the Court in *Patterson* approved for use in § 1981 actions the Title VII intentional yet inferential disparate *treatment* mode of proof first outlined in McDonnell Douglas Corporation v. Green (1973). Those requirements continue to be routinely applied to actions under § 1981.

Yet at times one encounters some suggestion in the cases that the showing of intent required in § 1981 cases by *General Building Contractors* in practice demands somewhat more "direct" evidence of discrimination than would usually be required under Title VII. And it remains uncertain whether, in § 1981 "mixed motive" situations, the courts will hew to the complete-defense approach mandated for at least some constitutional violations in actions under § 1983; to the more limited defense mandated by the 1991 Civil Rights Act for post-November 21, 1991 employment practices that violate Title VII; or to the complete defense stipulated by the Supreme Court in *Price Waterhouse v. Hopkins,* which governed Title VII violations before they were modified by the 1991 Act. The uncertainty is fueled by the fact that the 1991 Act, which in other respects expressly and materially modifies § 1981, refers only to Title VII, not to § 1981, in the provisions that modify *Price Waterhouse*.

Section 1981 has also been read more narrowly than Title VII with respect to the ability of plaintiffs to assert the rights of third parties. The problem has recently arisen in connection with suits by "testers" to challenge discriminatory referrals by employment agencies. Testers have been defined as persons of the opposite race "equipped with fake credentials intended to be comparable" who apply for employment to an agency or employer without an intention to accept an offer if one is forthcoming. The typical ensuing claim is that the employment agency, on grounds of race, failed to refer the African–American (or female) tester but did refer the other (white or male) tester. Title VII provides that any "person claiming to be aggrieved" by an unlawful employment practice may, after exhausting administrative remedies, sue such an agency in court. Consequently, testers may be able to state a Title VII claim despite their own lack of a bona fide interest in employment.

By contrast, the text of § 1981 suggests that only a person deprived of what is otherwise a legal right to make or enforce a contract has standing. Reasoning that testers could not have enforced an employment contract offer because of the material misrepresentations of fact they made to the defendant employment agency about their intentions to secure employment, several appellate courts have held that tester plaintiffs cannot state a claim for damages under § 1981.

By its terms, § 1981 protects only the contractual relationship, and the class of persons who can sue is therefore generally limited to those wishing to enter in, or remain in, that relationship. Thus a shareholder may not maintain such an action for harm caused to her corporation, unless the defendant's conduct that injures the corporation causes distinct injury to the shareholder. The corporation itself probably does have standing if it is an indirect target of racial discrimination in contracting, for example when it suffers loss profits resulting from unlawful discrimination aimed at a member of a class protected under § 1981.

This standing problem, however, should be distinguished from the question of how broadly a violation of the plaintiff's own rights under § 1981 may be defined in relation to discriminatory actions immediately directed against another. Here the courts have shown considerable flexibility, permitting the assertion of § 1981 claims where intimate or associational rights of the plaintiff are allegedly invaded by a defendant whose conduct was aimed at third parties. A related, but distinct question is whether the defendant must be the party with whom the plaintiff contracts or seeks to contract. Courts have answered this question in the negative, holding § 1981 is violated by a racially motivated interference with a plaintiff's right to enter into contracts with nonwhites and by third parties' attempts to punish the plaintiff for making such contracts.

When a customer complains of racial discrimination by an employee of a retailer, the employer can be held vicariously liable for the acts of the employee if the employee was acting within the scope of the employment. Unlike sexual harassment employment cases, in these public accommodation § 1981 cases, it is no defense to respondeat superior liability that the customer suffered the discrimination at the hands of a low-level clerk.

A plaintiff makes out a prima facie case under § 1981 of discrimination in hotel accommodations when she demonstrates that (1) she is a member of a protected class, (2) she sought to enter into or had a contract with a hotel for accommodations, (3) she met the hotel's standard requirements for occupancy, and (4) she was denied accommodations that were available to guests outside of the protected class.

The Supreme Court initially directed the lower federal courts to borrow analogous state statutes of limitations in actions under § 1981, and has held that pursuing Title VII administrative procedures does not toll the § 1981 statute of limitations. The Court explained that in actions under the Reconstruction Civil Rights Acts, the forum state's "personal injury" statute of limitations should apply; and the particular period the court should borrow is the state's general or residual statute on personal injury claims rather than, for example, a statute geared specifically to intentional torts.

But subsequently Congress enacted 28 U.S.C. § 1658(a), a 4–year "catchall" statute of limitations governing claims "arising under an Act of Congress enacted after [December 1, 1990]." One such post-December 1, 1990 statute is the Civil Rights Act of 1991, which, as discussed later in this subsection, amended § 1981 by overruling the Supreme Court's decision in Patterson v. McLean Credit Union (1989) and thus restoring the application of § 1981 to terms and conditions of employment—like on-the-job harassment, failure to promote, demotion, and discharge—arising after initial contract formation. The question that then divided five circuit courts of appeals was whether a § 1981 claim asserting racial discrimination respecting a post-hire term of employment—that is, a claim made possible only by the Civil Rights Act of 1991's overruling of *Patterson*—was eligible for § 1658's 4–year statute of limitations even though the underlying statute that the 1991 Act amended, Section 1981, pre-dated December 1, 1990 by 124 years.

In Jones v. R.R. Donnelley & Sons Company (2004), the Court held that it is. The Court concluded that a cause of action "aris[es] under an Act of Congress enacted after" December 1, 1990—and is therefore governed by § 1658's 4–year limitations period—if the particular plaintiff's claims were made possible by a post–1990 enactment. Because the

Jones petitioners' hostile work environment, wrongful termination, and failure-to-transfer claims alleged § 1981 violations that, under *Patterson*, would not have stated a claim before December 1, 1990, but were actionable by virtue of the Civil Rights Act of 1991 amendments, they "ar[ose] under" the 1991 amendments to § 1981 and accordingly fit within the terms of § 1658. Because the vast majority of claims under Section 1981, indeed virtually all such claims other than alleged racially discriminatory refusals to hire, depend on the 1991 amendments to § 1981 that overruled *Patterson*, almost all Section 1981 claims will now be eligible for § 1658's generous 4–year limitations period, regardless of shorter limitations periods of the forum state. By contrast, claims under the other Reconstruction Acts, principally claims under Sections 1982, 1983, and 1985, will remain subject to the forum state's general or residual limitations period governing claims of personal injury, because the rights created by those statutes have not been substantively amended after § 1658's cutoff of December 1, 1990.

It appears likely that the liberal approach to claim accrual embraced by the Supreme Court in National Railroad Passenger Corporation v. Morgan (2002) for "hostile environment" claims of racial or sexual harassment under Title VII will be extended to similar § 1981 claims as well.

Title 42 U.S.C.A. § 1977A(a)(1), added by § 102 of the Civil Rights Act of 1991, provides that damages under Title VII are recoverable only if the complainant "cannot recover" under § 1981. But the EEOC, relying on the Sponsors' Interpretive Memorandum, has interpreted that language to bar only double recovery for the same injury, not parallel proceedings under the two statutes. Putative plaintiffs with intentional race discrimination claims against employers large enough to be covered by and not exempt from Title VII can therefore apparently choose whether to proceed under Title VII or § 1981 or both.

That choice will be heavily influenced by the availability of unlimited compensatory and punitive damages under § 1981, free of Title VII's variable caps, and by the immediate access to court under § 1981, free of the Title VII state and federal administrative prerequisite requirements with their rather early filing deadlines. Some such claimants, however, who, despite the availability of attorneys' fees, are unable to attract counsel might nevertheless prefer the Title VII route, because by statute the EEOC is expected to assist with investigation and conciliation.

In practice, however, § 1981 will usually look more attractive. Procedurally and remedially, the Reconstruction Civil Rights Acts, § 1981 in particular, may hold several attractions over Title VII. For one, no administrative exhaustion is required. Second, both the national 4–year limitations period that now governs most new Section 1981 claims, and the applicable limitation periods still borrowed from state law to govern the rest, are normally longer than the usual 180–day or 240/300–day Title VII deadline for filing charges with federal or state agencies. Third, although jury trials are now available under either statute with respect to claims of intentional discrimination, the nineteenth-century statutes offer compensatory and punitive damages unlimited in amount; even after the Civil Rights Act of 1991, Title VII plaintiffs who prove intentional discrimination are subject to caps on those damages that vary with the number of employees working for the defendant employer. In one respect, Title VII lines up precisely with § 1983 and § 1981: punitive damages are not available against a defendant government entity.

But what if the § 1981 defendant is able to prove something akin to what the Supreme Court's Mt. Healthy City School

Dist. Bd. of Educ. v. Doyle (1977), decision encourages § 1983 defendants to prove: that the challenged employment action would have been taken for lawful reasons independent of the racial component of the employer's overall motivation? The effect of this showing under § 1983 appears to be (except with respect to procedural due process and certain express or facial equal protection violations) that no federal law violation is established and the defendant may not be mulcted in damages. Under Title VII, as amended in 1991, the defendant who makes this "same-decision" showing is relieved only of retroactive, monetary relief; she is still considered to have violated the law and is therefore subject to prospective relief and attorneys' fees. The 1991 amendments to Title VII did not, however, make the same amendment to § 1981 or the ADEA, although it amended those statutes in other respects. Consequently, the post–*Mt. Healthy*, pre–1991 regime governing § 1981 defendants who carry the showing—a complete defense to liability—is therefore still likely to prevail in most circuits. And under that regime the § 1981 defendant may escape without liability, whereas the Title VII discrimination plaintiff (although perhaps not the Title VII retaliation plaintiff) will establish a violation and thereby have an opportunity to receive declaratory and injunctive relief and, in turn, attorney's fees as a "prevailing party." Indeed, even if the Section 1981 defendant fails to plead the defense affirmatively, it may be preserved if mentioned in the pretrial order.

A potential plaintiff with an intentional race discrimination claim actionable under both statutes may prefer Title VII if she cannot afford counsel and believes that state or federal agency administrative processing of her charge will induce her employer to settle. In addition, it remains possible, to an as yet uncertain extent, for a plaintiff who cannot prove intentional discrimination and would therefore fail under § 1981 to succeed under Title VII by establishing that an employer's neutral practice had a disproportionate adverse impact on her group and that the employer cannot justify the practice as a matter of job relatedness and business necessity.

In actions against state and local government employers, it appears increasingly likely, as discussed in detail in the *"Jett"* sections that follow, that § 1981 is not available on its own terms and instead the plaintiff must surmount the additional proof requirements and defenses available under § 1983. If this is so, then Title VII may once again become a more attractive option for asserting intentional race discrimination claims against state or local government employers. And Title VII would appear to be the *only* remedy for race discrimination in federal employment, which has been held outside the reach of § 1981.

In Patterson v. McLean Credit Union (1989), the Court held that discriminatory conduct directed against an employee after her initial hiring falls outside the right granted by § 1981 to "make" a contract free from racial discrimination. The 1991 legislation overturns this decision and thereby restores 42 U.S.C.A. § 1981 as a forceful supplementary vehicle for redressing race or ancestry discrimination in contracting, although only when the defendant's conduct is shown, by direct or indirect evidence, to be *intentional*. The legislation provides that the right to "make" a contract extends beyond initial formation to include "performance, modification and termination" and thus reaches not only dismissal but also ongoing terms and conditions of employment, probably including retaliation and race-based harassment.

The 1991 legislation likely restores § 1981 post-hiring retaliation claims by overturning *Patterson*. The contours of such a claim, however, remain unclear. The Eleventh Circuit, for example, revived a § 1981 post-hiring retaliation claim by a black plaintiff alleging that she was terminated for filing an

EEOC charge for race discrimination, but rejected a claim by a white plaintiff fired for complaining of racial slurs about blacks. In general, the retaliatory conduct, to be actionable, must respond to an employee's assertion of rights protected by Section 1981. Thus the claim would fail if the underlying discrimination were based on religion, a ground that per se is probably not protected by § 1981. The Seventh Circuit requires a type of double causation: in order for retaliation to be actionable under § 1981, the plaintiff must show that the defendant interfered with his right to enforce the contract on account of race, and the plaintiff must then show that the retaliation itself had a racial motivation. Daniels v. Pipefitters' Ass'n Local Union No. 597 (7th Cir.1991). However, this double causation requirement is suspect; the party complaining of retaliation need not also be a member of a protected group.

Another emerging Title VII proof requirement—that the plaintiff show a substantial or material adverse impact on terms and conditions of employment—has sometimes been held inapplicable to Reconstruction Act claims. And the Eleventh Circuit has held that neither the BFOQ nor business necessity defenses, available in some circumstances under Title VII, will defeat a § 1981 claim. The court stated that the business necessity defense is available only to claims of disparate impact, a claim not cognizable under § 1981, which requires proof of intentional discrimination. And a BFOQ defense, the court noted, is not available to a charge of racial discrimination.

Section 1981 contains no threshold numerical requirement for employer coverage. In the course of considering the amendments, Congress observed that § 1981 constitutes the only protection against race or ancestry discrimination for those millions of applicants or employees whose employers are too small to be covered by Title VII. Despite this understanding, the amendments make no attempt to protect those applicants or employees against the other forms of discrimination prohibited by Title VII, that is, sex, religion, or national origin, or against race discrimination resulting solely from the effects of a neutral practice. Indeed, by capping Title VII damages, while leaving uncapped the compensatory and punitive damages recoverable under § 1981, Congress implicitly expresses greater concern with intentional race discrimination than with unintentional discrimination or intentional discrimination based on Title VII's other prohibited grounds.

In § 1981 disparate treatment discrimination cases, courts commonly permit the showing of intent requisite under the Reconstruction Acts to be made inferentially, that is, through the *McDonnell Douglas/Burdine/St. Mary's* formula of shifting evidentiary burdens that is paradigmatic under Title VII. Similarly, once a plaintiff has established a prima face case of retaliation under § 1981, most circuits will consider *McDonnell Douglas* inferential evidence to discredit any neutral employer reason for the adverse action at issue. Nevertheless, there have been rumblings of discontent with the dominant view that treats such inferential evidence as an adequate foundation not only for liability but also for punitive damages. The Supreme Court's decision in Kolstad v. American Dental Association (1999), should put an end to these rumblings, while at the same time reaffirming that punitive damages do depend on a showing of either malice or reckless disregard of legal obligations, in addition to evidence of intentional discrimination. While proof requirements for § 1981 discrimination or retaliation claims are rather stringent, and in all cases require evidence of intentional conduct, all such claims in federal court enjoy the benefit of liberal Federal Rules notice pleading.

While the damages caps in 42 U.S.C.A. § 1981a limit the recovery of compensatory and punitive damages available under Title VII, they do not limit the recovery available to plaintiffs who prevail under the amended § 1981. For this reason, plaintiffs complaining under both Title VII and § 1981 of underlying intentional race or ancestry discrimination may be well advised to pursue a related retaliation claim under § 1981, as well as Title VII. But to prevail under § 1981, the retaliation plaintiff must show that the defendant took action against him in reprisal for plaintiff's assertion of one of the rights protected by § 1981—i.e., the right to be free of interference in the making or enforcement of contracts because of race or ancestry, and not, for example, gender, a prohibited ground only under Title VII. And the plaintiff who has tried primary discrimination or retaliation claims under both Title VII and § 1981 and receives a favorable jury verdict may bear the additional burden of demonstrating to the court that the jury accepted her § 1981 claim if she hopes to avoid the Title VII cap on damages.

Section 1981, in sum, is ordinarily superior to Title VII as a remedy for intentional, race-based discrimination in employment. Nevertheless, there are at least five situations, two of them relatively common, in which the advocate contemplating a race-based employment discrimination claim should endure Title VII's procedural prerequisites and limitations on damages rather than proceed under Section 1981 alone. The first of these, relatively rare, is where Section 1981 is unavailable because the plaintiff alleges unintentional discrimination—that is, where the plaintiff's sole complaint is that the employer utilized one or more neutral employment practices (tests, height-weight requirements, no-spouse rule) that had a disproportionate adverse impact on a group defined by race. That claim is actionable under Title VII, although it is subject to the elaborate and notoriously vague affirmative defense described by the 1991 amendments to that statute.

A second situation is quite common. Plaintiff has an intentional race-based employment discrimination claim actionable under Section 1981 but fears that the finder of fact will determine that the employer acted with mixed lawful and unlawful motives and would have taken action against the plaintiff (not hired, not promoted, disciplined, or fired her) based on the lawful ground alone. Authority under Section 1981, drawing on comparable Supreme Court rulings under Section 1983, treats this "same-decision" affirmative defense as a complete defense to liability, not merely a limitation on remedy. By contrast, the mixed-motive Title VII plaintiff alleging intentional discrimination (and perhaps retaliation) remains eligible for prospective (mainly injunctive) relief and, in turn, attorney's fees even if the defense succeeds.

Third, another relatively common circumstance, is the plaintiff who sues state or local governments for intentional, race-based employment discrimination under Section 1981. He may have to show that the adverse action was taken against him by a final policymaking official or otherwise as a matter of agency "policy"—a difficult proof hurdle imported into Section 1981 from Section 1983 cases against local government by the Supreme Court's *Jett* decision, which appears to have survived the 1991 amendments to Section 1981. The difficulty is that the typical employment discrimination claim alleges adverse action inflicted ad hoc by a lower-ranking government agent rather than through an official agency policy or by a top policymaker. When asserted against a state or local government employer, therefore, such a claim will fare far better under Title VII: except for hostile environment harassment, that statute imposes respondeat superior liability on the employer for the acts of low-ranking supervisors and managers, with no additional required proof of "policy." If, as seems likely, *Jett* survives the 1991 amendments, there can be no respondeat superior liability against units of local or state government arising from claims asserting liability based on violations of § 1981.

Fourth, the unrepresented plaintiff, or plaintiff of low means, may choose to pursue a Title VII claim, at least initially, to capitalize on any free assistance in investigation or settlement that may be provided by the regional office of the Equal Employment Opportunity Commission. Pre-suit resort to the EEOC is mandated in actions under Title VII, but EEOC is not available for the processing of claims under the Reconstruction Civil Rights Acts.

Fifth, where the claim is brought by someone other than the injured employee, so that the plaintiff is asserting the right of a third party, broader standing has been recognized under Title VII than under Section 1981.

The vast majority of § 1981 claims, including those arising from employment, assert violations of the "same right ... to make and enforce contracts" clause. A few, however, are brought under the "equal benefit" clause, which provides a claim where a plaintiff can demonstrate that a defendant, motivated by racial animosity, has deprived or attempted to deprive him of "the full and equal benefit" of a law or proceedings "for the security of persons and property." It is well established, of course, that the *contracts* clause applies to purely private conduct; indeed, ironically, the private § 1981 defendant, definitively held subject to § 1981 claims only in 1976, may be worse off than his public counterpart, for he does not enjoy the qualified immunity defense enjoyed by individual § 1981 state actor defendants sued for damages in their individual capacities or the *Jett* advantages that may accrue to state actor defendants sued in their official capacities. The circuit decisions disagree, however, whether the *equal benefit* claim reaches private defendants. Section 1981(c), added in 1991, provides: "The rights protected by this section are protected against impairment *by nongovernmental discrimination* and impairment under color of State law," and that language refers to rights protected by the section as a whole, without excepting the equal benefit clause. Despite the seeming clarity of that language, the few circuits to have addressed the question are divided as to whether state action is required for an equal benefit clause claim governed by the amended statute.

Although *Patterson* reaffirmed the *Runyon* ruling that extended § 1981's application to the private sector, it also sharply restricted the scope of § 1981 claims. The Court recognized that § 1981 protects the right to "enforce" contracts; an employer is therefore prohibited from discriminating on the basis of race or national origin so as to impede the enforcement of contract rights. But five justices also ruled that the statutory prohibition on racial or ethnic discrimination in the "making" of private employment contracts does not extend to conduct occurring after the employment relation is established. Thus the Court held employer racial "harassment," fostering or tolerating a discriminatory work environment, outside the ambit of the statute.

The Civil Rights Act of 1991 overrules the *Patterson* limitation on the scope of the right to "make and enforce" contracts, although only prospectively. Section 101 of the Civil Rights Act of 1991 adds to § 1981 the following new subsection:

(b) For purposes of this section, the term "make and enforce contracts" includes the making, performance, modification, and termination of contracts, and the enjoyment of all benefits, privileges, terms, and conditions of the contractual relationship.

The sweeping text of this addition appears to equate the sphere in which contract discrimination is forbidden by

§ 1981 with the wide ambit of the terms and conditions of employment protected under Title VII. In particular, it is now clear that claims of race-based harassment and discharge are once again actionable under § 1981.

In Jett v. Dallas Independent School District (1989) the Court reigned in § 1981 as an independent, free-standing source of redress in actions against local and almost surely also state governments as well. Plaintiffs sometimes bring race discrimination claims against state and local government entities under § 1981 in the hope of skirting the rigors of the § 1983 "official policy" limitation declared by Monell v. Department of Social Services (1978) and thus prevailing with *respondeat superior*-type vicarious liability. But the Court held in *Jett* that municipalities are liable under § 1981 only if they would be liable under the more stringent standards of § 1983. The five-member majority considered it unlikely that Congress intended for § 1981, enacted in 1866 and re-enacted in 1870, to subject state instrumentalities to liability on laxer terms than those which Congress would expressly mandate for them only a year later, in 1871, with the enactment of § 1983.

The Court's reasoning in *Jett* appears in part anachronistic and in part disingenuous. First, it was far from clear when § 1983 was enacted that it reached municipalities, the kind of state unit defending in *Jett*. It was not until more than a century later, with *Monell*, that local government entities were declared to be among the "persons" subject to § 1983 liability on any terms; and only in *Monell* itself did the Court hold that liability contingent on the presence of "policy," a term not found in the statute's text and therefore presumably absent from the minds of its framers in 1871.

The Court had held in Will v. Michigan Dep't of State Police (1989) that states *eo nomine* are *not* liable under *§ 1983*, in either state or federal court; instead the federal law violations of states were held redressable under that statute only indirectly, through actions against individual state officials for prospective relief.

In an apparent attempt to overrule *Jett*, Congress in § 101 of the Civil Rights Act of 1991 appended to § 1981 the following paragraph:

(c) The rights protected by this section are protected against impairment by nongovernmental discrimination and impairment under color of State law.

The protection against impairment by nongovernmental discrimination simply codifies the *Runyon* holding, reaffirmed by *Patterson*, that § 1981 extends to purely private, as well as governmental, discrimination. Indeed the Sponsors' Interpretive Memorandum, identifies *only* this purpose for the entire new paragraph (c). Does the paragraph's last clause, then, asserting that the rights protected by § 1981 are protected from "impairment under color of State law," overrule *Jett*? Perhaps not, for that decision never denied that the § 1981 right to be free of race discrimination in contracting was enforceable to some degree against state and local government. It held only that in actions against those entities the § 1981 plaintiff must establish the "policy" element of the § 1983 prima facie case. On this reading, and a "plain text" approach to statutory interpretation, the Supreme Court might find that the final clause of section (c) actually codifies rather than overrules *Jett*.

Jett, if it has not been legislatively overruled, could have far-reaching restrictive implications. Suppose the *Jett* limitation of § 1981 claims to Section 1983 proof survives judicial construction of new § 1981(c) and the limitation is definitively held applicable to cases against state as well as local government defendants. Would *Jett* then entirely preclude § 1981 claims against states *eo nomine* because after *Will* those claims now fail under § 1983? If so, states could not be subjected to damages for violations of federal rights under either § 1983 or § 1981. Per *Will*, plaintiffs would instead be remitted to § 1983 claims against individual state officials for prospective relief, and then would prevail only if they could prove that the officials were implementing established state policy or custom.

With its decisions in *Will* and *Jett*, the Supreme Court imposed significant restrictions on plaintiffs alleging intentional race discrimination and seeking redress against state and local governments under, respectively, 42 U.S.C.A. § 1983 and 42 U.S.C.A. § 1981. The Civil Rights Act of 1991 casts some doubt on the continued vitality of *Jett*. How the federal courts interpret the 1991 Act as applied to *Jett* will determine whether and to what degree such a plaintiff can pursue remedies against government under § 1981, or only under § 1983.

If the 1991 Act is construed to overrule *Jett*, a plaintiff with an intentional race discrimination claim against a state or local government employer can make a claim under § 1981, unencumbered by the "policy" proof demanded by § 1983. This § 1981 claim could be against all "state action" defendants, local governmental entities as well as the states themselves.

But if, as is more likely, and as several circuits have held, *Jett* is not overruled by the 1991 Act and is extended to claims against state entities, a plaintiff with an intentional race discrimination claim against any state or local government defendant will be somewhat hamstrung. She may perhaps still pursue a claim under § 1981, probably even against the state. At a minimum, the 1991 Act confirms that § 1981 furnishes a *right* to be free of racial discrimination in contracting that may not be impaired "under color of state law," including presumably by the state itself. But to recover the plaintiff would have to meet the proof requirements of § 1983 by showing that her injury was inflicted by a formal government policy, a local policymaking official, or through "deliberate indifference." And state defendants sued in their individual capacity for § 1981 violations asserted through § 1983 of course have available the § 1983 defense of qualified immunity.

A third possible scenario will result if *Jett* is held not to have been overruled by the 1991 Act, but is held to apply only to local government defendants. Because *Will*, decided earlier in the same week as *Jett*, clearly precluded § 1983 claims against states, *Jett's* broad language may be subordinated to *Jett's* logic, and its holding would then likely impinge only on § 1981 claims against local governments. Under this interpretation, an employee with an intentional race discrimination claim could use § 1981 "neat" to state a claim against *state* governments (subject to a 11th Amendment or sovereign immunity defense) but would remain obliged to meet § 1983's "policy" requirement when seeking redress under § 1981 from *local* government defendants.

Unless Congress acts to overrule *Will*, only plaintiffs challenging the conduct of municipal or other local, as opposed to state or federal, governments may now be able to take advantage of the immediate court access and generous remedies afforded by the Reconstruction Civil Rights Acts; and even those plaintiffs may have to meet the formidable new requirements of § 1983. Yet when a *private* defendant intentionally refuses, because of race or ancestry, to execute or perform a contract, the unsuccessful applicant will still clearly have a claim under § 1981, in accordance with new paragraph (c); and after the overruling of *Patterson* by new paragraph (b), that claim will once again secure the right to make and enforce contracts without discrimination across the entire spectrum of the contractual relationship. The ironic residue is that § 1981 claims against government defendants are probably not (in the case of states) or simply not (in the case of the federal government) actionable, and (in the case of local governments) can probably succeed only on stricter (i.e., § 1983) proof terms than claims against private sector defendants—this despite the fact that, until *Runyon* was decided in 1976, private defendants were not thought subject to suit under § 1981 at all.

The federal courts' role in enforcing the Reconstruction Civil Rights Acts has also been diminished by liberal application of the doctrines of *res judicata* and collateral estoppel. The Supreme Court has found no policy of § 1983 that warrants denying state judgments their normal preclusive effect in federal court under the Full Faith and Credit Statute. These judgments now therefore bar civil rights claims from relitigation to the same extent as in the forum state's courts. Indeed, relying on federal common law, the Supreme Court has even approved the preclusion of Civil Rights Acts claims by unreviewed quasi-judicial determinations of state administrative agencies. University of Tenn. v. Elliott (1986).

The Supreme Court has in the past several decades both breathed new life into the civil rights legislation enacted after the Civil War and then taken steps to curtail the resulting claims. After expanding the §§ 1981 and 1982 concept of "race", and bringing purely private conduct within the reach of those statutes, the Court demanded proof of intent in *General Building Contractors,* and in *Jett* imported restrictive § 1983 liability requirements into § 1981 claims against government defendants. Only Congress' overruling of the restrictive *Patterson* reading of the incidents of contract reached by § 1981 saved that statute from falling into virtual desuetude.

Meanwhile, after its pioneering extension of § 1983 liability to the unauthorized as well as sanctioned acts of government employees in *Monroe v. Pope* (1961) the Court has clamped down on claims against individual defendants by affording them an ever more generous defense of qualified immunity. The Court apparently learned from *Monroe* the lesson that expansive terms of liability under § 1983 will invite large numbers of federal court lawsuits. For when it subjected government entities to § 1983 liability in *Monell*, it simultaneously instituted restrictive checks in the latter part of the same opinion. The prima facie "policy" requirement announced by *Monell* has since been even more strictly reformulated in subsequent cases involving constitutional violations stemming from affirmative official misconduct as well as for violations occasioned by flagrant failures to act. And the Court has found it necessary to temper the reached the "and laws" language of § 1983, so that today claims based on the violation of a federal statute, are subject to "privacy rights" and "comprehensive remedies" limitations.

As with *Monell*'s holding that official "policy" or "custom" is prerequisite to the § 1983 liability of government entities, so with the Court's decision in Griffin v. Breckenridge (1971), that § 1985(3) could impose liability on private as well as public conspirators: the Court, anticipating that many ordinary multi-defendant torts could be transmuted into federal constitutional conspiracy cases, found in the statute's protection of "equal rights" a requirement that the plaintiff must show invidious racial or otherwise class-based animus. Later decisions would clarify that the "otherwise" does not extend beyond race to include economic motivation, United Brotherhood of Carpenters and Joiners v. Scott (1983), and that conspiracies limited to private actors violate § 1985(3) only if they invade the two constitutional rights protected against purely private interference—the interstate right to travel and freedom from involuntary servitude. Bray v. Alexandria Women's Health Clinic (1993). And while the Court has not clarified whether § 1985(3) remedies the conspiratorial deprivation of rights secured by federal statutes, it has precluded the use of § 1985(3) if the right in question is redressable under another federal statute. Great Am. Fed. S & L Ass'n v. Novotony (1979). Finally, actions against a state, state agency or sub-state entity functioning on behalf of the state that are brought under § 1985, like those under § 1981, are subject to the defense of Eleventh Amendment immunity.

The Court's Section 1983 and 1985(3) decisions are discussed in detail in Lewis and Norman, Civil Rights Law and Practice (Thomson/West 2d ed.2004).

3.　SECTION 1983

Section 1983 authorizes actions at law or suits in equity against any "person" for the deprivation of rights, privileges or immunities secured by the federal Constitution or laws, so long as the defendant acted "under color of" state law, custom or usage. For most employment discrimination claimants, § 1983 is of less utility than § 1981. First, it vindicates only rights, notably equal protection, protected by the U.S. Constitution or other federal statutes. Second, deprivations of those rights are actionable only if imposed "under color of" state law. Third, while the Supreme Court has held that municipalities and other local governments are "persons," and hence appropriate defendants, for purposes of § 1983, it simultaneously concluded that municipalities are not subject to liability vicariously, through *respondeat superior.* Monell v. Department of Social Services of City of New York (1978).

Instead, local government entities are responsible only for conduct composing a well established entity "custom"; for official policies or actions taken or approved by employees with "final policymaking authority," a question to be decided by the court before trial by reference to local law; or for omissions so likely to result in unconstitutional harm as to amount to "deliberate indifference." On the "final policymaking official" requirement, see Pembaur v. Cincinnati (1986) (plurality opinion); St. Louis v. Praprotnik (1988) (plurality opinion); and Jett v. Dallas Independent School District (1989) (5-member majority opinion).

The § 1983 liability of individual government employees, state or local, has been sharply circumscribed by a series of Supreme Court rulings expanding the range of absolute immunity for government officials respecting conduct constituting a legislative, judicial or prosecutorial function, and by an increasingly generous brand of qualified immunity for discretionary executive or administrative acts. See generally Forrester v. White (1988) (judicial immunity); Burns v. Reed (1991) (prosecutorial immunity); Harlow v. Fitzgerald (1982) and Anderson v. Creighton (1987) (qualified immunity).

Despite these obstacles, § 1983 presents the tempting prospect of uncapped compensatory damages, as opposed to the capped compensatory damages under Title VII. And while Title VII does not support claims against individual employer agents like supervisors, § 1983 does; and it subjects them not only to uncapped compensatory damages but in appropriate cases to punitive awards as well. The United States Supreme Court has yet to decide whether Title VII provides the exclusive remedy for employment discrimination against state actors, thus impliedly preempting § 1983. But the federal circuit courts are largely in accord that the mere availability of a Title VII claim does not altogether preempt a § 1983 claim arising from the same facts. But see Hughes v. Bedsole (4th Cir.1995). Most, however, also hold that the § 1983 employment discrimination plaintiff cannot rest simply on the "and laws" branch of that statute, which provides a remedy for action under color of state law that violates a federal statutory right. See, e.g., Pontarelli v. Stone (1st Cir.1991). This means that in general § 1983 can be used to challenge only employment discrimination that violates the Equal Protection or Due Process Clauses of the Constitution, rather than Title VII alone. But see Wu v. Thomas (11th Cir.1989).

Discrimination actionable under Title VII's "disparate treatment" theory may be vindicated through § 1983, because that kind of intentional discrimination could also violate the Equal Protection Clause. By contrast, employer conduct that violates only the Title VII "neutral practice/disparate impact" theory fails to show the intentional discrimination requisite for a violation of the Equal Protection Clause. See Washington v. Davis (1976).

4. WHETHER § 1981 PLAINTIFFS SUING STATE AND LOCAL GOVERNMENT EMPLOYERS MUST MEET THE ADDITIONAL PROOF REQUIREMENTS OF § 1983

Title VII would appear to be the *only* remedy for race discrimination in federal employment, which has been held outside the reach of § 1981. Lee v. Hughes (11th Cir.1998). In actions against state and local government employers, there is some doubt whether § 1981 is available on its own terms, or whether the plaintiff must also surmount the additional proof requirements and defenses available of § 1983. If the latter, then Title VII might once again become a more attractive option than § 1981.

The uncertainty stems from the Court's decision in Jett v. Dallas Independent School Dist. (1989). There the Court imposed the significant additional restrictions that confront § 1983 plaintiffs on plaintiffs seeking redress against state and local governments under § 1981. The Court held in Jett that "the express 'action at law' provided by Section 1983 . . . provides the exclusive federal damages remedy for the violation of the *rights* guaranteed by Section 1981 when the claim is pressed against a state actor." Accordingly, the § 1981 plaintiff must show that the violation of his § 1981 "right to make contracts" was caused by a "custom" or "policy" or by "deliberate indifference" of the kind required by Section 1983. By engrafting § 1983 limitations on to actions enforcing § 1981 rights, *Jett* may also defeat any § 1981 claim against a State. This is because the Supreme Court has held that a state in its own name is not even a suable "person" under Section 1983. Will v. Michigan Department of State Police.

Yet the Civil Rights Act of 1991 casts doubt on the continued vitality of *Jett.* § 101 adds the following new subparagraph to § 1981:

> (c) The rights protected by this section are protected against impairment by nongovernmental discrimination *and impairment under color of state law.* (codified at 42 U.S.C.A. § 1981(c)) (emphasis added).

A few early reported cases addressing the issue held or implied that this section effectively overruled *Jett.* But the simple statement that § 1981 protects against "impairment under color of state law" does not really contradict *Jett,* which assumed that a plaintiff suing a state or local government employer could assert a claim under § 1981, not just § 1983. What *Jett* did demand was that the plaintiff bringing a § 1981 claim against a government entity satisfy § 1983's "policy" requirement for entity liability. Viewed this way, the language of new § 1981(c) arguably codifies, rather than overrules, *Jett.* Moreover, the legislative history of the 1991 Act lacks any stated intention to overrule Jett, despite the express statement found elsewhere in that history to overrule other Supreme Court rulings. Several recent circuit decisions have therefore assumed or concluded that Jett is still vital notwithstanding § 1981(c). See, e.g., Federation of African American Contractors v. Oakland, Calif. (9th Cir.1996).

5.   *BIVENS* CLAIMS ASSERTED DIRECTLY UNDER THE U.S. CONSTITUTION

In limited circumstances the Constitution provides direct protection against certain forms of employment discrimination. The Fifth Amendment prohibits federal government deprivations of life, liberty, or property without due process; the Fourteenth Amendment prohibits the same deprivations by state and local governments. The Fourteenth Amendment also prohibits states from denying the equal protection of the laws; this prohibition has been judicially extended to federal action as part of the Fifth Amendment right of due process. See Bolling v. Sharpe (1954).

The Court has recognized an implied private right of action against individual federal agents for Constitutional violations. Bivens v. Six Unknown Named Agents of Fed. Bureau of Narcotics (1971), It has also upheld a "Bivens" claim for employment discrimination against a member of Congress under the equal protection component of the 5th amendment's due process clause. Davis v. Passman (1979) Individual federal officers sued under Bivens receive the same immunities available to individual state and local officers sued under § 1983. See, e.g., *Harlow*; *Butz v. Economou* (1978). The Supreme Court has declined to recognized a similar implied constitutional claim against federal agencies.

The Court has also crafted an exception to *Bivens*-based suits that radically reduces its utility as a remedy for employment discrimination. It has refused to imply a *Bivens* claim against a federal officer where the government action in question is subject to an elaborate statutory remedial scheme, even when the alternative does not afford as generous a remedy, or perhaps any remedy, against the offending agent. Schweiker v. Chilicky (1988); United States v. Stanley (1987). Most federal employees work for an agency that is a covered "employer" within § 717 of Title VII, 42 U.S.C. § 2000e–16, and therefore enjoy the protection against discrimination afforded by that statute. See Brown v. General Services Administration (1976). Accordingly, those employees may not maintain a *Bivens* claim alleging unconstitutional employment discrimination remediable by Title VII.

Even for employment claims other than discrimination, the Supreme Court has held that Congress' complete occupation of the federal personnel field is a "special factor" counseling against the *Bivens* damages remedy in matters related to "federal personnel policy." Bush v. Lucas (1983). After enactment of the Civil Service Reform Act ("CSRA"), the Court rejected a claim under the Back Pay Act that would have indirectly provided for review of adverse federal personnel action by a court that was not an "appropriate authority" to review that action under CSRA. The Court concluded that Congress intended to withhold such review by failing to provide for it in the CSRA, which it deemed a comprehensive and exhaustive charter of protections and remedies for federal employees. United States v. Fausto (1988).

Following the Court's lead, the circuits have routinely denied federal employees review of adverse agency action under *Bivens,* the Back Pay Act, the Administrative Procedure Act or other statutory remedies, against U.S. agencies or individual federal officers, except to the extent authorized by CSRA. See, e.g., Ayrault v. Pena (7th Cir.1995). Thus a federal employee in a service not covered by Title VII (e.g., the judiciary) has no *Bivens* damages remedy even though he has no other congressionally enacted judicial or administrative procedure for vindicating a claim of unconstitutional race discrimination. See Lee v. Hughes (11th Cir.1998).

In recent years at least 21 states and Puerto Rico have recognized counterparts to *Bivens* claims under state constitutions—17 through an implied cause of action approved by the highest court of the state, and 4 others by statute. See Donoghue and Edelstein, "Life After Brown: The Future of State Constitutional Tort Actions in New York," 42 New York Law School L. Rev. 447 (1998). In employment settings these claims may become impliedly precluded by other remedies as with federal employees' attempts to use *Bivens*. But a state cause of action for employment discrimination gives rise to a property interest that may not be impaired without Fourteenth Amendment due process. Logan v. Zimmerman Brush Co. (1982). And government actions that create "suspect classifications" potentially violate the equal protection standards of the Fifth and Fourteenth Amendments. See National Education Association v. South Carolina (1978); Califano v. Goldfarb (1977). Public employees' First Amendment claims are increasingly constrained by decisions heavily weighting the government employer's interest in efficient management and discipline. See Waters v. Churchill (1994).

6. SECTION 1985(3)

Section 1985(3) is a purely remedial statute that, like § 1983 but unlike § 1981, creates no substantive rights itself. Great Am. Fed. S & L Ass'n v. Novotny (1979). Its "deprivation" clause, by far the most frequently litigated, provides a federal cause of action for damages for the redress of conspiracies that have the purpose and result of "depriving either directly or indirectly, any person or class of persons of the equal protection of the laws, or of equal privileges and immunities under the laws...." The Supreme Court has not decided if § 1985(3) supports a prayer for injunctive relief. Bray v. Alexandria Women's Health Clinic (1993).

The conspiracy elements are standard, requiring an agreement by two or more distinct persons or entities to engage in conduct that resulted in the deprivation of the requisite rights, plus some overt act in furtherance of that agreement. In general, § 1985(3) is not violated by discussions, agreements, or actions taken between two or more individuals who serve the same corporate or other entity. Wright v. Illinois Dept. of Children & Family Services (7th Cir.1994).

The question of what rights are protected has proven more difficult. Paving the way for damage actions against purely private actors, the Supreme Court has held that state action is a required element if the particular right plaintiff invokes is itself dependent on state action. Griffin v. Breckenridge (1971). Because the First Amendment prohibits infringements only by government, a § 1985(3) claim against union members for conspiracy to deprive plaintiffs of rights to free speech and association failed for lack of evidence of state involvement. United Brotherhood of Carpenters and Joiners v. Scott (1983). But since virtually all rights protected by the U.S. Constitution also depend on state action, § 1985(3) reaches only those private conspiracies aimed at interfering with the two constitutional rights that are "protected against private, as well as official, encroachment." These are the Thirteenth Amendment right to be free from involuntary servitude and a limited right to interstate travel. *Bray.*

In *Griffin,* the Court added a distinct claim element that requires the plaintiff to show "some racial, or perhaps otherwise class-based, invidiously discriminatory animus behind the conspirators' action." The "animus" requirement applies to claims alleging government official as well as purely private conspiracies. Aulson v. Blanchard (1st Cir.1996). Conspiracies directed against groups defined by race or racial advocacy most clearly meet the class-based motivation or animus requirement of § 1985(3). *Griffin.* As under § 1981, however, the kind of "race" qualifying for protection is not always apparent. For example a circuit court has ruled that a target religious group containing both Jewish and non-Jewish members could not constitute a class for § 1985(3) purposes because of its racial diversity. Jews for Jesus, Inc. v. Jewish Community Relations Council of New York, Inc. (2d Cir.1992).

The "perhaps" language in *Griffin* suggested that certain non-racial yet still group-based motivations might also sustain a § 1985(3) claim. But the Court has held that conspiratorial conduct "motivated by economic or commercial animus" is outside the statute's reach. *Carpenters.* At a minimum, the target class is cognizable "only when it is comprised [sic] of a distinctive and identifiable group" whose members could be ascertained "by means of objective criteria." *Aulson.* There is no consensus whether conduct motivated by animus based on politics, gender or disability is actionable.

By analogy to the construction of § 1985(3)'s criminal counterpart, 18 U.S.C.A. § 241, the Court has also insisted that a § 1985(3) conspiracy must have the specific purpose, and not merely the effect, of interfering with a protected right. The defendants' conduct must be "aimed at" that right. *Bray.* So even assuming that women are a class that the statute protects from anti-female animus, the Supreme Court in *Bray* concluded that private anti-abortion protesters targeted women trying to enter a clinic not because the women were members of that class, but because they were seeking abortions. And the constitutional right to an abortion could not support the deprivation clause claim because that right, like most, is protected only against public, not private interference.

In sum, as long as the Court limits the protected target "class" to groups defined by race or the advocacy of racial views, § 1985(3) will seldom be needed when the conspirators include state actors: government officials today rarely conspire on racial grounds. And the statute will provide scant protection against the far more numerous purely private conspiracies, except the few designed to enslave or to infringe the right to interstate travel.

B. THE EQUAL PAY ACT OF 1963

The Equal Pay Act of 1963, 29 U.S.C.A. § 206(d) ("EPA"), requires "equal pay for equal work" within the same establishment regardless of sex. The concept of "equal work" lies at the heart of the Act. General comparisons between two jobs carrying unequal pay will not suffice to establish that work is "equal"; rather, demonstrating an EPA violation demands specific showings of equivalent skill, effort, and responsibility, as well as performance under similar working conditions. Once an inequality is found, however, it cannot be remedied by reducing the wages of the higher paid member of the other sex.

The EPA contains four affirmative defenses. It permits exceptions to the equal pay for equal work principle when differentials are pursuant to: (1) seniority systems; (2) merit systems; (3) systems which measure earnings by quantity or quality of production (incentive systems); or (4) factors other than sex.

1. EPA COVERAGE, THE PRIMA FACIE CASE AND AFFIRMATIVE DEFENSES

a. Coverage

Why would a plaintiff resort to the Equal Pay Act when Title VII proscribes sex discrimination in *all* terms and conditions of employment, not just for compensation between persons of different genders holding "equal" jobs? For starters, it may be the only game in town. EPA looks primarily to the Fair Labor Standards Act, 29 U.S.C.A. § 209 *et seq.* ("FLSA"), to which it is an amendment, for provisions on coverage, as well as enforcement. In sharp contrast to Title VII, EPA has no coverage threshold defined in terms of the employer's number of employees. Instead, it covers most employers of any size, unless the employer is in one of several specifically exempted industries. 29 U.S.C.A. § 213. These industries include certain fishing and agricultural businesses as well as small local newspapers.

An employee not in an exempted industry may assert an FLSA, and therefore an EPA claim if she has some contact with interstate commerce. This contact may be established by satisfying one of two requirements. The first concerns the nature of the work implicated by the plaintiff's claim. If the employee is "engaged in commerce" or produces "goods for commerce," the work is covered, no matter what the employer's size.

An alternative FLSA avenue protects employees who, though not themselves engaged in or producing goods for interstate commerce, work for nonexempt businesses that are. This alternative measure of FLSA coverage extends EPA's protection to persons employed by "enterprises" engaged in commerce or producing goods for commerce. Such enterprises will be deemed to meet the interstate commerce test if they (1) achieved certain sales volumes or (2) were part of certain industries specifically mentioned in FLSA.

A third approach, based on text unique to EPA, arguably reaches more broadly than the FLSA alternatives. It focuses on the relation between other employees' production and interstate commerce, without regard to the commerce involvement of the plaintiff or the defendant employer. The EPA prohibits employers that have "employees subject to" EPA from engaging in unequal pay discrimination against [other] "employees." 29 U.S.C.A. § 206(d)(1). Read literally, the EPA would therefore appear to protect all employees of employers that have at least two employees of different genders who are engaged in or producing goods for commerce, even if those employers are not FLSA "enterprises."

The Act defines an employer as "any person acting directly or indirectly in the interest of an employer in relation to an employee...." 29 U.S.C.A. § 203(d). Notwithstanding this definition, claims against supervisors or managers in their individual as distinct from official capacities are likely to be dismissed because in an individual capacity a defendant lacks control over the plaintiff's terms of employment. See Welch v. Laney (11th Cir.1995).

b. *Equal Work*

The first step in the plaintiff's prima facie case is to establish that the plaintiff performed work equal to that of another of the opposite sex. Job equivalence, as measured by skill, effort, responsibility, and working conditions, need not be precise, only substantial. Corning Glass Works v. Brennan (1974). The issue in *Corning Glass* was whether the employer violated the EPA by paying a higher base wage to male night shift inspectors than it paid to female day shift inspectors. Historically, Corning had paid higher wages to the night inspectors, who were then all male. After the enactment of the EPA, Corning opened both jobs to men and women, but a collective-bargaining agreement perpetuated the differential in favor of the night jobs. The Court defined "working conditions" to refer to a job's "hazards" and "surroundings," but not time of day, which the Court concluded did not render substantially equal working conditions unequal. Accordingly,

Corning had prima facie violated the EPA by paying women who worked days less than men who worked nights for equal work.

The circuit courts have similarly disregarded minor differences between jobs to find work "equal." See, e.g., Hein v. Oregon College of Education (9th Cir.1983). But when a plaintiff of one gender is not responsible for tasks important to the enterprise that are assigned to a comparator of the other gender, she does not perform equal work and therefore has no right to equal pay.

c. Unequal Pay

Another element of the plaintiff's prima facie case is a showing that the plaintiff is paid less than another of the opposite sex. First, the plaintiff must be paid a lesser "rate" of pay. Second, this rate must be compared with that of an individual of the opposite sex performing substantially similar work.

(1) EQUAL "RATE" OF PAY

Commissions worth less per sale to female than to male employees who provide the same total service to an employer's clientele violate the EPA because they yield women a lesser "rate." Bence v. Detroit Health Corp. (6th Cir.1983).

(2) THE NECESSITY OF A "COMPARATOR" WITHIN A SINGLE "ESTABLISHMENT"

In order to show unequal pay, there must be some comparison between the complaining individual and one of the opposite sex in a substantially similar position. The plaintiff, therefore, must demonstrate that an individual of the opposite sex received greater compensation for substantially the same job. This task is accomplished through the use of a comparator. The comparator may be one who held the job before the plaintiff, who replaced the plaintiff, or who held a substantially similar position contemporaneously with the plaintiff. See Brinkley–Obu v. Hughes Training, Inc. (4th Cir.1994). Finally, the comparator must also be employed in the same establishment as the plaintiff. These requirements may be subdivided into four components.

First, the comparator may not be hypothetical but rather a specific identifiable and better paid individual performing a job of substantially equal skill, effort, and responsibility. EEOC v. Liggett & Myers Inc. (4th Cir.1982). Where a plaintiff identified her male comparators in general terms as "any men who got any higher salary increases than [the plaintiff] did," the plaintiff failed to carry a prima facie case. Houck v. Virginia Polytechnic Institute and State University (4th Cir. 1993).

Second, the comparator must perform a substantially similar job. The court analyzes the job, not the qualification or performance characteristics of individual employees holding the job, and only the skill and qualifications actually needed to perform the job in question are considered. Miranda v. B & B Cash Grocery Store, Inc. (11th Cir.1992). Additionally, the examination rests on the primary, not the incidental or insubstantial job duties. Where the plaintiff performs substantially similar tasks but the comparator also has significant additional primary duties, the prima facie case fails. Mulhall v. Advance Security, Inc. (11th Cir.1994).

Third, the comparator may be a past, present or future employee in a substantially similar position. There can be a valid comparison between the plaintiff, a former "Vice–President, Administration," and a current "Vice–President, Controller" because financial concerns were essential to both jobs. But if the plaintiff cannot establish that the plaintiff's predecessor, successor, or contemporary was paid more for the same responsibilities, the plaintiff has failed to make a prima facie showing. Weiss v. Coca–Cola Bottling Co. of Chicago (7th Cir.1993).

Finally, the comparator must be an employee of the same "establishment" as the plaintiff. The Secretary of Labor has defined "establishment" to mean "a distinct physical place of business rather than … an entire business or 'enterprise' which may include several separate places of business." 29 C.F.R. § 1620.9(a) (1993). In "unusual circumstances," however, a single establishment can include more than one physical location. 29 C.F.R. § 1620.9(b) (1993).

When there is centralized control and administration, some courts have been willing to find a single EPA establishment despite several physical locations. See, e.g., Brennan v. Goose Creek Consolidated Indep. Sch. Dist. (5th Cir.1975). By contrast, other circuits have restricted the comparison of salaries to employees in one physical location when the local office where plaintiff worked made the ultimate hiring decision and, within a broad range determined by the central office, set specific salaries, Meeks v. Computer Associates International (11th Cir.1994); or where the employer conferred independent personnel decisionmaking authority on managers at the plaintiff's facility. Foster v. Arcata Associates, Inc. (9th Cir.1985).

d. The Employer's Defenses

Once a plaintiff has established a prima facie case, the employer bears the burden of producing evidence and persuading that the employment practice fits within one or more of EPA's 4 affirmative defenses. "Unequal pay" for equal work is permitted when the payment is made pursuant to (i) a seniority system, (ii) a merit system; (iii) a system which measures earnings by quantity or quality of production; or (iv) a differential based on any factor other than sex. 29 U.S.C.A. § 206(d)(1).

The burden of establishing one of the four affirmative defenses is "a heavy one," because the statutory exemptions are "narrowly construed." Indeed, a recent circuit opinion demonstrates that the employer's burden in EPA cases is heavier than that in a Title VII case, and, in at least one sense, the plaintiff's burden is lighter. Unlike in Title VII, once the employer proffers one of the four affirmative defenses, the burden to prove the defense remains with the employer. Compare this to the burden shifting scheme of Title VII pretext inferential proof cases, where the plaintiff must persuade that the defendant's proffered legitimate, nondiscriminatory reason for the adverse term or condition of employment is but a pretext for intentional discrimination. Moreover, under the EPA, the employer must submit evidence from which a reasonable factfinder could conclude not merely that the employer's proffered reasons could explain the wage disparity (as under the Title VII burden-shifting paradigm), but that the proffered reasons do in fact explain the wage disparity.

In Ryduchowski v. Port Authority of N.Y. and N.J. (2d Cir.2000), the Court reversed a grant of judgment as a matter of law after a plaintiff's verdict on her EPA claim. The appellate court found that the jury could have reasonably concluded that the defendant failed to meet its burden to establish that a valid merit system was in place and systematically administered.

Affirmative defenses (i)–(iii) above are rarely used. These three defenses specifically require a "system." This system need not be formalized or structured, but employees must know about it none-the-less. And a defendant asserting a seniority system affirmative defense must "be able to identify standards for measuring seniority which are systematically applied and observed." Irby v. Bittick (11th Cir.1995). Further, the system must be operated in good faith and not used as a way to maintain sex-based wage differences. The third defense, a system based on quality or quantity of production, has little independent vitality. First, if employees are paid the same "rate" for their work based on production, there is no EPA violation. Second, a quality or quantity system is so closely related to a merit system that it may have no separate significance. The majority of litigation in the area of affirmative defenses, therefore, has centered around the rather ambiguous defense (iv), "any factor other than sex."

Examples of "factors other than sex" include salary retention policies, prior salary, and economic benefit to the employer. See, e.g., Kouba v. Allstate Insurance Co. (9th Cir.1982). Another circuit has allowed reliance on prior salary only when other business considerations—such as the selectee's greater amount of experience in a closely related job—reasonably explain its utilization. *Irby.* A comparator's greater experience in similar positions remains a neutral, nondiscriminatory reason, even if the plaintiff has greater total service. See Lindale v. Tokheim Corp. (7th Cir. 1998). But regardless of other factors, where sex is even a "but for" cause, the EPA is violated. See Peters v. City of Shreveport (5th Cir.1987).

Another factor that has been approved as something "other than sex" is reliance on differential economic benefit to the employer of otherwise equal "male" and "female" jobs. Byrd v. Ronayne (1st Cir.1995) (alternative holding). A clothier could pay its salesmen more than its saleswomen, a controversial decision holds, where the men produced greater benefit to the employer because the men's clothing department generated higher profit margins and revenues. Hodgson v. Robert Hall Clothes, Inc. (3d Cir.1973). But compensation disparities keyed solely to gender-based actuarial differences are not saved by the "other than sex" exception. City of Los Angeles, Department of Water and Power v. Manhart (1978). The

Supreme Court has also rejected time of day as an "other than sex" defense. *Corning Glass.*

e.   Retaliation

The FLSA anti-retaliation provision, applicable by reference to EPA, prohibits retaliation in language more cramped than § 704 of Title VII. By offering protection against reprisal only to those who have "filed any complaint" or "instituted any proceeding," it does not in terms protect those who have made an informal on-the-job protest. But the federal judiciary views access to available avenues of protest of such importance that at least five circuit courts have nevertheless extended such protection to informal protesters. See EEOC v. Romeo Community Schools (6th Cir.1992). But see Lambert v. Genesee Hospital (2d Cir.1993). Consistent with the tradition under FLSA, it has been held that EPA authorizes compensatory and punitive damages for unlawful retaliation. Travis v. Gary Community Mental Health Center, Inc. (7th Cir.1990).

2.   ENFORCEMENT, LIMITATIONS, AND REMEDIES

a.   Enforcement

Although the EEOC has enforcement responsibility and may file civil actions under the EPA, a private plaintiff need not exhaust state or federal administrative remedies before proceeding to court. Under provisions of the FLSA that EPA incorporates by reference, the action may be brought in state or federal court against a private or public employer. 29 U.S.C.A. § 216(b). A suit may be brought under the EPA by an employee or the EEOC. The EPA grants authority to the Secretary of Labor to initiate suit against an employer for monetary damages or injunctive relief. The courts have upheld the constitutionality of a 1978 Presidential transfer of this authority to EEOC. See, e.g., EEOC v. Hernando Bank, Inc. (5th Cir.1984).

While under Title VII the EEOC must try to eliminate an unlawful practice through informal methods of conciliation, the EPA contains no similar provision. The Equal Pay Act, unlike Title VII, has no requirement of filing administrative complaints or awaiting administrative conciliation or determination. County of Washington v. Gunther (1981). Accordingly, courts have found no requirement of prior administrative filing or informal conciliation. See *Hernando Bank*.

An employee may initiate suit seeking monetary damages up until the point the EEOC files a complaint against the employer. If the EEOC files an action, the employee's right to sue or become a party to an action brought by other employees is terminated. The EEOC's suit is deemed to commence from the date a complaint is filed that names EEOC as a party plaintiff, or from the date the EEOC's name is added as a party plaintiff.

Suit may be brought individually or on behalf of a class. As under ADEA, if the suit is brought as a class action, each class member must consent in writing to become a party and the consent must be filed with the court. 29 U.S.C.A. § 216(b). Under either ADEA or EPA, therefore, a class action may not be pursued under Federal Rule of Civil Procedure 23. See Lachapelle v. Owens–Illinois, Inc. (5th Cir.1975).

b.   Limitations

The FLSA provides a two year statute of limitations for filing an EPA action, three years in the case of a "willful" violation. These statutes of limitations compare favorably from the plaintiff's perspective with the 180-day or 300-day administrative filing deadlines of Title VII, now also made applicable to ADEA.

The three-year limitations period for willful violations is available when an employer knows that, or recklessly disregards whether, its conduct violates the statute. See McLaughlin v. Richland Shoe Co. (1988). Willfulness under the FLSA refers to conduct that is more than merely negligent; yet the requisite willfulness for purposes of limitations may be found not just when the employer believes its conduct violates the statute, but also when the employer was merely indifferent to whether its conduct constituted a violation. Trans World Airlines, Inc. v. Thurston (1985); Walton v. United Consumers Club, Inc. (7th Cir.1986).

c. Continuing Violations

The judicially-created "continuing violations" doctrine provides certain plaintiffs an escape from the statute of limitations. The doctrine allows a court to take jurisdiction over a cause of action, or impose liability, for a discrete EPA violation that occurred outside the limitations period. Plaintiffs have invoked the doctrine under both the Equal Pay Act and Title VII, but the courts have afforded it a wider sweep in EPA cases. This is probably because of the nature of the sole EPA violation, which is predicated on unequal compensation, a practice that continues from paycheck to paycheck. Brinkley–Obu v. Hughes Training, Inc. (4th Cir.1994).

Because "each unequal paycheck is considered a separate violation of the Equal Pay Act, a cause of action may be brought for any or all violations occurring within the limitations period.... " Gandy v. Sullivan County (6th Cir.1994). The plaintiff took a position at a pay rate below that of her predecessor and was paid unequally for nine years before she filed suit. The defendant argued that the statute tolled three years after the first unequal paycheck. The court concluded that the action was not time-barred as long as at least one discriminatory act occurred within the limitations period. A majority of circuits concur with Gandy that an actionable EPA violation occurs each time an employee receives an "unequal" paycheck, not just when the first such paycheck is issued. See, e.g., Ashley v. Boyle's Famous Corned Beef Co. (8th Cir.1995).

d.   Remedies

EPA remedies are governed by two provisions of FLSA, 29 U.S.C.A. §§ 216 and 217. These sections authorize recovery not only of unlawfully withheld wages but also of an equal amount denominated "liquidated damages." An employee plaintiff may then recover unlawfully withheld wages, liquidated damages and attorney fees plus costs. Unlawfully withheld wages accrue from no earlier than two years prior to the filing of the complaint and continue until a court order. The accrual period begins three years prior to the filing of a complaint if the employer is found to have acted "willfully."

After the passage of the Portal-to-Portal Act of 1947, the imposition of liquidated damages in FLSA cases became discretionary with the trial judge. 29 U.S.C.A. § 260. She may not award liquidated damages when the employer proves "to the satisfaction of the court" that it acted in good faith and had a reasonable belief that its conduct did not violate FLSA. The burden is on the employer to show that it acted in the sincere and reasonable belief that its conduct was lawful.

3.   GENDER–BASED COMPENSATION DISCRIMINATION OUTSIDE THE REACH OF EPA BUT PROHIBITED BY TITLE VII

In *County of Washington v. Gunther*, the plaintiff challenged the employer's practice of intentionally setting the wage scale for female, but not male guards at a level substantially lower than recommended by its survey of outside markets. That decision was actionable, if at all, only under Title VII; EPA was not implicated because the male and female comparator jobs did not involve substantially equal work. Yet whether Title VII applied was doubtful in view of that part of Section 703(h), 42 U.S.C.A. § 2000e–2(h), known as the Bennett Amendment, which removes from Title VII's reach practices "authorized" by EPA. The Supreme Court held, however, that Title VII may regulate an intentionally discriminatory gender-based compensation practice that EPA does not prohibit—as well as the "unequal pay for equal work" claim that EPA does prohibit. In other words, the only compensation practices affirmatively "authorized" by the EPA, and therefore beyond the reach of Title VII by virtue of the Bennett Amendment, are those insulated by EPA's four affirmative defenses. This holding provides a remedy for intentional, gender-based compensation discrimination to a woman who holds a unique position and therefore cannot invoke EPA for lack of a male comparator.

Gunther provides little guidance, however, on key related questions about the scope of Title VII respecting gender-based compensation discrimination. May Title VII ban pay practices not prohibited by EPA where an employer intent to discriminate can be proved only inferentially, a la *McDonnell Douglas/Burdine*? Can Title VII reach compensation practices neutral on their face that have discriminatory gender impact? Or what if the employer has dual intentions, one intentionally discriminatory and another benign, as in *Price Waterhouse,* the landmark Title VII "mixed motives" decision?

4.   COMPARABLE WORTH

The comparable worth theory would mandate upward adjustment in the wage rates of all men and women holding jobs traditionally held predominantly by women, even absent wage discrimination between male and female employees whose work is "equal" or evidence of intentional discrimination based on gender. Plaintiffs would prove simply that a "woman's" job was of similar "worth" to the employer as a "man's" job, yet commanded lesser compensation. The revised wage level is supposed to represent a court's or legislature's evaluation of the job's "worth" to the employer.

EPA affords no relief for a comparable worth claim, because by hypothesis the plaintiff and the higher paid employee are performing non-"equal" jobs. The similarity is only in the "worth" of the respective jobs to the employer. The difficulty with a comparable worth challenge under Title VII is that the differences between the comparison jobs preclude the plaintiff from proving that she suffered intentional disparate treatment. Attempts to secure judicial recognition of the comparable worth theory by challenging the employer's pay system as a neutral practice with adverse impact on women have also been conspicuously unsuccessful. See American Federation of State, County, and Municipal Employees v. Washington (9th Cir.1985).

The Supreme Court has not addressed the issue of comparable worth. But in *County of Washington v. Gunther* the Court specifically noted that allowing the intentional disparate treatment claim there did not require it to make its own subjective assessment of the value of the male and female guard jobs.

Comparable worth claims will therefore probably still fail. Even if the plaintiff may base a prima facie case on the adverse impact of the "subjective" pay practice in question, the employer can assert a market-related justification that is likely to be adjudged a matter of business necessity. In the face of the pre–1991 case law that consistently rejected comparable worth claims, the silence of the Civil Rights Act of 1991 on the subject is a significant indication that Congress hews to the relatively narrow yardstick of nondiscrimination, eschewing gender-based minimum standards. Comparable worth has been endorsed by a few state legislatures, but most states continue to reject the notion that market-driven job wage rates equate to discrimination based on gender.

5.   CLAIMS COVERED BY TITLE VII AND EPA

Assume a case covered by both statutes, one involving "equal pay for equal work." Why would some plaintiffs resort to the Equal Pay Act, with its narrow proscription of only one kind of sex-based wage discrimination, when Title VII also prohibits other forms of sex-based wage discrimination and sex discrimination affecting other terms and conditions of employment? The answer lies in varying proof requirements and differences in enforcement and remedial schemes.

In an unequal pay for equal work situation, there are three potentially available ways of proving a Title VII claim. A plaintiff may offer "direct" evidence of gender discriminatory intent, evidence from which such discriminatory intent may be inferred, or evidence that establishes an EPA violation. The federal circuit decisions are divided over which of these proof modes is permissible or indispensable. Some courts require direct or express evidence of discriminatory intent to show an "equal pay" violation of Title VII. See EEOC v. Sears, Roebuck & Co. (7th Cir.1988); Plemer v. Parsons–Gilbane (5th Cir.1983). But see Fallon v. Illinois (7th Cir.1989). For these courts, then, the *Gunther* facts represent the outer limit of Title VII liability for gender-based discrimination in compensation.

On the other hand, several circuits have decided that the *McDonnell Douglas/Burdine* inferential evidence approach may be used to prove a Title VII violation of unequal pay for equal work. See, e.g., Miranda v. B & B Cash Grocery Store, Inc. (11th Cir.1992). These circuits, however, divide over whether the traditional Title VII allocation of burdens of proof, or the very different framework established by the EPA, controls. A slim majority consider Title VII and EPA claims completely independent; these courts require proof for each alleged violation that tracks the distinct elements and burden shifts of each statute. See Meeks v. Computer Associates International (11th Cir.1994). Other circuits, however, hold that a violation of the EPA is ipso facto a violation of Title VII; this means that the Title VII claim requires no independent evidence of intent, direct or indirect. See Korte v. Diemer (6th Cir.1990). Regulations promulgated by the EEOC support the latter view. 29 C.F.R. § 1620.27(a) (1993).

The difference between these approaches can substantially affect outcome. The prima facie case for an EPA claim is simply that the employer pays different wages to employees of the opposite sex for "equal work"—work requiring substantially equal skill, effort, and responsibility and performed under similar working conditions. Once the plaintiff has made this showing, the defendant bears the burden of establishing one of the affirmative defenses. There is no separate requirement under the EPA that the plaintiff offer evidence of intent to discriminate; in this sense the EPA is a "strict liability" statute. See *Meeks*.

By contrast, the standard, inferential prima facie evidence required to establish a Title VII individual disparate treatment claim begins with a showing that the plaintiff occupies a job similar to that of a higher paid member of the opposite sex. The defendant must then produce evidence of a legitimate nondiscriminatory reason for paying less. If the defendant does so, the plaintiff may prevail only by proving in a variety of ways that the employer intended to discriminate based on gender. *Burdine; McDonnell Douglas*. In sharp contrast to

EPA, employer intent is critical, and the Title VII plaintiff throughout the case bears the risk of nonpersuasion on the "ultimate" question of intentional disparate treatment because of sex. *St. Mary's.*

Until the 1991 Civil Rights Act amendments, these different approaches to the required elements of unequal pay for equal work claims under Title VII and EPA had minimal practical importance. The remedies under EPA were more congenial to the plaintiff than the remedies under Title VII, because EPA afforded the possibility of liquidated damages while Title VII remitted the plaintiff to back pay done. So the plaintiff with only an unequal pay work equal work claim usually took the EPA route, which was also easier to establish. But the 1991 amendments expanded the remedies under Title VII to include compensatory and punitive damages for intentional or "disparate treatment" violations; and most EPA violations fit that description, even if no direct evidence of intent is required. In circuits that equate the eased EPA proof standards with the more stringent Title VII standards, the plaintiff can now recover Title VII's potentially more generous remedies (compensation and punitive damages in addition to back and front pay) by carrying the lighter EPA burden.

C. THE AGE DISCRIMINATION IN EMPLOYMENT ACT OF 1967, AS AMENDED ("ADEA")

1. IN GENERAL

Age differs from race, sex, religion and national origin in that it lies on a continuum, and everyone who lives to be 40 crosses into the federally protected category. The universal vulnerability to age discrimination and consequent identification with its victims generated widespread political support for protection. This support found expression in ADEA remedies that, as originally enacted in 1967, were more generous than those afforded by Title VII as originally enacted in 1964. Indeed, in the 1960's Congress trusted juries to consider fairly claims of age discrimination, but not Title VII claims, and at least in part this is a reflection of the universality of aging. Initially, these factors also engendered sympathetic handling of age claims not only by juries but by the federal judiciary as well.

On the other hand, perhaps because of its very universality, there is a greater general willingness to acknowledge that some types of performance decline with advancing age than that work-related capabilities vary by gender, national origin, or race. Age discrimination is therefore seen as a less invidious form of discrimination; protection is seen as needed only from exaggerated, not from statistically supportable stereotypes, from "arbitrary" rather than all discrimination. Age Discrimination in Employment Act, 29 U.S.C.A. § 621, "Statement of Findings and Purpose."

In recent years, these latter attributes have come to the fore in legislative and judicial decisions, lessening or eliminating the previous relative advantage age discrimination plaintiffs enjoyed over their Title VII counterparts. Congress has retained the 20–employee threshold for employer coverage, while Title VII and the Americans with Disabilities Act apply to employers with only 15 or more employees. The Civil Rights Act of 1991 eased the Title VII plaintiff's burden of proving disparate treatment discrimination, especially for the common case where employer motives are mixed, but made no similar amendment to ADEA. Soon thereafter, the Supreme Court declared that the plaintiff's ultimate burden in an ADEA disparate treatment case is to demonstrate that the employer's reliance on age had a "determinative influence on the outcome"—a requirement more onerous than the Title VII plaintiff's burden, after the 1991 amendments, to show that race, sex, religion or national origin was a "motivating factor." Hazen Paper Co. v. Biggins (1993).

Hazen also puts in doubt whether the disproportionate adverse impact proof mode remains available under ADEA. Moreover, the ADEA defendant who carries the "same-decision" burden apparently still defeats liability altogether; in contrast, the 1991 Civil Rights Act subjects the Title VII defendant who carries that burden to potential liability for declaratory relief and attorneys' fees. Lower federal courts have explicitly permitted employers to defend ADEA claims by relying on the high cost of employing, and the declining productivity of older workers; the similar Title VII BFOQ defense has been in distinctly bad odor since the *Johnson Controls* decision and new § 703(k)(2). Finally, while the 1991 amendments gave the Title VII plaintiff virtual parity with the ADEA plaintiff with respect to a right to trial by jury, the ADEA monetary remedies originally authorized in 1970 (back pay and, for willful violations, an equal additional amount of "liquidated" damages) remain unchanged and have arguably been eclipsed by the more generous compensatory and punitive damages now available under Title VII.

2.   COVERAGE

The ADEA prohibits age discrimination against employees or job applicants who are 40 years of age or older. It is therefore clear that the plaintiff must be 40 at the time of the alleged unlawful employment practice. See, e.g., Doyle v. Suffolk County (2d Cir.1986). But what if the plaintiff compares his treatment to more favorable treatment received by a younger person who is also over 40? The Supreme Court has held that the ADEA plaintiff need not show that she was replaced by someone younger than forty. O'Connor v. Consolidated Coin Caterers Corp. (1996). Prima facie she need only produce evidence from which it may be inferred that the employer relied on the comparator's younger age in making the challenged decision. The Court added, however, that "such an inference cannot be drawn from the replacement of one worker with another worker insignificantly younger."

A related issue is whether over–40 employees, although clearly within the group protected from discrimination on the ground that they are too old, state a cognizable claim when they complain that they suffered discrimination because they were too young. In General Dynamics Land Systems, Inc. v. Cline (2004), the employer retained health care retirement benefits only for current employees exceeding age 50. This meant that employees younger than 50—including those within the ADEA protected group because older than 40—would not receive those benefits upon retiring. The Supreme Court, deeming it textually ambiguous whether the statute's protection from "age" discrimination was limited to those of older age, relied on legislative history suggesting Congress intended to protect older workers only. In brief, ADEA protects only relatively older workers (over 40) from discrimination favoring relatively younger ones (of any age).

An emerging and as yet unsettled question is whether the ADEA prohibits harassment on the basis of age. At least three other circuits have explicitly recognized such a claim. And the Fourth Circuit assumes the existence of a hostile environment claim under ADEA and explicates the prima facie case: "employee seeking to establish such claim was required to show that: (1) she was at least 40 years old; (2) she was harassed based on her age; (3) the harassment had the effect of unreasonably interfering with her work, creating an environment that was both objectively and subjectively hostile or offensive; and (4) she had some basis for imputing liability to her employer." Burns v. AAF–McQuay, Inc. (4th Cir.1999).

ADEA was amended in 1986 to remove the then current upper age limitation, 70, for the vast majority of covered employees. Thus, in general, ADEA prohibits mandatory retirement because of age at any age for covered employers. The most important surviving exception authorizes the mandatory retirement at age 65 of a highly compensated person "employed in a bona fide executive or a high policy making position" who has an "immediate, nonforfeitable annual retirement benefit" aggregating $44,000. ADEA § 12(c)(1), 29 U.S.C.A. § 631(c)(1). But to be "entitled" to that nonforfeitable benefit within the meaning of the exemption, and hence denied protection, it may not suffice that the executive is actually receiving in excess of $44,000. Two circuits have divided on whether payments in the requisite amount must be due and owing *at retirement* under the terms of a pension, profit-sharing, savings, or deferred compensation plan, or whether an employer may, on an ad hoc basis, purchase the right to discriminate by inflating the plaintiff's *post*-retirement income to push it over the $44,000 threshold.

Other exceptions formerly permitted the mandatory retirement of tenured college-and university-level professors and law enforcement officers and firefighters. They were subject to involuntary retirement at age 70 (professors) or, in the case of public safety officers, younger, at the local governments' discretion. But those exceptions expired December 31, 1993. Legislation re-established a retirement exemption with respect to the public safety officers. ADEA § 4(j), 29 U.S.C.A. § 623(j), as reenacted and amended by the Age Discrimination in Employment Amendments of 1996, Pub.L. 104–208, effective September 30, 1996. Similarly, in October 1998, a "safe harbor" provision was added to the ADEA under which institutions of higher education may offer to tenured faculty members, upon their voluntary retirement, supplemental benefits that are reduced or eliminated as employees age, subject to three conditions: (1) the institution must not implement any age-based reduction or cessation of benefits other than these supplemental benefits; (2) these supplemental benefits must be in addition to any retirement or severance benefits that have been available to tenured faculty members generally, independent of any early retirement or exit-incentive plan, within the preceding 365 days; and (3) any tenured faculty member who attains the minimum age and satisfies all non-age-based conditions for receiving such a supplemental benefit has an opportunity for at least 180 days to elect to retire and receive the maximum supplemental benefit that could then be elected by a younger but otherwise similarly situated employee, and must have the ability to delay retirement for at least 180 days after making that election. Higher Education Amendments of 1998, Pub.L. 105–244, § 941, 112 Stat. 1581 (1998).

ADEA covers "employers" who have 20 or more employees for each working day in each of 20 weeks in the current or preceding calendar year; labor unions having 25 members; and employment agencies. Hoekel v. Plumbing Planning Corp. (8th Cir.1994). As of July 1994, the numerical coverage threshold under the 1990 Americans with Disabilities Act has been coextensive with that under Title VII, namely 15 employees; this will mean that fewer persons will be protected from age than from the other major forms of discrimination, an irony given the previously broader scope of the prohibition against age discrimination. The Older American Act Amendments of 1984 specifically protect U.S. citizens "employed by an employer in a workplace in a foreign country." At a minimum this covers overseas employees of American corporations, and may also cover employees working at U.S. branches of foreign employers with more than 20 workers *worldwide*. State and local governments were included in the term "employer" by amendments in 1974, but the Supreme Court has since held that Congress lacked the authority under § 5 of the Fourteenth Amendment to abrogate the states' Eleventh Amendment immunity from ADEA suits in federal court. Kimel v. Florida Bd. of Regents (2000).

Elected officers of state and local government are excluded from the "employee" definitions and thus enjoy no protection under Title VII or ADEA. Moreover, until recently, these definitions also excluded from protection members of such officers' personal staffs, immediate advisors, and other appointees responsible for setting policy, unless they were subject to state or local civil service laws. Reasoning that Congress did not exclude judges from the class of excluded policymaking appointees with the specificity required to overcome the presumption of state sovereignty implicit in the Tenth Amendment, the Supreme Court held that they, like elected judges, were outside the protection of ADEA. Gregory v. Ashcroft (1991). The Civil Rights Act of 1991 overturns the result of *Gregory* and more generally protects the other, previously exempt appointees of elected officials by extending to them all "rights" and "protections" of both Title VII and ADEA, together with the "remedies" that would ordinarily be available in actions against state or local government—that is, all but punitive damages. But unlike other state or local government (or private) employees, whose charges are simply investigated and perhaps conciliated by EEOC and who are therefore entitled to a de novo hearing in state or federal court, these newly-covered government appointees are remitted to an adjudicatory hearing before EEOC, subject only to limited judicial review. Section 321(c) and (d).

Although the Act does not include the federal government within the definition of "employer," a separate provision requires that personnel actions affecting most federal employees 40 or older shall be made "free from any discrimination based on age." ADEA § 15, 29 U.S.C.A. § 633a. Specific provisions in other statutes authorize mandatory separation of federal air traffic controllers and law enforcement officers and firefighters at various specified ages, and it appears that only civilian members of the military departments are covered. Helm v. California (9th Cir.1983). EEOC has adjudicatory authority to resolve federal employees' age discrimination complaints. In contrast to federal employee complaints under Title VII, the age discrimination complainant may bypass any process available from his employing agency as well as from EEOC and proceed directly to federal court for a de novo hearing. A complainant making this choice need only give EEOC, within 180 days after the alleged unlawful employment practice, 30 days' notice of its intent to sue. ADEA § 15(c), (d), 29 U.S.C.A. § 633a(c), (d). The federal age discrimination complainant who chooses to initiate administrative review of the challenged decision will be deemed to have exhausted those remedies if the employing agency or EEOC has taken no action on a charge within 180 days of its filing. Alternatively, if the agency or EEOC reaches a decision, the complainant has 90 days within which to file a judicial action.

3. PROOF MODES

ADEA forbids age discrimination in hiring, firing or classifying employees or job applicants and in other "terms, conditions, or privileges of employment." 29 U.S.C.A. § 623(a)(1). It also bars age-related bias in employment advertisements or referrals. The prima facie theories of liability under ADEA parallel those of Title VII, from which its language was derived. Many cases involve express or direct evidence, such as statements attributed to management agents that the employer needs "new blood," strives to become "young, lean, and mean," or needs to purge itself of "old farts" or "dead wood." A supervisor's reference in the context of plaintiff's termination to cutting down "old, big trees so the little trees underneath can grow" qualified as direct evidence despite its metaphorical nature. Liability may not be predicated on such statements when they are merely "stray remarks in the workplace," by which courts usually mean that they are uttered by co-employees or low-level supervisors or are divorced from the decisional process affecting the particular plaintiff.

But express statements reflecting preference for youth or animus toward age lose their "stray" character and become actionable when announced by top executives or incorporated into official company planning documents or when uttered by a representative of management with decisionmaking authority with respect to the plaintiff. And the fact that such comments were made over a long period of time argues for rather than against their admissibility; while any particular comment may be remote in time from the alleged violation, as a whole the comments may show a pattern of age-based animus. Moreover, age-related remarks that can be linked to managers responsible for overseeing the implementation of a layoff are relevant as tending to show that the layoffs themselves were tainted by unlawful motivation. Armbruster v. Unisys Corp. (3d Cir.1994). Even if the slur or stray remark does not arise to the level of direct evidence necessary to allow the plaintiff to avoid the inferential proof mode, such evidence can support a determination that the employer's proffered legitimate non-discriminatory reason for the adverse employment action was an unlawful pretext for age discrimination.

One defense that seems to have particular potency in ADEA claims, perhaps even more than in actions under Title VII, is the "same actor" doctrine, which applies where the supervisor who imposed the employment detriment (e.g. firing) on the plaintiff is the same person who had hired him. Thus it may be difficult to believe that the employer developed a certain aversion to older people only two years after hiring one. Rand

v. CF Indus., Inc. (7th Cir.1994). In such circumstances, the plaintiff must show that this proffered justification is a pretext for age discrimination. Roper v. Peabody Coal Co. (7th Cir.1995). Similarly, if the decisionmaker is also a member of the protected group, an inference of age discrimination is weakened.

A more common mode of proof tracks the individual *McDonnell Douglas* disparate treatment case of the kind that also predominates under Title VII. In these cases employers have enjoyed particular success when the plaintiff's termination can be shown to have taken place as part of a comprehensive, economically motivated reduction in force ("RIF"). Because such a force reduction is itself a legitimate reason for termination, courts typically require plaintiffs discharged in those circumstances to produce "plus" evidence beyond the prima facie case tending to show that age was a factor in the challenged termination. In appellate decisions, one plaintiff carried that burden by offering evidence of two age-related comments by company officials in connection with the transfer of two younger employees into the department from which plaintiff had been downsized. Another succeeded by showing half-hearted efforts to place him in alternative positions for which he was qualified. Cronin v. Aetna Life Ins. Co. (2d Cir.1995). In the latter case, the company's statistical evidence tending to show that the organization as a whole was not age-discriminatory failed to conclusively negate the inference plaintiff's evidence raised that he individually had been treated unfavorably because of his age. If the plaintiff makes that showing, the employer must then come forward with an age-neutral justification for the discharge of the particular plaintiff—a neutral justification, that is, separate and apart from the fact that the termination took place as part of a reduction in force. Viola v. Philips Med. Sys. of N. Am. & N. Am. Philips Corp. (2d Cir.1994).

Indeed in some circuits the "RIFFed" plaintiff enjoys an easier burden than the "single-discharge" plaintiff. For example, she need only show that younger employees received more favorable treatment during a RIF, and not that her particular replacement was younger. The inference of discriminatory treatment is not drawn so lightly in a single-discharge case, in which there can be no assumption that job requirements are fungible, unless the single plaintiff's responsibilities are absorbed by others. Gadsby v. Norwalk Furniture Corp. (7th Cir.1995). In RIF cases the plaintiff's prima facie case may be similarly eased on the element of comparative qualifications.

The RIFFed plaintiff must show prima facie that one or more similarly situated persons below the age of 40, or at least younger than herself, were retained or hired shortly after plaintiff's layoff while she was dismissed despite having met the employer's legitimate performance expectations. Even then, the employer can avoid liability by offering evidence of a legitimate nondiscriminatory reason for retaining the younger workers, thereby casting on the plaintiff the final burden of demonstrating the pretextual nature of that justification. When an employer reduces its force for economic reasons, it generally incurs no duty to transfer laid off workers to other positions. However, if a job is currently available for which the plaintiff is qualified and the employer fills that job with a person outside the protected group, an inference of discrimination is permitted. Similarly, the inconsistent application of RIF criteria can suffice to show pretext. One circuit court has stressed that in analyzing RIF cases "the similarity of the jobs held by an older and younger employee is the touchstone for determining whether a lay-off of the older may be found to be an ADEA violation by a trier of fact." Burger v. New York Inst. of Tech. (2d Cir.1996). That same circuit delineates two types of actionable RIFs: cases that center on "who took the place of the covered employee," and those that center on whether the selection of RIFFed employees was influenced by an impermissible ground. Danzer v. Norden Sys., Inc. (2d Cir.1998).

As under Title VII, the more generalized and subjective the employer justification in response to a *McDonnell Douglas* prima facie case, the more vulnerable it is to a finding of "pretext." The Supreme Court's refinement of the Title VII "pretext" concept in the *St. Mary's Honor Center* decision has been adapted to actions under ADEA. Thus even though the employer's stated reason for its conduct is refuted by the evidence, the employer may be absolved of liability if the factfinder determines that the false explanation was not a cover for discrimination because of age. Wyvill v. United Cos. Life Ins. Co. (5th Cir.2000).

Relative to cases under Title VII, ADEA plaintiffs who attempted to show pretext solely by attempting to undermine the employer's stated legitimate reason may have anticipated even more exacting scrutiny under the *St. Mary's* standard, because their burden after *Hazen* has been to demonstrate that age is not merely a "motivating" but rather a "determinative" factor in the employer's decision. Perhaps because of this complicating consideration, the lower courts experienced at least as much difficulty in applying *St. Mary's* to ADEA cases as to actions under Title VII.

But the Supreme Court has resolved the post-*St. Mary's* debate favorably to plaintiffs, consistent with the approach taken by the majority of the circuit courts. In Reeves v. Sanderson Plumbing Products, Inc. (2000), an ADEA case, the Court, taking note of the differing *St. Mary's* passages, wrote that the jury may find the ultimate fact of discrimination on a prohibited ground simply from (1) evidence establishing a prima facie case, coupled with (2) "sufficient" evidence that the employer's asserted legitimate nondiscriminatory explanation is false. The Court considered this approach consistent with general evidence law: "the factfinder is entitled to consider a party's dishonesty about a material fact as 'affirmative evidence of guilt'"; and once the employer's asserted reason is rejected, unlawful discrimination "may well be the most likely alternative explanation." Of course, as *St. Mary's* had held, the jury may properly find liability in such a case only if properly charged that it must, from these two kinds of evidence, make dual *findings*: (1) that the reason or reasons offered by the employer for taking the adverse action against plaintiff were not its real reasons, and (2) that the employer's real reason was in fact the unlawful ground. To that extent the Court disapproved the circuit cases that had required plaintiffs to adduce evidence not only that the employer's asserted legitimate reason was false but also sufficient, independent *evidence* that the employer's actual reason was an unlawful one.

It should also be noted that Hazen Paper Co. v. Biggins (1993), held that an employer does not intentionally discriminate in violation of ADEA simply by making a decision based on a factor other than age—there, the fact that plaintiff was nearing pension eligibility—even if that factor strongly correlates with age. Thus firing an older worker to reduce high current salaries or future benefits, Dilla v. West (11th Cir. 1999); Broaddus v. Florida Power Corp. (11th Cir.1998); Anderson v. Baxter Healthcare Corp. (7th Cir.1994), making employment decisions based on employees' bad backs, Beith v. Nitrogen Products, Inc. (8th Cir.1993), choosing an older worker for termination because his eligibility for a pension would lessen the blow of the termination, Cruz–Ramos v. Puerto Rico Sun Oil Co. (1st Cir.2000), or distinguishing on the basis of seniority, Williams v. General Motors Corp. (5th Cir.1981), do not violate the Act even though in each case the distinguishing neutral feature may be more prevalent in older workers.

The *Hazen* opinion indicated that proof of discriminatory motive was critical to establish disparate treatment under ADEA. Relying on *Hazen*, circuit opinions sometimes insist that the plaintiff prove not only that the challenged practice denies benefits or imposes burdens because of age, but also an age-related "intent" or "discriminatory motive" or even "discriminatory animus" underlying the defendant's adoption of that practice. Lyon v. Ohio Educ. Ass'n and Professional Staff Union (6th Cir.1995). They differ sharply, however, over the kind of evidence that meets this state of mind requirement.

4. MIXED MOTIVES IN ADEA DISPARATE TREATMENT CASES

Where the plaintiff's evidence shows lawful as well as unlawful factors for the employer's conduct, ADEA plaintiffs must generally show that age was a determinative factor in the challenged employment decision; the employer must then carry the burden of persuading that it would have taken the same employment action independent of the unlawful component of its aggregate complex of reasons. See, e.g., Rose v. National Cash Register Corp. (6th Cir.1983). Where there is no employer admission of unlawfulness, and the evidence does not reveal an obviously unlawful motivation, the jury should be charged that the plaintiff must prove age played a "determinative" role in the challenged decision. That requires a showing, where the challenged decision proceeds from more than one motive, that age was a "but-for" cause of the decision; it does not require a showing that the unlawful factor was predominant. *Miller.* Although the "determining" or "determinative" factor requirement frequently appears in the ADEA opinions of the lower federal courts, it has been endorsed by the Supreme Court only indirectly or in passing. Simpler words recently recommended by the Seventh Circuit for jury instructions on this issue ask "whether age accounts for the decision—in other words, whether the same events would have transpired if the employee had been younger than 40 and everything else had been the same." Gehring v. Case Corp. (7th Cir.1994). See Umpleby v. Potter & Brumfield, Inc. (7th Cir.1995).

Key amendments made to Title VII made by Section 107 of the Civil Rights Act of 1991 shed light by way of contrast on the proof elements, defenses and remedies under ADEA. That section declares a Title VII unlawful employment practice established when the plaintiff demonstrates that employer reliance on protected group status was a "motivating factor" for "any" employment practice, "even though other factors also motivated the practice." Section 107, adding Title VII § 703(m), 42 U.S.C.A. § 2000e–2(m)(1988). Once plaintiff shows a discriminatory motivating factor, the Title VII defendant employer has the burden of demonstrating by a preponderance of the evidence "that it would have taken the same action in the absence of the impermissible motivating factor." Section 107(b), adding Title VII § 706(g), 42 U.S.C.A. § 2000e–5(g) (1972).

The text of these sections suggest, and the Supreme Court has now held, Desert Palace, Inc. v. Costa (U.S.2003), that the Title VII defendant's "same decision" burden is triggered not only by "direct" testimony of discriminatory motive, or substantial evidence that an employer agent, practice or policy treated the plaintiff adversely on a prohibited ground, but also by the more common and less telling *McDonnell Douglas/Burdine* "inferential" evidence that the plaintiff applied, was minimally qualified, and was rejected. Further, the defendant must carry the "same-decision" showing by a preponderance of the evidence. Section 104 (adding subsection 701(m) to Title VII, 42 U.S.C.A. § 2000e(m)). Finally, even if the defendant succeeds with "same-decision" showing, it does not escape liability entirely. Although the employer will not be liable for back or front pay or backward-looking damages, it is still deemed to have committed a law violation remediable by prospective relief and attorneys' fees. Section 107(b)(3) (adding paragraph (2)(B) to § 706(g) of Title VII, 42 U.S.C.A. § 2000e–5(g)).

It is unclear which if any of these important modifications to Title VII mixed-motive cases will ultimately be held to apply to actions under ADEA. Although other parts of the 1991 Act refer directly to ADEA, § 107 does not. If the omission is ultimately regarded as legislative oversight, the ADEA defendant, like the Title VII one, will be forced to carry the same-decision burden regardless of whether the plaintiff established prima facie that age was a "determinative" factor through "direct" evidence or the *McDonnell Douglas* inferential formula. Moreover, the employer who carries the "same-decision" burden will still have violated ADEA and be liable for prospective relief and attorneys' fees. But lower federal courts have instead been giving the 1991 Act a "plain text" reading, treating the absence of any reference to ADEA in § 107 as advertent. Accordingly, they consider ADEA mixed-motive cases to be governed by the pre–1991 Act Title VII regime of the *Price Waterhouse* plurality, as tightened up by concurring Justices White and O'Connor. Under that view the employer does not bear a "same-decision" burden unless the plaintiff's prima facie evidence of age-based motivation is "direct," "substantial," or both. See *Miller v. CIGNA Corp.* In addition, a defendant who does carry that burden will not be exposed to declaratory relief or attorneys' fees as under the amended Title VII, but will escape liability completely.

Of course if the ADEA plaintiff is really required to show prima facie that age was a "determinative" factor in the sense that "but-for" the employer's reliance on age it would not have taken the challenged action, then a "same-decision" defense could serve no sensible function. The employer who carried that defense would be negating exactly what the plaintiff had just proved! That lower courts continue to recognize a same-decision ADEA defense therefore suggests that a "determinative" factor, although more substantial in an employer's decisional calculus than a Title VII "motivating" factor, is nevertheless something less than a "but for" factor.

The individual disparate treatment evidence of age discrimination may be buttressed, as under Title VII, by statistical or anecdotal evidence or both that the employer systemically discriminates on a widespread, routine basis. See EEOC v. Western Electric (4th Cir.1983). But courts have required refined and technically significant statistical evidence and sometimes also anecdotal testimony by multiple individuals before they will conclude that the employer is responsible for a pattern or practice of discrimination.

5. DOES A "NEUTRAL PRACTICE/ADVERSE IMPACT" THEORY SURVIVE UNDER ADEA?

The neutral practice theory derived from the *Griggs v. Duke Power* interpretation of Title VII has until recently been widely recognized to be available to prove claims under ADEA. See, e.g., Abbott v. Federal Forge, Inc. (6th Cir.1990). But the continued utility of neutral practice/adverse impact proof in ADEA actions has been undermined by language in *Hazen Paper Co. v. Biggins,* a decision limited on its facts to defining age-based disparate treatment. Even if the impact case survives, the plaintiff must show that the employer's practice has significant adverse impact on protected group members vis-a-vis similarly situated employees younger than 40, not on subsets of the over-40 protected group. Lowe v. Commack Union Free School Dist. (2d Cir.1989). And employers have successfully cited cost factors in defending the adverse impact of neutral practices on older workers. One court precluded any use of the disparate impact theory to prove age discrimination resulting from across-the-board, cost-cutting measures implemented by a company in an effort to avoid bankruptcy. Finnegan v. Trans World Airlines, Inc. (7th Cir.1992).

More generally, ADEA complainants face the defense that apparently neutral requirements or benefits limitations that have disproportionate adverse impact on the basis of age are motivated by and are in fact conducive to cost reduction or productive efficiency. Consider, for example, employment compensation geared to years of service, which in turn is usually strongly correlated with age. That employer will incur higher average costs in employing relatively older workers. When the employer then lays off higher-paid employees or those with greater seniority because of the greater cost reductions it thereby achieves, is it unlawfully discriminating because of age? If so, is the form of discrimination express or simply the disparate effect of a neutral practice?

Where the covariance between compensation or seniority and age is overwhelming, most courts, until recently, treated a practice that selects employees for termination or forced early retirement on the basis of higher salary or greater service as a variety of express discrimination. These courts generally followed the EEOC's administrative interpretation which rejects the defense that cost savings is a "reasonable factor other than age" under § 4(f)(1) of the Act. See 29 C.F.R. § 1625.7(f)(1986) and Metz v. Transit Mix, Inc. (7th Cir.1987). But see EEOC v. Chrysler Corp. (6th Cir.1984). Even viewing such practices as neutral, some courts held that cost savings did not amount to a business necessity justifying the resulting adverse impact on protected group members. Leftwich v. Harris–Stowe State College (8th Cir.1983); Geller. Alternatively, they concluded that the defense failed because the employer bypassed available less restrictive means—for example, reducing the salaries of senior workers—to effect the desired savings. See *Metz*.

The Supreme Court may have rendered much of this law obsolete by holding that discrimination on the basis of a factor merely correlating with age—e.g., pension status, years of service or seniority—is not unlawful disparate treatment under the ADEA. *Hazen*. The employer in *Hazen* allegedly fired the plaintiff to prevent his pension benefits from vesting, which the Supreme Court agreed would violate ERISA. But the same conduct, standing alone, does not violate ADEA, the Court concluded, unless a particular employer is dually motivated by the employee's age as well as his pension status, or is shown to have treated pension status as a proxy for age. As guidance for determining whether an employer is motivated by the plaintiff's age, the Court described the "essence of what Congress sought to prohibit in the ADEA" as inaccurate, stigmatizing stereotyping based on the belief that older workers are less productive or efficient. It follows that if an employer fires an employee solely in order to reduce salary costs it is not intentionally discriminating on the basis of age, even if being older substantially correlates with higher compensation. Anderson v. Baxter Healthcare Corp. (7th Cir. 1994).

The Court in *Hazen* had no occasion to decide whether employer reliance on years of service or pension status, as distinct from age as such, could violate ADEA as an instance of disparate impact, for no disparate impact claim was made there. It is now more doubtful, however, that the current Court would answer that question affirmatively. The Court continues to view disparate treatment, as distinct from disproportionate adverse impact, as "the essence of what Congress sought to prohibit. . . ." Three justices in *Hazen* alluded to "substantial arguments that it is improper to carry over . . .

impact analysis from Title VII to the ADEA." Their logic seems to be that disproportionate adverse impact results because the neutral factor on which an employer relies correlates with age; accordingly, allowing the impact theory would undermine the Court's holding that employer reliance on factors correlated with age is not unlawful disparate treatment.

Long shadows cast by *Hazen* have doomed subsequent disparate impact claims. A school linked salary to work experience in a way that excluded over-40 applicants at 4.2 times the rate of younger applicants. Although the school's years-of-service factor was age-correlated, its salary policy was held "economically defensible and reasonable"; plaintiff therefore had the burden to "demonstrate that the reason given was a pretext for a stereotype-based rationale." EEOC v. Francis W. Parker School (7th Cir.1994). Other circuits have launched more frontal attacks on the ADEA impact claim, relying not just on *Hazen* but on Congress' failure, when it codified the Title VII impact theory in the 1991 Civil Rights Act, to add a parallel provision to the ADEA. See Ellis v. United Airlines, Inc. (10th Cir.1996).

Even when ADEA disparate impact claims are recognized, they are subject to a defense unavailable to the Title VII defendant. The provisions of the 1991 Civil Rights Act that restrict the impact defense by tying the employer's justification to the plaintiff's particular job as well as the overall business make no mention of the ADEA. So cost savings remains a defense to ADEA disproportionate adverse impact claims, even though that action is not related to the capability of an individual to perform a particular job. See Jones v. Unisys Corp. (10th Cir.1995).

6. RETALIATION

Section 623(d) of ADEA provides protection against retaliation in the same terms as § 704(a) of Title VII. Former employees, in particular those who have been discharged, are among the "employees" shielded by § 623(d). Passer v. American Chem. Soc'y (D.C.Cir.1991); E.E.O.C. v. Cosmair, Inc. (5th Cir.1987). Further, the employer need not have affected the terms or conditions of the former employment; withholding letters of recommendation or providing negative information to prospective employers may also constitute forbidden retaliation. *Passer*. The ADEA provision, like the Title VII counterpart, has been construed to shield a wide range of on-the-job "opposition" in addition to formal participation in ADEA proceedings. One circuit court has held, however, that retaliation against a plaintiff who filed an age discrimination claim is not cognizable under Title VII. Lennon v. Rubin (1st Cir. 1999).

7. THE OLDER WORKERS BENEFIT PROTECTION ACT

Prior to the 1990 enactment of the Older Workers Benefit Protection Act ("OWBPA"), § 4(f)(2) of the ADEA exempted employers from liability for "a bona fide employee benefit plan such as retirement, pension, or insurance plan, which is not a subterfuge to evade the purpose of [the ADEA]." 29 U.S.C.A. § 623(f)(2). The EEOC had interpreted this exemption to require a cost justification for any age discriminatory provision in an employee benefit plan. The interpretation required that any reduction in fringe benefits for older employees would be lawful only if the employer's actual cost of providing that benefit was higher for older employees than younger ones and the employer was spending the same amount for its older employees as its younger ones. Thus, an employer was permitted to reduce the health insurance coverage of an older employee only if the premiums for covering the worker were greater than those of covering a younger employee.

The Supreme Court, rejecting the unanimous position of the courts of appeals and the EEOC, gave former section 4(f)(2) an expansive reading. *Public Employees Retirement System of Ohio v. Betts.* First, the Court held that the exemption pertains to plans that regulate any fringe benefit (for example, disability plans) and not just to retirement, pension, or insurance plans. Second, as a matter of law, a plan provision adopted before an employer becomes subject to ADEA cannot be deemed a "subterfuge" to evade the Act's purposes. Third, even a plan provision adopted thereafter will not be considered a subterfuge except in the unlikely event that the plaintiff is able to prove that it was "intended to serve the purpose of discriminating in some nonfringe-benefit aspect of the employment relation," such as discrimination in hiring or compensation.

The OWBPA, enacted October 16, 1990, repeals the § 4(f)(2) exemption, reinstates the EEOC cost justification rule, and declares that employee benefit plans are covered by the ADEA's general prohibition against age discrimination. Specifically, the Act requires that "for each benefit or benefit package, the actual amount of payment made or cost incurred on behalf of an older worker [shall be] no less than that made or incurred on behalf of a younger work."

The OWBPA also expressly permits employers to follow the terms of a bona fide seniority system, provide for the attainment of a specified age as a condition of eligibility for a pension plan, and provide bona fide voluntary early retirement incentive plans. Such a voluntary plan is bona fide if it does not confer more valuable benefits on younger workers.

8. WAIVER OF RIGHTS OR CLAIMS UNDER THE ADEA AFTER OWBPA

Some employers have required employees to sign a release waiving all rights and claims, if any, under the ADEA as a condition to receiving severance benefits. Prior to the enactment of OWBPA, the ADEA did not state whether an employee could release her rights under the ADEA without supervision by the EEOC. Courts of Appeals, however, generally have upheld the validity of private releases so long as a waiver is "knowing and voluntary."

The OWBPA resolves this question by specifically permitting unsupervised releases (those not approved by EEOC), provided that: (1) the waiver is in writing and written in terms likely to be understood by the average individual eligible to participate in the plan (or by the individual herself); (2) the waiver specifically refers to the rights or claims arising under the ADEA; (3) the individual does not waive rights or claims that may arise *after* the waiver is executed (See Adams v. Philip Morris, Inc. (6th Cir.1995)); (4) the individual waives rights or claims only in exchange for additional consideration (that is, consideration in addition to anything of value the individual is already entitled to receive); (5) the individual is advised in writing to consult with an attorney prior to executing the waiver; (6) the individual is given at least 21 days in which to consider the agreement (the individual must be given 45 days if the waiver is requested in connection with an exit incentive or group termination program); (7) the agreement provides for a period of at least seven (7) days following execution to revoke the agreement and does not become effective until this period has expired; and (8) if the waiver is requested as part of an exit incentive or group termination program, the employer must inform the individual in writing (in understandable language) of: (a) any class or group of individuals covered by the program and any eligibility factors and time limits for the program; and (b) the job titles and ages of all individual eligible or selected for the program and those within the same job classification or organization unit not eligible or selected for the program.

Waivers are subject to attack as not "knowing and voluntary." See Griffin v. Kraft General Foods, Inc. (11th Cir.1995). No waiver or settlement of an EEOC or court action is considered "knowing or voluntary" unless the above requirements have been met and the individual is given a "reasonable period" in which to consider the settlement. The OWBPA imposes the burden of proof upon the proponent of the release to prove that the minimum statutory requirements for ADEA releases have been satisfied. And no waiver agreement affects the EEOC's ability to enforce the ADEA or an individual's right to file a charge or participate in an EEOC investigation or proceeding.

The Supreme Court has held that a release which fails to comply with OWBPA requirements does not bar an action under ADEA. The plaintiff's retention of consideration received for a waiver agreement does not ratify the waiver, and the employee need not tender back that consideration as a prerequisite to suit. Oubre v. Entergy Operations, Inc. (1998). EEOC has subsequently issued regulations on waiver of rights and claims under ADEA. 29 C.F.R. Pt. 1625 (1998).

Employer policies that require terminated employees to sign a general release of all claims to be eligible for enhanced severance benefits do not discriminate expressly, even though they may put pressure only on members of the over-40 protected group to waive rights under ADEA. The bundle of accrued claims that an over-40 employee would be required to release would not necessarily be worth more than the bundle released by any particular employee under 40. For example, more of the younger employees may be members of minority groups or women, who as such would be forfeiting distinct protection under other statutes that are part of the waiver package.

9. ADEA PROCEDURES

EEOC is charged with enforcement of the Act, and ADEA provides criminal penalties for intentional or willful interference with its processes. It investigates claims of age discrimination, attempts conciliation, and has the power to file civil actions. But individual actions are the major means of enforcement, and many ADEA procedures and remedies are borrowed from the Fair Labor Standards Act. See, e.g., EEOC v. Tire Kingdom, Inc. (11th Cir.1996).

The standards for administrative charge filing under ADEA are more relaxed than those under Title VII. The major superficial similarities are the twin requirements that a complainant file a charge of discrimination (1) with EEOC, within 180 days of an alleged violation, or within 300 days in a deferral state; and (2) with an appropriately empowered state agency, if one exists, which then must be deferred to for a maximum of 60 days or until it dismisses or surrenders jurisdiction. But EEOC itself is given only 60 days of deferral, in contrast to the 180 days specified by Title VII, and plaintiffs may then proceed to federal court without demanding or receiving a "right to sue" letter from that agency. If, however, the plaintiff awaits EEOC's right to sue notice, the action must be commenced, as under Title VII, within 90 days after the plaintiff receives it.

In addition, the Supreme Court has leniently construed the ADEA's apparent requirement that a state filing precede the filing of an ADEA action in federal court. A complainant's failure to file a state agency charge before commencing a federal action is not fatal; the federal court will simply stay its proceedings until a state charge is filed and the state deferral period elapses. Oscar Mayer & Co. v. Evans (1979). For this reason lower courts in ADEA cases have also not followed the approach taken by the Supreme Court's *Mohasco* decision under Title VII, which subtracts the 60-day state deferral period from the 300 EEOC filing deadline and thus effectively requires a state filing by day 240; the 300 days to file with EEOC in ADEA actions remains 300, rather than 240 days. Thelen v. Marc's Big Boy Corp. (7th Cir.1995).

Securities industry and other employees who have agreed individually to arbitrate statutory discrimination claims as a condition of employment have been held precluded by the Federal Arbitration Act ("FAA") from instituting judicial actions under ADEA without first exhausting the agreed upon arbitration procedures. Gilmer v. Interstate/Johnson Lane Corp. (1991). It remains unclear whether those employees will be precluded from resuming such stayed lawsuits after the issuance of an adverse arbitration award. Further, it is uncertain whether the compulsion attaches where the arbitration promise is contained in a collectively bargained agreement negotiated not by the putative plaintiff but by her union. See Chapter 19, Section G.4.

Until the Civil Rights Act of 1991, the plaintiff was required to initiate an ADEA action within the 2- or 3-year limitations period applicable under the Portal-to-Portal Act. But an amendment made by the Civil Rights Act of 1991 eliminates the Portal-to-Portal Act limitations periods. Section 115 instead requires EEOC, when it dismisses or otherwise terminates a proceeding, to notify the charging party, who then may (and must) bring a private action against the respondent within 90 days of receipt of that notice. That amendment was not made to shorten the statute of limitations on ADEA claims but rather to preserve them: EEOC had proven incapable of acting on many age discrimination claims before the former 2- or 3-year statutes expired. Sperling v. Hoffmann–La Roche, Inc. (3d Cir.1994). Nevertheless circuit courts, regarding the new 90-day provision as "procedural," have applied it to bar claims filed after the effective date of the 1991 Civil Rights Act even on claims accruing before that date. Garfield v. J.C. Nichols Real Estate (8th Cir.1995).

ADEA may be somewhat more restrictive than Title VII in one procedural respect, although probably largely in form. No ADEA class action may be maintained under Federal Rule 23, which in appropriate circumstances permits class members to be bound without their specific consent. But multiple plaintiffs may join together under Federal Rule 20; and "representative" actions are permitted under ADEA § 7(b), which incorporates by reference § 16(b) of FLSA, 29 U.S.C.A. § 216(b). The class representatives must frame their court complaint so as to notify the employer that it will have to defend an opt-in representative action. *Sperling.* (The Third Circuit has also insisted, as a prerequisite to an ADEA representative action, that the class representatives must have included a similar notice in their administrative charge filed with EEOC. Lusardi v. Lechner (3d Cir.1988)). Section 16(b) accordingly allows a would-be "class member" who has not filed a charge affirmatively to "opt in" the action by giving a written consent to joinder as a party plaintiff. The Supreme Court has authorized district courts to facilitate this process by ordering employers to produce the names and addresses of employees similarly situated to the representative and to issue a consent document approved in form by the court itself. Hoffmann–La Roche Inc. v. Sperling (1989). And the required degree of similarity between the allegations of the putative joiner and those of the named plaintiff is less than is required for FRCP 20(a) permissive joinder. K–Mart Corp. v. Helton (Ky.1995).

Further, paralleling the practice followed under Title VII in the case of true Rule 23 class actions, most circuit courts have adopted a "single-filing" rule that rather liberally permits would-be ADEA representees who have not filed timely charges with EEOC to piggyback on the timely filed charges of their co-joined individual plaintiffs or "representatives." See, e.g., Grayson v. K Mart Corp. (11th Cir.1996); Howlett v. Holiday Inns, Inc. (6th Cir.1995). But see Whalen v. W.R. Grace & Co. (3d Cir.1995).

10. ADEA REMEDIES

An individual may be awarded injunctive relief, back wages, statutory "liquidated" damages equal to the amount of back wages, attorney's fees, and costs. 29 U.S.C.A. § 626(b), incorporating by reference the remedies authorized under the Fair Labor Standards Act, 29 U.S.C.A. §§ 216–17. Although, as under Title VII, back pay is routinely available as a remedy for a proven ADEA violation, similar limitations on its scope apply. For example back pay will be denied for the period beginning after an employer eliminates the position from which plaintiff was terminated, provided it has not created a comparable position. Bartek v. Urban Redevelopment Authority of Pittsburgh (3d Cir.1989).

The circuits generally approve front pay as an ADEA remedy that is almost routinely available when needed. See, e.g., McKnight v. General Motors Corp. (7th Cir.1990). But see Blum v. Witco (3d Cir.1987) and Wells v. New Cherokee Corp. (6th Cir.1995). Its duration extends until the plaintiff fails to make reasonable efforts to secure substantially equivalent employment or until he obtains or is offered such employment, or until a date the court determines his job would no longer be available, or plaintiff would have quit. See Dominic v. Consolidated Edison Co. of N.Y., Inc. (2d Cir.1987).

Since the age 70 cap on the class protected by ADEA was removed effective January 1, 1987, it is theoretically possible for front pay to continue indefinitely, or at least for the duration of an employee's lifetime as predicted by a standard mortality table. But an employer's normal retirement age may well serve as a practical cap on the duration of what would otherwise be an astronomical total amount of front pay. Olitsky v. Spencer Gifts, Inc. (5th Cir.1992).

Liquidated damages equal to the compensatory back pay award are available under ADEA in the same circumstances as they are available under the EPA, i.e., when the violation is "willful" within the meaning of the FLSA. This means that the double award is available only if the employer knows that its employment practice violates ADEA or recklessly disregards whether its conduct will violate the Act; it is not enough that the employer knows that the Act is potentially applicable to the practice in question. *Trans World Airlines, Inc. v. Thurston.* Employer conduct must be more than merely voluntary and negligent to constitute a willful violation, but need not involve the kind of egregiousness or malice that most circuits require for punitive damages under Title VII or ADA. The Supreme Court specifically rejects these additional requirements. *Hazen Paper Co. v. Biggins.*

Hazen also made it clear that the *Thurston* definition of willfulness applies to cases concerning alleged ad hoc disparate treatment against individual employees, as well as to alleged disparate treatment resulting from the kind of formal policy at issue in *Thurston*. But the Court also wrote that an employer "who knowingly relies on age" does not "invariably" commit a knowing or reckless violation of the ADEA. This is because the Court's test finds willfulness only when the employer knows that or recklessly disregards whether it is violating the prohibitions of the statute, not simply when it knowingly takes age into account. Specifically, the Court in *Hazen* sought to preserve "two tiers of liability" in ADEA cases by finding liability for back pay whenever an intentional violation is established, but denying liquidated damages even for intentional violations when "an employer incorrectly but in good faith and nonrecklessly" believes that its conduct is not prohibited or is affirmatively authorized by the statute.

Consequently, while conduct constituting a constructive discharge is by its nature serious, aggravated and almost surely intentional, it does not follow that every such violation is willful. Peterson v. Insurance Co. of North America (2d Cir. 1994). Some violations, however—unlawful retaliation is an example—may inherently involve knowledge or reckless disregard of the prohibitions of the statute, so liquidated damages should follow as a matter of course from a finding of liability. Compare Edwards v. Board of Regents (11th Cir.1993) with Starceski v. Westinghouse Electric (3d Cir.1995) and Grant v. Hazelett Strip–Casting Corp. (2d Cir.1989).

Although a 1978 amendment clarifies that jury trials are available on liquidated damages claims as well as on claims for lost wages, there are unresolved legal questions about the computation of the liquidated damages award. The major issue is whether the doubling should be based on the full compensatory award, including front pay, replacement of lost pension income, and other fringe benefits or, as one circuit has held, should be limited to the amount of back pay. Compare Bruno v. W.B. Saunders Co. (3d Cir.1989) with Blim v. Western Electric Co. (10th Cir.1984).

The circuits also disagree whether, when liquidated damages are awarded, the court may additionally award front pay. See Walther v. Lone Star Gas Co. (5th Cir.1992). A similar debate surrounds prejudgment interest. Courts that, despite *Thurston,* view liquidated damages as at least partly compensatory reject prejudgment interest, holding that the plaintiff who receives both would be overcompensated. See McCann v. Texas City Refining, Inc. (5th Cir.1993). Courts that consider liquidated damages as the ADEA's substitute for punitive damages allow prejudgment interest in addition. Starceski; Reichman v. Bonsignore, Brignati and Mazzotta (2d Cir.1987). The latter view is fortified by the Supreme Court's reaffirmation that ADEA liquidated damages are designed to be punitive. Commissioner v. Schleier (1994).

Despite *Hazen's* confirmation that ADEA authorizes "legal remedies," the Civil Rights Act of 1991 gives Title VII plaintiffs alleging disparate treatment important remedies that the circuit courts have uniformly held unavailable under ADEA: compensatory and punitive damages. See Moskowitz v. Trustees of Purdue University (7th Cir.1993). But state law claims authorizing compensatory or punitive damages may often be joined with ADEA claims. See Sanchez v. Puerto Rico Oil Co. (1st Cir.1994).

Accordingly, while it could be said categorically before the 1991 Act that an ADEA plaintiff was remedially better situated than a claimant under Title VII, that is no longer necessarily true. To be awarded more than back and, with luck, front pay, the ADEA plaintiff must prove wilfulness; and even then she is likely to receive an award equal to only back pay doubled, or at best twice the amount of back and front pay combined. By contrast, the Title VII plaintiff, by showing no more than an intentional violation, may now recover not just back and front pay but compensatory damages, although those will be capped in amounts that vary with the size of the defendant's employee complement. Only when she seeks punitive damages must the Title VII plaintiff show something akin to ADEA wilfulness. On the other hand, the 1991 Act caps the sum of compensatory and punitive damages available under Title VII, while there is no absolute cap on the size of ADEA liquidated damages. An ADEA plaintiff who recovers a very large award of back pay, front pay or both may accordingly still find that his liquidated damages exceed the capped amount a Title VII counterpart could recover by way of compensatory and punitive damages.

The 1991 Act denies successful ADEA plaintiffs, unlike their Title VII counterparts, more than a nominal recovery at the statutory rate for the fees of expert witnesses. James v. Sears, Roebuck and Co. (10th Cir.1994). And in contrast to § 706(k) of Title VII, ADEA, per the FLSA, authorizes attorneys' fees only to "plaintiffs," not "prevailing parties." Thus even a prevailing ADEA defendant who can make the extraordinary showing of frivolousness demanded by the Christiansburg Garment interpretation of § 706(k) of Title VII may not be entitled to an award of attorneys' fees from the plaintiff.

D. SEX DISCRIMINATION IN FEDERALLY FUNDED EDUCATION PROGRAMS: TITLE IX

Title IX of the Civil Rights Act of 1964 redresses sex discrimination in employment, as well as in admissions and general educational activities, by federally funded education programs. North Haven Bd. of Educ. v. Bell (1982). Title VI of that Act prohibits discrimination based on race, color, or national origin in federally funded programs or activities. 42 U.S.C.A. §§ 2000d–2000d–4a. But Title VI does not reach employment practices except where a primary objective of the federal assistance is to provide employment. 42 U.S.C.A. § 2000d–3. Accordingly, even though many judicially developed liability and remedy standards are used interchangably in cases under both Titles, discussion here will be limited to Title IX.

Title IX's primary prohibition provides that . . .

No person in the United States shall, on the basis of sex, be excluded from participation in, be denied the benefit of, or be subjected to discrimination under any education program or activity receiving Federal financial assistance. . . . 20 U.S.C.A. § 1681. See also 20 U.S.C.A. § 1684 (prohibiting discrimination because of blindness or severe visual impairment).

Federal assistance includes grants, loans, or contracts other than those of insurance or guaranty. 20 U.S.C.A. § 1682. See 20 U.S.C.A. § 1685 (contracts of insurance or guaranty). One holding of Grove City College v. Bell (1984), that federal assistance funneled directly to students constitutes "assistance" to the students' educational institutions, thus triggering Title IX regulation of programs or of the institution itself, appears undisturbed either by subsequent decisions or by the 1987 Civil Rights Restoration Act discussed immediately below.

1.   COVERED PROGRAMS OR ACTIVITIES

Lower courts had held that discrimination in any Title IX "program or activity" within an institution receiving federal assistance was a violation of Title IX, even if the particular discriminatory program was not the subject of the assistance. But in *Grove City College,* the Supreme Court interpreted the phrase "program or activity" narrowly, holding that Title IX prohibited discrimination only in the particular educational program or activity receiving the federal assistance, not in all the educational programs and activities conducted by the institution receiving such assistance. The Civil Rights Restoration Act of 1987 overturned this holding by defining the "program or activity" covered by Title IX to include "all" of a recipient's operations. 20 U.S.C.A. § 1687.

So where federal aid is extended to any program within a college, university or other public system of elementary, secondary or higher education, the entire institution or system is covered by the prohibitions of Title IX. 42 U.S.C.A. § 1687(2)(B). See Yusuf v. Vassar College (2d Cir.1994). Where a state and local government department (or agency) other than a school receives federal aid for an educational program or activity, and the funds stay within that particular department, only that department is subject to Title IX sanctions; but if the aid is distributed to other departments or agencies, all entities that receive it are covered. 42 U.S.C.A. § 1687(1)(B). Finally, a private corporation that receives aid as a whole or that provides a public service would fall under Title IX; but the entire corporation may not be covered if the federal funds are extended to only a geographically separate facility. 42 U.S.C.A. § 1687(3)(B).

2. EXEMPTIONS

Title IX redresses sex discrimination in employment by federally funded education institutions. See *North Haven Bd. of Educ.* The Restoration Act exempts entities controlled by religious organizations from Title IX coverage if the application of Title IX's ban on sex discrimination would conflict with the organization's religious tenets. 20 U.S.C.A. § 1687(4).

3. ELEMENTS OF A PRIVATE ACTION UNDER TITLE IX

The Supreme Court has implied a private right of action under Title IX. Cannon v. University of Chicago (1979). The right of action appears to extend to claims of sex discrimination in employment, for example claims by teachers against school districts. See Preston v. Commonwealth of Va. (4th Cir.1994) The preceding statement must be qualified, however, because a Supreme Court decision holding Title IX applicable to employment practices did not specifically consider whether a violation would give rise to a private right of action. See *North Haven Bd. of Educ. v. Bell.* Thus a debate is emerging in the circuit decisions over whether the existence of a detailed judicial remedy for employment discrimination under Title VII of the 1964 Civil Rights Act (amended as of 1991 to permit compensatory and punitive damages subject to statutory caps) forecloses a judicially implied remedy for employment discrimination under Title IX with respect to gender-discriminatory practices of federally funded education institutions that are actionable under Title VII. Compare Lakoski v. James (5th Cir.1995) with Lipsett v. University of Puerto Rico (1st Cir.1988).

Even if a school district is subject to a private damages action under Title IX for gender-discriminatory employment practices, the scope of such liability is unclear. The Supreme Court has held in a case involving a teacher's sexual abuse of a student that no damages remedy lies against the education entity unless an official with authority to end the discrimination had actual knowledge of the unlawful discrimination and failed adequately to respond. Gebser v. Lago Vista Ind. Sch. Dist. (1998). Presumably some teachers with gender-based employment discrimination claims could meet this strict standard, but only if the harassment was committed by, or came to the attention of, a principal or other high-ranking administrative official. Liability would be considerably broader, and could more readily reach co-worker harassment of teachers, if the stringent *Gebser* actual knowledge standard is limited to the student-plaintiff context. Then employee plaintiffs might be able to utilize the broader standards of entity liability developed under Title VII.

The administrative regulations promulgated under Title IX, like those under Title VI, prohibit discrimination resulting from facially neutral policies that have gender-discriminatory effect as well as intentional discrimination based on gender. See 34 C.F.R. § 106.21(b)(2). Lower courts have applied the impact principle to Title IX actions when the plaintiff distinctly pleads a violation of the applicable implementing regulations, as distinct from the statute alone. See, e.g., Mabry v. State Bd. of Community Colleges & Occupational Educ. (10th Cir.1987).

A related uncertain question is whether individual supervisors and managers, as distinct from institutional educational federal funds recipients, are separately subject to Title IX liability. A majority of the few decisions on point hold that they are not. See,e.g., Lipsett v. University of Puerto Rico (1st Cir.1988). But see Mennone v. Gordon (D.Conn.1995). Creative plaintiffs' counsel have attempted to skirt this obstacle by suing educational officials individually for Title IX violations under the "and laws" branch of § 1983, with mixed success. Compare Seamons v. Snow (10th Cir.1996), with Pfeiffer v. Marion Center Area Sch. Dist. (3d Cir.1990) and *Mennone v. Gordon.*

4. DAMAGES

The Supreme Court has held that a successful Title IX plaintiff is eligible for all traditional legal and equitable relief that may be appropriate, damages as well as back pay and prospective relief. Franklin v. Gwinnett County Public Schools (1992). Further, the Civil Rights Remedies Equalization Amendment of 1986 permits federal courts to award retrospective relief under, among other statutes, Titles VI and IX, against a state or state agency, expressly abrogating their Eleventh Amendment immunity. 42 U.S.C.A. § 2000d–7(b). Because *Franklin* concerned intentional discrimination, it is unclear what the effect of its broad language may be on damages in Title IX cases challenging neutral practices. *Franklin* has been limited, however, by a Supreme Court decision barring punitive damages under Title IX. *Barnes v. Gorman* (2002).

E.   COSTS AND FEES: FEDERAL RULE OF CIVIL PROCEDURE 54(d), THE CIVIL RIGHTS ATTORNEY'S FEES AWARDS ACT, AND FEDERAL RULE 68

1.   RECOVERING COSTS OF SUIT: F.R.C.P. 54(D)

Unlike attorney's fees under Title VII or § 1988, which as we shall see are ordinarily awardable only to prevailing plaintiffs, either side that prevails is presumptively entitled to costs under Fed.R.Civ.P. 54(d). Indeed the argument has been rejected that a losing Title VII plaintiff may be assessed costs only on the same terms as she should be assessed fees—that is, when the claim was frivolous, unreasonable, or without foundation. The awarding of costs lies within the sound discretion of the district court and may be denied where the award would be inequitable.

The "costs" recoverable by any prevailing party are limited, however, to items specified by a separate federal statute, 28 U.S.C.A. § 1920. These include clerk and marshal fees, fees by court reporters for transcripts "necessarily obtained for use in the case;" printing disbursements and witness fees; specified docket fees; and fees for court-appointed experts and certain interpreters. Most important, "costs" as used in Rule 54(d) do *not* include the prevailing party's attorney's fees. This is consistent with the ordinary "American rule" which, as explained by the Supreme Court, calls for each side to pay its own lawyer, win or lose, unless there is specific statutory authority for fee "shifting."

2. ATTORNEY'S FEES FOR PREVAILING PARTIES: THE CIVIL RIGHTS ATTORNEY'S FEES AWARDS ACT

The Civil Rights Attorney's Fees Awards Act (the "Act"), a 1976 amendment to 42 U.S.C.A. § 1988, permits a discretionary award of attorney's fees, in a "reasonable" amount, as part of the costs recoverable by prevailing parties, other than the United States, in any action or proceeding pursuant to 42 U.S.C.A. §§ 1981, 1982, 1983, 1985, and 1986, as well as Titles VI and IX. The purpose of the award is to enable plaintiffs to attract competent legal counsel; perhaps that is why fees have been denied for lawyers' public relations efforts on behalf of their clients. Halderman v. Pennhurst State Sch. & Hosp. (3d Cir.1995). The Act parallels separate statutory authority to award attorney's fees to prevailing parties in actions under the Rehabilitation Act of 1973, the Age Discrimination in Employment Act, the Equal Pay Act, the Clean Water Act, the Fair Labor Standards Act, and under Title VII. In fact, over a hundred separate statutes allow for court awarded attorney's fees. The principles governing eligibility for and computation of awards are largely interchangeable among these statutes.

Although a plaintiff must receive at least some relief on the merits in order to become a "prevailing party" eligible for fees, success on a "significant issue," even if it is not a "central" one, will suffice. But opinion is divided as to whether fee eligibility depends upon the plaintiff's having prevailed on a claim under one of the § 1988–referenced federal statutes, rather than a related claim under state law. A plaintiff adjudged to be a prevailing party should ordinarily receive a fee award absent "special circumstances," such as the plaintiff's egregious misconduct, e.g. Patricia P. v. Board of Educ. of Oak Park (7th Cir.2000). These circumstances are rarely found. But *pro se* plaintiffs who also happen to be attorneys have been ruled ineligible for a fee award. Kay v. Ehrler (1991). And a plaintiff who recovers only nominal damages, although a prevailing party, may be entitled to no fee award if those damages represent only a slight degree of success achieved in the litigation. Farrar v. Hobby (1992).

To achieve success on a "significant issue" and thus "prevail" so as to be eligible for fees, the plaintiff need only obtain some relief which changes his legal relationship with the defendant and is more than merely technical or *de minimis*. Hewitt v. Helms (1987). In general, if the relief plaintiff initially seeks is "of the same general type" as the relief eventually obtained, plaintiff may be considered a prevailing party. Lyte v. Sara Lee Corp. (2d Cir.1991). An injunction requiring a company to correct a racially intimidating work atmosphere, for example, has sufficed as the predicate for a fee award to a plaintiff who lost on most of his individual claims of race discrimination. Ruffin v. Great Dane Trailers (11th Cir.1992). But in applying this standard, courts have sometimes resorted to a highly subjective appraisal of plaintiff's original objective in bringing suit, denying fees where that objective was not obtained.

A finding of a violation under § 1983 may lead to an award of nominal damages where the predicate constitutional violation is "absolute," that is not dependent upon the merits of the plaintiff's substantive assertions or the magnitude of injury resulting from a violation. Such damages may now be available under Title VII, which provides for certain kinds of legal relief since its amendment by the Civil Rights Act of 1991. Whether such nominal damages can serve as a springboard for § 1988 attorney's fees was the subject of conflict among the circuits.

In Farrar v. Hobby (1992), the Supreme Court attempted to resolve this conflict, but did so somewhat oddly. It formally conferred prevailing party status on plaintiffs who recover only nominal damages, but did so under standards that fix the amount of a reasonable attorney's fee at zero when their degree of success is slight. The Court confirmed that "a plaintiff 'prevails' when actual relief on the merits of his claim materially alters the legal relationship between the parties by modifying the defendant's behavior in a way that directly benefits the plaintiff"; and it acknowledged that even a judgment for only nominal damages "modifies the defendant's behavior for the plaintiff's benefit by forcing the defendant to pay an amount of money he otherwise would not pay." But it then drained this conclusion of practical significance under most circumstances by adding that when a plaintiff, having failed to prove an essential element of a claim for monetary relief, recovers only nominal damages, "the only reasonable fee is usually no fee at all."

In Carey v. Piphus (1978), the Court had found that nominal damages must be available for deprivations of "absolute" rights like procedural due process because of "the importance to organized society that those rights be scrupulously observed." After *Farrar*, however, it is difficult to understand how, where there is little or no actual economic or emotional injury, the Court contemplates that such rights will be enforced if attorney's fees are only theoretically and not practically available to plaintiffs who successfully prosecute suits for their violation. One possibility is that lower courts will limit *Farrar* to its facts: no jury specification of the constitutional right violated and no specific jury finding that the defendant's conduct caused the plaintiff's (nominal) damages. In one case, for example, a jury specifically found that a municipality's policy regarding excessive police force resulted in $1 of harm to an otherwise unsympathetic plaintiff, and the city disciplined an officer and modified its policy during the litigation. Upholding a fee award of $66,535, the appellate

court distinguished *Farrar*, concluding that the finding bene-
fitted the department and the community and might have
collateral estoppel effect in subsequent litigation. Wilcox v.
City Reno (9th Cir.1994). These distinctions, however, seem a
thin evasion of *Farrar*. Plaintiffs could create them routinely
by requesting special interrogatories concerning the right violated and causation, and the jury would presumably find
causation whenever it awarded damages, even nominal ones.
Another evasive tactic has been specifically rebuffed: if the
plaintiff's lawyer first asks for nominal damages at the end of
trial, when things look bleak for his client, the plaintiff who
then recovers $1, while technically prevailing, will fail to
recover fees by virtue of *Farrar*. Romberg v. Nichols (9th
Cir.1995). But a small damages award is not necessarily
conclusive on the issue of fees. Because there is no federal
small claims court and no amount in controversy requirement
in civil rights cases, the Seventh Circuit instructs courts to
determine whether the plaintiff aimed high and fell short, in
which case *Farrar* may deprive the prevailing plaintiff of a fee,
Cole v. Wodziak (7th Cir.1999), or whether it was simply a
small claim and was tried accordingly. Hyde v. Small (7th
Cir.1997). Other courts resist a literal adherence to *Farrar*,
awarding fees even where plaintiff's monetary recovery falls
many multiples short of what she sought. Brandau v. State of
Kansas (10th Cir.1999). These courts follow Justice O'Connor's *Farrar* concurrence in weighing the difference between
the judgment sought and that obtained, the significance of the
legal issue on which plaintiff prevailed, and the lawsuit's
public purpose. Other lower courts, at the opposite end of the
spectrum, indulge a virtually insuperable presumption that
the only reasonable fee to the prevailing party is zero where
plaintiff recovers nominal damages alone after having sought
compensatory and/or punitive damages initially, e.g. Pouillon

v. Little (6th Cir.2003); Johnson v. City of Aiken (4th Cir. 2002).

Another possibility, somewhat uncertain, is that the recovery of nominal damages may permit the § 1983 plaintiff to recover punitive damages otherwise warranted by a malicious or aggravated violation of procedural due process. But is there a more reliable general incentive for a lawyer to pursue a § 1983 case involving an "ordinary" constitutional or federal statutory violation in what promises to be a case of "mixed motives"—that is, where she anticipates that the defendant could carry the Mt. Healthy City School District Bd. of Education v. Doyle (1977) burden of demonstrating that it would have subjected the plaintiff to the same loss or deprivation for a lawful reason or reasons wholly independent of a substantial federally unlawful motive? In those cases there is probably no constitutional or federal statutory "violation," and hence no possible monetary relief on the merits or, accordingly, attorney's fees.

On the other hand, what if the plaintiff from the outset seeks no compensatory or punitive damages, only declaratory relief or an injunction, and recovers one? Has he not then achieved substantial, indeed entire success on the merits? And what if there are multiple claims? It is clear enough that a plaintiff's recovery of compensatory damages on fewer than all of the claims not only makes him technically prevailing but also entitles him to attorney's fees, although only with respect to the hours reasonably expended in pursuit of the successful claim or claims. Blum v. Stenson (1984). Or suppose the plaintiff prevails on several claims, obtaining only nominal damages on each? In this situation a circuit has ruled that the plaintiff is not a prevailing party. Peters v. Polk County Mem'l Hosp. (5th Cir.1993). The decisions struggle to define whether a plaintiff's "primary" goal was recovery of substantial monetary damages or merely injunctive relief to vindicate constitutional rights; if the former, then a "reasonable" fee may be nothing at all where the defendant's conduct is altered but no monetary relief is obtained.

Farrar left unresolved a related question: can one become a prevailing party without having obtained, in the Supreme Court's words, a "consent decree, enforceable judgment or settlement," but simply because the filing of a lawsuit proved to be the "catalyst" that brought about some of the lawsuit's objectives? This theory would require the plaintiff to prove that the legal action is causally linked to the relief obtained by settlement or defendant's unilateral action, and that the defendant's change in position was required by law and not merely gratuitous.

In a 5–4 decision, the Supreme Court, rejecting the view of twelve of the thirteen circuit courts that had ruled on the question, held in Buckhannon Board and Care Home, Inc. v. West Virginia Dep't of Health and Human Resources (2001) that even a plaintiff who demonstrates that his suit for injunctive relief was the "catalyst" for the defendant's "voluntary" midsuit abandonment or modification of a challenged practice is not a "prevailing party" within the meaning of federal fee-shifting statutes, and so is ineligible for court-ordered attorneys' fees, unless he is awarded some *judicial* relief. The majority ruled that the plaintiff must receive a "judgment" or "some relief by the court" to fit within the statutory term "prevailing party." Although the holding technically extends only to actions under the Fair Housing Amendments Act and the Americans With Disabilities Act, circuit courts, consistent with language in *Buckhannon*, have extended the *Buckhannon* holding to actions under any of the Reconstruction Civil Rights Acts, notably Section 1983, under which prevailing parties are eligible for fees pursuant to the Civil Rights Attorneys' Fees Act of 1976, 42 U.S.C.A. § 1988, as well as to the contemporary employment discrimination statutes, and other civil rights statutes like the Individuals With Disabilities Education Act. Indeed, a growing consensus has developed that *Buckhannon* applies to fee awards under any statute with "prevailing party" language, e.g. Thomas v. National Science Foundation (D.C. Cir.2003) but not to awards under statutes that hinge recovery of fees on other language, e.g. Sierra Club v. Environmental Protections Agency (D.C. Cir.2003).

The majority did agree that settlements enforced through consent decrees, as well as formal determinations of liability on the merits, will count as judicial relief qualifying the plaintiff for prevailing party status, because each effects a court-ordered change in the legal relationship between the parties. Cody v. Hillard (8th Cir.2002). Absent those formal judicial rulings, circuit courts are somewhat at sea as to what judicial involvement is necessary.

The ruling should have little practical consequence in damage-only cases, since no change in a defendant's challenged practices can moot such a case. But the settlement posture of plaintiff's counsel is drastically affected to the extent her client seeks declaratory or injunctive relief. The ruling pressures plaintiff's counsel in such cases to negotiate for attorney fees at the same time she negotiates for relief accruing only to her client, raising the specter of conflict with the client's interests. Or she could attempt to lessen client conflicts by negotiating on behalf of her client alone but insisting as a condition of settlement that any resulting agreement be embodied in a consent decree or consent judgment—which clearly qualify under *Buckhannon* for "prevailing party" status and hence for court-ordered fee eligibility. But if the defendant is unwilling to have an agreement providing relief to the plaintiff memorialized in a court order or judgment, plaintiff and plaintiff's counsel run the risk of losing any statutory fee award if they reach a partial settlement not inclusive of fees.

The circuits are split on the degree of judicial memorialization or enforcement of a private settlement that qualifies plaintiff as a "prevailing party" in the wake of *Buckhannon*.

It has been argued that the *Farrar* limitation, while applicable to all cases under the Reconstruction civil rights acts, is wholly inapplicable to "mixed-motive" cases under Title VII or the ADA. The argument is based on Section 706(g)(2)(B), added by the 1991 Civil Rights Act, which specifically authorizes an award of attorney's fees under those statutes even when the employer makes the "same-decision" showing—that is, where the plaintiff has had only partial success. But an appellate court has rejected that argument, observing that both the decision to award and the amount of attorney's fees are discretionary under Section 706(g)(2)(B) just as under Section 1988, the provision construed in *Farrar*. And it wrote that plaintiff's rejection of a settlement offer is one factor the court may take into account in deciding the appropriate amount of a fee award. Sheppard v. Riverview Nursing Ctr. (4th Cir.1996).

Recoverability of fees for services performed in a preliminary administrative proceeding depends in part on whether the proceeding is optional or mandatory. If the state or local administrative proceeding is mandated, as it is under Title VII, fees for legal services performed in that hearing can be recovered in an independent Title VII action. This is because the state or local administrative proceedings in a deferral state, and the EEOC proceedings in any state, qualify as a "proceeding under this subchapter" within the meaning of Title VII § 706(k). New York Gaslight Club, Inc. v. Carey (1980). If the prior administrative hearing is optional, however, fees are generally not awarded because such a hearing is not considered an "action or proceeding to enforce" civil rights under the language of § 1988. For example, because a plaintiff is not required to exhaust his administrative remedies before bringing a § 1983 action, Patsy v. Florida Bd. of Regents (1982), services performed in administrative proceedings on § 1983 claims are not compensable under § 1988. Webb v. Dyer County Bd of Educ. (1985). Sometimes, however, where the administrative work is "useful and of a type ordinarily necessary to advance the civil rights litigation," fees may be awarded (supra Webb 1985). In Pennsylvania v. Delaware Valley Citizens' Council for Clean Air (1986) ("*Delaware I*"), the Court applied this exception so as to allow fees. The *Delaware I* Court found that post-judgment administrative proceedings, held to enforce a consent decree, were "crucial to the vindication of [plaintiff's] rights," and concluded that the attorney's services performed for those proceedings were compensable.

But it remains unsettled whether, or under what circumstances, a plaintiff who achieves complete merits relief through settlement or decision in pre-litigation administrative proceedings may pursue a judicial action seeking only compensation for the attorney's fees she incurred in the pre-suit proceedings. After all, in the leading case upholding an action for fees incurred in prior administrative proceedings under Title VII, New York Gaslight Club, Inc. v. Carey (1980), the plaintiff's action for fees was coupled with a claim on the merits. Yet the Eighth Circuit subsequently extended *Carey* to encompass Title VII actions brought solely to recover fees incurred in prior administrative proceedings. In Jones v. American State Bank (8th Cir.1988), the parties settled plaintiff's pregnancy discrimination claim during the administrative proceedings, but the state deferral agency denied attorney's fees as unavailable under state law. The Eighth Circuit affirmed the federal district court's award of fees under Section 706(k). It reasoned that because, as the Supreme Court stressed repeatedly in *Carey*, the state deferral agency proceeding was mandated by Title VII and complementary to the federal statutory scheme, the administrative proceeding constituted an "action or proceeding" for which fees might be awarded within the meaning of § 706(k).

In so holding, the Eighth Circuit treated *Jones* as distinguishable from a post-*Carey* Supreme Court decision, North Carolina Department of Transportation v. Crest Street Community Council (1986). There the Supreme Court erected a distinct barrier to recovering attorney's fees for services performed in optional administrative proceedings followed by fees-only lawsuits under any of the *civil rights* statutes for which fees are recoverable under *42 U.S.C.A. § 1988*. The Court in *Crest* held that, regardless of whether negotiations following the filing of an optional administrative complaint under Title VI are themselves "proceedings to enforce" that statute, § 1988 does not authorize the recovery of fees incurred in *any* pre-suit administrative proceedings unless a judicial action is filed that also seeks relief on the merits.

The Court in *Crest* relied on language in § 1988, absent from Section 706(k) of Title VII, stipulating that fees may be awarded only "in the action or proceeding to enforce" the listed civil rights laws, including Title VI. It concluded that the judicial action in which fees are sought, and not just the pre-litigation administrative agency proceedings for which they are sought, must qualify as an "action or proceeding to enforce a provision" of Title VI (or any of the other civil rights statutes listed in § 1988). And it further concluded that a judicial action for fees alone could not be considered an action "to enforce" such a provision. Accordingly, it insisted that *under § 1988*, an award of fees for pre-suit administrative agency work is authorized only if a party prevails on a *merits-based* claim under one of the referenced civil rights statutes in a *judicial action* filed concurrently with, or subsequent to, the administrative proceedings. *Crest* did, however, recognize that if the ensuing judicial action meets this definition of a "proceeding to enforce" a § 1988 statute, a court "may still award attorney's fees for time spent on administrative proceedings to enforce the civil rights claim prior to the litigation." In fact, so long as the civil rights plaintiff files a judicial action seeking merits relief, she may recover in that action fees for whatever attorney's work at the administrative stage was "useful and of a type ordinarily necessary to advance the civil rights litigation to the stage it reached before settlement"—regardless of whether the underlying administrative proceeding is characterized as a "proceeding to enforce" one of the § 1988 statutes.

Fees may be awarded *pendente lite* when a plaintiff achieves some durable interim relief on the merits, for example an injunction that works some permanent change in the legal relations between the parties. Hanrahan v. Hampton (1980). More generally the Supreme Court has approved the award of fees pendente lite to a party who has obtained some relief on the merits at trial or on appeal. Hewitt v. Helms (1987). But plaintiffs did not acquire prevailing party status by virtue of obtaining an injunction pending appeal that merely preserved the status quo in a circuit that determines the propriety of such injunctions principally by balancing the equities and harms attendant on granting or denying relief, rather than by weighing the merits. LaRouche v. Kezer (2d Cir.1994). And attorney's fees for preliminary injunctive relief have been denied where the injunction is ultimately reversed on appeal, the party having obtained that injunction then being regarded as not having prevailed. N.A.A.C.P. v. Detroit Police Officers Ass'n (6th Cir.1995). After *Buckhannon*, there is dispute in the circuits as to whether a plaintiff who obtains only a preliminary injunction, even one that is unappealed or that survives appeal, is a "prevailing party" who has obtained some judicial relief that changes the legal relationship between the parties.

Attorney's fees may be awarded for services necessary to implement or enforce a consent decree that resulted from earlier, successful litigation. Eirhart v. Libbey–Owens Ford Co. (7th Cir.1993). And a prevailing party may also recover, to the degree of her success, fees for services rendered in an unsuccessful judicial action if she ultimately prevails in a subsequent related judicial action. Cabrales v. County of Los Angeles (9th Cir.1991).

To calculate the amount of a "reasonable" award of attorney's fees the court must arrive first at a "lodestar" figure that represents a reasonable hourly rate multiplied by the number of hours reasonably expended on matters on which the plaintiff prevailed. Blum v. Stenson (1984); Hensley v. Eckerhart (1983). Both the reasonable hours and reasonable rates questions are committed to the discretion of the district courts, Zuchel v. City and County of Denver (10th Cir.1993), although elements of legal analysis integral to their decisions are reviewable de novo. Oviatt v. Pearce (9th Cir.1992). Fees sought by the plaintiff that are attributable to attorney time clearly devoted only to unsuccessful claims will be deducted from the overall request. Green v. Torres (2d Cir.2004). And a high number of hours in a case with a relatively modest claim for compensatory damages has been sharply reduced. Gumbhir v. Curators of Univ. of Missouri (8th Cir.1998). But where a party prevails on only one of multiple legal claims rooted in the same factual nucleus, fees should not be reduced automatically. Roberts v. Roadway Exp., Inc. (10th Cir.1998). Instead, so long as the plaintiff has obtained "excellent" relief, he should recover a fully compensatory fee encompassing all hours reasonably expended on the litigation; Villano v. City of Boynton (11th Cir.2001), less than "excellent" but still "substantial" relief may warrant a fee reduction in proportion to plaintiff's overall degree of success (Hensley, supra). By not reducing the fee award simply because the plaintiff fails to prevail on every contention, this approach encourages plaintiff's counsel to advance alternative grounds for relief as authorized by F.R.C.P. 8(e). Similarly, time should not be deducted for unsuccessful but reasonable arguments made in support of a successful claim. Jaffee v. Redmond (7th Cir. 1998).

Time spent in establishing the prevailing party's entitlement to a fee award under § 1988 is itself compensable. But such requests for "fees-on-fees" are themselves subject to reduction in proportion to the degree by which the "merits fees" award was discounted, as a percentage of merits fees claimed. For example, where plaintiffs recovered 87.2% of the fees claimed for work related to the underlying merits of the action, a reduction of 12.8%, their lodestar award for the fees incurred in petitioning for those fees was also disallowed by 12.8%. Thompson v. Gomez (9th Cir.1995).

Even with respect to claims on which the plaintiff prevailed, fees may not be awarded for hours that are "excessive, redundant, or otherwise unnecessary." (Hensley, supra). The court will carefully scrutinize plaintiff's counsel's time records in the post-judgment hearing, if any, on attorney's fees to determine which hours were reasonably necessary to the outcome on successful claims. Miller v. Woodharbor Molding & Millworks, Inc. (8th Cir.1999).

The Court in Blum v. Stenson (1984) held that the lodestar is based on market rates in the relevant community, and therefore fees awardable to nonprofit legal services organizations may not be limited to actual costs. Similarly, fee awards may compensate for the work of law clerks and paralegals, again at market rates. Missouri v. Jenkins (1989). To say that the lodestar rate is based on rates prevailing in the relevant community masks two difficult sub issues: *which lawyer's* rate in a diverse legal community where lawyers of differing experience, special skills, and reputation enjoy different degrees of market power; and *which community's* rate where a lawyer from one community performs services in another with a significantly different prevailing market average. *Blum* seems to rest on the premise that the appropriate market rate for § 1988 purposes is "the opportunity cost of that time, the income foregone by [the lawyer in] representing this plaintiff." Gusman v. Unisys Corp. (7th Cir.1993). It follows that an established billing rate of the prevailing party's lawyer deserves significant weight. Thus a district court erred in compensating the prevailing plaintiff's counsel in an excessive force case at the lower rate that the defendant city paid lawyers to defend those cases. Trevino v. Gates (9th Cir.1996).

Another difficult task facing a court in calculating a lodestar is to identify the issues on which plaintiff prevailed and in turn the number of hours counsel reasonably expended on those issues. In this sense degree of success is a critical component of the ultimate fee award. But a lodestar-based fee award need not be proportionate to the amount of damages a plaintiff recovers with respect to a successful issue. Riverside v. Rivera (1986).

Attorney's fees may be augmented to compensate for delay in payment (as distinct from risk of nonpayment or "contingency"—to be discussed below). Risk of delay is compensated "either by basing the award on current rates or by adjusting the fee based on historical rates to reflect its present value." Missouri v. Jenkins (1989).

The Eleventh Amendment does not bar that adjustment in an action against a state. More generally, by the terms of the Civil Rights Attorneys' Fees Act of 1976, 42 U.S.C.A. § 1988(b), the Amendment does not bar fees against the state to the prevailing party, other than the United States, in any action or proceeding to enforce a provision of any of the Reconstruction Acts or Title VI of the Civil Rights Act of 1964 or Title IX . Such fees constitute an item of "costs" under the language of § 1988 and may therefore be recovered from a state even in federal court, notwithstanding the Eleventh Amendment. The significance of this statutory abrogation has diminished since 1989, when the Court held in Will v. Michigan Dept. of State Police (1989) that states sued in their own name are not proper defendants under § 1983. Nevertheless, the Civil Rights Act of 1976 continues to have significance in the reduced class of § 1983 actions challenging state action that *Will* approves, i.e., official-capacity actions against named state officials for prospective or injunctive relief.

Additional adjustment factors to the lodestar include the novelty and difficulty of the questions presented, the extent to which the demands of the case preclude other legal employment, the undesirability of the case, awards in similar cases, and the experience, reputation, and ability of the attorneys. Circuit courts have been reluctant to approve reduction in the amount of an award below the lodestar because of erroneous "billing judgment" by a plaintiff's lawyer in spending considerable time pursuing a claim that a district court considered relatively simple. Quaratino v. Tiffany & Co. (2d Cir.1999); Robinson v. City of Edmond (10th Cir.1998). These adjustment factors may refine but cannot substitute for the basic multiplication of a reasonable billing rate by the number of hours reasonably expended on successful claims. Similarly, the attorney's fee award may not be limited by a contingent-fee arrangement that yields a lesser sum than the lodestar. Blanchard v. Bergeron (1989).

In Evans v. Jeff D. (1986), the Court approved the practice of compulsory waiver of attorney's fees by settlement. FRCP 23 requires district court approval of class action settlements. Parties are free to negotiate the terms of a settlement and may waive statutorily authorized attorney's fees. The Court held that § 1988 does not interfere with that freedom. The

Civil Rights Act of 1991 leaves *Evans* intact. The Court in *Evans* did, however, leave open the possibility that a defendant's insistence that the plaintiff waive an attorney's fee award under § 1988, while not violating federal law, might violate local law or ethical prohibitions; and a few jurisdictions have on occasion so held. In addition, it is undecided whether a city or county's uniform policy of insisting on waiver of § 1988 fees as a condition of settling any federal civil rights action unlawfully conflicts with the policies of § 1988.

Venegas v. Mitchell (1990), treats the effect of a § 1988 fee award on the plaintiff's contractual arrangement with his own attorney. It holds that § 1988 does not invalidate a contingent fee agreement providing for payments substantially in excess of the reasonable fee recoverable from the defendant. That is, § 1988 controls only the relationship between the losing defendant and the prevailing plaintiff, not between the plaintiff and plaintiff's own attorney. Although under general § 1988 principles plaintiff's own portion of a recovery may not include amounts she has agreed to pay her attorney that exceed the "reasonable" amounts recoverable as attorney's fees from the defendant, *Venegas* also reinforces a plaintiff's capacity to secure counsel of her choice by upholding the integrity of the private fee agreement. This decision has been applied to actions under Title VII as well. Gobert v. U.S. Dept. of the Interior (5th Cir.2003). On the other hand, the plaintiff's attorney's fee award under § 1988 may not be absolutely limited by a contingent-fee arrangement that calls for a lesser sum than the lodestar. (Blanchard, supra).

Previously, a prevailing plaintiff was not entitled to have its expert witnesses compensated by the losing party, absent contractual or statutory authority stating otherwise. Crawford Fitting Co. v. J.T. Gibbons (1987). In West Virginia Univ. Hosps. v. Casey (1991), the Court held that § 1988 does not authorize the recovery of expert witness fees. They are limited to the amount designated for all witnesses, $30 per day. The Civil Rights Act of 1991, which includes expert fees as a part of an attorney's fee award under Title VII, reverses *West Virginia Univ. Hosps. v. Casey* in part. The Act authorizes expert witness fees in actions or proceedings to enforce provisions of § 1981 and § 1981a, but not § 1983. Of course, the Supreme Court has already included certain related costs, e.g., those for law clerks and paralegals, as part of the attorney's fees recoverable under § 1988. Missouri v. Jenkins (1989).

Depending on the circuit, post-judgment interest on attorney's fees may begin to accrue either from the date of the judgment that unconditionally entitled the prevailing party to reasonable attorney's fees, Associated General Contractors of Ohio, Inc. v. Drabik (6th Cir.2000); Friend v. Kolodzieczak (9th Cir.1995); BankAtlantic v. Blythe Eastman Pain Webber, Inc. (11th Cir.1994); Jenkins v. State of Missouri (8th Cir. 1991); Mathis v. Spears (Fed.Cir.1998); Copper Liquor, Inc. v. Adolph Coors Co. (5th Cir.1983) or from the date that the award of attorney's fees is quantified. Eaves v. County of Cape May (3d Cir.2001); Mid American Fed. Sav. & Loan Assoc. v. Shearson/American Express, Inc. (10th Cir.1992).

There is a strong presumption that the lodestar represents a reasonable fee, and any upward or downward adjustments may take into account only those factors not used in arriving at the lodestar. Hensley, supra. In any event the lodestar may not be adjusted upward by a "multiplier" to compensate for an attorney's risk of loss, or "contingency"—as distinct from the loss caused by delay—unless perhaps evidence is produced to show that the possibility of an enhanced fee was required in order to attract counsel. Pennsylvania v. Delaware Citizens' Council for Clean Air 1987 (Delaware II). The Court in *Delaware II* rendered a 4–1–4 decision on the issue of the availability of contingency multipliers. As a result of this splintered decision, lower courts attempted to implement the views of

Justice O'Connor. Justice O'Connor would allow an enhancement for risk when an applicant has shown that: (1) the degree to which the relevant market compensates for risk in contingent fee litigation as a class, and (2) but for the enhancement, he would have faced "substantial difficulties" in securing counsel in the relevant market.

A decision of the Supreme Court, Burlington v. Dague (1992), appears to be in favor of flatly precluding contingency enhancement. Although the underlying claims at issue were brought under modern environmental statutes, the Court's opinion and citations to cases, including *King v. Palmer* (D.C. Cir.1991), in which fees were sought under § 1988 or Title VII, strongly suggest that the holding applies to fee applications under the latter statutes as well.

What if, as a result of *Dague* or otherwise, a putative plaintiff cannot attract counsel? Section 706(f)(1)(B) authorizes the court, upon application and under such circumstances as it deems just, to "appoint an attorney" for a complainant and authorize commencement of the action without fees, costs, or security. And what if the court is unable, after diligent effort, to locate a lawyer willing to take the case without up-front compensation? There is authority that § 706(f)(1)(B) may be read to require the coercive appointment of counsel; this reading is partly justified by the fact that the unwilling lawyer may ultimately be compensated as the result of a statutory award of attorney's fees if his client prevails. E.g. Scott v. Tyson Foods Inc. (8th Cir.1991); Bradshaw v. U.S. District Court (9th Cir.1984); Bradshaw v. Zoological Soc. of San Diego (9th Cir.1981).

While a prevailing plaintiff is ordinarily to be awarded attorney's fees in all but special circumstances, the Supreme Court in Christiansburg Garment Co. v. EEOC (1978) has interpreted § 706(k) to preclude attorney's fees to a prevailing defendant unless the plaintiff's action was "frivolous, unreasonable, or without foundation." This appears to mean that a fee award to a prevailing defendant is unwarranted where the plaintiff's claim, although plainly flawed, is colorable. The plaintiff's failure to establish a prima facie case, the unprecedented nature of a claim, the defendant's offer of a settlement, or the dismissal of an action before trial all figure in determining whether a claim is sufficiently frivolous, unreasonable, or groundless to justify taxing attorney's fees against a plaintiff. E.g. Bass v. E.I. Dupont de Nemours & Co. (4th Cir.2003). If the defendant can show that a plaintiff asserted a claim in subjective bad faith, the case for awarding the defendant his attorney's fees is stronger. But the circumstances warranting fees to a prevailing defendant must be truly exceptional, so much so that a trial court does not abuse its discretion in denying such fees even if no reason is stated for the denial. Maag v. Wessler (9th Cir.1993). And where EEOC is the plaintiff, it is not even enough for the defendant seeking attorney's fees to show that EEOC failed to present credible evidence of discrimination. In such a case the defendant has the even more difficult burden of demonstrating that EEOC should have "anticipated at the outset that none of its evidence of discriminatory conduct was credible" or unreasonably believed that it had made adequate efforts to conciliate. EEOC v. Bruno's Restaurant (9th Cir.1993). It is difficult to imagine a situation in which the defendant could carry that showing.

If the standard for prevailing plaintiffs announced in *Farrar* were the test of whether a defendant is a "prevailing party," the defendant might qualify for fees when the plaintiff voluntarily dismisses her suit with prejudice even before a decision on the merits by motion for summary judgment or at trial. Such a dismissal does, after all, alter the legal relationship between the parties to the benefit of the defendant. To show the frivolousness, unreasonableness, or groundlessness demanded by *Christiansburg*, the defendant must ordinarily have prevailed summarily on the pleadings or on a motion for summary judgment on the merits, e.g., Le Blanc–Sternberg v. Fletcher (2d Cir.1998). On the other hand, the granting of a summary judgment motion does not ensure fees. Riddle v. Egensperger (6th Cir.2001). Yet a denial of a defendant's summary judgment motion does not necessarily prevent its recovering attorney's fees under the *Christiansburg* standard if plaintiff should have realized, from subsequent pretrial discovery, that his claim was groundless. Flowers v. Jefferson Hospital Ass'n (8th Cir.1995). The prevailing defendant eligible for fees under *Christiansburg* may, like the prevailing plaintiff, also recover the reasonable fees and expenses incurred in proceedings to collect the underlying fee award should plaintiff decline to pay it. Vukadinovich v. McCarthy (7th Cir.1995).

The Equal Access to Justice Act, unlike § 1988 and its Title VII counterpart, provides for fee awards to prevailing defendants when the plaintiff's claim is merely groundless but not frivolous, if the unsuccessful plaintiff is the U.S. government. The circuit courts are in conflict concerning whether EAJA is available in actions under statutes (like the Reconstruction Acts and Title VII) that have their own fee-shifting statutes. Nowd v. Rubin (1st Cir.1996); Gavette v. Office of Personnel Management (Fed. Cir.1986); Escobar Ruiz v. INS (9th Cir. 1986). The circuits that have visited the issue thus far have allowed a prevailing defendant to recover fees from the government under the ADEA which has no fee-shifting provision for prevailing defendants. And even where EAJA applies, a defendant employer will not be entitled to fees if the evidence presented by EEOC as plaintiff, although seriously flawed, is supported by anecdotal evidence, e.g. EEOC v. O & G Spring & Wire Forms Specialty Co. (7th Cir.1994).

The *Christiansburg* test has been applied to govern the award of attorney's fees against unsuccessful intervenors. The

Supreme Court characterized as "particularly welcome" a union's intervention challenging a proposed settlement of a sex discrimination action in order to protect "the legitimate expectations of . . . [male] employees innocent of any wrongdoing." Independent Federation of Flight Attendants v. Zipes (1989). The decision encouraged intervention by holding that intervenors would be liable for plaintiffs' costs of defending a settlement only when the intervention is "frivolous, unreasonable, or without foundation." In effect, then, intervention becomes *per se* a "special circumstance" that warrants denial of a fee award to a prevailing plaintiff. The Civil Rights Act of 1991 leaves this approach intact. In actions under the ADEA, several circuits have required prevailing defendants to show not that plaintiff's claim was objectively frivolous, but that it was brought in bad faith. Turlington v. Atlanta Gas Light Co. (11th Cir.1998).

3. RULE 68 OFFERS OF JUDGMENT

Federal Rule 68 authorizes the defendant, at any time more than 10 days before trial, to "offer to allow judgment to be taken against [it] . . . for the money or property . . . specified in the offer, with costs then accrued." It then provides that, if the offer is not accepted and a judgment obtained by the plaintiff "is not more favorable than the offer, the offeree must pay the costs incurred after the making of the offer." On its face, then, Rule 68 merely relieves a defendant who makes such an offer that is not accepted by the plaintiff and equaled or exceeded by a final judgment from what would otherwise be its liability for the "costs" routinely taxable under Federal Rule of Civil Procedure 54(d) in favor of prevailing parties in any federal civil action. Such an offer is valid even when it is conditioned upon acceptance of its terms by all plaintiffs, and a settlement agreement counts as a "judgment" that triggers the cost-shifting permitted by Rule 68.

Rule 54(d) costs, however, are relatively minor, as they are universally understood not to include attorney's fees. The real bite of Rule 68 in civil rights and employment discrimination actions results from the interplay of that rule with the provisions in Title VII and § 1988 that call for an award of "a reasonable attorney's fee *as part of the costs*." Importing the italicized language into the word "costs" as it appears in Rule 68, the Supreme Court in Marek v. Chesny (1985) held that a defendant's offer of judgment in a civil rights action governed by statutory provisions for attorney's fees can shift what would otherwise be the losing defendant's liability for the prevailing plaintiff's attorney's fees, as well as ordinary costs. Specifically, a Rule 68 offer that meets the requirements of that Rule relieves the losing defendant of liability for the plaintiff's post-offer attorney's fees as well as her ordinary costs of litigation. This holding greatly increases the defendant's incentive to make a Rule 68 offer, and the Civil Rights Act of 1991 leaves *Marek* intact. The *Marek* holding goes well beyond actions under the Reconstruction Civil Rights statutes governed by § 1988. In Lyte v. Sara Lee Corp. (2d Cir.1991), the court held that attorney's fees are a part of the "costs" shifted by a defendant's offer of judgment under FRCP 68 in actions under any statute that allows fee awards as a "part of," rather than "in addition to" "costs," which would include those under Title VII but not under ADEA.

The defendant's offer, to avoid liability for costs and fees to the prevailing plaintiff, must, in the words of Rule 68, include the plaintiff's "costs then accrued," that is, up until the time of the offer. The "costs" that must be included in the offer—like the "costs" mentioned in the subsequent phrase of Rule 68 that shifts liability for attorney's fees if the offer is rejected—have been held to include the amount of the plaintiff's attorney's fees accrued at the time of the offer. This is because a prevailing plaintiff would, absent an offer, ordinarily be entitled by judgment to an award of attorney's fees for pre-offer work. Accordingly, those fees, together with ordinary costs, must be added to the judgment to calculate the total received by judgment that the offer must equal or exceed to shift post-offer costs and fees under Rule 68. Where an offer no longer exceeded, in fact was slightly less than, the amount of plaintiff's judgment once pre-offer attorney's fees were added to the judgment, the Rule 68 requirement that the offer equal or exceed the judgment was held not met and the defendant was therefore subject to the usual assessment of costs and fees owed a prevailing plaintiff, including those incurred after the making of its offer. Scheeler v. Crane Co. (8th Cir.1994).

In another case, the offer promised not only "costs then accrued," as prescribed by Rule 68, but also "reasonable attorney fees as determined by the court." Holland v. Roeser (9th Cir.1994). The Ninth Circuit construed the language of the offer to authorize a district judge's award of attorney's fees for plaintiffs' counsel's preparation of a fee petition *after* they accepted the offer, even though under Rule 68 costs, and hence, under *Marek*, fees, are halted by a successful offer. The court indicated that if the defendant had offered to pay only plaintiff's "costs then accrued," the offer would have clearly and unambiguously limited plaintiff's fees to the full extent that *Marek* and Rule 68 permit. The decision points up the necessity for defendant's counsel to draft tightly worded offers that not only meet Rule 68's strictures but also stay within them. A majority of circuits that have confronted the question have held that any waiver of or limitation on attorney's fees in actions under statutes providing for the recovery of fees by prevailing plaintiffs must be "clear and unambiguous." E.g. Ellis v. University of Kansas Med. Ctr. (10th Cir.1998); Jennings v. Metropolitan Government of Nashville (6th Cir.1983). Similarly, a circuit court has ruled ineffective a Rule 68 offer that failed to apportion the offer among the multiple plaintiffs. By advising only that the offered sum was "to be divided among all three plaintiffs," the offer failed to give the notice each required to evaluate whether to accept. Gavoni v. Dobbs House, Inc. (7th Cir.1999).

The inclusion of attorney's fees in the Rule 68 post-offer "costs" that the plaintiff may be precluded from recovering assumes that the underlying fee statute includes "attorney's fees" within the definition of "costs." That is the case with most fee statutes, including § 1988, and the principal Title VII fee provision, Section 706(k). By contrast, since the "mixed-motive" remedies section of Title VII, Section 706(g)(2)(B), refers to "costs" and "attorney's fees" distinctly and separately, attorney's fees will not be counted as part of the post-offer Rule 68 "costs" a plaintiff is barred from recovering where the entitlement to fees flows only from that section. Sheppard v. Riverview Nursing Ctr. (4th Cir.1996). The same is true under ADEA.

Likewise, at least one circuit has held that attorney's fees are not shifted as part of costs in ADA actions because the text of the ADA does not define attorney's fees as part of costs. Webb v. James (7th Cir.1998). In an ADA action, "the court or agency, in its discretion, may allow the prevailing party ... a reasonable attorney's fee, including litigation expenses, *and* costs." Under this section, then, Congress did not define costs to include fees for the purposes of the ADA. Therefore, an offer that mentions only "costs" and is silent on the issue of fees cannot relieve the defendant of its statutory liability for fees (Webb, supra).

Can Rule 68 be used not just to relieve the defendant of cost and fee liability to a prevailing plaintiff but as the basis for an award of attorney's fees to a prevailing defendant? If so, Rule 68 could serve as the defendant's end run around the *Chris-*

tiansburg Garment test applicable to claims under the Reconstruction Acts and employment discrimination statutes. That is, a defendant would become eligible for attorney's fees simply by submitting what proves to be a shrewd offer of judgment in cases where the plaintiff has prevailed and therefore defendant has not shown the groundlessness, frivolousness, or subjective bad faith the Supreme Court has required. But the circuits to have considered the issue have all rejected this argument in civil rights and employment discrimination actions governed by *Christianburg Garment's* plaintiff-tilted interpretation of "prevailing party." They confirm that FRCP 68, while a one-way street available only to defendants, helps them only if the plaintiff prevails, Delta Air Lines, Inc. v. August (1981), and then only by relieving them of what would otherwise be their liability for plaintiff's costs and fees, and enabling them to receive costs, not by making them eligible for a fee award themselves, e.g., Le v. University of Pennsylvania (3d Cir.2003).

By contrast, there is also complete consensus among the circuits to have decided the issue that where an employment discrimination or civil rights plaintiff's trial recovery (plus court-ordered pre-offer costs and fees) does not exceed the defendant's rejected Rule 68 offer, the defendant is entitled to an award from plaintiff of its post-offer *costs*, i.e., excluding post-offer fees, e.g., Pouillon v. Little (6th Cir.2003); Crossman v. Marcoccio (1st Cir.1986). The decisions thus read the Rule 68 requirement that the offeree "pay the costs incurred after the making of the offer" to mean not just that offeree bear its own post-offer costs but that it be ordered to pay those of the offeror. These courts find no tension between FRCP 54(d), which awards presumptive but still discretionary costs only to prevailing parties, and this application of FRCP 68, which mandates costs to a non-prevailing defendant that submitted a

Rule 68 offer that was successful in the sense that plaintiff, after rejecting it, could not recover more at trial.

If, however, as the circuits agree, plaintiffs who fail to surpass at trial a Rule 68 offer they rejected must pay post-offer defense costs; and if Rule 68 "costs," per *Marek*, are defined by reference to the underlying statute awarding costs and/or fees to prevailing parties; and if, as is true of Section 1988, in the case of civil rights actions, and Section 706(k), in the cases of Title VII actions, the underlying statutes authorize the recovery of fees as part of "costs"; then shouldn't Rule 68 also require the plaintiff to pay the defendant's post-offer *fees*? The circuit decisions summarized above have all rejected this syllogism. They stress the statement in *Marek* that "the term 'costs' in Rule 68 was intended to refer [only] to all costs *properly awardable* under the relevant substantive statute . . ." And fees to a defendant where Rule 68 is triggered would not be properly awardable under Sections 1988 or 706(k) for two reasons. First, those statutes authorize fees only to prevailing parties, whereas Rule 68 is triggered only where the plaintiff, not the defendant, has prevailed. Second, *Christiansburg Garment* interprets those statutes to mean that a defendant can be a prevailing party only where the plaintiff's claim is frivolous, unreasonable or without foundation, and that will certainly not be the case in the Rule 68 situation under examination, where the plaintiff has to some degree prevailed.

In brief, Rule 68 is triggered when the sum of plaintiff's trial recovery, plus her pre-offer costs and fees as awarded by the court, fails to exceed defendant's offer. When the Rule is triggered in civil rights or employment discrimination cases, the Rule denies the plaintiff eligibility for the post-offer costs or fees she would ordinarily be awarded by virtue of the underlying applicable fee-authorizing statute; and it also requires the plaintiff-offeree to pay the defendant-offeror the latter's post-offer costs, but not fees.

Courts have generally held that Rule 68 offers of judgment may not be revoked during the 10–day period set by the Rule, e.g., Webb v. James (7th Cir.1998); Richardson v. National R.R. Passenger Corp. (D.C. Cir.1995). Moreover, rescission may not be an available remedy for mutual mistakes because the mandatory language of Rule 68, requiring that the clerk "shall enter judgment" upon the filing of an offer, removes discretion from the trial court as to whether to enter judgment upon the filing of the accepted offer. Webb, supra. Relief from a judgment entered as a result of a Rule 68 offer and acceptance may be available under Rule 60. Rule 60(b) provides in relevant part that "[o]n motion and upon such terms as are just, the court may relieve a party or a party's legal representative from a final judgment order or proceeding for the following reasons: (1) mistake, inadvertence, surprise, or excusable neglect; . . . (3) fraud (whether heretofore denominated intrinsic or extrinsic), misrepresentation, or other misconduct of an adverse party; (4) the judgment is void; . . . or (6) any other reason justifying relief from the operation of the judgment." Webb, supra. On the other hand, a defendant who fails to renew an offer of judgment on retrial of an action remains eligible for Rule 68 costs from the plaintiff if on retrial the plaintiff's judgment is for less than the amount of the offer. Pouillon, supra.

F. DISABILITY DISCRIMINATION: THE AMERICANS WITH DISABILITIES ACT OF 1990 AND THE REHABILITATION ACT OF 1973

Title I of The Americans With Disabilities Act of 1990 ("ADA") represents the first comprehensive national legislation banning employment discrimination on the basis of physical or mental disability. Like Title VII, ADA prohibits not only intentional or "disparate treatment" discrimination on the part of covered employers—those with 15 or more employees—but also generally applied, facially "neutral" employment tests, practices or standards that have a disproportionate adverse impact on the disabled. The latter may be justified only if the employer shows them to be "job-related and consistent with business necessity." One set of neutral practices—medical inquiries or examinations (other than those testing for the use of illegal drugs)—is specifically outlawed until an offer of employment is made; thereafter, actual employment may be conditioned on the results of medical history questions and examinations, but those must meet the job-relatedness/business necessity requirement, and their results must be held confidential. But while pre-offer inquiries to applicants concerning the existence or severity of a disability are prohibited, employers may ask whether the employee can perform essential job-related functions.

The ADA is distinct from standard employment discrimination laws in its affirmative additional requirement that employers provide "qualified" disabled individuals "reasonable accommodation." An individual is "qualified" if, with or without such accommodation, she can perform the "essential" (not all) functions of the job in question. The employer bears the burden of showing the infeasibility, excessive cost, or other undue hardship involved in providing the accommodation proposed by the disabled employee.

In this respect and others ADA is an outgrowth of § 504 of the Rehabilitation Act of 1973, 29 U.S.C. § 701 et seq. ("RHA"), which prohibits federal funds recipients from excluding or discriminating against any "otherwise qualified handicapped individual" in "any program or activity receiving federal financial assistance." See generally, U.S. Department of Labor website: http://www.dol.gov/asp/programs/guide/disable.htm. The Civil Rights Restoration Act of 1987 effectively banned discrimination in all the recipient institution's operations, not merely in programs or activities for which federal assistance is granted. RHA Section 504 is enforced by the administrative procedures of Title VI, which may lead to termination of funding or refusal to extend future assistance.

In 1974, Congress amended the definition of "handicapped individual" for Section 504 purposes to include not just those with actual physical impairments, "but also those who are regarded as impaired and who, as a result, are substantially limited in a major life activity...." School Board of Nassau County v. Arline (1987). Moreover, a person suffering impairment of major life activities from tuberculosis is considered handicapped even though his disease is contagious. But to be eligible for relief, a plaintiff must generally also be "otherwise qualified," or able to perform the "essential functions" of the particular job. And while inability to function may not be inferred simply from the fact of a handicap, a tuberculosis sufferer may not be "otherwise qualified" if his contagion poses "a serious health threat to others."

The ADA, and decisions construing it, adhere for the most part to the RHA model, expanding it to private employment. The ADA excludes from coverage as employers wholly owned United States corporations and tax-exempt private membership clubs. An employer may require that every employee be qualified to perform the "essential functions" of a job (the phrase is part of the definition of a "qualified person" with a disability); but the judgment whether a disabled employee can so perform must take into account feasible "reasonable accommodations." So employers can continue to require that all applicants and employees, including those with disabilities, be able, or with reasonable accommodation be enabled, to perform the essential, i.e., non-marginal functions of the job in question. Although applicants for Social Security disability benefits must also be disabled to be eligible, disability within the meaning of that act does not inquire if the applicant could fulfill the functions of a particular job after receiving reasonable accommodation. Accordingly, most circuits have held that application for or receipt of social security benefits will not by itself defeat an ADA claim through the doctrine of judicial estoppel. See decisions summarized in Rascon v. U.S. West Communications, Inc. (10th Cir.1998).

The determination of whether a person is qualified should be made at the time of an employment action, for example, hiring or promotion. The "qualification" of an applicant should not be based on the possibility that the employee or applicant will become incapacitated and unqualified in the future. And the ADA frowns on paternalistic concerns about what would be best for the person with the disability, since these serve to foreclose employment opportunities.

Under the ADA an employer remains free to select the most qualified applicant available and to make decisions based on reasons unrelated to the existence or consequence of a disability. Employment decisions must not have the purpose or effect of subjecting a qualified individual with a disability to discrimination based on that disability. The non-discrimination concept does not prohibit an employer from devising physical or other job criteria or tests for a job so long as the criteria and tests are job-related and consistent with job necessity. Even a nondiscriminating employer, however, must on an applicant's or employee's request determine whether a reasonable accommodation would enable the disabled person to perform the essential functions of the job without imposing an undue hardship on the business.

Title I prohibits discrimination by employers, unions, employment agencies and union-management committees against "any qualified individual with a disability" regarding any term, condition or privilege of employment.

Section 3(2) of the ADA defines "disability" as:

(1) a mental or physical impairment that substantially limits one or more of an individual's "major life activities";

(2) a record of having such an impairment; or

(3) being regarded as having such an impairment. ADA § 3, 42 U.S.C.A. § 12102.

See generally, Toyota Motor Mfg. v. Williams (2002); Sutton v. United Air Lines, Inc. (1999).

Section 101(8) of the ADA explains that a "qualified" disabled person is "an individual with a disability who with or without reasonable accommodation, can perform the essential functions of the employment position that such individual holds or desires." This prohibition extends to job applications, hiring, advancement, discharge, compensation, training, or other terms of employment. Section 102(a). Job descriptions are considered primary evidence in establishing the scope of essential functions. Section 101(8).

Title I's broad anti-discrimination policy blends the concepts of equal treatment and affirmative support. Thus an employer may not: (1) classify a disabled applicant or employee in a way that adversely affects the opportunities or status of the person; (2) participate in an arrangement with another organization that has the effect of discriminating against the disabled individual; (3) utilize standards, criteria, or methods of administration that have the effect of discriminating on the basis of the disability or perpetuating discrimination by others subject to common administrative control; (4) exclude or deny equal jobs or benefits to an individual because she has a relationship with a disabled individual; (5) use standards or tests that screen out or tend to screen out an individual with disabilities (unless the standard is job-related and consistent with business necessity); (6) use tests whose results reflect the impairment of the individual rather than the skills or aptitude of the test-taker; or (7) fail to make reasonable accommodations to the known physical or mental limitations of an otherwise qualified individual (unless the accommodation would impose undue hardship.) § 102(b).

The ADA does not exclude infected or contagious applicants or employees from its definition of the "qualified individual with a disability" who is entitled to reasonable accommodation. See Bragdon v. Abbott (1998). Claims of disability must be evaluated on a case by case basis. Albertson's, Inc. v. Kirkingburg (1999).

Section 103 of ADA does allow employers the defense of showing that such a person poses a "direct threat to the health or safety of other individuals in the workplace" and that his safe performance "cannot be accomplished by reasonable accommodation...." See Chevron U.S.A. Inc. v. Echazabal (2002).

The Act neither prohibits nor authorizes testing for illegal drugs, although such tests are not considered medical examinations and accordingly may be conducted even prior to a job offer. Employers may ban the use of illegal drugs and alcohol at the workplace and may hold alcoholics and drug users to the same qualifications and job performance standards as other employees, even if unsatisfactory performance is related to alcoholism.

Section 501(c) provides that ADA may not be construed to restrict a health care provider from classifying or administering risks unless it does so as a "subterfuge" to evade the purposes of the Act.

CHAPTER 21

MISCELLANEOUS EMPLOYEE PROTECTION LAWS

A. EMPLOYEE RETIREMENT INCOME SECURITY ACT OF 1974 (ERISA)

Congress enacted the Employee Retirement Income Security Act, 29 U.S.C.A. § 1001 et seq., for the purpose of safeguarding employee retirement and pension benefits. The act established minimum standards for employee participation, vesting standards which create nonforfeitable rights, and funding guidelines. Generally speaking, federal laws preempt all state laws and causes of action which relate to ERISA pension or welfare plans, directly or indirectly. Ellenburg v. Brockway, Inc. (9th Cir.1985). For example, ERISA preempts state tort and contract actions involving ERISA covered plans. See e.g., Jackson v. Martin Marietta Corp. (11th Cir.1986) (contract); Dependahl v. Falstaff Brewing Corp. (8th Cir.1981) (tort). As a result of preemption, damages in an ERISA proceeding are limited, but attorney's fees are recoverable. Punitives are not allowed. Massachusetts Mut. Life Ins. Co. v. Russell (1985). Investments are regulated, and minimum standards of fiduciary conduct for trustees and administrators are established, with civil and criminal enforcement measures provided. See generally, U.S. Department of Labor website: http://www. dol.gov/asp/programs/guide/erisa.htm.

ERISA plan administrators have a special fiduciary relationship toward plan participants and beneficiaries. Most federal courts of appeal had applied an arbitrary and capricious standard of review to decisions of plan administration denying benefits. However, the Supreme Court in Firestone Tire & Rubber Co. v. Bruch (1989), placed limits on the utilization of this standard of review, and provided for de novo review, unless a plan expressly grants the necessary discretion to an administrator to construe terms and determine benefits. It should be pointed out that if an employer is found to have acted as a fiduciary toward its employees in misleading them about their benefits, recovery becomes much easier. Varity Corp. v. Howe (1996). Payment of pensions has been assured through the Pension Benefit Guaranty Corporation, which administers the termination insurance provisions. The Retiree Benefits Bankruptcy Protection Act of 1988 also affords workers health, disability, and life insurance protection from insolvent businesses. See Conison, Employee Benefit Plans in a Nutshell (3d ed. Thomson/West 2004).

B. NATIONAL LABOR RELATIONS ACT

The National Labor Relations Act, as amended, primarily governs employer-union relations. The act grants employees important rights to create or become members of unions, to choose representatives and to bargain collectively, and to engage in or refrain from "concerted activities" for mutual aid and protection. This concerted activity protection is afforded non-union employees, and the National Labor Relations Board (NLRB) frequently intervenes to protect non-union employees so long as their activities are related to wage or working conditions. For example, NLRB involvement based upon "concerted activity" could arise in an employment situation if an employee solicited additional employee support for a group health insurance plan. See Edward Blankstein, Inc. v. NLRB (3d Cir.1980). For a more complete summary of the various federal legislation regulating unions, management, strikes, boycotts, etc., see D. Leslie, Labor Law in a Nutshell (3d Ed. 1992).

C. LABOR MANAGEMENT RELATIONS ACT

The National Labor Relations Board ("NLRB"), in administering the Labor Management Relations Act ("LMRA"), may encounter unlawful discrimination during union representation campaigns, certifications, fair representation disputes, duty to bargain situations, or other unfair labor practice proceedings. A certified union's duty of fair representation may be enforced by aggrieved black union members or applicants for union membership in private federal damages actions, Steele v. Louisville & Nashville Railroad (1944), and probably in NLRB unfair labor practice proceedings. See Del-Costello v. International Brotherhood of Teamsters (1983). But minority employees are not protected from union discipline when, bypassing their union, they raise employment discrimination grievances directly with an employer. Emporium Capwell Co. v. The Western Addition Community Organization (1975). An employer probably has a duty to bargain over employment discrimination issues, but employer discrimination standing alone will not constitute an unfair labor practice absent a link between the employer's alleged discriminatory conduct and interference with rights conferred by the LMRA. See Jubilee Mfg. Co. (1973).

Although election results may be overturned if either a union or an employer has appealed directly to race hatred during a campaign, a union is not foreclosed from invoking the election procedures of the LMRA because it has a history of racial discrimination. Compare Sewell Mfg. Co., (1962) with Handy Andy, Inc., (1977). Some courts of appeals, however, have found that the NLRB is constitutionally compelled to withhold certification from an illegally discriminating union.

See NLRB v. Heavy Lift Serv., Inc. (5th Cir.1979); NLRB v. Mansion House Center Management Corp. (8th Cir.1973). In any event, the Board may revoke a union's certification if it breaches the duty of fair representation by engaging in discriminatory practices. See generally, U.S. Department of Labor website: http://www.dol.gov/asp/programs/guide/unions.htm.

D. FEDERAL CONSTRUCTION PROJECTS

Two important federal acts protect workers employed on federal construction projects. The Miller Act contains a performance bond requirement, and the act permits persons supplying labor and materials to sue in federal district court to collect monies owed for unpaid wages or supplies. The Copeland or "Kickback" Act prohibits by criminal penalty any attempt to force or induce workers to pay kickbacks from wages under federal construction contracts. See generally, U.S. Department of Labor website: http://www.dol.gov/asp/programs/guide/kickback.htm.

E. EXECUTIVE ORDERS

A number of Executive Orders issued under the authority of the President prohibit employment discrimination. These orders usually establish federal policy in a particular area, require affirmative action programs, and specify responsibility for enforcement. No private rights of action are created, and enforcement and implementation are usually left to the executive agency or department involved.

By far the most important for present purposes is Executive Order 11246. As amended, it prohibits employment discrimination by government contractors on grounds of race, religion, sex, or national origin. It also demands that contractors take "affirmative action" by means of "goals" and "timetables" to boost the representation of protected group members in major job categories to levels that reflect the availability of qualified members of the protected group. There is no specific legislative basis for the Order, but lower courts have followed the lead of the Third Circuit in holding that Congress should be "deemed to have granted" the President the "general authority" to so protect federal interests. Contractors Ass'n v. Secretary of Labor (3rd Cir.1971). See generally, U.S. Department of Labor websites: http://www.dol.gov/asp/programs/guide/discrim.htm; and http://www.dol.gov/asp/programs/guide/discron.htm.

Executive Order 11141 prohibits age discrimination by government contractors and subcontractors; Executive Order 11478 prohibits race, color, religion, sex, national origin, handicap, and age discrimination by the federal government. Other executive orders establish coordinated enforcement efforts and special programs for minority and women's enterprises.

F. FOREIGN BOYCOTT LAWS

The Export Administration Act of 1969, as amended, popularly known as the Foreign Boycott Laws, 50 U.S.C.A.App. § 2407, authorizes the President to prohibit the facilitating of discrimination by foreign governments against "any United States person" on the basis of race, religion, sex or national origin. It also expressly prohibits furnishing racial, religious, gender, or national origin information about any "United States person," or any owner, officer, director, or employee of such person. Violations of the Act or regulations promulgated under it can result in criminal penalties.

G. FEDERAL CREDIT LAWS

The Consumer Credit Protection Act, Title III, prohibits the discharge of an employee because of a garnishment for any one indebtedness. See generally, U.S. Department of Labor website: http://www.dol.gov/asp/programs/guide/garnish.htm. The Consumer Credit Protection Act, Title VI (called the Fair Credit Reporting Act) regulates the use of credit reports for employment purposes. It should be noted that state laws frequently regulate garnishments. Additionally, blacklisting, employer statements and "service letters" relating to former employees are often areas of state regulation. Some states also regulate or prohibit wage assignments.

H. JURY SERVICE

The Jury System Improvement Act of 1968, as amended, protects any employee's job security in the event the employee is called to serve on a federal jury. See Shea v. County of Rockland (2d Cir.1987) (damages are limited to economic losses). A number of states have enacted similar employee protection laws for state jury service.

I. UNJUST DISCHARGES

Traditionally, the employment at-will concept freely allowed the employer or the employee to terminate the employment relationship at any time and for any reason without further obligation. See Adair v. United States (1908). However, recent litigation and legislation concerning wrongful terminations or unjust discharges have dramatically changed this entire area of the law. See generally, Smith v. Atlas Off–Shore Boat Service, Inc. (5th Cir.1981); Mont. Code Ann. §§ 39–2–901, et seq.

The common-law doctrine of employment-at-will has been the subject of rapid revision by state and federal legislation and judicial decision. Federal and state laws concerning unions, civil service employees, and fair employment give certain classes of employees fairly comprehensive protection from certain types of discharges.

The following theories or laws may provide an employee with a remedy for an unjust discharge or wrongful termination: (1) violation of public policy; see Sheets v. Teddy's Frosted Foods, Inc. (1980) (discussion of illegal act and whistleblowing); (2) breach of an implied contract of employment, usually based upon employment handbooks or oral representations; see Toussaint v. Blue Cross & Blue Shield (1980) (handbook); Schipani v. Ford Motor Co. (1981) (oral representations can override written disclaimers); (3) breach of implied covenant of good faith and fair dealing; see Wagenseller v. Scottsdale Memorial Hospital (1985); (4) breach of express employment contract; (5) promissory estoppel; see Grouse v. Group Health Plan, Inc. (1981) (job change in reliance on employment offer that was later revoked); (6) common law tort actions growing out of the discharge, including but not limited to prima facie tort, intentional infliction of emotional distress, fraud, defamation, tortious interference with contract, invasion of privacy; some jurisdictions recognize a separate tort action for the discharge itself, under the headings of wrongful discharge, retaliatory discharge, abusive discharge, or unjust discharge, etc.; and (7) state and federal statutory protections.

A non-exclusive list of federal statutory protections against discharge includes: the Labor Management Relations Act, 29 U.S.C.A. § 141 et seq.; Age Discrimination in Employment Act, 29 U.S.C.A. § 621 et seq.; Rehabilitation Act of 1973, 29 U.S.C.A. §§ 701, 796i; Equal Pay Act, 29 U.S.C.A. § 206(d); Civil Rights Act of 1964, 42 U.S.C.A. § 2000e–17; Civil Rights

Act of 1866, 42 U.S.C.A. § 1981; Civil Rights Act of 1871, 42 U.S.C.A. § 1983; Alcohol Abuse and Alcoholism Prevention Treatment and Rehabilitation Program for Government and Other Employees Act, 42 U.S.C.A. § 290 dd; Vietnam Era Veterans' Readjustment Assistance Act of 1974, 38 U.S.C.A. § 2011 et seq.; Occupational Safety and Health Act, 29 U.S.C.A. § 660; Mine Safety and Health Act, 30 U.S.C.A. § 815; Railroad Safety Act, 45 U.S.C.A. § 441; Longshore and Harbor Workers' Compensation Act, 33 U.S.C.A. § 948; Selective Service Act, 38 U.S.C.A. § 2021; Vocational Rehabilitation Act, 29 U.S.C.A. § 793; Energy Reorganization Act, 45 U.S.C.A. § 5851; Consumer Protection Act, 15 U.S.C.A. § 1674; Employee Polygraph Protection Act, 29 U.S.C.A. § 2001 et seq.; Whistleblower Protection Act of 1989, 5 U.S.C.A. §§ 1213–1222, 2302 (see generally, U.S. Department of Labor website: http://www.dol.gov/asp/programs/guide/whistle.htm); Bankruptcy Act, 11 U.S.C.A. § 525(b); Clean Air Act, 42 U.S.C.A. § 7622; Toxic Substances Control Act, 15 U.S.C.A. § 2622; Federal Water Pollution Control Act, 33 U.S.C.A. § 1367; Solid Waste Disposal Act, 42 U.S.C.A. § 6971; Comprehensive Environmental Response, Compensation and Liability Act, 42 U.S.C.A. § 9610; Civil Service Reform Act, 5 U.S.C.A. § 2303; Fair Labor Standards Act, 29 U.S.C.A. § 215(a)(3); Migrant and Seasonal Agricultural Worker Protection Act, 29 U.S.C.A. § 1855; Trade Act of 1974, 19 U.S.C.A. § 2394; Worker Adjustment and Retraining Notification Act, 29 U.S.C.A. § 2101; and the Employee Retirement Income Security Act of 1974, 29 U.S.C.A. §§ 1140, 1141. It should also be noted that the Sarbanes–Oxley Act of 2002 provided whistleblower protection for employees of publicity traded companies. 18 U.S.C.A. § 1514A.

In a similar fashion, but in a less comprehensive manner, many states have begun to enact protections against discharge. Traditionally, state unjust discharge actions that involve claims by union employees covered by a collective bargaining agreement, may be the subject of preemption under § 301 of the Labor Management Relations Act, 29 U.S.C.A. § 185 et seq. However, state tort claims, independent of the collective bargaining agreement, are not subject to preemption. Lingle v. Norge Div. of Magic Chef, Inc. (1988).

J. DRUGS IN THE WORKPLACE

Public and private sector drug testing of employees has generated increased litigation and legislation in recent years. This area of the law involves sensitive issues of employee privacy versus employer concern for safety and health. For example, Congress passed the Drug Free Workplace Act of 1988, 41 U.S.C.A. § 701 et seq., to force most federal contractors to establish, supervise, and maintain an employee drug program designed to eliminate the use of drugs in the workplace. See also Skinner v. Railway Labor Executives' Ass'n. (1989); National Treasury Employees Union v. Von Raab (1989).

The National Labor Relations Board views drug testing as a mandatory subject of bargaining when union represented employees are involved. Johnson–Bateman Co. (1989).

K. POLYGRAPHS

For the most part, the Employee Polygraph Protection Act of 1988, 29 U.S.C.A. § 2001, prohibits the use of polygraphs by employers with regard to job applicants or employees. Limited exceptions are made for some government contractors, some providers of security services, some drug industries, and some instances involving employee crime. The act is administered by the Secretary of Labor, and employees are given a private right of action. See generally, U.S. Department of Labor website: http://www.dol.gov/asp/programs/guide/eppa.htm.

L. NOTICE OF PLANT CLOSINGS

Most lay-offs or plant closings by employers with 100 or more employees are subject to the notice requirements of the Worker Adjustment and Retraining Notification Act of 1988, 29 U.S.C.A. § 2101. Employers must give 60 days notice to the employees' union or to the employees in the absence of a union, prior to such actions. Failure to comply with the act can result in employer liability for backpay and benefits to employees, and the imposition of fines. Enforcement actions are to be brought in federal district court. See generally, U.S. Department of Labor website: http://www.dol.gov/asp/programs/guide/layoffs.htm.

M. MIGRANT FARM WORKERS

The Migrant and Seasonal Agricultural Worker Protection Act, 29 U.S.C.A. § 1801 et seq., attempts to regulate migrant and seasonal farm labor by requiring farm labor contractor registration; by regulating workers safety, housing, and transportation; and by requiring employers to keep certain records. Enforcement provisions include a private right of action for act violations. See Barrett v. Adams Fruit Co. (11th Cir.1989) (act preempts exclusive remedy provision of Florida's workers' compensation law). See generally, U.S. Department of Labor website: http://www.dol.gov/asp/programs/guide/mspa.htm.

N. CONTAGIOUS DISEASES IN THE WORK PLACE

Contagious disease in the workplace, and the increasing number of employees with AIDS (Acquired Immune Deficiency

Syndrome), have focused attention on new employer-employee legal issues in recent years.

Of great importance to workers with diseases are medical benefits that are usually protected by the Employee Retirement Income Security Act of 1974, (ERISA) 29 U.S.C.A. § 1140. ERISA protected benefits plans may afford relief from acts of discrimination in connection with discontinuation of health insurance, denial of disability payments or pensions, or forced retirements.

It should also be noted that the Occupational Safety and Health Act, (OSHA) 29 U.S.C.A. § 651 et seq., imposes duties upon employers to provide safe workplaces free from recognized hazards, which can include contagious and other diseases.

An employer who discloses that a worker has a contagious disease may face common law claims for invasion of privacy. Also, states that have adopted fair employment practices laws in the handicap area may offer workers an additional remedy for discrimination. Finally, an employer could face state tort liability for any intentional exposure of workers to contagious diseases. See Chapters 3, 8, supra. Furthermore, the employer could be liable for third-party harm by way of negligent hiring and retention of workers with contagious diseases.

O. FAMILY AND MEDICAL LEAVE

The Family and Medical Leave Act of 1993, 29 U.S.C.A. §§ 2601, et seq., mandates covered employers to give up to 12 weeks of unpaid job protected leave to eligible employees for certain family and medical reasons. Leave must be granted for: child care after births or adoptions; care of a spouse, child, or parent with a serious health condition; and any serious health condition of the employee that prohibits job performance. See generally, U.S. Department of Labor website: http://www.dol.gov/asp/programs/guide/fmla.htm.

P. VIOLENCE AGAINST WOMEN

The Violence Against Women Act of 1994, 42 U.S.C.A. § 13981, provided a civil rights cause of action for violent crimes with a gender motive. This Act is aimed at individual defendants; however, the Supreme Court held the Act unconstitutional in United States v. Morrison (2000).

Q. UNIFORMED SERVICES PERSONNEL

No federal anti-discrimination laws applicable to the private sector have been enacted by Congress to protect homosexuals and lesbians from discrimination; however, there has been a federal effort to assist such individuals in the non-disclosure of their preferences upon entry into the military. See Pub. L. 103–160, approved Nov. 30, 1993, 107 Stat. 1670.

Congress enacted special legislation for Vietnam veterans (38 U.S.C.A. § 4212), which requires contractors to use affirmative action plans to hire, promote and train qualified Vietnam era veterans. Congress also guaranteed reemployment rights for service members (38 U.S.C.A. § 4301–4333) and generally prohibited discrimination against them. See generally, U.S. Department of Labor websites: http://www.dol.gov/asp/programs/guide/vietvets.htm; http://www.dol.gov/asp/programs/guide/userra.htm.

It should be noted that the Servicemembers Civil Relief Act (Soldiers' and Sailors Civil Relief Act of 1940, as amended), 50 U.S.C.A. App. §§ 501–596, provides important protections to service members from lawsuits and legal process.

*

INDEX

References are to Pages

511

ARISING OUT OF EMPLOYMENT
See also, Risks
Generally, 55–65
Acts of God, 56, 60
Assault, 61–62
Dangers imported by co-employee, 61
Heart cases, 63
Heat and cold, injuries from, 60
Horseplay, 62–63
Idiopathic fall, 64–65
Imported dangers doctrine, 61
Pre-existing injury or disease, 63–64
Proximate cause, 58
Rescue, accident incident to, 69–70
Risks, generally, 55–65
Suicide, 71–72
Unexplained accidents and deaths, 64–65

ARMED FORCES
See, Military Personnel

ARTIFICIAL LIMBS
Accident vs. injury, 57, 73
Special statutory provisions, 73

ASBESTOSIS
Special statutory coverage, 77–78

ASSAULT
Arising out of employment, 61–62

ASSUMPTION OF RISK
See also, Federal Employers' Liability Act
Employers' Liability Acts, effect of, 4–5, 13–15
Erosion of defense, 13–14
Federal Employers' Liability Act, 13–15
Non-delegable duties, 4
Origin of doctrine, 4

ATTORNEYS
See also, Attorney's Fees
As employee vs. independent contractor, 49–50
Workers' compensation coverage of, 49–50

ATTORNEY'S FEES AND COSTS
Civil Rights Acts, Reconstruction, 466
Civil Rights Attorney's Fees Awards Act and amendment, 466–467
Denial of, under Federal Rule of Civil Procedure 68, 486–492
Federal Rule of Civil Procedure 54(d), 466–467, 486–492
Federal Rule of Civil Procedure 68, 486–492
Fee shifting statutes and waiver, 486–492

CHARITABLE EMPLOYERS
See, Employer

CHILD
 See also, Minor Employees
Death benefits, 82–83, 97–98
Illegitimate, 82–83
Stepchild, right to compensation, 82–83

CIVIL RIGHTS ACTS, RECONSTRUCTION
 See also, Job Anti-discrimination Legislation, Title VII of the 1964 Civil
  Rights Act
Acts of 1866, 1870, 1871, 380–381
Attorney's fees, 466–467
Bivens claims, 408–410
Costs, 465
Fourteenth Amendment, 410
Proof requirements of Section 1983 in Section 1981 suits, 406–408
Section 1981, 381–404
Section 1983, 404–406
Section 1985(3), 410–413
Thirteenth Amendment, 380

CO-EMPLOYEES
 See also, Fellow Servant Rule
As third party, 35–37, 117–118
Danger imported by, 61
Dual capacity, where physician, 38–39
Immunity, 35
Liability of, 35
Physician, 38–39

COMMON LAW RECOVERY SYSTEM
 See also, Tort Liability of Employer
Remedies, 1–2
Replaced by state compensation legislation, 7–11

COMPARATIVE FAULT
Federal Employers' Liability Act, 14
Replaced contributory negligence, 14

COMPENSATION NEUROSIS
As occupational disease, 73–74
Causally connected to risk of employment, 73–74
Compensation for, 73–74

CONCURRENT EMPLOYERS
See, Employer

†